NINE DOG WINTER

OTHER BOOKS
BY BRUCE T. BATCHELOR

YUKON CHANNEL CHARTS
Sternwheeler-style Strip Maps of the Historic Yukon River

DOGTEAM TO DAWSON
The Quest for the Cosmic Bannock

BOOK MARKETING DEMYSTIFIED
Enjoy discovering the optimal way to sell your self-published book!

BUCHMARKETING OHNE GEHEIMNISSE
Entdecken Sie den besten Weg, Ihr selbstverlegtes Buch zu verkaufen!

OF MIKES AND ME 1940–'64
Stories from the broadcast life and times of Lew Short [co-author]

THE LOST WHOLE MOOSE CATALOGUE
A Yukon Way of Knowledge [anthology co-editor, contributor]

NINE DOG
WINTER

BRUCE T. BATCHELOR

Agio
PUBLISHING HOUSE

Agio
PUBLISHING HOUSE

151 Howe Street, Victoria BC Canada V8V 4K5

Thanks to Jill Bauer for her clever drawings of our
dogs. Maps drawn by Marsha Batchelor. All other
sketches and diagrams by the author. Thanks to
Cor Guimond for photos on pages 126 and 349; all
other photos by the author and Marsha, except as
indicated. *Cover photo: our sled dog Dawson*

*For rights information and bulk orders, please
contact:* info@agiopublishing.com *or go to*
www.agiopublishing.com

Nine Dog Winter
ISBN 978-1-897435-17-5 (trade paperback)
ISBN 987-1-897435-18-2 (electronic edition)

For more information, we invite you to visit
www.NineDogWinter-book.com

Printed on acid-free paper that includes no fibre
from endangered forests. Agio Publishing House is a
socially responsible company, measuring success on
a triple-bottom-line basis.

10   9   8   7   6   5   4   3   2   1 a

DEDICATION

To Marsha, of course! *You were – and always will be – amazing.*
To our Yukon wilderness neighbours, and our nine furry mutts. *Thank you all.*
And to our outdoors-loving son, Dan. *May your life be blessed with crisp air.*

TABLE OF CONTENTS

APPENDICES

CHAPTER ONE

WHAT TO DO ABOUT A DREAM

I was having a difficult time trying to sleep. Mosquitoes were bouncing on the tent's roof as if it was their own private trampoline. Fishing my watch out of a boot beside my sleeping bag, I checked the time: one o'clock in the morning. The sky was disgustingly daylight.

My campsite overlooked a tiny, sub-Arctic lake teeming with rowdy birds. A half-dozen species were squawking, cooing, warbling, gobbling and quacking at each other, terribly pleased to have flown all the way to the Yukon where there was certainly no lack of bugs to eat. Yet it wasn't this noisy, natural celebration of spring that was keeping me awake, it was the thought of going *dog mushing*. This weird notion was really messing with my mind.

The concept of owning sled dogs had been lurking in my subconscious over the years, slowly growing until, at this opportune moment, it had emerged as a full-fledged compulsion. All I could think about was dropping everything, rearranging my whole life, and moving off to the remotest corners of Canada's Yukon Territory to go winter camping with huskies.

Over the past two weeks, I had been on a working holiday in Whitehorse, revising a map book of the Yukon River. The first edition, which I published five years before in 1975, had sold out and the summer canoeists were clamouring for more copies. A week before, when I was redrafting some critical bends and sandbars by referring to aerial photographs, a friend had slipped a few old winter shots into the slide projector tray. There on the screen was the tiny dome-shaped cabin I once lived in near Whitehorse. The piles of canoes and firewood surrounding the building were covered with so much snow they looked like landscaped shrubbery. Smoke was rising straight up from the chimney so it had to be Minus Twenty Fahrenheit or colder when the photograph was taken. Cross-country skis were propped in a snow bank by the door; the odd-looking, orange-and-white puppy posing in the doorway was Casey, my pet and best friend. He has always been a ham for pictures.

As I looked at that image, the hibernating dream began stirring in my head, though I wouldn't realize this until too late to stop it. The next slides were typical scenes of the Yukon Sourdough Rendezvous, the grand carnival held in the territorial capital every February. There were flour-packing contests, a beauty pageant, Gold Rush era costumes, sourdough pancake breakfasts and… sled dog races.

Dozens of teams were gathered on the river ice for the start and I could pick out a few friends' teams in the photos. Jean's was on the left, Cor's beside them, and next was Jon and his crew. I caught myself wondering why I'd never owned a pack of dogs too. The old excuses of mess, noise, time and money seemed insignificant as the romantic, snowy images glittered on the screen.

During the next few days, while I revamped the canoeists' guidebook, my dream began to assert itself. Out of the blue, I would blurt out a question about building harnessing or bending boards for a toboggan. People looked at me strangely. After all, it was May with daytime temperatures pushing into the 70s.

My plan had been to return to Vancouver Island to resume my fledgling journalist career as soon as this book was off the presses. I'd thought living in the Yukon was a long-finished chapter in my life. Since then, there had been a different story for me on the coast, with another cast of characters and a new plot. Yet here I was back in the North, lying in my tent, sleepless at the thought of spending a winter way off in the bush with my own dog team, going on camping expeditions, visiting with trappers and learning about living at Sixty Degrees Below Zero.

Perhaps all Canadians harbour genetically-transferred, idealist impulses to relive a pioneering lifestyle. If so, very few of us put these instincts into thoughts, fewer into words, and only the rare soul is compelled into action. Yet a full-fledged obsession had me clearly and completely in its grasp; I'm not sure I was really being given an option. The thought occurred to me that this might be quite dangerous – not everyone returns from his or her romantic Yukon dreams. However, the next message from my subconscious was to have faith in my luck.

Two days later, I found myself walking thirty-two miles in a thunderstorm, then sleeping under a spruce tree near the base of a mountain. Come daylight, I rolled up my soggy sleeping bag, poured water from my boots, ate an apple, and hiked up into the clouds. Following a steep ridge, I eventually climbed above the weather and could look for peaks and other landmarks. A few craggy features matched the lines on my now-mushy topographic map, so I knew this was the right mountain.

From her fire tower high atop One Ace Mountain [on the BC-Yukon border near Watson Lake], Marsha coordinated communications with planes, fire crews and other lookout towers.

Another half hour's scrambling brought renewed doubts, as I was near the summit and hadn't seen any sign of human habitation. Happily, the last rise revealed a small ledge, upon which were perched a white outhouse, an ecstatic floppy-eared puppy, a many-windowed hut with an impressive array of antennae wires, and – standing in the doorway – my future wife. Marsha McGillis was grinning and shaking her head in disbelief while the black-and-tan dog was sniffing my wet boots and wriggling its whole body in delight.

A forest fire tower might be an unlikely place to discuss dog mushing, but we did just that. I explained I needed a good heater to keep me warm on this winter adventure. Marsha has since said it was not really fair of me to proposition her like that: she hadn't seen a man for weeks and was susceptible to any offer.

Whether asking was ethical or not, by the time I climbed down the mountain three days later, Marsha had agreed to be my partner for the winter ahead. Her year-old puppy Tyhee would be one of the many dogs we would need.

CHAPTER TWO

MAKING READY

As soon as Marsha could join me on Vancouver Island in early August, we set to work drawing up food lists and deciding on equipment. From my previous experiences in the North, I had a fair idea about cold weather camping equipment. Marsha had worked as a park ranger and camp cook, and had taken home economics and wildland recreation courses at college. Between us, we had enough opinions to cover just about any eventuality. Unfortunately, we were a trifle short on cash. Marsha and I had met the winter before while working as group leaders for Katimavik, a low-paying, government-sponsored youth project, and neither of us had much money saved.

Tight finances forced us to rely heavily on our chief assets: time and energy. The next two months would be spent scrounging, bargain hunting and building. If we couldn't buy an item on the cheap, we made it. Some articles we hand-crafted because traditional models were no longer commercially available. We aimed for simplicity of design and time-tested materials, but kept our eyes open for worthwhile technological advances. To push our pennies further, we bought raw materials from wholesalers and manufacturers in Vancouver and Victoria, avoiding the high mark-ups in northern stores.

We toured second-hand stores with a vengeance, but finally had to commit ourselves to making our own dog harnesses, dog packs, chains and collars, portable kennels, toboggans, one sleeping bag, anoraks, mitts, gauntlets, socks, vests.... The list seemed to go on forever and so did the projects. A few items wouldn't get finished until we were in our cabin.

Although starting from scratch to make our outfit was exhausting, it gave us a thorough understanding of, and confidence in, our equipment. A delightful side-effect from all this industry was the boost to our self-images: we felt so capable.

Finished or not, at the end of September, everything we had would go to the

Yukon with us in our '70 Ford pick-up truck or on the trailer to be towed behind. The truck was a rusty, battered beast I bought when fed up with looking at used trucks. On the sixth day of walking the streets of Vancouver, classified ads in hand, searching for anything we could afford, I pounce on a deal just before midnight. Come morning, I had to try the key in four trucks parked in that lot before finding the one I'd paid for. Buying a vehicle after dark isn't recommended for anyone caring about aesthetics, but we were aiming for *sturdy*. Seeing the old Ford now in the light of day, I told myself *Furd* (as Marsha dubbed it) projected a certain air of being dependable. Furd's previous life was hauling plants, rocks and soil for a landscaping firm – the box was heavily dented. My main worry was the chatter already noticeable in the clutch. For thousands of miles through British Columbia and on up the dusty Alaska Highway, this old warrior would have to pull a flat deck trailer, both vehicles heaped with our winter necessities. As for appearances, we would have Furd so piled and draped with supplies on the trip North no one would notice the cancer eating at the wheel wells or the rippled fenders.

I had pinpointed a destination for us, but it was difficult to arrange actual accommodation from thousands of miles away. After many canoe trips on the Yukon's rivers, my favourite area was the confluence of the Pelly and Yukon rivers. We ordered some large-scale topographic maps and climate reports to give us more info. The signs all looked good: there were abandoned mining roads and wagon trails galore in the hills for our dog travels, and a sparse population of trappers and homesteaders, the closest ones living within a half-day's travel. From the weather records, we could expect a knee-high covering of snow during an average winter, and plenty of cold temperatures. We shivered at mentions of Seventy Below Zero!

The weather was that much above zero on Vancouver Island in early September. My parents, who lived at Qualicum Beach, had offered the use of their house for the month while they went off on holidays. I doubt they imagined what was going to happen.

Qualicum Beach is a sleepy village, populated mostly by retired folks. The centre of activity is a golf course overlooking Georgia Strait. From the fairways, one can look over the wide, sandy beach and glassy blue waters to the snowcapped Coastal Rockies. Sport fishermen troll between the anchored yachts while killer whales cavort in their wake. The residents spend their days at tea parties and cocktail gatherings when they are not themselves fishing, golfing or hosting relatives from less attractive areas of Canada.

A mountain of cardboard boxes covered by a canvas tarpaulin appeared on the front lawn. Beside my primer-painted and ailing '71 Plymouth Valiant was parked the newly-acquired pick-up, and behind that a rusty flat-bed trailer bought from a fellow who'd used it to haul cedar shake bolts. Our dogs, Casey, Tyhee and the newcomer Loki, were chained to the porch. I'd just bought a stack of plywood and – with help from our carpenter friend and former Yukoner, Barry Barlow – was constructing kennels to fit on the truck and trailer. With chain saw roaring, Skil saw whining, hammers pounding, engines revving, dogs howling and the living room stereo blaring country music, we were beginning to attract a little attention from the neighbours. They closed their windows.

Taking advantage of sales on apples and pears from the Okanagan Valley, we decided to do some large-scale fruit drying. Marsha borrowed a library book on making your own solar fruit dehydrator.

"This is too complicated," she decided, "and definitely too expensive. Let's just use some large pans, or some screens, or —"

Before I knew it, she had me taking down all the window screens in the house for temporary drying racks. When I dragged the garden hose over to wash the dust off them, Marsha called out that she had another idea. Following the sound of running water, I found her naked in the shower stall, scrubbing screens with a bristle brush.

We arranged the screens in the patio and driveway, elevated on blocks to permit air circulation beneath the fruit. By thinly slicing the apples and pears, and directing an oscillating fan over the screens, we had each batch dehydrated in two days. At night, the neighbours could watch us carry all the screens inside to be spread around the house, where the drying would continue, safe from the dew. Next morning, as they had crumpets and tea, the procession would be reversed for their entertainment.

My parents' closest friends began finding the queerest excuses to drop in and check on our activities from close range.

"They must feel an obligation to Mom and Dad to see that no irreparable damage is being done," I explained to Marsha. "All our comings and goings must be unsettling for them."

"I think everyone is more interested in our going than our comings," she suggested. "At least, their first question seems to be *When are you leaving?*"

To Hank Bennett from two lots up, we proudly displayed our latest find.

"I salvaged this deerskin from a doe killed on the highway last week," I proudly told him. "We're tanning it with a vinegar and ashes solution. We'll be able to use the leather this winter."

"I'm glad you didn't pay money for that stinky thing," he said and looked sideways at me. "Ever tanned a deer hide before?"

"Nope," I admitted. "But how hard can it be?"

That rhetorical question *How hard can it be?* became somewhat of a rallying call for our many preparations.

Meanwhile, our dogs, frustrated by the heat and bored of being chained, were taking out their anxieties on Dad's cherished lawn. Before we noticed, Casey had burrowed under the thornless blackberries in pursuit, perhaps, of some prehistoric bone. Tyhee excavated a patch of grass and tunnelled beneath the porch with no apparent intent apart from a love of digging. When we moved them beside the garage, they proceeded to scoop out great potholes in the gravel driveway.

We were making good progress on our preparations, locating much of the materials and information right in the immediate area. Harnesses would obviously be a most important item for a winter of dog mushing, so finding or making these was high on our list of priorities. We wanted to have a reliable, simple style that would be suitable for freighting large loads.

Essentially, there were two main styles of draught gear for dogs used in the North: *collar harness* and *siwash harness*. The *collar harness* was essentially a scaled-down model of draught horse harnessing. It was the standard for working teams when the important factor was power, not speed. The teams that had transported the mails, for example, would have hauled massive loads through the worst conditions. Gold Rush era stories tell of travellers waiting at roadhouses after a big snowstorm for the mail team to come through and break trail to the next settlement. The dogs of those yarns were huge beasts, part Malemute, crossed with Saint Bernard, Labrador, Newfoundlander and wolf, outfitted in padded collars and tandem traces. The Mounted Police dog teams used these collar harnesses as well.

The more commonly-seen style over the few years I'd spent in the North was the lighter *siwash harness*. This version was made of nylon or cotton webbing – crossed around the dog's body and padded lightly across the chest. All the racing teams used these, and an increasing number of trappers too. The dogs had greater freedom of movement in siwash harnesses, which was important for running a race, though the consensus I'd gathered was that this gear was not suitable for heavy freighting.

When I first started to train Casey as a pup, I sewed him a siwash from pieces of lampwick and seatbelt webbing. I learned hardly anyone was building their own siwashes any more, because it was almost as cheap to mail-order them ready-made.

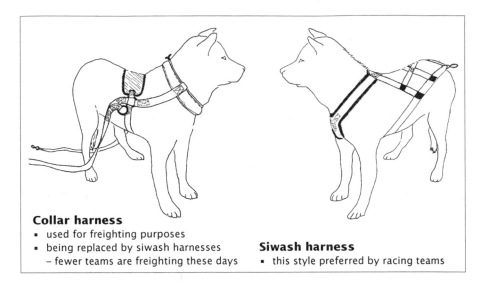

Collar harness
- used for freighting purposes
- being replaced by siwash harnesses
  – fewer teams are freighting these days

Siwash harness
- this style preferred by racing teams

"How could we order harnesses if we don't know the sizes of the other dogs we're going to get?" Marsha wanted to know. "These order forms have blanks for a half-dozen measurements."

"I'd rather try collar-type freighting harnesses this winter," I suggested, "though I haven't been able to locate a supplier. The demand seems to have dropped to the point that cobblers aren't making them any more. I guess they're all concentrating on making horse gear now."

My affliction for things traditional was coming out again. I'd envisioned dogs transporting us on extended camping trips. The loads were bound to be heavy and the trails unpacked. I had one old collar harness I'd brought back from the Yukon years ago and we took this to a cobbler in Coombs, near Qualicum, to get a quote on having harnesses custom made. His price, for cutting, forming, stitching and stuffing the collars, and sewing all the traces, including the cost of all materials, was a very reasonable $40 per harness if we helped with some of the labour. But having so little money, we decided to make them ourselves, using scrounged leather and straw. The process turned out to be neither quick nor simple. If we'd known in advance what all was entailed, we'd surely have borrowed money and taken the cobbler up on his offer.

For a collar pattern, I consulted library books on horse harness making, thinking we could simply scale down their patterns. In the meantime, Marsha had gingerly taken apart the ancient collar to see how it had been assembled. The leather and straw had, over its history, absorbed the odours of goodness knows how many sled dogs; when released, the stench was overpowering. We retreated while Tyhee wagged her tail in appreciation.

Our final collars would be made of tanned leather which was stitched to a thin steel rod and stuffed with oat straw. One saddlery text opined that rye straw was the ultimate, but we settled on oat straw we scythed from a sympathetic farmer's field. *[For step-by-step instructions, please see Appendix I.]*

For traces, we substituted nylon webbing for the leather strapping used in previous eras. We would leave the tugs and backbands to measure and stitch later when we had all the dogs in front of us. *[For diagrams, see Appendix I.]*

We had acquired all the materials and were fumbling with a glover's needle and pliers to stitch the first collar, when Dad's fishing buddy dropped in for a surprise inspection. Colonel Norm Jeffries surveyed the situation and called for a halt.

"That's not how you do it!" he roared. "You bring that collar over to my house at four o'clock and I'll show you how it is done."

When I arrived, Col. Jeffries had located his father's sewing kit and was ready to demonstrate the two-needle method of stitching leather. His father was a harness maker in the British Army and later served in the Mounted Police.

"This is the proper way to sew," Col. Jeffries declared. "If one of the threads breaks, the second will hold."

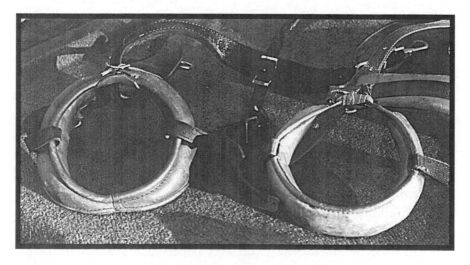

Note the contoured shape of the left collar –
reminiscent of a draught-horse's harness –
while the right one is what we referred to as donut-shaped.

He lent us the kit to work with, and I found the antique awl and knee vise a joy to work with. A faster, easier method of stitching heavy leather or webbing would have been to use a sewing awl, which makes a running stitch like a sewing machine. With this latter method, however, both threads may come loose if one breaks.

I had barely mastered proper two-needle form, when my grandfather heard what we were up to. He showed up with a glover's palm to use instead of a thimble. Then he produced some pig bristles and bees wax to demonstrate how a real purist stitches. Leatherworkers shunned needles for centuries, preferring to form the bristle into the thread to make a stiff end for poking through the hole made by an awl. After an educational, but frustrating hour rolling bristles and linen thread on my thigh, I decided we'd better settle on being half-pure if the collars were ever to get finished.

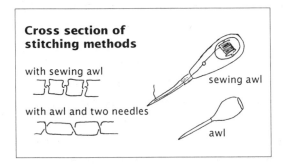

Cross section of stitching methods

with sewing awl

with awl and two needles

sewing awl

awl

Traces would have to take a lot of wear and tear, being constantly flexed and strained, twisted and turned. They would get dragged through slush and dog doo, rubbed against trees, urinated on and gnawed. We were not too confident about the light nylon webbing we were using, for it was even thin enough to be sewn on Mom's sewing machine. Marsha sat for hours measuring all the lengths of webbing, pinning them together, and stitching them at the places that didn't have to wait for a custom measurement. She was rubbing her fingers raw on the traces while I was getting blisters from pushing the awl and yanking on the thread to make the collars.

"Maybe we should have mail-ordered the other type," sighed Marsha.

"Yeah, but think of the specialized technical training you're getting," I kidded. "And there's no tuition charge."

We had the saddlery business down pat by the end of the month, but only three harnesses actually finished. The partially assembled traces were in a spaghetti-like tangle, stored in an empty kennel box on the trailer. The straw rolls and leather were kept handy, in case there was a dull moment during the long safari ahead of us. Marsha had already penned names on the first three completed harnesses.

"This one's for Tyhee Maquillée," she announced grandly, draping it over her German Shepherd and Siberian Husky cross. The puppy had filled out considerably and now weighed fifty-five pounds. She would never get too big, though, because her growth had been stunted by the strain of carrying puppies from her first heat.

Tyhee's long nose and skinny tail would set her apart in any gathering of northern dogs, but she had the necessary thick coat and big paws. Around her eyes were patches of tan which had given rise to her fancy surname, *Maquillée*, a French word meaning *a female who wears make-up*.

"Loki, you old mongrel, come try this on," I called when Marsha pulled out the second harness. "You've seen a freight collar before, I'm told."

Loki was a gift to us from friends who were building a ferro-cement fishing boat near Courtenay. Mel Hart and Laurie Murray had Loki as combination pet and watchdog while construction was under way, but now the *Lamplighter III* was almost finished. Soon they would be heading out to sea and would have no room on board for the dog. Mel said a previous owner had used Loki in harness in the Cassiar, B.C. area, so we were glad to have acquired a veteran. When we'd gone to the boatworks to fetch him, Marsha had mistaken Loki's fuzziness and lopsided grin for teddy bear friendliness. When she mussed his fur and playfully wrestled his head, Loki suddenly roared and snapped at her face. Marsha stumbled back out of his chain's reach and we surveyed the damage: two bruise marks on her forehead and two at her jaw line. I turned my attention to Loki: he was lying down meekly, knowing he had made a horrific mistake. I reprimanded him, determined he remember not to get rough with us humans. He'd impressed upon us not to let down our guard with huskies.

Loki was a much-scarred and sturdy-looking dog, about Casey's height. He weighed about five pounds more than Tyhee and the same amount less than Casey. He and Casey growled a lot the first two days together before settling down as comrades, with Casey apparently the alpha male of this pack of three.

Casey and I had been together for five years, since I acquired him as a pup in Whitehorse. He had some experience in harness, mostly from pulling a small toboggan behind me when I first tried winter camping and travelling on cross-country skis. For the record, Casey had actually run in the Sourdough Rendezvous races one year while being dog-sat by my buddy, Jon Rudolph. Jon had assembled a gang of borrowed pets and strays just to try the sport. At the starting line, the announcer described these dogs as, "—not really Malamutes, not really Siberian Huskies. Ah, let's call them *just friends*."

Casey would be a good choice for a silly team. Almost all sled dogs are black and white, with a few dogs showing some brown or beige markings. My pet was bright orange with white trim, and clownish in demeanour. Somewhere he'd picked up a nickname of *The Poofer*.

"Here's your collar to try on, Poofer," Marsha called to Casey. He rolled on his back to suggest he'd rather have his tummy scratched. Marsha laughed and shook her head, saying, "Some lead dog you are going to be!"

Indeed, unless we could buy an already-trained leader in the Yukon, Casey the Poofer would have to be the first dog in my team. He appeared to lack a winner's driving determination, but could understand a few basic commands and would do in a pinch. I had hopes Tyhee would have the temperament to lead Marsha's team, because we had decided two teams would be better than one. This would allow us to take more equipment and supplies on long winter camping trips. Since we could anticipate having up to a dozen dogs between the two squads, there were still nine collars to be stitched. My blistered fingers ached at the thought.

CHAPTER THREE

AND AWAY WE GO...

My parents returned just in time to see us off. We had the cavalcade stretched out on the street, with **Valerie** the blue Valiant lined up in front of our homely truck-and-trailer rig. **Marsha** would be driving the car as far as Victoria for delivery to its new owner, our friend Barry Barlow. All our worldly possessions were tucked somewhere into the canvas-covered mountain on the trailer or crammed under the canoes on the half-ton pick-up. Why we were taking the canoes no one was quite sure, but they added a finishing touch, like a top hat to a tuxedo. I had been carting these two battered canoes around the country for so long that a move just wouldn't have seemed right without them.

The kennel boxes were crowded on the trailer with barely space to open the ten compartment doors. Taking advantage of every available nook and cranny, we had stuffed supplies in all but three of the little rooms. Now came the dogs' chance to try out their travelling quarters. With Mom's camera clicking, we proudly walked Casey, Tyhee and Loki from their excavation sites to the trailer.

They were dubious. Tyhee jumped into the back of the pick-up truck, while Casey made it clear he would prefer to sit in the driver's seat. Loki crawled under the trailer.

"Aw, come on, you guys," I pleaded with them. "You're spoiling a very dramatic moment."

One by one, we manhandled the reluctant canines into their boxes. Loki gave us a scare when he bared his teeth and snapped at Marsha, but he submitted meekly after I cuffed him on the snout. It was disturbing to think about introducing nine strange dogs to this routine; our own pets were hard enough to manage.

"You'd better stop at a butcher and stock up on bones to make those compartments more enticing," Dad suggested.

"Good idea," I said, as I gave him a good-bye hug.

The neighbours were peeking out their windows, no doubt relieved we were

The metal rims on Marsha's sunglasses are taped so they won't freeze to her cheek skin when she's out in the extreme cold.

finally leaving. To us, the feeling was more one of disbelief. We had been planning and working so hard to make this moment possible, and the departure time was finally here.

Mom gasped, ran into the house and, a moment later, reappeared with a shopping bag. She handed it to Marsha and gave her a kiss. "I almost forgot," Mom said, indicating the contents. "I packed you a lunch. Just some sandwiches to snack on. And some biscuits for the dogs."

I drove slowly down the street, watching the trailer in the wide outside mirrors to see how it would behave. In those reflectors, I could see Mom and Dad waving and smiling. I felt the sadness that comes with departures, and my eyes misted over.

"They certainly will have a few things to remember us by," I thought, feeling a flush of embarrassment as an image of the dogs' diggings flashed into my mind. What didn't occurred to me then was another reminder we'd overlooked in our cleanup. Come the rains of January, hundreds of oat seeds from the straw we'd cut for the collar stuffing would be uncurling their first leaves and growing up through the gravel driveway.

We slept that night in Victoria, the *Garden City,* at Barry's home. The dogs were tethered out in the trees of a vacant lot next door to his apartment building. The condominiums towering overhead must have intimidated these country dogs, because they settled down immediately, each curling into a furry ball to sleep beside his or her water pan.

On the ferry crossing to Vancouver they were, by contrast, excited and noisy. We chained them to various parts of the truck to allow them a chance to stretch and breathe after the confinement of their kennels. Each had a ham bone for entertainment, and fresh water.

As Casey paced at his chain's end, we realized the effect the dogs were having on the other passengers. The heavy chains, thick collars, shaggy fur, powerful teeth pulverizing the large bones, the manner in which Casey and Loki strutted for any audience, all combined to make them appear bigger and wilder and curiously savage for this inter-city passage. They were drawing a crowd.

Then an unsuspecting pensioner ambled up with a miniature poodle in tow. He had barely said, "Look, Tiger," when our dogs spotted his little pet. All three lunged forward with fangs flashing. Terrifying growls echoed off the steel hull, while their jerking rocked the truck on its springs.

The poor man looked as if he'd have gladly jumped overboard if he could have freed himself from the leash tangled around his ankles. But Tiger was made of sterner stuff. He growled right back at Casey. Then, demonstrating a mastery of the art of taunting, the bold little pooch peed on a car tire inches outside of Casey's chain radius. That done, he walked defiantly away, jittery owner in tow.

Next time I checked on the dogs, my orange pet was still straining to sniff that tire. Tiger was small, but he wasn't dumb.

By nightfall, we'd gone only as far as Haney, where we pulled into a campground, our nerves frazzled. Driving the ungainly load through city traffic had been no picnic. Tomorrow we'd get a taste of the open road. That is, tomorrow, and the next day, and the next.... At reasonable speeds, and barring breakdowns, we had over fifty hours of driving ahead of us to reach Whitehorse.

"There is one aspect of the journey I'm looking forward to right now," Marsha muttered as we scurried about in the headlights' glare to set up our tent. "As we drive northward, we'll be getting out of this soggy coastal climate!" Staying that rainy night in Haney was like camping inside a car wash.

We left southern B.C. in late September, and had the highways largely to ourselves. The summer tourist traffic had long since gone home.

Autumn seemed synonymous with harvest on the fertile Fraser River valley

Travelling kennels or 'Dog Boxes'

and a time for late haying in the golden Cariboo region. Yet as we passed out of the Bulkley Valley near Hazelton and touched the first gravel roads, we became progressively more aware of the desolation of this season in the North. Leaves had long ago quit the deciduous trees and the colourful roadside displays of wild roses and fireweed existed only on the guidebook covers. The country was shrouded in drabness, mourning the loss of summer or, perhaps, dreading the approach of winter. One could sense a desperation in the air.

The days were getting noticeably shorter as the latitude increased. Darkness would descend like a dense curtain. There was no snow yet to mirror the star-light and no moon this week. Only the eerie, beautiful flicker of Northern Lights distracted us from the hypnotizing swath of Furd's high beams sweeping over the endless gravel ahead. The spruce trees and rock bluffs flashed by on either side like disjoint rushes of a movie. Where ground water was undermining the roadbed, we crawled along at 10 miles per hour, weaving around deep ruts and mush-holes. At one point, our headlights illuminated the ancient wreckage of two eighteen-wheelers that had underestimated this highway and become their own burnt, twisted memorials.

When we were both too cross-eyed and dizzy to continue, we'd pull off and camp in a gravel pit or at a picnic area, sleeping on a tarp beside the truck, under a heap of sleeping bags, blankets and stars. The nights were nose-nipping cold and clear. The fabled northern mosquito and black fly slept deep in the muskeg moss to arise only when the sun was high overhead and our dust-caked vehicle had resumed its journey.

By now, we wouldn't have minded a few rainstorms. On and on through the dust we drove. Being passed by another traveller was a nerve-shattering event. Each vehicle threw up a billowing beige cloud of fine dust which hung in the still air like dirty cotton candy. For seconds after a truck swept by, we would be driving blind, trusting only that the road was clear for the next hundred yards until visibility was restored. Everyone had their headlights turned on night and day, trying to minimize the chances of a head-on collision in the blind moments.

The powdery, flour-like dust found its way into the cab from under the floorboards, around the windows, even through cracks in the dashboard. Though dust was settling democratically in our every pore, the discomfort we felt inside the truck must have been slight compared to what the poor dogs were enduring. Dust clouds almost hid the trailer and its kennels from view, no doubt coating their lungs with the same brown layer that the cargo wore. While we had the truck suspension and seat springs to cushion the bumps, there was only a bit of straw on the kennel floor to absorb the constant jarring for them.

"We've got to do something," Marsha insisted on the second day since leaving pavement. "Those dogs will hate us if we keep this up."

"What are our choices?" I asked. "They won't all fit in the cab with us, and the back of the truck is full. If they stand on top of the canoes, one of them will probably fall off and get killed."

"We could always move one of the two kennel boxes forward to the back of the truck. It is less dusty there."

"And move all that's in the truck box onto the trailer? Do you know how long that would take?"

By the next gravel pit, she had me convinced and we pulled off to start the tedious transfer of dirty equipment. Fortunately, we'd planned ahead and any food or delicate items were well wrapped in airtight bundles of plastic or canvas. We trusted that the contents of these grimy sacks were still clean.

Having moved the boxes, I thought our kennel problems were over for a while, when Casey created a new challenge. He chewed the plywood around the little breathing hole in his door until the opening was just large enough to get his head out, but not back in without hurting his ears. He set up a terrible racket, and the more he struggled, the worse he impaled himself on the jagged edges of the gnawed hole. At length, after many calming words, interspersed with the odd threat when we got impatient with him, Casey's head was back in the box and I could repair the door, while Marsha checked his ears for external injury.

The best temporary solution I could effect on the spot was to drill holes around the opening and weave wire back and forth, forming a crude mesh. Even if Casey hadn't learned a lesson from this event, the wire would slow him down. Once we got to Whitehorse, I could get some steel mesh to fasten inside all the doors to avoid this happening with the other dogs.

"The Poofer isn't hurt, except for his dignity," Marsha reported as I put my tool box away. "We'd better not play with his ears for a few days. They'll be a bit sore."

Each day travelled meant we were closer to our dream and each town fed our excitement. Every gas pump and tumbledown café announced itself as *On the Route to the North* or *Gateway to the Yukon* or some such slogan. They could have saved their words; it was obvious where we were. The brisk air, the snowcapped mountains, the clear skies; one could really feel the North.

At Teslin, an Indian village beside a glittering lake, we allowed ourselves a mental pat on the back. We were finally in the Yukon River's watershed. Had we the time, we could have put in our canoes here, and floated down the Teslin River, on down the Yukon to reach our destination near the mouth of the Pelly. We'd come a long way.

Teslin Lake is part of a two-thousand-mile-long waterway which starts in these mountains and becomes a wide, awesomely powerful river. The Yukon River flows northward to the Arctic Circle, then westward through central Alaska into the Bering Sea. Except for a handful of towns and small villages, like this one, the banks are wilderness. There are fewer people living along the Yukon River's banks now than at any time in recorded history.

There have been Indians living and travelling through the Yukon for twenty thousand years, if you can believe old bones and carbon dating techniques. They evolved a culture that allowed them to thrive despite the incredibly harsh winters. Each year was a cycle of migration between the best harvest areas. The harvest was mostly fishing and hunting plus a little berry-picking. Salmon were caught in nets woven from spruce roots or captured in corrals formed by pounding stakes across a stream bed. The people would dry fish for winter food, just like we did with our apples and pears.

Moose gathered on the islands and flatlands along the rivers in the autumn for rutting and again in the spring for calving. The Indians killed them with bow and arrow or spears, or caught them in large snares. When the caribou migrated across the rivers, they were easy targets for hunters in skin boats. The Indians here depended on moose, caribou and salmon for their food, clothing, shelter – in much the same way that the Plains Indians depended upon the buffalo.

Most of the year, the people would live in hunting groups of only a few families. So the annual large gatherings at good fishing spots must have been a time of great excitement. This was their chance to arrange marriages, trade information and tools, play games, celebrate births and mourn the dead. In later years, bands of Indians from the coast of Alaska began to show up, bringing Russian knives,

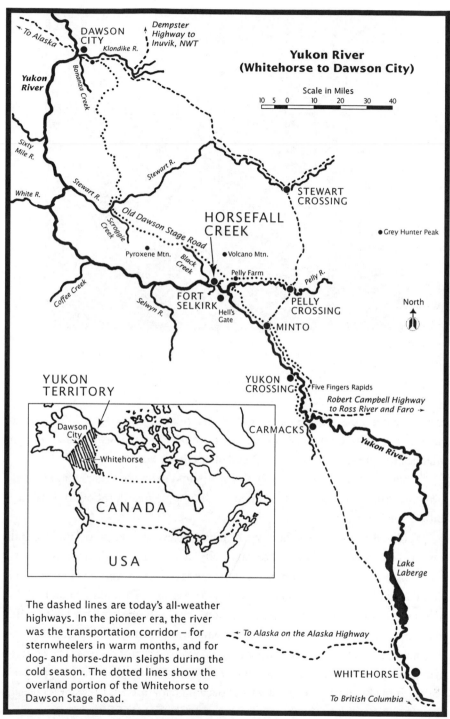

Yukon River
(Whitehorse to Dawson City)

Scale in Miles

10 5 0   10   20   30   40

To Alaska

DAWSON CITY

Klondike R.

Dempster Highway to Inuvik, NWT

Yukon River

Bonanza Creek

Sixty Mile R.

White R.

Stewart R.

Stewart R.

Stewart R.

STEWART CROSSING

Old Dawson Stage Road

Scroggie Creek

HORSEFALL CREEK

Grey Hunter Peak

Pyroxene Mtn.

Black Creek

Volcano Mtn.

Coffee Creek

Pelly Farm

Pelly R.

FORT SELKIRK

Selwyn R.

Hell's Gate

PELLY CROSSING

North

MINTO

YUKON TERRITORY

YUKON CROSSING

Five Fingers Rapids

Robert Campbell Highway to Ross River and Faro →

Dawson City

Whitehorse

CARMACKS

CANADA

Yukon River

USA

Lake Laberge

The dashed lines are today's all-weather highways. In the pioneer era, the river was the transportation corridor – for sternwheelers in warm months, and for dog- and horse-drawn sleighs during the cold season. The dotted lines show the overland portion of the Whitehorse to Dawson Stage Road.

← To Alaska on the Alaska Highway

WHITEHORSE

To British Columbia

See page 103 for close-up of Horsefall area.

*Marsha and Tyhee take a break from the dusty driving up the Alaska
Highway to savour the flavour of water at Teslin Lake.*

copper kettles, beads, blankets and eventually guns, to trade for furs. Imagine the
change it made to their lives to suddenly have iron tools, guns to hunt with, and
matches to light their fires. The cultural shock must have been tremendous.

"What about the Hudson's Bay Company and their voyageurs and all that?"
asked Marsha as the dusty miles rolled by. "I thought that Fort Selkirk was originally a fur trading post."

"Yep, that's right near where we're going, if everything pans out. The Indians used the junction of the Yukon and Pelly as a trading and gathering spot for
centuries before Robert Campbell and his crew claimed it for the Hudson's Bay
Company in 1848. But Campbell didn't have much luck. The coastal Indians didn't
like trading competition, so they burned down the buildings, and the Hudson Bay
men beat a hasty retreat back over the mountains to eastern Canada."

The next bunch of whites to see the Yukon were gold prospectors. They filtered
in over the mountains and up the river from Alaska. The big discovery happened in
1896, off the Klondike River, near what became Dawson City. Tens of thousands
of people flooded into the territory to get in on the gold find.

"That would be when the Yukon River started to have big paddlewheelers, like the tourism pictures always show," Marsha said, "and the *Gold Rush of 1898* and miners climbing in a long line up to the Chilcoot Pass. Diamond-Tooth Gertie and Klondike Kate. Jack London's *Call of the Wild* and *White Fang*. We had to read those in school."

"You've got it. And most of those stampeders floated down the Yukon River on rafts and small boats to Dawson City. The big steamboats brought in the heavy equipment and most of the food for the boom town. One book I found in the archives when I was writing that canoeing guidebook listed the names of hundreds of boats working the river during the Gold Rush. There must have been traffic jams in places."

"It would have been pretty quiet in the winter around the place where we're going to stay, wouldn't it?" Marsha prompted.

"For the first few years of the Gold Rush, any winter traffic was dog-powered. Then a road was cut paralleling the river for a horse-drawn stage or sleigh which carried the mail and a few hearty passengers, but it was nothing like the activity of the summer. That old road is still there and we'll be driving our dogs over it this winter," I said. "Since an all-weather highway was built in the 1950s from the railhead at Whitehorse to Dawson and the other mining towns, the stage road has been deserted. The riverboat fleets have all retired, too, because they couldn't compete with trucks driving on that new highway."

"Who lives along the river now?"

"Hardly anyone. Almost all the Indians moved to towns along the highway. A lot of their men cut wood for the riverboats until the boats were beached. About that time the fur prices nose-dived, so they had little choice but to move to wherever the government agents wanted them to settle, and try to fit in with the white man's culture."

"Hey! Look at that whiteman culture up ahead," Marsha whooped.

It was hard to believe, but there was paved road in front of us. We had reached Whitehorse's city limits. Our tires passed from the gravel onto the smooth blacktop, and a strange silence engulfed the truck.

"Ahhh!" Marsha sighed. "That's sooooo nice."

CHAPTER FOUR

FINDING A CABIN AND ONE MORE DOG

At Whitehorse, we were lucky to have friends who would lodge us and help find the items still on our shopping lists. Jon Rudolph and Carol Racz's cabin was a few miles out of town, and we could tie up our three mutts in the yard beside Jon's pack of sled dogs.

Old Furd, showing an impressive sense of timing, didn't break down until we reached Jon's driveway, leaving us close to help. We nursed the ailing vehicle until it could be driven back into town, but a mechanic's verdict there sounded gloomy. The chattering clutch had chewed itself to pieces. The bill would be hundreds of dollars.

"Do we invest money into a sick old beast like this," I pondered aloud, "or borrow money from somewhere and buy another one?"

"How can you say that?" Marsha scolded. "If Furd heard you he might think he isn't appreciated and break down in some awful place next time."

Faced with logic like that, I clearly had no choice but to agree to the repairs.

While the truck was undergoing surgery to transplant various internal organs, I found a phone book and placed a few calls to people I knew from previous canoe trips on the Yukon. A fisherman's summer cabin near our destination might be available for a modest rent, I learned, but it *would require a little fixing up and a good sweeping out.* We could go look it over before we decided, but should be on guard for bears: the area around the fish camp was, reportedly, *thick with the bastards.*

We were ecstatic! Although there remained, of course, the condition of the cabin to check, it had to be better than wintering in a wall tent. We immediately decided to do a reconnaissance of our future home as soon as Furd was ready. Our plans were running smoothly; the next step would be finding sled dogs. I got another handful of coins for the payphone....

Because of my dog experience, albeit limited, in the Yukon, Marsha placed me nominally in charge of recruitment. I had my own theories about what size and breeding made a good sled dog – thoughts certainly neither original nor complete. While living in the North, I'd watched the races, listened to the bar-room discussions, read a few books on the subject, and tagged along while friends tried their hand with teams. Now, I was pumping everyone available for ideas and information about the availability of dogs, the latest racing sled developments, methods of training, care and feeding and, especially, how the old-timers ran their teams. I was trying to simplify, to demystify, to grasp the bare essentials.

Sled dogs come in a surprising variety of shapes and sizes. Originally any dog who worked well was kept, and failures were put into the dog food pot. Fighting would also weed out weaker dogs. Over the centuries, the people in each area developed their own breed of canine genetically suited for local needs and conditions. For example, the Malemute tribe's dogs were twice the size of those used by the Siberians, but each breed had its advantages. Generally, the larger dogs were used in deeper snow, hauling tougher loads, while the lighter mutts were bred for speed on the wind-packed snow over the tundra and sea ice.

In the central Yukon, the native Indians had dogs mostly as pack animals, seldom using them for draught until the period of contact with the white men. The particular strain of dogs bred in this area was subsequently lost, overwhelmed by the veritable zoo of canines that came in with the stampeders during the great Gold Rush of 1898.

Early in the 20th century, organizations in Europe and America established show standards for a few northern breeds: the Malemute, Samoyed and Siberian. Other types, such as the Esquimo, Mackenzie Husky, Greenland and Manitoba, were mentioned in journals but weren't given breed status. Unfortunately, the standards for kennel-raised dogs (colour of eyes, shape of tail and ears, and other cosmetic considerations) had little to do with actual pulling ability. With kennel owners breeding and in-breeding for appearance only, the evolutionary processes were short-circuited and the so-called pure-bred strains lost their vigour. Although in recent years some breeders had been revitalizing their registered lines by using them in races and weeding out the unfit, the winning teams rarely included any registered pure-bred dogs.

For our winter transportation, I wanted mongrels, because they were less prone to congenital defects and diseases, and often had better temperaments. We needed dogs big enough to wade through loose snow, yet not slow, meandering brutes, like St. Bernard-size dogs could be. It was important they all be about the same build too, so one pup wouldn't be forced to make two steps for a larger dog's single stride. Lean, well-proportioned dogs, weighing from fifty to seventy-five pounds, were my ideal.

We phoned every musher in the Whitehorse area who had a telephone, but no one had extra dogs at this time of year. A couple of people suggested I try again in a few months, after the first races of the season, when a few culls would be up for grabs. We couldn't wait that long.

Our next avenue was the local dog pound. We wandered in and made the mistake of telling the attendant we were seeking homeless mutts for our dog teams.

"Are you *DOG MUSHERS?*" she asked, making it sound as if we could be child molesters.

"We want to be," I said. "Why? Does it make a difference in cost?"

"You can't have *any* dogs! It's the rules. I can't give up a dog for adoption to a dog musher."

"How come?" asked Marsha.

"It is the policy. The rules. Some dog mushers chain up their dogs to a tree and hardly feed them. *And they beat them.*"

She was making me feel bad, so I shifted the topic to her volunteer work. "You keep this place so clean and tidy. I bet the dogs like it here. What do you do if no one wants to adopt them as pets?"

"Oh," the attendant said casually, "we shoot them."

After twenty minutes of discussing the matter and assuring her I'd only been joking about being a nasty musher and that we *dearly wanted a pet or two to play with in the snow,* Marsha and I got a peek at the orphaned darlings.

Only one dog looked anything like my ideal and he was rather on the fat side. He was a shaggy black-and-white mutt, about Casey's height and length but thicker through the chest. His pointed snout and silky hair could have been from a Collie heritage, but the big bones must have been from some sturdier breed stock. There was a thick layer of body fat all over him, so I figured he would be cheap to feed for the first while, until we trimmed him down to working shape.

"We'll take this guy," I called to the lady.

"*—as a pet,*" Marsha quickly added.

Five minutes, many triplicate forms and $40 later, the new dog was in the back of Furd. We decided on the way back to Jon and Carol's to christen our newest recruit *Hinglish* because of his large boney cranium. Some French Canadians refer to English Canadians as square heads, or *les têtes carrées*, or sometimes *les maudits Hinglish.*

Hinglish whined and whimpered constantly for the first few days, clearly not used to being chained. The commands to *sit, lie down* and *shake a paw* were

We rescued Hinglish from the Whitehorse pound.
He was shaggy and cuddly in both looks and personality.

familiar to him, leading us to assume he'd been a house pet before his stint at the pound. He was good-natured and friendly, though terribly frightened of the other dogs. I judged Hinglish to be between one and two years old.

Leaving the four dogs, the trailer and a mountain of equipment with our Whitehorse friends, we headed off in Furd the next morning for our reconnaissance mission into the Fort Selkirk area. With the rebuilt clutch and lightened load, the old truck handled like a sports car, zipping along the Klondike Highway with nary a cough nor sputter. It appeared the money spent on repairs had been well invested.

The cabin we planned to examine was on Horsefall Creek, which flows into the Yukon River some six miles below the confluence with the Pelly River. We could travel in by truck from the main highway some thirty miles on a narrow side-road which ran parallel to the Pelly. From the road's end, we would have a nine-mile hike to the Horsefall fish camp.

Both highway and side-road were clear and dry, so we made good time, parking the truck just after one o'clock. By the end of this road was an old farm, established during the Gold Rush. Now operated by brothers Dick and Hugh Bradley, the Pelly River Ranch was the most northerly cattle farm in Canada. The Bradleys offered to look after the truck, but insisted on first filling us up with gallons of tea. I pumped Hugh, who made a point of knowing such local history, for the story behind the name *Horsefall*.

"Well, there weren't any horses involved," he explained with a grin, "at least, not in the name itself. There was a modest homestead on that river flat and the people's name was Hosfel or Horsfall. The creek name is a corruption of the family name. Apparently the man was an Englishman and his wife was Native Indian. From what I can find out, the wife – we can call her Mrs. Horsfall – was very highly regarded by everyone. The husband was said to be a prospector and wandered about, leaving her to raise the children mostly on her own."

Early in the century, Joe Horsfall ran a hotel and store at Fort Selkirk at the downriver end of the town. In 1910, the Horsfalls' two-year-old son set the store on fire while playing with matches, and died soon after from his burns. Not long after the tragedy, the family moved downriver to set up their small farm homestead. There were four daughters, but no other sons.

"That's so sad. Perhaps the loss of the son severely depressed the father," I said. "That might explain his wandering about in the bush after being so industrious before."

"And what's the cabin like?" asked Marsha. "Is it part of the old homestead? That might be spooky."

"The original buildings are pretty much fallen down by now," Dick spoke up from where he sat on the cot. "The cabin you'll be looking at was only built a few years back. It's not big, but that'll make it warmer for you when the weather starts pushing Sixty or Seventy Below around Christmas."

Our enthusiasm, fuelled by the caffeine in the black tea, was too much to allow more conversation. We thanked the farmers, confirmed our directions on a topo map, and hiked off along the shore.

The sky was clear and the air fresh; it was ideal weather for walking. We carried light packs, with only our sleeping bags, coats, a bit of food and a rifle. After thousands of miles of dusty driving, these moments were an exhilarating treat. It was heavenly to not be bogged down by either our tons of possessions or our menagerie of animals for one whole day. With eager steps, we fairly danced through the forest.

The trail we followed headed away from the Pelly at the end of the farm fields, branching onto the old Dawson overland stage road. About five miles farther on, we swung onto a narrow wagon trail which would take us to Horsefall. As we walked, we tried to imagine how the forest would look after the first snowfall, and especially how this trail would be for driving our dog teams.

"What if we can't get any more dogs?" asked Marsha. "I don't like snowmobiles."

"We'll find lots of dogs," I said optimistically. "Don't worry."

The grade changed gradually until we were descending from the forest plateau country, the trail progressively steeper and steeper as we approached the Yukon River. High basalt rock bluffs frame the Yukon valley all along this stretch of river; our route snaked down a narrow

We were a great match at Pelly River Ranch. Dick Bradley loved to tell stories, and I loved to listen!

draw carved into these cliffs by Horsefall Creek. The creek itself was a dry, rocky bed, crossing and re-crossing our path. We thought about driving charging dog teams down this wild incline.

"Should be interesting," I commented, trying to be nonchalant.

"*Interesting*, my ass," muttered Marsha. "We'd better build good brakes."

At the base of the cliffs was a wedge-shaped flat, formed over the eons by the buildup of river silt onto the creek's delta. The trees were mostly willows, many quite knurled and gnarled. Locally, these twisted hardwoods were called *diamond willow*, because of diamond-shaped splits in their bark. In patches there were some evergreens, mostly white spruce, plus a few black spruce at the margins of the swampier ground. Wild grass was knee-high everywhere between the willows, attesting to the fertility of the soil.

We were noting the different types of animal excreta on the trail to appreciate the hiding, warm-blooded inhabitants of Horsefall flat when we spied one pile that stopped us in our tracks. A mound of bear excreta, chock full of bright red berries, confirmed the resident status of at least one bruin. The pile was old, but still unnerving.

I levered a bullet into the chamber of my rifle. I'd never had any problems with bears before, partly because I stayed away from them as best I could. This flat might be too small for that tactic. We cautiously made our way along the narrow trail, forcing a little chattering conversation to announce our presence.

We found the low, shabby cabin slumped in a clearing like yesterday's soggy sandwich. It was no architectural beauty and the yard around it resembled a war zone. Underfoot everywhere were spent bullet casings and tattered shotgun shells, lending a neo-Vimy Ridge decor to the scene. Discarded gas drums and plastic oil bottle targets bloomed like weeds. The cabin door and windows were boarded over and a cart was barricaded against the door. I imagined this bunker was what Hollywood filmmakers would build for a Mad Trapper's shoot-out with the Mounties.

Once inside, we had to stoop. The ceiling was so low I could only stand erect near the ridgepole. Marsha was suddenly happy to be shorter.

"It's not so bad," she laughed. "You'll just have to sit down a lot."

Heaps of old clothing tactfully hid the furniture. An ancient outboard motor was propped up against, and leaking oil onto, a tall stack of girlie magazines. The bench beside was overflowing with the rest of the library: gun club journals, hunting magazines and police novels. Tools and spare parts were sprinkled over the floor, at least as far back into the cabin as I immediately cared to venture. The windows were covered with plywood and plank shutters, making it hard to see much more.

We effected the removal of the bear protection with an axe handle, and stowed all the shutters around back. Inside again, we could now find the cookstove, bright red with rust, and the kitchen table, buried under tottering columns of soiled dinnerware and encrusted cook pots. Petrified baked beans with a shaggy topping of blue mold remained as evidence of the last meal served, yet never eaten. Even the mice, who had ripped apart the Kool-aid packages and camped in the Aunt Jemima bag, had passed up on those beans. They had defecated everywhere else but there was a clear area all around the putrid chili.

Cautiously we poked around, gingerly peering under tables and beds, never sure what all might be living under the jumble of greasy garments and personal effects. The most pleasant surprise was a large, deep root cellar under a trapdoor in the plank flooring. The other plus was the cookstove, which appeared intact, save for one missing firewall. We'd be able to rectify that absence by substituting a piece of scrap metal from the battlefield outside.

"What do you think?" I asked my partner when we were safely out in the sunshine.

"We could probably do everyone a favour and burn it down," Marsha grimaced, "— but we'll make it liveable."

If we wanted to live on this river flat, it was either here or in a tent. Examined from that perspective, the cabin looked much better.

"Welcome to your new home," I said with a hug.

Pacing off the wall measurements, I found the cabin to be twenty feet by sixteen feet using outside dimensions. Minus the thickness of the logs, this left less than nineteen by fifteen inside. The height was about seven feet under the ridge, but decreased to less than five feet tall along the side walls. The two windows were positioned too low to see through when I stood up, but offered a decent view toward the south and the west if one were seated.

"Now if we could clean and bleach the floor planks, so they would reflect the light from those windows, it would make this place much brighter—" Marsha was wandering about, talking to herself, already planning our attack. She and I examined every facet of the place to assess what could be moved, rebuilt, insulated, thrown out, cleaned, constructed or replaced. We needed an exhaustive list of supplies and tools for transforming this neglected hovel into a winter home.

A high priority on the *to-do list* was eviction of present occupants. We decided upon a two-fold plan: we would try to remove temptation, and deliver damnation should that fail. Our defensive supplies would consist of Marsha's collection of big glass jars, metal bread boxes and cookie tins. For an offensive capability, we put *mouse traps* on the list.

With night closing in upon us and the air chilling rapidly, we focused our attention on the cabin's two heat sources. Apart from the cookstove, there was a heater crudely welded from a 45-gallon fuel drum. Theses type of wood burners were called barrel stoves or *pigs* in the North and had a reputation for burning uncontrollably hot whenever the mood struck them, transforming any cabin into a sauna. A better place for a pig was in a warehouse or large garage that needed a lot of thermal output, and could use the huge firebox to advantage. For this little cabin, though, we'd have to get either a smaller heater or a full wardrobe of bathing suits.

Before lighting a fire in the drum, I had a sudden thought and rapped on the chimney pipe. A great wad of black, caked creosote fell onto my carefully arranged kindling.

"Yikes!" I cried, and banged again. A new rush of debris showered down from above. Tracing the flow of the pipes, it became apparent to me why there was so much creosote buildup. The smoke was compelled to rise, turn a right-angle, run slightly downhill for eight feet, pass through the log wall, then bend another 90 degrees before ending a few inches under the eaves.

Wishing we had done so before we were cold, we disassembled the chimney arrangement and emptied all the stack residue into cardboard boxes. There was enough to fill a bushel basket. I doubt we could have lit a fire without igniting all this creosote and possibly razing the cabin. We decided then and there to make a new chimney going straight up through the roof for whatever replacement heater we brought in.

Rather than fiddle any more with the big heater, we opted for lighting the cookstove. It wouldn't be able to hold a fire all night, but we had warm sleeping bags and only needed to get the immediate chill off our bones. The cookstove chimney, we noted happily, rose straight as a flagpole. Marsha banged on it and there was scarcely a trickle of soot dislodged.

Routinely examining the stove, Marsha checked the oven lever and draft controls, and then opened the oven itself. Inside was a pile of half-burnt sticks and a dozen spent matches. Someone, probably a tourist canoeing the river, had stopped here and tried to light the cookstove by making a fire in the oven!

Thanking that urbanite for the kindling, we soon had a blaze crackling in the firebox and were warming our hands over the red-hot glow of the cast-iron top. When our bodies were warmed and our spirits rejuvenated by the stove's heat, Marsha pulled out the list again and started us off on another session of *What if we do this here?* and *We'll need a thingy over there.*

An hour later, fed and snuggled deep in sleeping bags and blankets, we were still adding to the list.

CHAPTER FIVE

FANTASTIC FURD SHOWS HIS STUFF

By next morning, we had two full pages of entries on the to-do list. Ideas raced around in our heads like kids loose at a carnival. There would certainly be no shortage of chores this winter. We walked the nine miles back out to the farm scarcely talking, but the babble of thoughts was almost deafening. There were a million and one details to remember for the all-important move to the cabin.

It was now late October and the first snow had yet to come. Without the snow's insulation, the ground had frozen rock-hard, even where the trail passed through swampy sections. Daytime temperatures were well below freezing, pushing the frost-line deeper with every passing hour. Perhaps, we mused, our pick-up truck could make it from the farm all the way in to the cabin with a load of supplies. With chains for extra traction, and a hand winch to help on steep hills, it might be possible if the snow held off. The hills ruled out any thoughts about bringing in the trailer, but even one truckload would save us dozens of trips freighting from the farmyard with the dog teams. The dog food to be brought to the cabin would, by itself, weigh over a ton.

When one's mind is occupied, the time passes quickly. With the three-hour hike soon behind us, we fired up old Furd, thanked the farmers and headed along the side-road toward the highway. Our plan of the moment was to return to Whitehorse, where we'd pack a load, then rush back to attempt the cart trail into Horsefall. It would be a race against winter. One good snowfall would cut us off.

One tremendously important errand had to be looked after first: stopping in the Indian village of Pelly Crossing to order winter footwear. Mrs. Lizzie Hager was renown in the region for her well-made moccasins, so we sought out directions to her house.

After negotiating a price of $50 a pair, she had us put on thick woollen socks and stand on a newspaper. Then she traced the outline of our feet to make a pattern. We asked her to use the best native-tanned moose hide for the soles, but agreed that canvas would be fine for the uppers. It was important to get smoke-tanned leather as it was more durable and also wouldn't frost on the inside as commercially-tanned leather would.

We learned that the Yukon Indians don't refer to winter moccasins as *mukluks*, which is an Inuit (Eskimo) word for similar footwear made from sealskin. Our order was for *work moccasins*, which would be plain, as opposed to *town moccasins*, which would have beading and fur trim. We needed two pairs each, so we could change them when wet. Mrs. Hager said it would take an evening to make each pair.

Naturally, her family was curious about our plans for the winter, and stood around us while all the moccasin negotiations were happening. I asked her husband about buying dogs in the village. This prompted a great deal of chatter in both English and the Indian language between father and sons, and Lizzie and another lady. They paused every once in a while to ask us a detail about our pasts or plans, but gave no sign of passing judgement either on us or on our dreams. When we were leaving, Mr. Hager's words were to *come back in one week, when those moccasins are ready, and we'll see about dogs.* We thanked him for his trouble, but didn't get our hopes up too high.

Casey must have recognized Furd's rattling as we drove up to Jon's cabin near Whitehorse five hours later. Jumping and yipping at the end of his chain, he had the dog lot in an uproar, with Jon's pooches and ours all howling, barking and growling. They seemed glad for a break in the dull routine of life on a chain. Tails were thumping up dust clouds and one fellow was pacing back and forth with his food dish in his mouth. Trees were being watered and ears were being scratched. Tyhee was standing on her hind legs and pawing the air. Loki was snapping his teeth and shaking his head. Hinglish had wound his chain completely around a tree and was looking a little blue in the face from lack of air. How different life would be for all of them when the rest of winter arrived; cold weather without snow was not much fun for a sled dog.

When we went into town, I appeased one worry and bought us a propane lighting system. Our home-to-be was so small and dingy I was sure we'd both go quite mad before the winter was out if we didn't have some high-powered lights. Propane lighting is bright, though rather harsh and quite noisy. It was necessary to have a few auxiliary kerosene lanterns too because of the difficulty with propane *freezing* at extremely cold temperatures. If it is colder than -45 degrees Fahrenheit, propane in outside storage tanks won't actually freeze solid but it will thicken and no longer flow through pipes or hoses into the cabin. Kerosene is not affected by low temperatures.

Max Fraser, a longtime friend, offered a remedy for the cold weather problem. Propane tanks are usually stored away from the cabin because of the danger of leaking gas creeping inside the cabin and causing an explosion and fire. Since this gas is heavier then air, Max suggested we could keep our tanks in an insulated shed against the cabin wall as long as there was adequate ventilation at the bottom for leaking gas to escape and dissipate away. Another old buddy, Greg Skuce, said that pouring a kettlefull of boiling water over the tank to warm the fuel will give temporary reprieve during a cold snap. He claimed the water trick works for *about three hours at Fifty Below.*

For insulating the glass windows, we tracked down some of the expensive, clear type of rolled plastic. This was twice the price of ordinary poly but I felt it would be important to our state of mind to have a real view instead of a foggy glow. Still worried about windows, we decided an extra one would be cheery, and scrounged a discarded multi-pane window from a long-abandoned cabin.

It took the two of us three long days in town before we had all the items on our winter list checked off. The truck was pretty full. As a finishing touch, I lashed two lengths of double-walled, insulated chimney pipe and a sheet-metal airtight heater on the top of the heap. This decidedly gave the load a look of *everything but the kitchen sink.*

Ready or not, it was time to go. There was a hint of snow in the black clouds drifting in from the coast.

Only a mile past the Pelly Farm, on the first steep hill, the truck was spinning its tires and chewing deep ruts in the sandy trail. To put chains on the tires, we had to first cautiously roll back down to a nearly level spot. Furd's wide, outside mirrors had been an early casualty, shattering when they were slammed against the cab by branches. To see behind, I had my head out the window and had to quickly pull it back in whenever a branch threatened to literally wipe the expression off my face.

"Not a good start," I growled. "First damn hill and this crummy truck poops out."

"Relax," Marsha said. She always became annoyingly pleasant whenever I got frustrated. "Furd's a *good truck.* We'll make it somehow."

After blocking the front wheels with rocks, we wriggled in the dust under the back end, freezing our fingertips on the cold chains and skinning knuckles on the fasteners. Of course, when I sat up too soon, I cracked my head on the wheel-well.

However, our labour was not in vain as the truck was soon underway once more, and clamouring up the wickedest of grades like a bull moose in rut. Although Furd was not a four-wheel-drive, it was now performing better than had it been.

"Yipee, Furd! *Yeehaw!!*" Marsha shrieked. She kept pounding the dashboard and cheering, betraying clearly her next-door-to-the-rodeo-grounds childhood. The bouncier the ride got, the louder Marsha hollered. *"Yeehawww!"*

The old wagon track had seemed fairly wide to us when we walked in, but there was barely room for the truck to squeeze through. Knee-high willows were scraping every vestige of Alaska Highway dust from the underside, while the pine and poplar saplings that crowded the route were removing the chrome trim strips and a fair amount of paint from the fenders and doors. One headlight was impaled and ripped from its socket by a spear-sized pole that had been lying half-buried in the trail and sprang up like a jungle tiger trap. Our hopes of getting a decent resale price for the truck after the winter were fast fading. The reality of saving so many pack or toboggan loads, however, seemed more important at the moment.

A half-dozen times we had to interrupt the fun, proceeding ahead on foot to scout out the best approach to a creek crossing. Where the route was too narrow around corners, we went to work with axe and swede saw to remove a few trees. Luck seemed to be riding with us, though, as we never got badly mired in the muskeg or wrapped around a tree. In what seemed like only a half-hour, we had traversed the forest and, with brakes a-smoking, cruised down the last section onto Horsefall Creek flat. There was the cabin, looking no better than before, but a welcome sight, nonetheless. I checked the time on our alarm clock and gave a whistle of surprise: the trip had taken four hours!

The clouds politely waited until the truck was unloaded – no small feat – before blessing us with the first flakes of the season. As the tempo of the storm picked up, we found ourselves digging frantically through the cargo for kerosene lanterns, wicks, globes and fuel. Darkness was descending rapidly tonight, with the precipitation blocking any hint of a sunset.

"There is nothing like a raging blizzard to make one appreciate a shelter," I chuckled as Marsha gave me a quick hug in agreement.

We sat in the soft glow of the lanterns, eating a scratch supper from the first two cans we found, and felt grateful to have this odd little cabin for our home. Even the mess and the mice were tolerable for a little while, if only because we could see past them to a time when we could totally relax in here.

There was a healthy blanket of snow on the ground by sunrise. The storm had abated, and we were getting our first clear view of our chosen environment in its new clothes. Every stump wore a white bowler hat and even the thinnest of branches was balancing an armload of fluffy flakes. The narrow path to the river bank was a tunnel of snow-laden trees, each bough poised delicately to tip its load down our necks. We put up the hoods on our anoraks and ran through, leaving a miniature snowstorm in our wake.

My heart never fails to flutter at the sight of the Yukon River. Chock-full of slushy ice crystals, it looked more like a flow of lava, boiling and bubbling as the current rolled over subsurface obstacles. The immense span of river here was intimidating: over half a mile wide at this point. From the vibrations under our feet, we could appreciate the colossal energy of millions of tons of water and silt in motion. The current was an impressive four knots – faster than a person's walk.

In the bays and backwaters of the near shoreline, the slush was gathering and crowding together as the first step towards sealing the river's surface. The cakes and flakes of ice were molded into a spiral pattern by the eddying current. With each passing day, they were being packed more firmly, while the mass gradually was extending, bit by bit, across from the shore.

The sips of water we tasted were so cold our teeth ached. Its temperature made rather sobering the thought of trusting an ice cover for our travels later this winter.

With our respects paid to the mighty Yukon, we scuffled our way along the snowy path to the truck. The veteran of many miles was barely recognizable; Furd was no longer dusty-brown. I swept the hood and windshield clear of snow and climbed in. First try, the engine roared to life, anxious, I believed, to tackle the trip out. The plan of the moment was to drive Furd up the steep trail to the plateau before the snow become deeper and trapped the truck down on the river flat. We'd leave the truck there, then return on foot to Horsefall to unpack and sort for a day before heading back to Whitehorse to fetch the dogs.

"Furd, you've only got one more return trip to make," I whispered. "Up the ravine trail today. Then tomorrow let's go get Casey and his buddies and bring them to the farm. After that, you can rest all winter beside the barn. We'll get those dogs to do all the work. It'll serve them right for peeing on your tires."

The pep talk was good for only two hundred yards. Somehow, we'd become high-centred on a big boulder at the creek crossing. One back wheel was spinning wildly.

That particular problem was not hard to solve. After we jacked up the back end and rolled rocks under the high tire, the truck could crawl forward. However, we'd lost our momentum and the bank was too steep to drive up without a run at it. To make matters worse, we couldn't back out of the deep creek bed for the same reason.

Now was the time to try the portable winch. This small, hand-powered, mechanical advantage device was known as a *come-a-long*. We spooled out all the cable, hooking one end to the truck's frame and the other to a tree. Thirty cranks later, the truck was still stuck, but the tree was quite mobile. We set up again, this time to a clump of larger trees. To ensure we wouldn't break the winch, we were using a double purchase, which meant we had to crank twice as much to move the truck as with a direct pull. Every ten minutes, we'd have made about two paces of progress up the incline when there would be no more cable to crank in. So we would block the wheels, pull out all the cable and hook to new trees further up the slope.

It seemed to take forever, but eventually we gained enough ground and could let the internal combustion motor take over the work. Before moving on, we loaded some boulders into the truck box to give us weight for better traction. Mentally crossing my fingers, I eased away and up the winding track. The snow made the ground slippery and neither of us wanted another episode with the come-a-long. Cautiously we crawled up the draw, squeezing between the willows, hugging the sidehill and straddling the deepest ruts.

Gaining the summit, we stopped the truck to stretch ourselves. Both of us were tight through the shoulders from all the pushing on the dashboard we'd been doing to encourage Furd along. Cross-country driving, we decided, was not an easy sport on vehicles, nor on the occupants.

Walking back down to the cabin, we allowed ourselves the liberty of gaping like tourists at the scenery, and of stopping often to examine animal tracks that crossed the cart ruts. From the frequency of rabbit prints, it looked as if this would be a good year for the trappers: lynx would be plentiful with so much of their favourite food around.

By next morning we were feeling quite refreshed. Unpacking had proven to be fun and we'd had a good sleep. Our tummies full of a tasty brunch fried on the cookstove, we started hiking up the trail toward the truck. We congratulated ourselves at timing the truck move just right – there were three more inches of white flakes on the ground from a overnight storm.

We'd only walked a few minutes before Marsha gasped and pointed to tracks in the fresh snow. The paws marks were as big as my pac boots, with well-defined claw prints. *"Grizzly,"* she whispered.

The bruin had come from the south end of the Horsefall flat, passing within a hundred paces of our cabin. It appeared he was heading for the hills, intent on finding a hibernation spot before more snow accumulated. Without our rifle on this hike, we could do little but hope he wasn't planning on a bedtime snack. With Marsha holding her breath most of the time, we followed his footprints to within sight of Furd – at which point the bear tracks headed due north.

The descent in Furd off the plateau down Farm Creek went without incident and the side-road gave us no problems, but by the time we reached Pelly Crossing there was only an hour of daylight left. The trip to Whitehorse was another 180-odd miles and we debated about stopping in at Hagers' to check on our moccasins. Luckily, we decided to invest the time.

"No, those moccasins are going to take another two, maybe three, days," Mr. Hager told us. "But it's good you stopped. Tommy McGinty's got too many dogs and you gotta tell him right away if you're gonna take two. Tomorrow, maybe it'll be too late, he might shoot them. He's got too many for himself."

One of his sons volunteered to take a note to McGinty's house that we'd pick up the dogs in two days, after we'd been to Whitehorse to fetch our four mutts and the rest of our gear.

"How many do you want?" Lizzie asked us then.

"We've got six if Tommy McGinty can give us two," I explained. "We'd like enough for five, maybe six, dogs each."

"Are you going to have your own team?" Lizzie asked Marsha.

"I'm going to try."

Lizzie looked pleased. She glanced over to her husband, then spoke up again. "Well, we're not going to use those two black-and-white dogs out back. You can take them and train them for us, but you have to give them back in the spring. My son, Jimmy, wants to use them for sled dogs, but I don't think he's got time this year."

She paused for a moment, then added, "Maybe that one by the side of the house you could take, too. The one that's named Peggy."

We had a cup of tea to solemnize the transaction, agreeing we'd give Jimmy three harnesses in the spring. This last idea was Mr. Hager's.

"After all," he said merrily, "you're not gonna need those harnesses if you go back to the South. There is no snow to run dogs in Vancouver!"

In the fading light we inspected the offered dogs. The two black-and-white dogs were a squirrelly pair of Siberian Huskies. They looked like pure-bred racing dogs, high-strung and each a bit over forty pounds.

"This one's Jeff," Jimmy Hager was saying, shining a flashlight at the one with more white on his face, "and this one's Mutt. They're brothers. Watch out for this one. He'll bite you if he gets a chance."

Marsha looked at the dogs and shook her head. "They're smaller than Tyhee!" she whispered to me. "Are they going to be any good?"

"What other choice is there?" I whispered back. "No one else is offering us dogs, and it's getting late. Who knows what the McGinty dogs will look like."

"This one's a lead dog," Jimmy called and we hurried over to look. "Peggy's really fast," he added, shining his light on a tiny, collie-like mongrel. "Got peg legs but *goes like stink.*"

Peggy was certainly an attractive dog, with long silky hair, dainty features, and a proud plume of a tail. The obvious problem was that she was even smaller than the other two. Peggy likely weighed thirty pounds at most.

"But her legs are so short!" Marsha protested. "She'll get lost in the deep snow."

"Peggy's really tough." Young Jimmy's brown face was almost invisible in the shadows, but his wide grin was quite evident. "The three go together."

Faced with a subtle all-or-nothing decision, I shrugged and decided to give the little guys a try. "We'll be back in a few days to get them. Same time as we pick up the moccasins."

"You're gonna like 'em," he assured us. "They'll *go like heck.*"

Driving the highway was easier now there was some snow. In the winter, the Yukon highway crews don't try to plough the roads clear. Instead they use graders to shape the snowfall and let the traffic pound it into a hard, smooth surface. As long as the temperature stayed cold, the traction on the snow was as good, or better, than on the gravel. For night travel, the white landscape lit up in our headlights' glare as if it was an airport runway.

When we cruised into Whitehorse at midnight, we were still scratching our heads and pondering our dog situation.

"Were those dogs really as small as I remember them?" I wondered aloud.

Marsha made a grim face. "What's getting me is that we've already accepted two other dogs we haven't even seen!"

All we could do was shake our heads and laugh at ourselves.

"So much for my *ideal* matched sled dogs!"

CHAPTER SIX

MUSH... PLEASE?

What we really needed at this point was a break. Just one day off, not worrying about dogs or about going into the bush, would have done us a world of good. Tired and frazzled after months of preparations, we were starting to get a bit wired around the edges, nagging and snapping at each other. Still, we were anxious to get settled, our goal finally within sight. So, *pretending we didn't know any better*, off we went as soon as all errands were attended to and the truck was packed for its last trip.

The trailer would stay at Jon and Carol's until spring. The road into their cabin was already so deep with snow there was some doubt whether we'd have been able to pull it out, even had we wanted to. For the past two days, it had been snowing almost non-stop. Judging by the weather reports on the CBC radio, our Fort Selkirk area was getting a real dumping. One account said there was eight inches on the ground at Pelly Crossing. That meant the dogs would get their first chance to show their stuff today.

The Klondike Highway was in good driving condition. Graders had been out around the clock, keeping the surface groomed. The giant ore-hauling trucks from the mines at Keno, Elsa and Faro had pounded the new snow rock-hard. We sped along at 50 m.p.h. with confidence, meeting only four vehicles on the long haul to Pelly Crossing.

At the Hagers' house in the village, we picked up our moccasins and their three dogs. The footwear had a strong smoky aroma from the tanning process the Indian women use. After scraping all the fat and meat from a raw moose hide, and rubbing it with the animal's brains, wood smoke is used to condition the hide. The entire process takes weeks, and is such hard work that not many of the people still do their own tanning. The resulting leather, though, is a magnificent product: soft, thick and yet incredibly durable. We would come to appreciate the smoke scent as *the smell of warm feet*. Mrs. Hager had used moose sinew to sew all the seams, it being tougher than cotton thread.

The dogs the Hagers were lending to us – Mutt, Jeff and Peggy – were not at all pleased about being jammed into the dog boxes on the truck. Though there was plenty of room for them, the darkness and strangeness seemed to scare them. When Jeff started crying, his brother burst into frantic yelping. Peggy started barking in high-pitched yips and scratched at the door. Mutt was trying to gnaw on the window screen until we finally located a stash of butcher's scraps and distracted him with a section of leg bone. These three dogs were hyperactive compared to our four. I could tell that hooking up these novices was going to be interesting, to say the least.

When we went to fetch the other two promised dogs at Tommy McGinty's house, no one was home. Around back were a half-dozen dog houses which had recently been used, but there were no dogs here now. A neighbour told us he thought Tommy and his wife were *off at their trapline*. He didn't know anything about two dogs we were supposed to pick up.

"Why don't you go see them?" he suggested. "His trapline is near Minto."

A quick conference was held in the truck cab. Minto was a ghost town five miles off the main highway. We had passed the turn-off a half-hour before reaching Pelly Crossing. Should we drive back there? Were we too late to get the dogs anyway? It was now well past noon and we still had thirty miles of side-road before the Bradleys' farm and nine miles of travel by dog team after that. We opted to leave the question of McGinty dogs for another day. Maybe one of us could travel the distance back to the village by dog sled later in the week to check on the offer. We left a note, saying we were still interested, and headed off down the farm road.

No grader had been on the side-road, but our truck had little trouble crunching through the loose snow. Tire chains made a tremendous difference, giving us a powerful bite down to the gravel base. When we checked on the dogs at the halfway point, they had all settled in nicely, except Mutt, who had ripped the screen from his window and had enlarged the hole considerably. We thwarted his escape attempt by moving him to Peggy's box, where he had to start all over. To make room, we brought Peggy up into the truck cab with us.

About a mile later, as that dog's fur began to thaw in the truck's heat, we found ourselves gagging at the unbelievable stench of this little dog. We halted the expedition.

"I'll put her with Casey in his box," I called over my shoulder to Marsha. "They will be crowded but won't fight 'cuz she's a female."

There was a brief baring of teeth and throaty growls, but I didn't stick around to hear the rest.

At the old farm, we parked Furd and immediately began hauling out harnesses and packs. The dogs set up a dreadful racket, demanding to be released, but we were sure we couldn't let them all out yet without having a gang fight on our hands. The bone bag was empty and there were no more tricks up our sleeves, so, enduring the din, we continued organizing the adventure ahead.

Our plan was for Marsha to hike off ahead with three loose dogs. I would wait a while, then follow with the other four dogs pulling the toboggan. It was just a children's snow toboggan, eight feet long, with neither handlebars nor brake. All the raw materials for constructing two oak freight toboggans had already gone in to the cabin on Furd's one load, and there had been no time yet to bend the boards and assemble them. This one would have to do for the first few trips. Because there was no brake, I didn't dare use more than four dogs. Even four might be scary. Hoping it would slow them down, I piled a huge load of supplies on board.

Marsha picked out gentle Hinglish, her pet Tyhee and little Peggy as the three she could manage best.

"Hinglish is male, so he shouldn't fight with the other two," she said. "And Peggy, even though she's female, seems to get along fine with Tyhee."

"That reminds me," I broke in. "We forgot to ask the Hagers when Peggy goes into heat."

"Boy, these dogs are noisy enough now," moaned Marsha. "Just wait until there's a dog in heat around!"

With a hug and a see-you-later, we released Marsha's charges and she set off along the trail. The dogs were leaping and bouncing through the fluffy snow, pausing to roll in it and sniff bushes. They would, no doubt, cover many times the distance Marsha would walk before they all reached the cabin. Her single trail was obliterated by their zig-zagging prints, checking out all the neighbourhood news.

"Don't run me over," she called and waved goodbye.

"See you in a little while," I yelled back.

By this time, Dick and Hugh Bradley had come out to watch my debut as a dog musher. Both men love telling jokes and stories and they were obviously sizing up the situation for material. The look on their faces said *this is going to make a classic story!*

"No brake, eh?" Hugh commented.

"Could be a wild ride," grinned Dick.

They helped hold the dogs from tangling themselves and fighting while I adjusted the harnesses. Casey was in lead, then Jeff and Mutt, with Loki in wheel position, closest to the toboggan.

"Let 'er rip," I said to the men. "Okay, Casey. *Let's GO!*"

Casey spun around and pounced on Jeff. Loki jerked the toboggan forward and bit into Mutt's neck. Fur was flying and teeth gnashing. Mutt was squealing in fright, but Jeff had managed to roll Casey over and was chewing on his leg. Loki looked up from gnawing on Mutt, saw a tempting sight and chomped onto Jeff's tail. With Loki molesting his rear, and Casey attacking from the front, Jeff was in a real fix until we were able to drag the pile apart by pulling on harnesses and prodding with a stick.

Blood was trickling down Casey's left foreleg and was splattered over Jeff's face. Neither dog seemed the least bit concerned by their punctures, though, so I too ignored the wounds.

"Should I run beside Casey for the first twenty feet, Bruce?" Hugh offered. "Just until he gets the idea?" He was being very diplomatic by not giggling.

"Please. I'd really appreciate it."

With my ego already bruised, I wanted to be gone before they began laughing out loud. So much for the *ideal musher* with his *ideal dogs*.

I knelt on the bundles and grasped firmly the rope that would trail behind as a last chance lifeline should I fall off. Hugh got the convoy rolling and stepped aside. Casey followed him off the trail, but Jeff kept on going straight. This tripped up the orange lead dog, who was dragged backwards until I could get us stopped.

I ran up, straightened him out, and gave a quick pep talk. He should have known better: he'd been in harness before and had even led on occasion. Then Loki nudged my elbow and I realized he had crowded in on us, trapping Jeff and Mutt in a net-like tangle of traces.

When I finally had them all in line again, Casey led away like a professional. The two Indian dogs wanted to run faster than Casey did, so there was a bit of snarling happening each time Jeff came abreast of Casey, but we were on our way.

If each disaster is a potential lesson to learn, my education in dog driving surely advanced to at least a PhD that afternoon, evening and night. The next calamity was a break in Mutt's traces. Loki and I were left with the toboggan as the other three raced ahead still in harness, pretending not to hear me, nor to notice the difference in drag behind them. Good old Loki and I had a nice chat as we towed the load up the steepest hill, me drenched in sweat and he puffing away like a veteran of many wars. We caught up to the rest of the troops where they were wrapped

He looked sweet, but Mutt was much more aggressive than his litter-mate Jeff. Mutt ripped open Tyhee's belly when she playfully grabbed at his bone.

around a tree trunk, all glaring furiously at the squirrel taunting them just out of reach. I used some rope to repair the traces and vowed to hand-stitch all joins as soon as we got to the cabin. The sewing machine stitching clearly wasn't going to be strong enough.

Ten minutes further along, I learned the importance of having *idiot strings* on mittens. The temperature was dropping with the sun's departure and one mitt was missing. By switching the remaining mitt from hand to hand, and keeping the other hand in a pocket, I managed to keep from freezing, but just barely. By now, I was walking behind or beside the toboggan, because the dogs refused to pull my weight. They'd go on strike and lie down if I rode. Being their first outing of the year, I felt it important to set a proper tone for the season, but they had already determined who was boss. Yelling only made them wince; my pleading prompted them to roll over; threatening with a stick set them to cowering and grovelling. My repertoire was exhausted. As long as they moved forward, I rationalized, we'd eventually make it to Horsefall. We could work on finesse another day.

For a long time, they pulled slowly and I walked. Then Jeff curled up in a fetal position and refused to move. The others pulled him for a few feet, slowing with each passing step, until they gave up entirely. I propped him up on four legs and stood beside him, trembling with fury. Ever so slowly, he sank back down. Immediately, I grabbed him up and plunked him on his feet again. He gradually crumpled. I hoisted him up. He wilted. I stood him up... We continued this for probably twenty minutes. At last, he stood until I could get the other dogs to move the heavy toboggan and start us down the trail. But after three steps, Jeff turned back into jelly.

I sat on the curl of the toboggan, wondering if crying would help. Jeff was cringing, expecting me to grab him at any moment. I decided to let him stew for a while.

Loki licked my hand. "What more can go wrong, Loki?" I asked, giving his ears a scratch. "I'm sorry to make you part of this mess. At least you're a good dog."

Casey was sitting out front, watching this and wagging his tail to hear me talking pleasantly. "And, you're a good dog, too, Poofer," I said to him, "but a bit lazy at times." He smiled and yawned.

Then I noticed Jeff had wriggled almost out of his harness! I leapt up and made a dive for him, but grabbed only air as the crafty Siberian sprang to the side and bounded off into the trees. For a pathetic basket case a few minutes ago, he displayed amazing energy. Jeff was leaping about the forest like a merry fawn.

This was another lesson for me; I understood the importance of cinching the belly strap tightly.

Jeff's absence did improve the team situation greatly, though, because the others were suddenly inspired, wanting to run along as well. By waiting until Jeff was some distance down the trail, I could get them to pull toward the cabin without difficulty. Whenever the loose dog came near, I would throw a stick to keep him out front. The trick worked well until it was too dark to see.

The dogs must have known where Jeff was all the time, because their ears would perk up and swivel around at noises in the woods. Casey was now wandering from rut to rut with his nose quivering, following the trail of Marsha and her three dogs. I walked behind the load, holding the rope in one hand and keeping the other inside my parka. Branches clawed at my face in the darkness, but I could only bow my head and trudge on, wishing we hadn't left both flashlights at the cabin.

When the moon rose, I could see more details. The white bluff on our right meant we were another mile from the fork where a path toward Black Creek led off. After that, the trail would begin its drop to the valley floor. By winter's end, we would know this route like the back of our hands. Right now, I wasn't much in the mood for sightseeing.

After what seemed an eternity, we were at the top of the long draw in the cliffs. There was enough loose snow on the trail to slow us down to the point where, if I sat straddling the load and dragged both feet, we were barely under control. I had a pole tucked under one arm and was leaning hard on it as another drag. My three beasts, fairly played out and uninspired by this stage, never gathered more momentum than I could handle.

The lights of the cabin were beacons of salvation. Smoke was billowing from the cookstove chimney and heat waves shimmered in the open doorway. Marsha had her mitts on and was outside ready to chain up the team.

"I knew you were coming," she said, kissing my cheek. "Jeff got here a few minutes ago."

Before I could make a reply, a brawl erupted. Both Casey and Loki had turned on poor Mutt and had him pinned to the ground. We grabbed their harnesses and wrenched them apart to save the little Siberian from becoming dog food. His nose was cut and ear ripped but otherwise he was intact. I didn't have the energy left to scold the culprits. They must have realized my feelings when I chained them to the closest trees, and headed into the cabin without even a pat on their heads or a comment of thanks for their work.

I flopped onto the bed and lay there for five minutes before I had the strength to sit up for a mug of hot soup.

"Thanks," I gasped. "You can't imagine how glad I am to finally be here."

"I was getting a little worried," Marsha admitted, massaging my shoulders. "What took you so long?"

CHAPTER SEVEN

KITCHEN PATROL

The sound of bacon sizzling on a hot griddle edged into my dreams. But nowhere, in images of endless trudging beside the toboggan, ferocious dog fighting, cursing and yelling, exhausting climbing and nerve-racking descent, did the sounds of breakfast make sense. When the maple smell finally reached my nose, it was too vivid to sleep through.

Marsha had a big feed of bacon and eggs waiting in the warming oven and was toasting rye bread on the cast-iron stove top. The teapot was already on the table, with a bag of rosehips brewing inside. She knew the way to my heart.

It was my good fortune to have paired with an excellent cook. Marsha had run ski hill kitchens, cooked for B.C. Forestry camps and studied home economics in college. Right from the start, she wanted to set a high standard in preparing our food. For an hour before starting breakfast, she'd sorted through the kitchen boxes and organized her working area. Lying beside her plate was a list of renovation ideas to bring the kitchen up to snuff.

"Hey, I didn't tell you about what happened to me on my walk in," she said suddenly. "You fell asleep before I had a chance. It was *scary.*"

My mouth was full of toast; I gave a questioning grunt.

"The dogs were running every which way and off into the forest. Then they'd come charging out of the bush, making great *ARRRAH* noises as they attacked each other. It was all in fun, though. They weren't really fighting."

"That was the scary part?"

"No, *Silly*, not that part. Sometimes it would sort of surprise me. But it wasn't really scary," she explained, sipping on her cup of tea and drawing out the story. "Tyhee stayed with me most of the time, so I wasn't always alone. And little Peggy kept trying to walk between my legs—I think Peggy is afraid of Hinglish. He isn't very nice to her and sometimes they growl at each other."

"That's strange," I offered, "for a male and female not to get along."

"Yeah, well, that's not what I wanted to tell you. You see: I was right near the summit of the trail, walking all by myself. The snow was clear in front of me, not a footprint anywhere— and, suddenly, there were these *HUGE BEAR TRACKS!* They were *grizzly*, for sure. Same as last trip. You could see the distinct claw marks and they were a lot wider than my hand stretched out." Marsha was so excited telling this, her face flushed as she continued.

"I was so scared. I waited for the dogs. And hoped. And worried... Then Hinglish came bounding out behind me like he was the bear! I almost dropped dead. I kept him right beside me after that."

"What about the bear tracks?" I asked. "Which way were they going?"

"He'd come up the trail from Horsefall. Where I came to the tracks, they led off the path and headed north through the bush. We followed his tracks back *all the way to our cabin door.* And his tracks were fresh—it snowed the night before last and they were made since then."

"There must be a few prints still visible where we didn't trample them last night," I muttered. "Let's see if we can find one."

We went out in our shirts to examine the area near the river bank. The prints were disturbingly clear. The morning air was also chilling, so we didn't stay long before hustling back into the cabin's warmth.

"Those are certainly big," I agreed. "Wonder if this is the same fellow whose prints and poop we saw last trip?"

"Whoever he is, let's hope he's found a nice cave somewhere and is already hibernating," said Marsha. "He didn't appear to cause any damage, but he sure knows the way to our cabin."

With Marsha's good cooking, I'd no doubt that any bear not hibernating would want to be a regular at our table.

Today, to have a fresh start at the kitchen, we shovelled all the former occupants' debris into cardboard boxes and stored them outside, under the eaves. We had neither the patience, nor strong enough stomachs, to sort out the possibly useful from the disposable. Next came a thorough bleaching of the log walls, table top and plank floor. The rickety shelves were taken down and stored until we could rebuild them.

With so little space and only part of it usable because of the low roof, Marsha had to juggle the placement of table, shelves and counters as if this was a jig saw puzzle with too many pieces. We both gave high priority to creating a comfortable kitchen atmosphere, knowing that, in our simple life, preparing and eating meals would be not merely a necessity but also a major source of our entertainment.

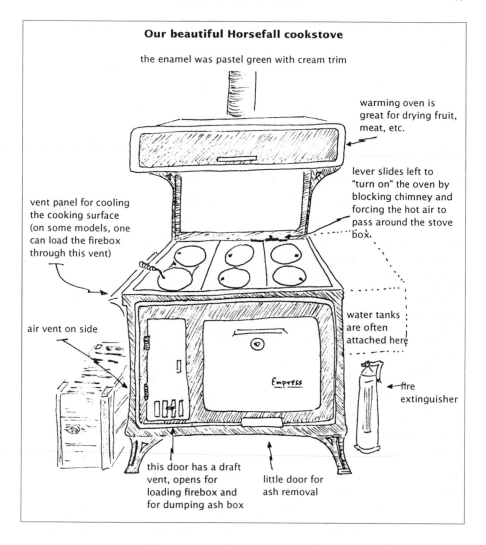

Our beautiful Horsefall cookstove

the enamel was pastel green with cream trim

warming oven is great for drying fruit, meat, etc.

lever slides left to "turn on" the oven by blocking chimney and forcing the hot air to pass around the stove box.

vent panel for cooling the cooking surface (on some models, one can load the firebox through this vent)

water tanks are often attached here

air vent on side

Empress

fire extinguisher

this door has a draft vent, opens for loading firebox and for dumping ash box

little door for ash removal

Later that morning I fled from the cabin, leaving Marsha to draw up her plans. There was the pleasant task of scouting out likely stands of firewood, and of planning access trails to them, that would keep me busy for a few hours. I stalked dead white spruce with great stealth, spied from the cliff's edge on likely driftwood jammed on the upstream point of gravel bars, and tiptoed through unsuspecting, but nonetheless trembling poplars. The few valiant birch trees on our side of the valley could be spared for seed stock, as there was plenty of the other species to thin from our forest.

After lunch, I cleared deadfall from a game path that would become part of a network of hauling trails. Using dogs for pulling the wood from the forest meant we could easily detour around most obstacles in our way, so much of my time was spent removing eye-level branches.

Marsha presented me, upon my return to the cabin, with a full wall of rebuilt shelves, a customized table and a swollen thumb. She had shortened the table's legs so it wouldn't block the low kitchen window. This made everything in the kitchen in proportion, as if dwarfs or goblins lived here. After we shortened the chairs considerably, we could fit right in, and now see quite well out the window while we ate.

Spurred on by Marsha's industry, we tackled the idea of a counter which would have a sink, shelves underneath, and would divide the bedroom off from the kitchen. It seemed funny to refer to the *kitchen*, the *bedroom* and the *living room* in this one space. By candlelight, we drew up many differing versions, knowing the winning design needed to be made of the various bits of plywood and two-by-fours available.

Next morning, we sawed and hammered our choice together. It stuck out from the side wall halfway down the cabin, like a hip-high peninsula. We knew to put in strong bracing so the counter would be able to withstand the ferocity of kneading bread dough. The shelves were open on both sides to serve as kitchen cupboards on one side, and as room to store clothes on the bedroom side. We sanded the top quite smooth before applying three coats of urethane plastic sealer. The glossy finish reflected light like a mirror and was a cinch to wipe clean.

Perhaps we were being fussy, but we wanted a kitchen sink, even though there would be neither running water nor outside drain for the waste water. Making do with the resources at hand, a ten-gallon fuel drum was recycled as our sink. I performed surgery with a cold chisel and hammer, dissecting at one of the circular ridges and saving only the top third. This was fastened under a circular hole in the counter, the ragged, chiselled edge safely back from the opening in the wood. The drum's bung hole would be the drain, and the bung could be screwed in from the inside to be the stopper. A flexible pouring spout was screwed in from underneath to direct waste water into a slop pail stationed below.

For food storage, the cabin offered the cavernous root cellar, with a trap door and a long, rickety ladder for access. It was a dank and scary place. I was always imagining dreadful things buried under the loose, silty floor. When I told Marsha about a strange murder in 1926, just downriver from our place, where the body was hidden in a root cellar, her interest in going down the ladder promptly evaporated. Still, the cellar would work well, keeping our vegetables, eggs and canned goods cool, yet not frozen. We cached all the dog food in the cellar too, and still had plenty of room available.

Marsha grating cheese by the low kitchen window at the front of the cabin.
It was hot standing beside the cookstove!

Yet for those many times a day when I needed one carrot to grate into a salad, or Marsha wanted some canned milk for her tea, the cellar was rather inconvenient. By the time a flashlight had been located, and someone had descended the shaky ladder, we might have forgotten what it was we wanted. For a while, we kept a few items in a box near the door. Unfortunately, the temperature range there was too wide: we'd have soured milk beside a frozen orange. We puzzled over all kinds of elaborate solutions, until we saw the obvious.

I got out the chainsaw, and carved two lines across the floor boards. *Plunk, plunk, plunk* went the planks as they dropped into the sub-floor space. We fished them out to make a trap door for our new mini-cellar. I framed around the opening to support the door, then scooped out enough dirt to make room for an orange crate. Marsha lined this box with tin and observed that it was *the best darn fridge for miles around.* Our kitchen was coming along nicely.

The heart of old-time kitchens was always the cookstove. Small wonder this was such a popular focus, because in many pioneer homes this was the only source of heat. One can picture little hands held out to warm up on a frosty morning, a row of munchkins watching oatmeal porridge bubbling and burping in a cast-iron pot. The friendly smell of wood smoke, mingling with the rich aroma of chicory coffee, would have been their summons to breakfast.

The old cookstove in our cabin was not the fanciest ever made, but it was no plain Jane either. Enamelled in pastel green, with some gently flowing but discreet trim, it had an overhead warming oven, and had once sported a circulating water heater. The water tank had been removed, no doubt because the heat exchanger pipes had been allowed to burn out. These pipes had run along the firebox walls, the water moving inside by convection as it heated.

To minimize temperature fluctuations in the oven, we placed bricks on the oven floor, and a knuckle-deep layer of sand over the top of the oven box. Both helped by retaining heat, increasing the thermal inertia. Since the oven door thermometer was correct only when the fire was out, we had to learn to gauge the oven temperature with our hands. If one could leave a hand inside, it was only warm [200 to 300 degrees Fahrenheit]; a hand in, but back out after a few seconds meant medium heat [325 to 375 degrees]; anything above 375 degrees was too hot to leave a bare hand in at all. The back corner nearest the firebox was the hottest place, and the opposite corner was the coolest.

Our warming oven's temperature fluctuated too much for rising bread dough, but it was an ideal place for drying fruit, vegetables or stripped meat.

We treated the cast top of the cookstove as if it were a cast-iron frying pan. To restore it, we lifted the surface rust with a wire brush and whisked it away, then brushed on cooking oil and baked it in to season the metal. This was a smoky procedure, so the cabin door had to be propped open for a while to flush out the fumes. Once blackened, the top required only occasional wiping with oil. We preferred cooking oil because we made toast directly on the stove and didn't know if the commercial stove polishes were edible. The trick to keeping toast from sticking was to dust a little salt on the stove first. A wire rack placed on the cast-iron top created a cooler spot for simmering soups, even if the stove surface was blistering hot.

Cooking on a wood stove is a lot more time-consuming than using an electric range, but the results justified the efforts. Bread was baked as it should be: golden

This is little Peggy, likely anticipating the evening meal, getting ready to play a regular part in the evening's howl.

and crusty. Pies had an unimaginable lightness. Moose roasts and Yorkshire puddings, baked spuds and steamed carrots. Each feast made us wonder about the *rough life* this was supposed to be, out here in the wilds.

On our third night in the cabin, Marsha had cooked a roast, and we toasted our good fortunes with a glass of French wine. From our places at the dwarf table, we could look out the window and see the full moon breaking through the clouds, washing the dog lot in bluish silver. The dogs were particularly restless because we hadn't exercised them since our trip in. When the vivid lunar face suddenly confronted the team, they reacted as true Northerners....

Mutt threw back his head and let out a shrill howl. Abruptly, he stopped to look around. The others were motionless, their eyes fixed on the bold Siberian. Then Peggy tilted her pointed nose at the sky and daintily voiced a series of pitiful pleas which drew the others from their trance. In seconds, all seven were pouring their hearts out like an off-key chorus of wolves and coyotes. To this fine serenade, we raised our glasses once more, and toasted this time to our furry companions.

While Marsha was pouring more wine, I stared out the window at Peggy performing a strange ritual. She raised her leg to pee on a tree. Then, this time while Marsha was also watching, Peggy watered two more places. Each time she lifted her leg.

"That's not right," I said. "How come she isn't squatting to pee?"

"I think we have this dog all wrong," Marsha had a twinkle in her eye. "Our pretty Peggy very definitely has a peter," she announced with great delight. "Peggy is a male! We need to call him *Peter* instead."

Our next toast was to the Pelly Crossing Indians and their sense of humour. I now knew why Lizzie and her son, Jimmy, had been giggling so much when we took the dogs from them. The joke was on us.

It would be a source of endless conjecturing about how stinky Peggy/Peter and macho Casey had shared a cramped dog box during that drive in on the farm side-road without tearing each other to pieces.

CHAPTER EIGHT

TRAINING THE DOGS,
AND FETCHING TWO MORE

For the first weeks at the cabin, we used the kiddie toboggan as our sole vehicle. There was so much to do, cutting and hauling firewood, fixing the cabin, and making chains and harnesses, we had no time to construct the freight toboggans. As an interim measure, I modified the small toboggan by bolting on a plywood backboard, pole handlebars and a brake. This gave me better control over the rig, an essential requirement for dog training sessions. The brake was similar to ones that would go on our freight toboggans: an iron claw bolted to a piece of plywood hinged to the tail of the vehicle, where the driver could step on it. We soon learned this drag was most effective if applied in short bursts to jerk the dogs off stride and slow them down. The handlebars and backboard were held together with twists of wire, a quick substitute for the rawhide strips, or *babiche*, a pioneer craftsman would have used. This diminutive rig, though rickety, was sufficient for introductory runs and occasional trips to the truck for more loads of supplies.

The descriptions other mushers gave us of training new dogs to harness weren't elaborate. Most other team owners, though, had veteran dogs to teach newcomers by example. If the older dogs were well-trained and enjoyed work, the youngsters usually picked up the good attitude. A seasoned crew would bully any rookie who was consistently spoiling their runs. With only one trainee, the others would, by their sheer numbers, control when to start, stop and turn. This took pressure off the new dog, so the musher could concentrate on encouraging him to pull well and stay in line. Unfortunately, our rookies outnumbered our veterans; some dog was always fouled up, turning classes into a nightmare.

As time permitted, I would take one dog out alone, and give him some individual coaching while he hauled in a light load of firewood. Some dogs had to be taught to keep their heads down and lean into the work. Though time in the

Casey was such a ham for photos – very striking with his orange and white fluffy coat and grand curling tail. He loved being in lead, but would leave the pulling to the others whenever possible.

harness could be enjoyable, I stressed that this was not play, either. A slap on the ear with a leather mitt usually got the idea across about who was boss. The trick was to do some positive encouraging, instilling respect and trust between us.

Driving dogs was, especially in the initial stages, very, very frustrating. When seven dogs were all conspiring to exasperate the musher, they would succeed. We took solace in the descriptions we heard about other mushers who were far more brutal with their dogs than we were. The euphemism for hitting dogs, in mushers' jargon, was *tuning them up,* as in *giving the team a tune-up.* It seemed that even the meekest person would discover a Mr. Hyde side when training a dog team, letting fly with some colourful language.

Once, when we came up to the old farm on the Pelly, Hugh popped his head out the door and asked cheerily, "Welcome. We heard you coming a ways back. Which dog is named *Bastard*?"

A musher not only needs to have great patience when training sled dogs, but he also must have a good imagination. I explained this to Marsha by telling her how Casey learned to be a great lead dog.

"How did he learn? It might be difficult for you to picture him as a scrawny, thirty-pound puppy, nervous and shy, fluffy and furry, with floppy paws, flapping ears, and a perpetually puzzled expression on his face. Casey was just six months old at that point. If he has grown much smarter over these five years, this must be partly my doing, because I was his teacher, his mentor of mushing, you might say.

"At the time," I continued, revelling in the role of raconteur, "I was living in a log shack near Whitehorse. There were nicely packed trails through the forest, ideal for cross-country skiing and snowshoeing or – I kept thinking – for dog sledding. It was already January and I was impatient for my puppy to grow to the point of usefulness. Most mushers agree that up to the age of one-and-a-half years, a dog's bones are too soft and pliable for pulling. Permanent damage or distortion could result from strenuously working a puppy. I could, however, see no danger in some light advance training. Indeed, one old Indian told me he harnesses up his first year pups, each one pulling a small block of wood, so the young dog gets used to wearing a harness and becomes clever about traces."

"So you had Casey dragging a block around," Marsha said. "Was that all?"

"Oh, no. He had to learn commands too. Since he was the only dog, he would be the leader," I explained. "Casey needed to distinguish between right and left, or *gee* and *haw* as mushers say in the Yukon. Since there was no other dog to show him by example, the task of teaching fell squarely on my shoulders."

"I can just imagine you crawling around the floor, wearing a harness, and responding to your own commands of gee and haw," Marsha laughed. I didn't find the idea terribly funny, but Marsha continued laughing until there were tears streaming down her cheeks.

"I devised a method of teaching commands worthy of a doctor of clinical psychology," I said, over her giggles. "Just like rewarding a caged rat or guinea pig for performing the correct task, I would use raisins to induce the appropriate response from Casey. Raisins were perfect because Casey loved them and – if given singly – it would require a great many successes before he was full."

"Did Casey have to push a button or run a maze to get a raisin, then?"

"It was like this: I would have Casey sit before me and then I offered him a choice between left or right clenched fist while repeating one of the commands.

He had to choose the correct side by motioning in that direction with his body or his head. To add a touch of realism, I dressed him in a puppy-size harness. Now, I was clever enough to realize that my left was his right and vice versa, so when I said *Gee*, the correct response would be his right – or my left – fist. If he nudged the correct fist with his snout, he got a raisin reward. The wrong hand had no reward. Psychologists, who love fancy words, call this *operant conditioning*."

"How'd the Poofer do?"

"The speed at which he mastered this lesson astonished me. Within minutes, he was choosing the appropriate direction every time! I was quite sure I had the canine equivalent of Einstein until, with the last raisin, while I was myself trying to remember whether *gee* was left or right and to me or him, he chose the raisin hand before my command. He had been using not his head, but his nose!"

"Sounds to me like he was smarter than you," Marsha quipped. "Or clairvoyant! Maybe you could have tried crawling around in a harness after all."

"Yes, well, the first evening had not been a complete loss," I continued, "because at least I was now quite proficient at gee and haw and could even transpose for someone facing me."

"Yes, you could also drop raisins along the trail in advance and I'm sure Casey would have followed them."

"Well, I bet he would have. Next evening, as I got out a sticky clump of raisins and separated it into singles on the table, Casey was beside himself in delight. While I tried to ignore him, he began offering me his paw, then the other, then both, and rolled over. Nuzzling my leg, now lifting my elbow with his snout, all the while he was banging his tail on the table leg, on the chair, and on the rug – the latter raising great clouds of dust. He was wagging so vehemently his whole body was rippling. If he had stood up while wagging, he would have looked like a belly dancer."

"In other words: he was ready to *Play The Game*," said Marsha.

"Exactly. But I had introduced a new twist. Now there was a raisin in each fist. Sniffing was no longer going to work! The correct choice would still win him one dehydrated grape, but a blunder meant instead a light rap on the snout. I added this last part as *negative conditioning* in our psychology experiment.

"'Gee, Casey,' I would say. '*Gee*. No, the other one. That's right, good boy.'

"'Now, haw, Casey, *haw*... Good!'

"And so we worked for twenty minutes each night, putting a considerable dent in my winter supply of raisins. Eventually my star pupil was getting the command correct on about eighty percent of the tries. This was good enough, or there would not be enough raisins left to put into the porridge. And surely, I thought, he would improve when actually pulling a sled."

"I guess eighty percent is pretty good," muttered Marsha. "Casey isn't terribly clever about anything else."

"That night, I dreamed of dog mushing: I could see myself being swept along, gliding 'round the corners, raising a great fantail of snowflakes in our wake. Out front of the team, galloping down hills and charging up the rises, was Casey the Wonder Dog! Strong, valiant, wise. Responding instantly to my whispered commands: 'Gee, Casey. That's it, big fella... Haw... Gee... Haw....'

"Come morning, I was too anxious even to wait for breakfast. After banging last night's snowfall from my little toboggan and tying his harness out front, I inserted my bouncing puppy in the appropriate loops and we headed down the trail together. Ahead was the first junction: to the left was town, the right trail went to the lake. Would he do alright? There was no time for last minute coaching, he was on his own now."

Marsha was listening, spellbound. I knew she was silently hoping the puppy would prove a success.

"I let him reach the forks ahead of me," I continued, "mindful of the day when I would be commanding while riding the toboggan instead of walking behind it.

"'Gee, Casey,' I called out.

"He hesitated.

"'Gee. *GEE!* Go right.'

"He looked first to the left and then to the right. I could almost feel the intense concentration.

"'That's it. That's it,' I prompted. 'Go gee! *Gee!*'

"Now his tail began to wag slowly. He glanced over his shoulder and his mouth dropped open in a kind of puppy-dog smile.

"Then he trotted back to me and, with a poke of his nose, chose my left mitt."

After a week of training the dogs and working around the cabin, it was the day marked on the calendar for a special trip to the farm. On my previous run out to the truck, I'd arranged with Dick Bradley to have him check in at Tommy McGinty's when he went to Pelly Crossing to deliver some beef, using our pick-up for the trip. The plan was for me to mush over with the two most experienced dogs, Casey and Loki, taking two extra harnesses in case Dick could bring us back more dogs. Dick predicted he might be late, so I planned to overnight at the farmhouse.

In my usual disorganized manner, I put off leaving until it was mid-afternoon.

In the late fall, the days were not only short, but rather halfhearted as well. At best, the sky was only dusk-bright; at no time did the sun ever fully appear from behind the mountains. However the trail to the farm was pretty obvious, so I did not anticipate any problem finding my way. Casey would be leading and could smell his way to the chicken coops even in the dark.

I jogged behind the empty toboggan up the hills, and pushed with one leg on the flat stretches to help the duo out. Though we made good progress in the fading light, by the time we were on the farm flat, I might as well have had a bag over my head for all I could see. The waning moon would not be up for hours, and the starlight was filtered out by the canopy of overhanging branches. My job now consisted entirely of hanging onto the backboard and ducking head-level limbs.

Unfortunately, I snuck a peek at the wrong moment and received a quick slap across the face by a malicious sapling. Something felt wrong, so I halted the dogs and cautiously peered around in the near-darkness. Then I closed one eye and looked again. As I feared, I had lost one contact lens, flicked neatly from my eye by that last branch.

Cursing my stupidity for not wearing glasses, I checked in the tool pouch for a flashlight. No flashlight. There was nothing else I could do but make a few kick-marks in the snow as a reference, and continue, seeing half of very little.

Dick and his wife Marjorie weren't back from their town trip yet, so Hugh and I ate supper without them in Hugh's riverside cabin. The tasty, farm-raised beef had a therapeutic effect on my temper. By now, I had removed the remaining contact lens and was wearing my glasses. When I griped about how glasses fog up after being worn in the cold, Hugh offered the solution.

"Mine don't fog up when I wear them," the gentle farmer said earnestly, "because I wear them in my pocket!"

To illustrate, when he ducked outside to throw a bone to the nearest dog, first he carefully removed his spectacles and stowed them in his shirt pocket.

"Never have any problem this way," he added, only then breaking the deadpan expression with a wide grin.

"Fine for you maybe," I replied, helping myself to more boiled spuds. "But I'm so blind without my glasses or lenses, that I'd have a hard time finding my pocket. I'll have to mail-order some more contacts."

Our evening was spent like a pair of pioneer sourdough prospectors, exchanging anecdotes and advice, while mending a shirt [Hugh] and stitching a harness collar [me]. Hugh had been living on this farm for almost twenty years, so he had plenty of fodder for his tales.

Just after midnight, I took my leave and headed for the main farmhouse where

Dick lived and I could bunk in. My head was swimming from both the caffeine and the grand yarns that Hugh had been spinning. Using a candle to light my way, I climbed over a sleeping cat and pet dog, and settled into bed in the upstairs guest bedroom. In a moment, I was fast asleep.

Dick pulled in around one o'clock, the rattling of tire chains rousing me from my slumber. I pulled on some clothes and hurried down to help unload groceries and see what he'd brought us. Shielding my eyes to look past the headlights' glare, I could make out the shapes of two dogs in the back of the truck.

"This dog's name is Dawson and he's only a pup," Dick said, passing me a rusty-tan armful of hysteria. "Old Tommy McGinty said to go easy with him at first, because he's just playful. He's not very big, is he?"

Young Dawson smelled strongly of smoked salmon. I hoped he wouldn't mind our meals as we would be hard pressed to come up with ones as odiferous as his last one. He was about Jeff's size, with a stocky body and sturdy legs. I couldn't figure out exactly what his breeding was, but his fur was short, dense and a touch wiry. The head was quite square and the ears short and pointed. It was his eyes, though, that caught your attention: they were slanted, like an oriental's, and bright orange as plum sauce. When Dawson grinned, he looked quite devilish.

I chained the pup to a fence post, and went back to check on his partner.

"This one's name is..." Dick's voice trailed off as he struggled to remember. "It was something like Larry... or Joe... *Gees*, I don't remember at all. Maybe it'll come to me in the morning."

The dog calmly uncurled from his nest between the boxes, and stretched. He was a blond mongrel with the boney head of a Malemute and the body of a gazelle. It was a lumpy gazelle at that. His legs seemed to go on forever. Bones stuck out everywhere: knobby knees, pronounced rib cage and massive skull. His ears and face were laced with scars and one lip hung a little crooked.

"Looks like he fights a lot," I remarked.

"And loses every time," Dick added merrily. "He must be taller than Casey, but he doesn't appear to weigh much."

The anonymous dog was friendly enough and very obedient. He offered no resistance when I led him over beside Dawson and chained him there for the remainder of the night. When I poured out a few scoops of dry dog food for them, neither dog was interested. The tall one barely looked up from his curled sleep while Dawson wouldn't stop digging at the snow, struggling with the chain and whimpering.

"Did you bring that little wee dog – what's its name – *Peggy* with you this trip?" Dick asked, still looking at the strange, tall dog.

"No," I said, realizing what he was thinking. The Pelly Indians had lent us not only the shortest dog in the village, but now we had the tallest as well.

Next morning, I had Casey pull me back along the trail to my reference marks in the snow. I wasn't too hopeful about finding the lost contact lens but thought I might as well search while hacking down the offending branches. Wearing my glasses now, I had two focused eyes and the morning's sparkling light to help me. Within seconds of our arrival, I spied a pale blue speck on the snow: my missing lens! At this moment I decided what to call the tall, blond dog— he'd brought good fortune so he would be called *Lucky*.

Meanwhile, Casey was having good fortune too: he snorfled under a snow bank and pulled up a piece of some long-dead rodent. I sat on the toboggan curl for a few minutes to give him a chance to enjoy the snack.

Back at the farm, I hooked up the other three animals and loaded on four 44-lbs. sacks of dog food from the dwindling cache in the back of Furd. Dawson was frantic about the harness and soon had twisted himself into a tight tangle. No sooner did I have him right, but Casey and Loki attacked Lucky. I soon realized why Lucky was so scarred: he wouldn't fight back at all. Instead, he screamed like a banshee. After I separated the three, everyone was tail-wagging happy, so perhaps Lucky merely had to be initiated into the pack.

Meanwhile Dawson was trying to chew his way to freedom. Since I had no spare harness, I took no chances and fastened a choke chain around his neck and tied it ahead to the next dog's harness. It was long enough so Dawson wouldn't choke as long as he didn't pull back. After thirty seconds of blue-tongued struggling, he acquiesced and behaved. Then, half the way home, he got bored with ambling along and began pulling like a veteran. With his help, and me walking up the steep hills, we had our cargo to Horsefall Creek in a touch over two and a half hours, well before dark and a near-record time.

CHAPTER NINE

MAKING A COSY NEST

As the days shortened, and the mercury in the thermometer sank lower and lower, we were well motivated to improve our log home. When the weeks of Fifty and Sixty Below Zero came, we would have to be ready.

Remembering all the creosote that had been lodged in the barrel heater's meandering pipes, we ran a chimney straight up through a *jack* – which is normally a factory-fabricated metal cylinder designed to create a generous airspace between the hot pipes and the roofing materials where they intersect. I used a five-gallon pail instead, with a double-walled, asbestos-lined *Selkirk Brand* pipe inside that. The gap between pail and pipe was stuffed with fibreglass insulation.

The new heater to replace the pig was a sheet metal bargain that cost $40, locally referred to as an *airtight*. The body was an oval-shaped, upright cylinder. Wood was loaded after pivoting aside the lid from a large opening on the top. A second opening on top was for the chimney pipe and there was an adjustable air intake lower down on the front. The basic pattern had been around since the Gold Rush era.

Although the airtight was less temperamental than the 45-gallon pig, it also required judicious supervision to prevent the dancing, smoke-puffing, red-hot overburn that could happen from loading a too-explosive combination of fuels. Dry, split wood burned too hot to be used by itself, so we mixed in half-dry and green pieces to moderate the rate of combustion. As the winter progressed, we became quite proficient at loading the right size, species and dryness of fuel. The placement within the fire chamber also affected the combustion: a densely-packed fire burned very hot, and half-rounds burned faster lying on edge than placed flat. Also, dry wood piled on top of green was like a time bomb, ready to burn extremely hot when the green wood was mostly consumed. Green wood over dry, on the other hand, burned steadily over a long time.

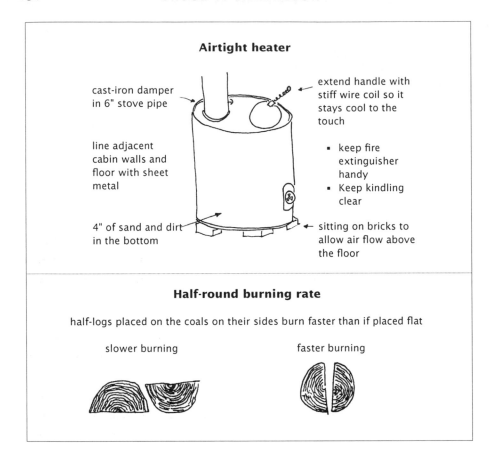

Airtight heater

cast-iron damper in 6" stove pipe

extend handle with stiff wire coil so it stays cool to the touch

line adjacent cabin walls and floor with sheet metal

- keep fire extinguisher handy
- Keep kindling clear

4" of sand and dirt in the bottom

sitting on bricks to allow air flow above the floor

Half-round burning rate

half-logs placed on the coals on their sides burn faster than if placed flat

slower burning

faster burning

To anyone unfamiliar with wood stove consciousness, our intermittent conversations throughout the day would have been curious—

"What kind of wood did you just load in?" Marsha would ask suddenly. "I want to do a laundry this morning and need to heat a tub of water on the airtight."

"It was that fairly wet poplar I cut last week."

"Did you bring it inside last night?"

"Yes, so it should burn faster than if the wood was cold."

"Was there a good bed of coals left from last night, or will the fire take a while to catch?"

—and so on.

The cookstove needed mostly split, dry wood. As a result, the chimney on the cookstove rarely had any creosote buildup. By contrast, the airtight would burn just about anything, from rotten stumps to unsplit, green logs. To minimize the danger of a chimney fire, we would have a hot fire at least once a day to burn out the pipes' accumulations before there was enough creosote to be dangerous.

Also, every two weeks I'd climb up on the roof and dangle a dog chain inside the pipes, rattling and twisting it to scour off any stubborn buildup.

As a precaution against igniting the walls or floor, we lined the area around both wood burners with thin metal sheets. The cheapest we could find, and the lightest to freight, were aluminium offset press plates from a printer's shop in Whitehorse. The design printed was still visible on these metal sheets, but it gave the cabin a cheery decor to be wallpapered in metal etchings from the RCMP's children's colouring book.

Because our cabin was so tiny, it didn't matter if every nook and cranny was perfectly insulated or not. With the cookstove providing generous blasts of heat at meal times, the airtight could be *shut down* (intake and damper closed) for most of the day. When bread was baking, the cabin door had to be left ajar to cool the cabin. It was novel to us city-raised folk to feel the air uncomfortably hot at eye level, while a Forty Below fog was rolling across the floor from the doorway and chilling our toes.

During nights that were Thirty Below or colder, one of us would get up around three or four o'clock to reload the airtight, so the cabin would be comfortably warm come morning. The fire could have been set to burn slower, but we needed plenty of heat, so left the intake vent slightly open.

Living primitively taught us to conserve our resources. Our fuel, food and water all had to be hauled to the cabin by dog team, so waste meant more trips. In the case of our firewood, the musher always worked far harder than the dogs, because the mutts didn't do the falling, bucking, loading, unloading, splitting or stacking, or even put on their own harnesses! All they did was *pull*. We did the rest.

Once we had a stockpile of food and cordwood on hand, we could relax on those fronts, but it was not so with water. Every day we needed to refill our containers, or at least clear out the water hole to keep it from freezing shut. Laundry and bathing required large quantities of water, and there was also dishwashing, baking and dog meals.

At our cabin, our water was drawn from a hole in the river ice, but out camping we would melt chunks of ice if they were available. Melting snow was the last resort because that required much more fuel than melting ice, and many trips with a pot to gather enough snow. Depending on how densely it was packed, snow took up as much as ten times the volume it would have after melting.

Cutting the water hole through the ice was a half-day job by midwinter when the river was frozen four feet thick. We could have augered a small hole, but it

Moving water

- hauling water in 3 gallon buckets is easier with a carrying yoke

- plastic "garbage bags" in buckets minimizes the wave action and spilling... (even old leaky bags work great)

Bath time

smaller bucket for feet

galvanized wash tub

"Nice to eat a bowl of yoghurt with raisins, nuts and dates while soaking!"

...two bodies later, with the same water, it was...

Laundry time!

Dancing on the clothes to agitate them

would have been frozen solid by morning. The pits we dug were over three feet across, designed to last a week whatever the temperature.

We made the most of every drop of water we hauled into the cabin: the weekly laundry followed literally *on the heels* of our baths. After two bodies were washed, the water would be a trifle grey, but it was fine for washing one batch of lighter coloured clothes and pre-washing the darks. The second bather stayed in the tub and stomped on the laundry to supply the agitation. Clothes lasted longer and were warmer if they were clean and thoroughly rinsed of soap. Marsha theorized dirt and salts chafed the materials, and grease or soap made the fibres pack down and lose their insulating ability.

The cabin air was so dry that clothes dried quickly, so we didn't have to strain our hands wringing out the clothes too thoroughly. All but the thickest woollens would be dry in one day. Clothes would dry if hung outside, even with temperatures well below freezing, but this took too long to be practical and the expansion of the water when it froze was probably a strain on the material's fibres.

For light inside the cabin, our propane lights worked like a charm to keep us in pseudo daylight. For those weeks around Christmas when the sun was on vacation, having bright interior lighting would be essential for our sanity. We soon came to appreciate the help of a wash of white paint on a wall, or high-gloss varnish on a plywood counter. We hung maps and a gaudy, happy Chinese kite on the wall to brighten and liven up our confined quarters. Our cabin had been built from logs salvaged from a forest fire burn area, so the walls were a rich brown colour – homey but rather dark. We envied those neighbours who had, when building, taken the time to thoroughly peel green logs, keeping them clear and mildew-free. They were rewarded with the easiest-to-illuminate cabins of all. Yet, all coveting aside, our little place had become a cosy, comfortable hideaway. We were glad to have – and more than a touch proud of – our new home.

See Appendix II for more information about cabin life and chores.

CHAPTER TEN

COLD HANDS, WARM HEART

The last days for legally hunting moose were upon us long before we were ready to go off on a serious moose safari. There was no real toboggan, my sleeping bag kit was not yet assembled, more wood had to be cut and hauled, more dog food had to be freighted over from the farm, and countless other chores remained. This was really no time to be stalking the great brown beasts through the hills.

Nevertheless, visions of thick steaks, tender liver slices, boiled tongue, lean ground meat, chunks of hearty stew, braised ribs and roasted haunch were distracting me from the tasks at hand. I kept shells for the .30-30 in my pocket, and spent a half-hour at dawn and dusk with binoculars combing our area from a vantage point on the cliff. It would be an oddity for a moose to be down in the valley this late in the year, but I didn't want to miss an opportunity if one wanted to walk right into our kitchen.

Marsha caught me staring at the calendar with a far-away look. She knew what was on my mind.

"Look, we both can't leave this place to go off hunting. At least, not now. We don't have enough harnesses made to take all the dogs, even if we had toboggans," she said, putting her arm around my shoulder.

"I'm not sure that I could manage a moose by myself," I admitted sadly. "A dead bull could weigh two thousand pounds. If I shot one and he jumped into a lake, I'd need a come-a-long to winch the body out. Then I'd want knives, an axe, and game bags to put the organ meat into... I'd need a sleeping bag and a lantern, food for a couple of days, warm clothing, maybe a piece of canvas to sleep under, snowshoes or skis – I don't think I could carry half the stuff I'd need to do a proper job."

"Do you really need all that?"

"Let's put it this way: I don't want to shoot a moose and have all that meat go bad or be wasted because I can't butcher it promptly and bring it all to the cabin before the wolves and the ravens find the kill.

"I've scanned everywhere close to Horsefall," I lamented. "The moose must be high in the hills, at least a full day's walk from here. That's too far to pack a thousand pounds of meat."

But Marsha had a plan.

"How about you go off for a few nights with Don?" she decided. "I'll stay and guard the fort."

Don Mark was staying at the Bradleys' farm and working as the assistant on Dick's trapline. He had promised to drop in with our mail en route to his line camp in the Black Creek area. Don had four eager mutts and a short sled for his trapline transportation. His cabin was high enough in the hills that there just might be moose in the vicinity. And he'd need help manhandling any moose he hoped to get as well.

"Let's ask him when he comes," Marsha suggested. "It would be nice to have even half a moose."

Three mornings later, on the last day of November, Don and I set out on our quest for meat. I skied ahead, with a rifle slung over my shoulder and field glasses in my anorak pocket, the two articles making it hard to develop a good stride. I resigned myself to a fast shuffle along the packed trail up the ravine. Don was to give me a half-hour head start, as we figured I'd have a better chance of sneaking up on a browsing moose than he would with his rowdy dogs.

Marsha was excited to see us go. She muttered about *things to do* and was busily drawing designs on paper and screwing up her forehead in concentration about something. I imagined she was planning what to do with our five to eight hundred pounds of moose.

We had enough rice and beans to supply our basic protein needs, so having moose would be a luxury. Moose, though, would add variety and provide better nutrition for the cold weather than vegetables and grains could. Marsha had spoken for the antlers to make into buttons. Scraps and hooves could go toward feeding the dogs. Technically, it was illegal to feed any game meat to dogs that was fit for human consumption, but the law was rather vague about personal taste. None of the game wardens we asked knew whether stomach linings, brains and all the obscure parts, like nose and testicles – which were great delicacies to some cultures – fell into human or dog food categories. We would have to let our consciences be our guide.

The raw hide would be needed to cover the curls of our toboggans, if we were to achieve an authentic duplication of the pioneer toboggans. Applied wet, the hide would shrink and hold the curl tightly, as well as becoming a cushion for crashes.

At the turn-off from our main trail onto the path to Black Creek, I was surprised to find the route was already packed by a snowmobile. Peter Isaac, a trapper from Pelly Crossing, must have gone this way to his own trapline. Our route to Don's cabin would swing by Peter's first camp, then back up this side of Black Creek into the hills. The creek itself was the boundary between their trapping areas.

The packed trail was a godsend, saving me an immense amount of work. Instead of clomping through calf-deep snow, my skis now easily carried my weight over the corrugated snowmobile track. Consequently, I was able to enjoy a more entertaining pace, running up the rises and coasting down the drops. The effort was exhilarating and despite the nippy temperature I found myself sweating. Off came layers of clothing, which I tied around my waist, being careful to keep the rifle strap free.

Each time I stopped to add or subtract a garment, the faint tracks of mice and squirrels caught my attention. Everywhere in the bush, these smallest of warm-blooded animals had laid down networks of paths. To be able to interpret the meaning of this language of footprints must give trappers a deep satisfaction. Almost as plentiful were the signs of the Arctic hare, the shallowness of the prints showing the snowshoe effect of their oversized feet. Wherever Peter had cut a sapling to widen the trail, the bark had been completely stripped by these hungry critters. In return, they left dozens of round, brown pellets.

The tracks I was most eager to see were nowhere along this undulating route. Moose weren't venturing near this creek at all. Still, the skiing was fun so far, a relaxing change from the high-tension journeys with the dogs. Except for the creaking of bamboo poles and the swish of birch skis, the world was absolutely quiet.

Peter Isaac's camp was deep in the forest, and the yard was only a widening of the path. There was a log A-frame shelter built shoulder-high and banked over with moss and snow. At first, all one could see was a stove pipe in a mound. Peter appeared from a white canvas tent which was well camouflaged against the snowy background. Through the open tent flap, I caught a glimpse of bloody carcasses and stacks of furs.

"Oh," he said shyly, "it's you."

We'd met once, some years before at the farm, and he remembered me, which I found flattering. I followed him inside the log shelter and was almost overwhelmed by the heat. It wouldn't take much fuel for his airtight to warm this lean-to, whatever the outside temperature.

"Want some coffee?" asked Peter, wiping out a cup with a paper towel.

"Sure. Want a cookie?" I replied, proudly pulling a bag of Marsha's home-made granola cookies from my pocket. The largest piece to survive the trip was as big as a nickel.

Peter smiled and took a pinch of crumbs. I dug in too and we soon had the bag emptied. Then we ate a few of his *Pilot* biscuits, palm-sized discs of hard tack which had travelled much better.

Don arrived at that point and the subject turned from eating to trapping. My partner on this hunt had been setting traps as he came.

"Don't worry about seeing them," he assured me. "I used lots of survey ribbon to mark the locations. It's mostly so I can find them myself – so much of this bush looks the same, I'd hate to lose all my traps after the next snowfall covers them. It would be expensive – and a bit embarrassing!"

Peter showed the rookie trapper the furs he was drying in the wall tent. Some were stretched over long, tapered planks with the skin side out while others had the fur showing. Peter demonstrated to Don how to tell when the skin side is dry enough to turn the pelt inside-out.

"It feels like this lynx here," he said touching what had once belonged to a large cat. Like most Northerners we met, Peter pronounced the word as *link* even when referring to more than one lynx. Although he had been at this camp for only a few days, Peter had already caught three lynx and had one wolf stretched out to dry as well.

"Wolf are really hard to catch, I've been told. Is that true?" I asked Peter.

"Some people have a problem, I guess," he shrugged. "I don't know what they do wrong. Everyone set traps differently."

"What about my sets?" Don asked and the veteran tactfully explained the proper way to him, giving measurements in terms of the size of a fist, the span of a hand or the thickness of two fingers. To me, who had no experience with traps, the descriptions had no context, but Don was hanging on Peter's every word. No doubt Don's fortunes this winter would depend in large measure on how well he learned these tips.

Peter offered to go ahead of us on his snowmobile to spring the trail sets and snares on the portion of his line we would be travelling, so the dogs would be safe. He also promised to help Don make a few sets when they got to the younger trapper's territory.

Peter's yellow machine came to life with a roar and he knelt on the seat. "You want to ride?" he hollered over the din.

"No, I'll be fine on my skis," I yelled, shaking my head so he could get my meaning.

Don's dogs stampeded merrily after the noisy snowmobile, their claws throwing up snow as they charged around willow clumps. As his light sled bounced across the muskeg, Don had to hang on tightly to stay aboard.

I noticed the cold air as I started, but shrugged it off as an after-effect from being inside the over-heated shelter. It usually took a while to warm up when skiing, just to get the blood circulating, so I skied hard, pushing myself to make my body heat itself. Even with my light parka on, the air felt chilly through my chest.

My legs were a bit tight, almost tired. For a short while, I caught glimpses of Don's back disappearing around corners. Then I could only hear them across the marshes when the snowmobile revved as Peter guided it around fallen trees and up the creek bank. When the motor idled, I imagined that Peter was springing his sets and explaining trappers' secrets to Don. It was getting dusky and I pulled up my hood to force a little more body heat to my fingers.

At the head of the valley was the old Dawson Stage Road, and Don's cabin was a fair ways along that.

"At least," I consoled myself, "I can't get lost on the old road."

On and on, I plodded. By now my legs felt like lead weights. It was too dark to shoot, so the burden of the rifle was doubly annoying. My shoulder felt raw where the strap had been chafing, but I tried not to think about it.

Out on the stage road I felt my second wind coming and relaxed a little. Here the trees bordering our way had been cleared in a tractor-wide swath, so the danger of face-slapping branches was minimal. Trees grow so slowly in the Yukon that only waist-high saplings had grown up in the ten years since the last mining company bulldozer travelled this road.

I stomped up another hill, and another hill, thinking each one must be the last. The cabin's location had been described to me as *just before a little creek, at the bottom of an incline.*

"This must be it," I promised myself at the foot of each hill, but Don's sled tracks didn't turn off.

The light was now fading quickly. I could barely make out the imprints at the side of the road where snowmobile tracks pulled off beside the toboggan's smooth trace. There were footprints off into the brush, but this had to be where the two men had set a trap. The vehicle trails led on.

More hills and more false hopes. My legs were complaining with each deliberate step. They were telling me this was too far to be going for my first outing on skis this winter. The old muscles were soft from inactivity.

Finally I saw a light through the trees a long way off. "That must be the cabin," I promised myself.

But then the light moved. It was the headlight on Peter's snowmobile, returning to his camp. In moments, Peter was beside me.

"How much further?" I shouted to him.

"Two more hills, then over to the side in some big spruce," he called as the engine whined impatiently. "Not much light now."

That was an understatement: it was almost black by this point.

"Well, see you," he shouted, and nodded.

"See you."

He blasted away, the headlight carving a diminishing slice out of the night as his machine sped out of sight.

Trudging on, up two of the longest hills imaginable… I had my ski poles tucked under one arm so my hands could thaw out inside my parka pockets. The work mitts and thin leather overmitts weren't holding their own against the night air.

Finally I was at the small cabin. I could hear Don talking to his dogs as he passed out their dried salmon suppers. A candle was throwing a flickering glow out the open doorway. Don stepped into this light just as I arrived.

"Thought you must have got a moose," he said cheerfully, "because it took you so long."

"I honestly haven't thought about hunting for quite a few miles," I muttered, unclipping the long skis and unslinging my rifle. "I was only thinking about the fire you'd have going to greet me."

But there was still work to be done before that comfort could happen: a new airtight had to be installed and wood chopped. My rest would have to be postponed.

Without the weight of skis, walking was a pleasure. After splitting a few blocks of wood, my circulation was pumped up again, so my hands were no longer hurting. I took a bundle of kindling inside where Don was fitting stove pipe sections through a *jack* in the roof.

"You got any ideas how to make the holes in this last section of pipe, so I can stick this damper pin through?" Don asked. "Guess we could use a nail and hammer it with the back of the axe —"

"Just stand back," I said, cocking his .22 rifle.

"Hey! What are you doing?"

"This is designed to make holes, isn't it?"

Don retreated to the far wall.

I popped a perfect pair of holes for the damper pin, aiming so the bullet would embed itself into a log behind. [Thus are stories born. Don could tell folks about the time I was so cold I shot his poor airtight when it wasn't working.]

Later in the evening, with a feed of lentil stew in our bellies and the cabin warm enough we could take off our parkas, we sat on the rough pole bed and enjoyed a cup of tea. The taste was suspiciously like that of spruce needles, but we couldn't see well enough to fish the culprits out of the brew. Melting snow for drinking water could have yielded worse surprises.

His curiosity killing him, Don finally took a candle outside to read the temperature off the little thermometer he had attached to the backboard of his sled.

"Twenty-Four Below Fahrenheit," he reported, replacing the blanket hanging over the doorway. "A drop of twenty degrees from this morning."

This was the lowest so far this winter. Though we didn't admit it to each other, we were both somewhat thankful we hadn't seen a moose. It would have been pretty cold butchering out in the open tonight.

In the morning, we took a different route back to Horsefall. Don stopped often to set lynx and marten traps, but I skied steadily to stay warm. The temperature had slipped another two degrees. To keep my feet warm, I'd put a pair of socks overtop of the thin cross-country boots. Another pair of socks, with holes poked out for the thumbs, made an extra layer of mitten. Even so, my fingers felt alarmingly numb by the time I was gliding down the last run onto our creek flat.

"I've got to do something about this," I resolved, "or I'll lose a finger to frostbite sometime this winter."

The dogs had alerted Marsha of our impending arrival, so she was out in the yard to greet us. Casey was leaping in the air at the end of his chain, orchestrating the noisy welcome.

"Hi! Did you get anything?" Marsha asked the two frosty hunters. She had her hands on her hips and was looking past me, expecting to see Don's sled piled high with meat.

"No, just cold hands!" I moaned, fumbling out of my ski bindings.

"Well, at least that part's good," Marsha said with a smile.

Inside the cabin, I saw what she found amusing about my predicament. Lying on the bed was a newly-sewn pair of deerskin gauntlets, and beside them were some thick duffle liners! The leather Marsha had used was the hide we'd tanned back in Qualicum Beach. Being home-tanned, it would breathe well, like the Yukon Indians' smoke-tanned moosehide. While we were off looking for moose, Marsha was looking after her Bruce.

See Appendix III for instructions and patterns for making gauntlets, liners and dead sweater mitts.

When hunting didn't bring us any food for humans or dogs, the Pelly farmers came to the rescue. Dick and Hugh decided to slaughter six older cows to sell in Whitehorse. Last summer had been rather wet and cool, so there wasn't enough silage set aside to overwinter all their herd. Hence the need to cull some.

Butchering was strenuous work, so Hugh recruited me to help – I would work a few days in exchange for some meat and a case of eggs. The biggest payoff was that our dogs could have the heads, hoofs and various other parts for food.

The Bradleys had developed a fondness for these old cows, knowing their names, characters and lineage, so the actual killing was easier for me to face. Hugh explained the technique: "Mentally draw a line from the cow's left ear to the right eye, and from the right ear to the left eye. You shoot in the centre of the X, right where the lines cross."

Dick would tie a rope from the tractor to a cow's leg – in case I missed the mark and a wounded cow tried to stumble away. But we never needed this tether. One shot with the .22 and the beast would fall to its knees, then flop on its side in the snow quite dead.

Hugh would slide a large baking pan under the cow's neck, and slit the jugular vein. Blood gushed out and filled the pan, pumped by the heart's last few beats.

This blood we poured onto a plastic sheet that was draped over long parallel depressions in the snow – we'd tromped these troughs earlier with our snowpacs. When the blood froze, I had super-high-protein popsicles to take in sacks back to Horsefall. Over the winter we would chop these up and enrich the dog food.

Dick bandsawed the heads into quarters. "One of those ought to keep a husky occupied for a few weeks," he said.

When I asked about the lungs, Hugh said we could have those too, but only second-hand.

"Our chickens eat them," he explained with a grin, "and then you'll get their eggs."

CHAPTER ELEVEN

BUILDING A FREIGHT TOBOGGAN

B uilding our freight toboggans was an epic adventure in itself. My first attempt at this project during the summer had been a dismal failure of splintered wood, and we had only brought enough hardwood for one more try.

Learning about the process of bending wood had taken me into the field of shipbuilding because, although no one was making dog toboggans on Vancouver Island, every shipyard had tradesmen with experience in steam-bending ribs and planks. I jumped the gun, buying oak planks before I thoroughly understood the critical factors involved. The lumber purchased was unsuitable for *steam-bending* because it was kiln-dried, wasn't clear of knots, and was sawn on the wrong angle. For optimal bending, the choice wood would be air-dried (or still green), straight-grained and rift-sawn. We had to *boil* our boards to make them pliable enough to form around a frame.

Our thin planks required thirty minutes of actual boiling to loosen up. At that point though, the change was amazing – the boards suddenly became limp and pliable. After I rushed the steaming board to our bending frame, Marsha would pin the end in place and then drop dowels into the holes as clamps while I walked the plank around the frame.

See Appendix IV for details about building toboggans.

We created a hybrid old-new craft: wooden frame with hi-tech UHMW [ultra-high molecular weight] plastic as an added base. The design was long and narrow: well-suited for travel through the bush behind tandem (single file) dogs. Seen from above, the toboggan was slightly coffin-shaped, about 16 inches wide at maximum, 12" across at the curl and 15" at the back. The narrower curl ensured the ends of the outside boards would be tucked well inside, away from snagging branches. At the tail, the taper made the toboggan easier to steer. The twelve-foot long oak boards formed a vehicle about 9-1/2 feet in length. Of this overall length, about 8-1/2 feet would be *on the snow*. The rest would be the upsweep of the curl which allowed the front to ride up and over loose snow.

I copied the local Indians' design for backboard and handlebars, using willow poles fastened with bolts and strap hinges. Our brake was a hefty metal claw bolted to a square of hardwood plywood, that was in turn hinged to the tail. To slow the dogs, the musher could stomp on the claw for a pulsed drag.

Again following the Indians' pattern, we wired our curls to the top of the backboard. Then the sides were woven in with rope, tying the whole together like a suspension bridge. The toboggan could flex and snake along a trail, but each spot was supported to keep it from bending too far. A canvas tarp laid out and fastened to both wires formed a basket into which the cargo was placed.

Checking out retired toboggans, wear was most obvious in two places: near the tail (beneath the musher's weight), and where the upsweep starts. We reinforced our toboggans at these points to compensate for the thinness of our oak planks. By doubling the boards at these stress points we had the stiffness comparable to a well worn-in heavy toboggan.

Where we strengthened the upsweep, it was important to leave in the flexibility. We installed a leaf-spring system devised by Marsha after the first few major crashes. The reinforcing boards were left to slide through channels in the crossbars. On impact, these inside boards absorbed and dissipated much of the shock. *[See Appendix IV.]*

By the time I was finally drilling a last hole in the first toboggan and feeding a rope to the singletree spreader bar where the harnesses would be attached, a solid week's work was behind me. Using handsaws and a brace and bit on the oak boards had been slow work, a strain on arms and back. With the sparse daylight, we'd kept the propane lights on even at midday to help me see the pencil lines and guide holes. When meals were baking in the cookstove, I'd been roasted too, drenched in sweat while ripping boards clamped to the kitchen counter. Each night for a week we had removed a pile of tools from the bed to have a place to sleep, and each morning tripped over them en route to lighting the cookstove. The air held a pungent, though pleasant, smell of oak sawdust.

With the singletree in place, the completed craft was in front of me. I realized it would need modifications as we learned from upcoming experiences, but at last we were ready to cruise the forests in proper style. Building the second one would be much simpler now I had the techniques worked out. I felt dizzy with exhaustion, yet my head was also swollen with pride. I couldn't wait to drag it out into the dog lot to show the crew, perhaps for a champagne-anointed christening ceremony—

Most of the pooches didn't wake up for the unveiling. A few wagged their tails lazily and yawned, not at all impressed or eager to try it out. Even my partner Marsha stayed in bed for the dramatic reveal. Perhaps the hour was affecting their enthusiasm – after all, it was 3 o'clock in the wee hours of the morning.

The toboggans were expected to endure lots of rough use –
hauling firewood and slamming into the occasional tree.

CHAPTER TWELVE

A FIRST RIDE TO REMEMBER

For the first road test of the new toboggan, I chose the trail so familiar to my four dogs. Casey, Lucky, Mutt and Loki were conscripted to pull me to the truck parked back in the farmyard to fetch yet another load of dog food.

On each previous freight trip I had tried out one of Marsha's five dogs, to get an idea of individual potential. This was neither adequate training nor sufficient exercise for her squad, and each was clearly anxious to show his or her stuff today. Leaving the dog lot, with Tyhee along with us for her trial, we were serenaded for the first half-hour by the echoing wails and indignant howling of her frustrated team-mates.

Soon we were up the long hill and into the peaceful plateau forest. Winding through the frozen swamps and meadows, the toboggan undulated over the mounds of muskeg like a snake slithering over rocks. Its flexibility on corners was somewhat unsettling to me after being accustomed to the stiffness of the shorter kid's toboggan. But most surprising was the speed of the huge vehicle: with its white synthetic base, there was virtually no friction on the packed trail. I had to be alert on the brake to save wheel dog Loki the indignity of being overtaken.

Tyhee was excited and curious at every bend. Her long nose sniffed the air and the bushes flashing by, and – more than once – she got wacked by a branch when not looking ahead. During the run, I was encouraging her to pay attention to pulling though I didn't want to spoil her enthusiasm. She had lots of spunk compared to the others who were accustomed to this route and the slow, heavily-laden return trips in the late afternoon twilight.

By the end of the day, I had made a mental list of improvements for this toboggan and its soon-to-be-built sister craft. The screws holding the backboard hinges were working loose and should be replaced by bolts with lock-washers on the nuts. The light strap hinges fastening the handlebars were too flimsy to withstand the strains when I leaned heavily to wrestle us around tight corners. Already one hinge was bent and it would only be a matter of time before it cracked and broke. If we didn't have any heavier hinges at the cabin, I could forge metal brackets to hold these points. Exactly when I would get around to doing all these little tune-ups would, of course, depend on what else had to be done sooner. It had been a long time since I'd felt there was nothing to do. Six months ago, this life had been a romantic dream; now, in December, it was an amazing though exhausting reality.

As the familiar scenery slipped by heading back towards Horsefall, I strained my eyes for signs of moose or caribou. There were a few weeks left for Don to hunt on his trapper's extended license, and I wanted desperately to locate some meat for him to shoot. But there was not a hint of activity on this trail; we would have to go much further afield if we were to dine on game meat this winter.

When I pulled into the dog lot again, Marsha's crew kicked up a pitiful racket. Marsha herself looked rather envious as I handed over letters and passed on various bits of gossip from the farm.

"How about we go tomorrow for a run, taking all your dogs, and you can be the musher?" I suggested. "I'll help you get started. You've got to try driving the dogs sometime."

Shortly after noon the following day, we tied the toboggan's gee-line to a stout poplar and laid out five harnesses. The leader's collar was roped ahead to another tree so the crew would be held in line until all was ready. With the temperature hovering at Thirty-Eight Below, we hoped to minimize the time spent with mitts off handling metal clips. It was so cold the snow squeaked and felt like beach sand beneath our moccasins.

The dogs wouldn't cooperate. Dawson kept turning in circles and rolling over. He even did a headfirst somersault in his harness to show his exuberance. Peter – who used to be Peggy – was hooked up in front because the Hagers had said he was a leader. When I checked him out in lead on a trip to the farm, he had proven too cautious, possibly because of his fear of the bigger dogs behind him. We hoped he'd do better today with this smaller crew supporting him.

Tyhee rose up and clubbed with both paws any person or dog that passed. Her wiener-tail was swishing back and forth like an errant windshield wiper. The long nose was hard at work sniffing high and low and where it was none of her business.

Jeff tried to fight with Dawson, but we yanked them apart before they'd passed the bared fangs stage. In frustration, Jeff sank his teeth into his traces as soon as he was harnessed. Just as quickly, he felt on his ears the wrath of the fellow who'd stitched that harness. Wide-eyed and quivering, he crouched in anticipation of more fun.

Big shaggy Hinglish, at wheel, was vibrating with excitement and jerking mightily forward, backward and sideways, eager to go, and not too choosy about direction.

I was merrily explaining my theories to Marsha as we struggled with each frantic canine, but she was far too nervous to reply. The gravity of the situation was showing on her usually gay countenance – she was biting her lower lip and her brow was furrowed in concentration. Her moment of truth was nigh.

Keeping all five mutts facing front, with all limbs in proper locations inside the traces, was like juggling boomerangs. Their energy might have been fun for us too, if it hadn't been so cold that we wanted to be mushing rather than harnessing. We had to box ears all around before they settled down enough so we could consider leaving.

It was quickly agreed I should drive them out of the yard. Marsha held Peter and ran with him for the first ten steps, then let go and stepped aside. He abruptly turned and followed her off the trail while the others piled up behind. What a mess.

After a session of untangling, we tried again and this time it worked! I had both feet on the brake to slow us down while Marsha leapt aboard. Then it was full speed ahead, snow flying, dogs sprinting for the hill, the toboggan careening off the willows lining the trail. A flow of power – very raw energy – jerked on the toboggan as the dogs scrambled around corners and surged into the straightaways. The force of acceleration left me gasping, my lungs full of frozen air.

Whenever we halted for a dog to relieve himself, Marsha would run forward and straighten out any tangles, pat their heads and point Peter in the right direction. They pulled us easily up the steepest hill – something my four dogs had never done – and we turned onto the Black Creek trail. On this level pathway the crew really picked up speed. Marsha was crouched on the toboggan in the *basket* observing all this from close to ground-level.

"Do they always go this fast?" she called over the rasping noise of the toboggan grinding over dry snow. "This is so scary. It seems like ninety miles per hour from here!"

"It would be great if they always would," I hollered at her hood-covered ear. "I could be at the farm in under an hour."

I was too busy steering, braking and leaning out to the side to think about being fearful. Only a few strategically-placed snow banks and tilted snowmobile ruts kept us on the trail. Huge trees slid by only inches from us. I crouched behind the

Marsha guides her team through the birch forest up on the plateau. It was a special treat – we were out of the deep river valley and into the sunshine.

backboard to miss low branches that would slap the handlebars and be swung up to stomach level.

Then Peter saw a rabbit dart across the trail – and abruptly dove into a willow thicket in hot pursuit. Dawson followed, but chose a slightly different route. The rest collided with a tree and were, in turn, run over by the toboggan.

We seized this opportunity to reorganize them a bit, switching Hinglish up behind Peter. We also switched mushers.

With a casual *your turn*, I climbed into the basket and braced myself. Marsha said nothing, but I knew she was struggling to find courage to go through with the job. Here was her big chance.

"Are you ready?" she finally whispered to me.

"Yep. Let's go before they get tangled again," I whispered in reply.

"Okay!" she yelled. *"Let's GO!"*

The dogs took off, running like there was no tomorrow. The toboggan was literally flying at times. As we caromed down the tunnel of giant poplars, the sun flashed between the trees at us like a strobe light. I felt as if I was part of an early vintage movie, every movement choppy and surreal.

Displaying great bravado, we *yeehawed* like a couple of rodeo cowboys. Marsha shouted, while ducking for a low branch, that it seemed so easy, exciting and wonderful. She especially liked being up here on the higher ground where the sunshine wasn't being blocked by low hills and valley walls.

Meanwhile, my adrenaline was flowing and my heart ready to burst: the view – from dog level – was *absolutely terrifying*. The trail here was only a snowmobile's width across. We were barely missing huge trees. Monstrous cottonwoods loomed up on me, and were fended off by the handlebars. I couldn't stop myself from trying to steer from inside the basket, by leaning and dragging my hands in the snow, even though I knew how easily an arm could be broken if brushed by a tree. I told myself this again and again, but it was hard to just sit in that little cage and brace myself for the seemingly-inevitable crash.

These dogs hadn't been off their chains much for weeks so it took ages before they finally slowed to a walk. As a neurotic *basket case*, I wasn't disappointed when they did. I was so frazzled from the wild ride I wasn't even cold.

After a brief stop to sort out a rabbit-inspired tangle, we headed for home very pleased. I was hopeful we'd be able to finish in good style so as to set a positive tone for this team. We were now planning to use this squad to inspire mine into running more often. A touch of competition would do my plodders a world of good.

However the dogs only ran for a moment before they slowed again to a walk. They were no longer interested in pulling. Instead five pairs of eyes were scanning the bushes for bunnies.

At the top of the steep descent down the Horsefall Creek ravine, we switched places so I'd be steering down this tricky stretch. From a mile away and five hundred feet below us in elevation, we could plainly hear the howling of the other four dogs. The chorus leader, sounding dreadfully wronged, was unmistakably Casey. Marsha's team perked up their ears at the racket and eagerly leaned into their harnesses once again.

"Are you ready?" I whispered to Marsha.

"Are you on the brake?" she replied.

"It'll be okay," I said. "Don't worry. Just keep your arms and legs in and you can't get hurt."

I'd almost finished saying that when the dogs bolted forward and tore off down the hill. I held white-knuckled onto the handlebars and stood fully on the brake. Like a plough, it carved a neat furrow in the trail – but we weren't slowing down.

To reassure Marsha, I yelled a few halfhearted *yeehaws* as if I were in full control of this rollercoaster ride. I crouched low and leaned way out to the side, steering like a motorcycle sidecar rider. It was exciting and I was happy to see the team running again.

Glancing back, Marsha called, "Are you on the brake? *ARE YOU ON THE BRAKE?*"

"Yes. Yes. It's okay. Keep your arms and feet in."

And we kept gaining speed—

Though the toboggan was squeaking and groaning, and the dogs' feet sounded like thunder, I was able to hear an alarming cracking noise which cut through the din like a scratch on a record. As we rounded a corner, I was leaning, using all my weight to keep up high on the inside rut, when one of the handlebars broke away from the toboggan. A split-second later, the unbraced backboard tore from its other moorings and flopped into my hands. With the strangest, dream-like sensation, I toppled backwards, tumbling and rolling, catching glimpses of sky, trees, snow – and then of the dismembered toboggan heading for a tree.

For the whole descent, Marsha had been thoroughly terrified. As trees whizzed by, she could only brace herself. She had faith in my driving, though, and thought we would make it safely to the bottom.

As the toboggan neared a sharp bend in the trail, one giant spruce was looming closer and closer. She waited for me to steer. She waited as that spruce got bigger and bigger. She was shouting, *"Bruce! TURN!"* as the crash happened.

Marsha felt the toboggan breaking under her and saw all the dogs arrested in mid-stride by the tremendous jerk, then watched them fall on their faces. She herself had been pitched sharply forward, then slammed back down by the impact. Only at that point did she glance back and realize there were neither handlebars nor backboard behind her. And no driver!

The dogs picked themselves up and started yanking on their traces. Slowly the crippled toboggan started moving again, heading off downhill. Marsha dug in her heels as brakes on either side, fighting for control.

"Whoa! *WHOA, WHOA!*" she called to the dogs who – amazingly – did stop. They halted mostly though because they were tangled. Some were turned around, some pointed ahead, all a little dazed. Marsha was saying reassuring words to them when I arrived, carrying the missing toboggan parts.

"What happened to you?" she asked.

"I fell off when everything broke apart," I said sheepishly. "I guess those hinges weren't strong enough to hold the handlebars."

"Are you okay?"

"Me? Oh, I'm fine. How about you?"

"My bum aches but I think everything still works," she said.

Around her feet, the dogs were all wagging, so they couldn't have been too badly done by. The toboggan had one smashed board and a cracked crossbar, not to mention the missing backboard and brake. A day's carpentry work would put that right.

We still had to get us all home. Our first plan was for me to walk and hold a rope to slow us down, while Marsha braked with her feet. But the dogs were too strong for that.

Next, Marsha walked beside Peter to hold him to a calm speed. However I couldn't hold the other four back, and they eagerly dogpiled onto Peter. The toboggan ran over wheel dog Jeff, who was taking this all rather well, considering the number of times it had happened.

Tyhee, being the only female, wouldn't fight so we released her to lessen the numbers. This created instant mayhem as the others sprang to life and struggled to get free. Marsha volunteered to walk two of the remaining four down the hill, leaving me to bring on the toboggan and two very upset dogs.

I waited until Marsha was out of sight before trying my descent. Jeff and Dawson were frantic to go. I held the gee-line and hauled back to keep them to a safe pace. The resistance made them pull harder.

Up ahead, Marsha was getting tugged along at an unsettling rate, so she sat down. She was dragged in that posture over a couple of rude bumps before she managed to trip up her two escorts and have a chance to reassess her position. Before she came to any conclusions though, she heard a clattering from uphill and hauled Hinglish and Peter off the trail. Then she turned to see Dawson and Jeff barrelling down on her, toboggan flapping behind and no driver – once again. I was twenty yards behind, running and shouting and holding a length of rope in my hand.

Marsha sidestepped Dawson and grabbed his traces. She wasn't fast enough to also dodge Jeff though – the toboggan ploughed into the poor Siberian and then knocked them all over like so many bowling pins.

Now she had five very excited dogs wrapped around her. She was trying to keep them all apart though they were knotted together by their harnesses. Four of them were growling fiercely while Tyhee was right in the middle, wagging her tail and licking faces.

"It's okay! *It's OKAY!*" she shouted. "Calm down. *Calm DOWN! Hey*, cut that out! Be nice, *PLEASE!*"

When I finally caught up, we were able to untangle the crew without ruffling too many feathers, and averted the pending free-for-all. Since Peter and Hinglish hadn't fought on their stroll with Marsha, we gambled and set them free to run ahead with Tyhee. Marsha walked Dawson home, although it looked the other way around. Then Jeff and I hauled the toboggan, this time with my rope more securely tied.

At last our luck came through: there were no fights in progress when we arrived at the dog lot ten minutes later. One by one we cornered the loose dogs and marched them to their chains. Hooking them seemed to take forever. It was getting fairly dark and our cold fingers were clumsy from numbness. Finally, when nine pairs of eyes were next to their proper trees, we switched off the flashlight and retreated inside, shivering from chills and exhaustion. The toboggan and harnesses could stay where they lay until morning.

We flopped on the bed and lay there for a long while without talking. When she rolled over onto her back, Marsha let out a loud *OUCH,* discovering three distinct holes in her buttocks, red and welted.

"When you're fixing the toboggan," she said, rubbing and wincing, "don't forget to hacksaw off the bolt ends sticking up from the crossbars!"

I got up, stoked the airtight and then crawled back onto the bed.

There was no sign of life from the other occupant – I wasn't sure she was still awake.

Gently I whispered, "Congratulations, Marsha! How do you like being a dog musher?"

"It's a pain in the butt," she muttered.

I giggled.

"It's *NOT* funny," she said. "This really hurts."

There was a pause, then she started chuckling too.

CHAPTER THIRTEEN

IT'S A DOG'S LIFE

H aving a dog team was a full-time job – body and mind. Thoughts about those little beasties oozed through our minds until every corner was contaminated. Conversation on normal, sane topics would drift with uncanny certainty to such matters as worming pills or the relative merits of soya and oat meal for a dog's winter diet.

Much more was involved in having nine dogs than either of us had anticipated. Our care of them improved as we learned from other mushers we met, from books we consulted, and from the hairy critters themselves.

Because we had only one female, one of the questions we couldn't resolve was which sex were better sled dogs. Some mushers preferred females to males in their teams, although these drivers were in the minority.

One previous summer I'd visited Jared and Eddie Wilkinson, two old-timers who trapped north-west of Mayo. Jared had a team of all females and his brother had males with a female leader. Both thought females were decidedly smarter and had nicer dispositions. When I asked how females in heat affected a team's performance, Jared said it made no difference. Eddie smiled shyly and admitted his males picked up *a little enthusiasm.*

At the time of my visit, the brothers had just moved to an old trading post site and had cut back the wild roses and willows enough to have a potato patch. Their dogs were staked out on the far side of the garden. I asked if that was to scare rabbits and ground squirrels away from the crops. Eddie said that was a help, but the main reason was to clear more land. Sure enough, each dog had thoroughly trampled, chewed and uprooted every bit of plant life within his or her chain's reach. Next year the Wilkinsons could move the teams further back to extend their garden, and this new section would be well tilled and fertilized!

The Wilkinsons' dogs were thin, though healthy-looking. Eddie explained that working dogs should be lean, especially in the summer. Only pet owners let their animals get fat, he said. I stored this philosophy in the back of my mind, and followed it when we got our nine dogs. I wonder if we were *too* stingy with the food at times though and didn't get the performance from our dogs we could have.

See Appendix V for more information about care and feeding of sled dogs.

Oldtimers advised us to feed our dogs only in the evening because *they won't work on a full stomach*. On the colder mornings, however, it was a generally accepted practice to give each mutt a chunk of fat or beef tripe (donations from the Pelly Farm) to help them stay warm during the day.

Serving the hot supper mush was quite a spectacle. We couldn't lift the steaming bucket off the stove without some alert dog hearing and sounding the alarm. Since there were no neighbours close by, we let them kick up a tremendous racket at feeding time. Nine dogs would be leaping in the air, rolling in the snow, snapping at their neighbours, barking at us, or whimpering and whining. If a dog had a cute act, such as presenting a paw or doing somersaults, now was the time for exhibitions.

Mindful of changing the route to not play favourites, we'd walk around and dish out the odiferous entrée into their pans. If it was too hot to eat, the dog would grab the pan's edge with bared teeth and tip the mash in a long smear across the snow. Then he'd go back to the start of the smear and eat as it cooled. At Fifty Below, the first bit he'd dumped out would be already cool enough to lap up.

It was a measure of the fanaticism of dog owners that we might spend an hour with Don Mark earnestly discussing the subject of dog excreta. If the dog was fed correctly, there should not be a great quantity passed through. Don insisted to us that a mentally-balanced dog will confine his stools to one area, and a neurotic one will have his deposited all over. "Same as with humans," Don laughed. "Check to see if they've *got their shit together*."

Indeed the amateur dog psychologist might contemplate why some dog will try to process his and other dogs' stools a second time – my theory was that the dog was extremely bored or hungry, or both.

The treatment for intestinal worms was *Canoids*, an inexpensive prescription worm-poison. As with most parasite treatments, the procedure had to be carried out once to kill the adult worms and two weeks later to kill the next generation of immature worms.

The actual administration of the pills was a nerve-racking adventure. Some of our dogs had been so wild it took Marsha two weeks to teach them to *sit* for their suppers. Neither of us was enthusiastic about sticking our fingers into Mutt's or Jeff's mouth, to force on them pills they didn't want. But – necessity being a great motivator – we soon learned a safe way: with one hand under his chin, the fingers forcing his jaws open by squeezing between the rows of molars, it was then a matter of gathering the courage to put the other hand inside those gaping fangs. The pill had to be pushed down the throat, then the dog was coaxed to swallow by holding his jaws shut and stroking his throat. Some of our dogs were terribly clever at faking a swallow, while secretly tonguing the pill forward to be nonchalantly dropped in the snow as soon as we released the jaws.

Dawson, for some reason, was always infested with worms. Extra doses never cleared him out completely, so we tried some folk medicine. An almanac claimed raw garlic would de-worm a horse, so we figured it should fix a husky. A trapper told us oats would flush out the parasites as well. So, we fed the squirrelly little devil nothing but raw oats and bulbs of garlic for four days. At that point we stopped the treatment because Dawson had developed an insatiable thirst and outrageous breath. The tactic did appeared to clear him up for a few weeks though.

Dawson's breath might have caused a few dog fights, but we couldn't blame them all on the young rascal. The worst bout we had was when Marsha's team was having a disagreement, and my crew pulled their toboggan alongside and jumped in en masse. The harnesses got so tangled it was ages before we had all the combatants apart. At the very bottom of the dogpile was the poor old pacifist, Lucky. When teeth were flashing, fur was flying, and blood was splattering on the snow, it seemed the dogs intended to kill each other, but the real purposes probably were to defend their personal territory, to establish a *pecking order* (if the chickens don't mind the metaphor), and simply to be rowdy. Mushers who had many dogs to choose from, as they built up their teams, weeded out incorrigible fighters. At races, we never saw a scrap because the instigators hadn't graduated past the training sessions. Of course, we did not have extra dogs, so we made do with our nine and tried to discourage any pugnacious behaviour.

When breaking up a fight, my immediate impulse was to rush into the fracas and yell, *STOP IT!* But yelling did no good at all, and getting too close was dangerous. We had to learn to keep out of range of those sharp teeth. Instead, we yanked on tails, harnesses or chains, or grabbed a pole to pry and bash them apart. From the times I forgot to keep back, I received scars on forearm, wrist, palm, finger and knee. Their hide was a lot tougher than mine, it seemed.

After making harnesses, chains and collars for each dog, we ran out of steam and didn't devote much energy to building dog houses. Loki's last owners had told us of seeing shelters built by one Indian band for their sled dogs: they made a short picket fence for each dog by pounding a row of stakes into the ground. The dog was chained to one end of the fence and could sleep on whatever side was out of the wind.

We had that image in our minds when we pondered designs, as well as another extreme example from Dawson City. A few years before, I visited John Tapsell just as he finished a beautifully elaborate dog house. Carpentry was a winter hobby for John, so he had gone all out making fancy mitred corners and intricate gingerbread trim all around the door and windows. The little mansion had a peaked roof so the dog, Sherlock, could stand inside without stooping.

"This one is much classier than Sherlock's old one," John told me as four of us carried it from the shop out into the yard. When I asked what happened to the previous one, John grinned and said, "He ate it."

A day later, the door opening was half-again the size it had been. Two days later, the roof was off and in well-gnawed fragments. I was not around to witness the rest. Clearly, John and Sherlock had a symbiotic relationship: John wanted projects to practise his carpentry technique, and his dog certainly needed a steady supply of houses.

For us, the moral from these two examples was to build simply and sturdily. We made log shelters, each of which had only three walls and a flat, plywood roof. By using large diameter logs, we needed only one round for the walls. Corners were lap-notched and spiked. These shelters were very small, but the size helped the dogs stay warm if they chose to use them. Some of our dogs wouldn't stay inside these houses whatever the temperature, but they loved to lie on top.

Despite the hard work, living with dogs was rewarding and enjoyable. It was an education in so many ways. Each morning, the dogs would have a grand howl. We never tried to stop this but did insist they limit noise to once in the morning, their grand display at mealtime, and maybe an evening howl too if the moon was waxing full.

One of them would begin the howl. Not all could get the others to follow; Casey, Peter and Mutt were the chorus leaders. Tails would flop as the others listened to the first soloist. Then, curling their tails as high and tight as possible, they would join in. Each would have his neck stretched out, ears pinned back, mouth pursed and lips wrinkled. If one dog tried to ignore the routine, he'd only be able to hold out for a minute before being drawn in. Maybe the reluctant dog wouldn't get up from his sleeping spot, but still he'd throw back his head and warble along.

Each mutt howled differently. It was an insight into their characters, we be-

Tyhee dozes on her dog house in this springtime photo.

lieved, for they seemed to let down all barriers and pretences. Peter's howl was a series of high-pitched yips, like a coyote's call. Casey's whole body trembled like the skin on a stereo woofer. Mutt would parade as he yodelled. His litter-mate Jeff combined growls with a few teeth snaps. Lucky had a deep, dignified call, while Tyhee's was shrill and spooky. Dawson made silly noises because he was still a puppy. Our big clown Hinglish barked and wagged, wagged and barked, appearing both delighted and confused.

If having nine dogs was our full-time job, Marsha and I were entitled to enjoy it: not only did we let them howl, we often joined in ourselves. Mutt would look curiously at us, then start up again. The others never paused.

The dogs' howling came from down deep, from instincts, from their heritage. It was a vivid reminder their ancestors were wolves. As Marsha and I howled, I knew that in other eras people believed in their instincts and were attuned to the oneness of Nature. And this thought made me feel good. Where mankind was before, maybe we could rediscover. There was hope in the howling.

CHAPTER FOURTEEN

WARMING THOUGHTS
ON NOT-SO-WARM DAYS

As the thermometer dropped well below Zero and the days became even shorter, it would have been heavenly to sit inside looking out on a dozen cords of wood all split and stacked. Instead we had to be cutting just to have enough for next week. We paid for our late arrival at the cabin by the toll the elements took on our tools. Forty Below air made splitting firewood ever so easy, but axe handles became brittle, and metal heads chipped or cracked. Many an evening was spent whittling willow replacement handles, rasping wedges from the oak scraps left from toboggan construction, and filing chipped blades.

From Horsefall Creek's previous inhabitants, we learned the ultimate way to keep an axe head on securely. There was an axe left at the fish camp that some-one must have attacked in a complete frenzy when they couldn't wedge the head on tightly. On one side of the axe head was an impressive bullet hole, about .45 calibre! The edges of the metal had mushroomed into the wooden handle, almost riveting the head on. Why the handle wasn't shattered and what happened to any ricochet remained a mystery to us, but we did know this axe head doggedly refused to work loose.

Finally, on one bitterly cold morning, that handle broke and I had a heck of a time getting the stub out to replace it. Usually this removal could be done by sawing off what was left of the handle close to the head and shrinking the wood by charring it in the oven. For this stubborn case, I had to auger out much of the wood before the stub fell out in pieces.

See Appendix VI for information about gathering wood: putting on axe handles, sharpening for different purposes, splitting blocks of wood without chopping your foot, etc.

The hidden advantage of our late arrival and lack of already-cut firewood was that we were forced to venture forth into temperatures that might have otherwise kept us cabin-bound. Once we were wrapped in umpteen layers of woollens and goose down, we discovered we needn't have been apprehensive of the inevitable Fifty Below spell. The coldest day that winter, as we proudly reported in letters to our relatives, would be Sixty-Eight Below Zero.

On that record low day just before Christmas, we didn't let the temperature stop us from doing some holiday season visiting. It was too cold to work the dogs, but we were so used to being outside gathering wood and getting river water, that we decided to walk over to the Bradley farm for a break in routine.

With so many layers of clothes to put on, dressing took half an hour. We had cotton thermal-knit underwear beneath woollen underwear beneath heavy woollen loggers pants, and two pairs of woollen socks inside duffle liners inside our moose-hide moccasins. A long-sleeve cotton T-shirt and Vyella shirt and two sweaters felt sweaty-hot in the cabin's warmth, but we put on a parka and anorak as well. To be safe, we had scarves as well as toques to wear beneath the parka's hood. Our hands were toasty in woollen mitts, duffle liners and leather gauntlets.

When we left the cabin and pulled up the hood and rolled the fur ruff forward, our view of the world shrank to a soft-edged picture at the end of a dark tunnel of fur. We had to swivel our bodies completely to see one another, because peripheral vision was out of the question. Before long, though, our movement warmed us enough to allow us to roll back the ruffs a little and appreciate the winter landscape.

Behind us, the smoke from the well-banked fire in the airtight was rising dead straight from the pipe. From the cookstove's chimney, even though the draft and damper were closed, air was escaping fast enough to send heat waves shimmering high into the still air.

"Did you check on the lantern in the root cellar?" Marsha asked.

"Yep, lots of kerosene left and I topped it up to be sure it wouldn't go out while we're away," I replied. "The thermometer down there is hovering just above the freezing mark, so one lantern seems to generate exactly the right amount of heat."

The dogs were either in their shelters or curled up in the snow. Those who raised their heads to watch us go displayed halos of frost buildup on the fur around their faces. Whiskers were tipped in white. On a day like this, the crew was happy to stay at home and conserve their energy for staying warm. We had boosted their rations because of the temperature but a few of them were still losing weight.

"Look at poor Lucky," Marsha whispered. The blond mongrel was frightfully thin. "I give him all our table scraps and more mush than the other dogs, but he seems to be wasting away. What can we do?"

"Hope for warmer weather, I guess. Maybe it is because his fur isn't as thick as some of the others. Look at Hinglish: he seems to be getting fatter by the day."

As we climbed out of the valley, we left thoughts of the dogs and the coldest weather behind us. Because warm air rises, the plateau was easily ten degrees warmer. The sun was also hitting this level, while our portion of the valley was blocked by Victoria Rock Mountain and the hills around it.

We were being as quiet as the crunchy snow would allow, yet we saw no animals. Indeed, there seemed to be a total absence of fresh tracks or droppings along our trail. Only when we wandered off the main path through a thicket to pick some Labrador tea leaves did we see one set of rabbit prints and the faint track of a squirrel.

Even the birds were hiding at this temperature. The giant ravens, who often amused us with their repertoire of goofy noises, were nowhere to be seen. The Whiskey Jacks must have been huddled in some sheltered corner, with their grey feathers and down as ruffled and fluffed as possible. Our other friends – who we decided were Boreal Chickadees – had been absent for a few weeks now, so we assumed they had gone south or to the coast for their Christmas vacation. The forest was all our own.

Above the deep green spruce tops, the sky was a startling blue. At this extreme temperature, the air is invariably still: lifeless, yet vitalizing and fresh. The little hairs in our nostrils would freeze as we inhaled and be thawed by each warm sigh. Winter is my favourite season, as I love the crisp new days and the amazingly clear, starlit nights. For weeks, we had seen no clouds, save for a few feathery wisps of cirrus high in the jet-streams. Thousands of galaxies decorated our clear evening skies, flickering and pulsing at us from across the cosmos.

A sharp explosion echoed across the plateau as a tree trunk suddenly cracked under strain of the cold, magically choosing this very moment after enduring fifty other winters. Down in the valley below us, the river would be shifting and struggling under its burden of ice, letting anyone nearby hear its every move. The dull, deep, rolling rumbles and heart-stopping *wuummps* reminded both musher and dogs that passage across the frozen surface was not to be taken for granted. Though the ice grew thicker daily, beneath it was a liquid monster, ever gnawing away at the white highway and pushing up ridges of displeasure.

It was peaceful up on these hills, away from the surging energy of the Yukon

River and out of the valley's unrelenting gloom. Being in the direct sunshine – feeling its warmth and flow of life-giving power – rejuvenated our spirits. Out here in the open, any shivers of cabin fever wriggled through our bodies, passed through the cocoon of clothes and evaporated into the crisp air. Even at – perhaps especially at – these fantastic temperatures, we were learning to treat the winter around us as a friend and let it soothe and heal us.

Marsha reminded me our preparations were nearly complete and soon we'd be heading off on extended dog trips, needing to be ready for any weather conditions.

CHAPTER FIFTEEN

WORKING THROUGH THE YULE
ON OUR WINTER COSTUMES

Christmas was not very different from any other December day. After opening a few presents that had been mailed to us in care of the Bradleys at Pelly Farm, we had a lazy breakfast then ambled through the daily chores of splitting wood and attending to the water hole. Marsha fired up the cookstove to bake a mincemeat pie and some shortbreads, while I settled into the never-ending task of sewing and repairing our clothing.

Since December 21st, the daylight minutes were increasing steadily. Although it would be ages before direct sunshine would again strike our kitchen window, we found it encouraging to check our clock and note that the glow in the sky above the valley was five minutes longer with each passing day. We were anxious to be off exploring, and wanted to be ready for the first spell of travelling weather.

This morning, as I surveyed the piles of clothing in various stages of construction, alteration and restoration, the image of a beach in Mexico flashed across my mind.

"Imagine packing for a trip in Mexico," I said wistfully, "and only taking sandals and a swim suit. It would be so simple."

"Who needs to pack?" said Marsha. "I'll buy my swimsuit and some plastic sandals when we get there. When do we leave?"

"As soon as Santa brings the tickets – and someone to mind the dogs."

"Fine," Marsha smiled. "I'll finish baking this pie in case he's hungry when he arrives."

"Good idea. And I'll darn these socks in case he forgets to come."

Having proper clothing was vitally important to us in the North. Our outfits had to be functional, durable, simple and repairable so we mostly kept to the tried-and-true traditional costume. With only a few exceptions, our clothing was identical to that worn a hundred years before by fur traders and prospectors.

On our feet, we wore either moccasins or boot pacs. The foot part of our moccasins was made of neck leather, which is the toughest part of the moosehide. Mrs. Hager had given us the option of open canvas tops or tube-like closed ones which are suited to deep snow. We ended up getting two pairs of each.

When the weather is warmer than Zero, the snow is too wet for moccasins — one has to use pacs instead. Pacs were known by a variety of names: snow-pacs, leather-tops, Arctic boots and snowmobile boots, to mention a few. The lower part was rubber or a synthetic rubber, and the uppers were leather or heavy nylon. Pacs weren't nearly as warm as moccasins because our feet didn't flex in them when we walked. Also the condensation built up in these waterproof boots, so the liners were soon quite damp. Yet for quick chores around the cabin, or for evenings around an open campfire, pacs were convenient and practical.

When I asked trapper Eddie Wilkinson what he wore for winter footwear, he replied, "Indian moccasins with seven pair of socks in them."

He maintained that he never wore liners, always seven pairs of socks. So I bit, and asked why exactly seven.

"That," he said grandly, "is *so the holes don't all match up!*"

While we never used seven socks, we did have some liners which were hand-knit thick wool socks created by Marsha's mother as soon as she heard about our Yukon plans. There must have been lots of love knitted in with the *Buffalo* wool, because we never got cold feet while wearing them.

See Appendix VII for more about our choices in winter clothing.

We placed a felt insole inside the moccasin with these knitted liners to make them warmer. Despite all these layers of leather, felt insole, liners and two pairs of socks, wearing moccasins still felt like being in bare feet. Marsha was a former downhill ski addict who believed cold feet were an unavoidable part of winter – until she tried moccasins. If her feet went in warm, they would stay that way. If her toes were cold from inactivity, a short walk would exercise those tootsies and have them toasty in no time. Our moccasins were so light on our feet we were disappointed to have to wear the comparatively heavy and clumsy pac boots; we hoped for sub-Zero weather for all our camping trips.

The pants we needed for the coldest days were the heavy, full-cut, wool pants loggers and fishermen wear. Because they insulated so well, snow did not melt on them and any water splashed on merely beaded on the surface. These pants were too hot for strenuous activity, and for wearing at all on any but the coldest days. We had some lighter-weight woollen pants for strenuous outdoor work.

Cotton pants, such as denim jeans, were moderately warm if not fitted too tightly. Unfortunately we found that cotton tended to wick up moisture too readily, so wet cuffs meant the pant legs – and long undies underneath – were soon soaked up to the knees. When we skied in jeans, we wore waterproof gaiters, covering from the ankle to the knee, to alleviate the wicking problem.

Marsha's one pair of nylon-covered skiers' warm-up pants lasted about five minutes. Over-exuberant dogs tore the fabric to shreds with their claws, just in the process of saying hello.

Our anoraks were loose-fitting hooded pullovers made of coloured canvas. Drawings made by the earliest traders and explorers into the Yukon showed the native Yukoners wearing anoraks made of moose or caribou hide, cut to a long vee at the front and back. The decorations were done in dyed porcupine quills and the trim was leather fringe or fur.

The 100% cotton canvas Marsha used to make our anoraks stood up well to the rough use. Rip-stop nylon, which she initially considered, would have been too flimsy for the ravages of branches, sparks and dog claws.

Marsha had a parka insulated with *Thinsulate*. The outer shell was a cotton and polyester blend, and Marsha added a wolf fur ruff to the hood to make a breathing tunnel.

When our neighbour, Abbie Roberts, saw the trim on Marsha's parka, she laughed and slapped her knee.

"You're a smart white lady," proclaimed Abbie. "Lots of white ladies wear fox fur on their parkas. Indians don't wear fox, we only sell it to the white folks. It's better to use wolverine or wolf; they don't frost up when you breathe."

By the time Christmas rolled around, we felt we were masters of winter clothing and keeping ourselves warm. Our relatives obviously didn't share our confidence. Three separate parcels arrived, each bearing the same gift: *charcoal-fueled hand warmers!*

"Do you think," Marsha asked, looking at them again, "that we can trade these in on what we really want? Like tickets to Mexico?"

"I doubt it," I laughed. "But I can have a Merry Christmas wherever there is mincemeat pie."

"Well then, put away all that darning and mending," she said, "and start being merry, because Christmas dinner is ready and we get half a pie each for dessert unless Santa comes for his share."

CHAPTER SIXTEEN

ATTACK BY THE BACON BURGLAR

A dog's bark is one way he communicates. After two months wintering at our isolated log cabin with nine sled dogs, we came to understand some meaning in the different tones, pitches, warbles, volumes and frequencies. At least we thought we understood. Maybe this was just part of our developing cabin fever.

The dog who barked the most was Lucky, a classic ectomorph if ever there was one (he looked like a dinosaur skeleton draped in wet terrycloth). His message didn't seem urgent – the rhythm was too slow, the pitch too deep and the raspy tone reminiscent of someone slowly handsawing plywood. From the kitchen window, through a tiny spot that wasn't frosted opaque, we could watch him pacing forward, one-two-three steps until his chain tightened and jerked his head sideways. Then one-two-three long-legged steps backward, a clever quick shuffle of his floppy feet, and forward one-two-three jerk. And back again. He'd do this for hours, graphically illustrated by the four-inch deep rut he'd worn into the frozen ground beside his tree.

All the while, pacing and rasping, he would be staring intensely toward our cabin. Beside the door (and behind it when it opened outward) was the focus of Lucky's attention: a tin-covered wooden chest where we stored frozen foods. Off on our lonesome in the Yukon wilderness, we had no hydroelectricity to power a deep freeze, so Mother Nature provided the cold air to preserve our goodies. In our region, we could count on below freezing temperatures from November until March. With ice blocks, we hoped to extend that period of free cold storage into April.

For part of the winter, the freezer had no proper latch on its top-loading door, making it quite easy to lift with a mittened hand. Or a curious nose....

One night during the first week in January, when there was no moon and the nights seemed so dark and desperate, I was suddenly awakened by a banging and thumping on the cabin wall beside the door. The dogs abruptly burst into a tremendous uproar of serious and fierce barking. These messages were staccato-sharp and shrill. Chains rattled and were strained as the alarmed dogs raced and tore at their restraints.

I grabbed the flashlight and tried to piece the situation together. Something was getting into the freezer chest and, judging from the dogs' excitement, it wasn't anything small like a squirrel or weasel. I slipped on my boots and crossed the chilly room.

"What is it?" Marsha asked from behind me. "What's out there?"

"I dunno. But this should scare it away." I seized a hefty chunk of firewood and pounded on the wall.

"GET OUT OF THERE! *GO ON! GIT!*" I was trying to sound fierce.

There was silence… and then a renewed scurrying in the freezer.

I banged again, but the scratching and thumping kept up. What did this mean? This animal wasn't afraid of humans? Or was it too starved to have any fears?

I looked at Marsha for ideas. My mind raced through a mental list of mammals indigenous to our area.

"That's no small animal. And it isn't afraid of us. It must be a winter bear come out of hibernation. *Or a wolverine!*"

"But a wolverine wouldn't come so close with all our dogs, would it?" Marsha's eyes were big as saucers. "What can we do?"

I lifted the .30-30 Winchester rifle from its hook, checked the lever action, then cranked a live round into position. Lethal power was in my hands, and that grasp was none too steady. One quick pull and a mushrooming lead bullet would punch a fist-size hole through flesh and bone. I kept the barrel pointed down and moved cautiously. I wanted to make sure that any flesh and bone being pierced was neither mine nor Marsha's.

Outside it would be black as the ace of spades, so there was only one way to sight the rifle. I held the flashlight against the barrel with my left hand. The rifle could now be crudely aimed by pointing the flashlight at the prey.

"Stand well back," I told Marsha, though she was keeping her distance already. "I'll kick open the cabin door first and maybe it'll run away. If that doesn't work, I'll have to go outside to see behind the door. I'll stand to the right."

Only a squeeze and a twitch of that trigger – I mustn't be startled into shooting too soon, yet I had to be ready. In my mind, I was visualizing a wolverine in our bacon. Long yellow claws ripping through our winter's grub; razor-sharp claws that could kill a bear; claws that made me very aware my legs were bare above

Lucky looked like he'd been in lots of fights... and lost them all.
He was obedient and a good team dog.
If put in lead position, he'd turn into a trembling statue of worry.

my pac boots. But there was no time to put on heavy pants – I had to go now. I kicked the door.

With a creak, then a thud, the door opened and banged against the freezer chest. The scurrying noise stopped. But there was no sound of an evacuation.

I waited, then took a deep breath and ran out and pointed the beam and barrel at the chest. The lid was ajar a few inches. All was silent. I held the rifle very tightly.

My heart pounding, my arms tense, I kept the flashlight directed on the narrow gap. There was a brief glint of white fur. Then the scratching inside started again, even more frantic than before.

Once more there was a flash of light fur, but with a stripe of bright blue across it. Blue?!? Now I was really puzzled.

All at once, the answer came to me. I stepped forward and flipped up the lid with my boot.

"What is it?" Marsha's voice whispered to me from deep inside the cabin.

"Lucky."

He was doing a frenzied gnaw job on a rock-hard slab of bacon, fully aware his parking meter in Pork Heaven was now reading *EXPIRED*. If he were half as aware of how close he had come to being a dead albino wolverine, it might have spoiled his appetite.

I grabbed the blue webbing collar, helped his long frame out of the freezer, and walked him past the other dogs to his tree. His clip and chain were still intact. Somehow the G-clip had undone itself, perhaps when rubbed against the tree. I fastened it again to his collar and patted the big fellow on his bony head.

"Glad I didn't shoot you, Lucky," I told him. "Be more careful next time."

Marsha had done a quick once-over of the freezer contents and it appeared that part of one slab of bacon was the only loss. She closed the lid and lifted the chopping block up on top of it.

"We need a proper lock on this thing," she said sleepily.

Back inside, I carefully ejected the bullet from the .30-30 and slipped it back down into the magazine. My fingers were shaking a little as I hung the rifle on its hook. I'd rather not have to handle guns; the sheer destructive power unnerves me.

It took us a while to get back to sleep.

Next day, Lucky was barking again. We knew he was trying to communicate. There had to be some meaning to those raspy, slow barks. He was pacing: one-two-three, jerk on the chain, and back. He had jerked so many times the bright blue collar was wearing away his neck fur on that side. And, always, he was looking toward the cabin, to near the door. His distinctive bark, we now understood, was the dog word for *BACON*.

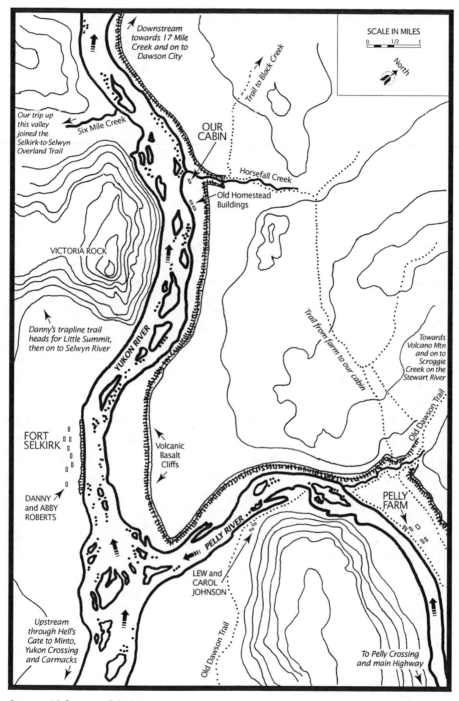

SCALE IN MILES
0   1/2   1

North

Downstream towards 17 Mile Creek and on to Dawson City

Trail to Black Creek

Our trip up this valley joined the Selkirk-to-Selwyn Overland Trail

Six Mile Creek

OUR CABIN

Horsefall Creek

Old Homestead Buildings

VICTORIA ROCK

Danny's trapline trail heads for Little Summit, then on to Selwyn River

YUKON RIVER

Trail from farm to our cabin

Towards Volcano Mtn and on to Scroggie Creek on the Stewart River

Old Dawson Trail

FORT SELKIRK

Volcanic Basalt Cliffs

DANNY and ABBY ROBERTS

PELLY FARM

PELLY RIVER

LEW and CAROL JOHNSON

Upstream through Hell's Gate to Minto, Yukon Crossing and Carmacks

Old Dawson Trail

To Pelly Crossing and main Highway

See page 19 for map of the larger area.

CHAPTER SEVENTEEN

THUMBS UP AND FROZEN

One day in early January, Marsha and I decided to make a trail across the wide river so we could explore the far bank. We were uneasy about wandering too far out on the frozen surface even though our water hole was now cut through ice over an arm's length deep. Though isolated parts of the Yukon River were still open, roaring ominously from behind screens of ice fog, we mustered up courage and ventured forth.

The river had frozen relatively smoothly this winter, much better for sled travel than in previous years. In places, surges of overflow water had flooded over vast tracks of jumbled ice blocks, transforming much of the river's surface into a softly undulating, white playground.

We took long poles both to tap on the ice to judge its soundness and to keep us from going under should we happen to break through. Hopefully the pole would straddle the hole. As well, we roped ourselves together, so one of us could pull the other out from a distance. As a further insurance, we decided to let a dog or three walk ahead to test the capability of the frozen river surface to support us humans.

For Casey, Loki and Tyhee, this was great fun to be running loose, especially with the other six howling so indignantly. The chosen trio kicked up their heels and rolled in the snow like puppies, playing tag around the trees and chasing each other in wide circles out on the ice. We had wanted to have Tyhee, in particular, with us to pay her some personal attention. Marsha's pet hadn't been performing at all well in harness.

"Seems too distracted to be a leader," said Marsha. "I'm sure she's bright enough, but her attention span is about five seconds long. She's more interested in rabbits than following the trail."

Tyhee was having a rough time making the adjustment from pet to working dog. We'd been warned the two concepts were mutually exclusive, so we were trying to treat her just like the rest of the dogs. We kept her chained like the rest, to avoid fights and to have her more keen on pulling. Having all our dogs intact and in working condition was of paramount importance. Yet Tyhee seemed to miss the special treatment Marsha had given her as a puppy and was refusing to fully cooperate in harness.

"Maybe what she needs is more love," Marsha opined. "I need to play with her, have her sit and give a paw, sit and stay, fetch a stick – that sort of thing. She needs to do something right for a change, and get a reward instead of all these scoldings. We've got to reassure her we're nice guys and still love her even though she is a working dog now."

Strangely Casey, who was also a pet, was one of our best dogs. We figured he'd opted to work extra hard to gain attention and reward. It was lucky for us he'd chosen this behaviour because he was our only leader who responded to commands. As such, he was invaluable.

Dear old Loki had been the pet to many different owners, and working dog to others, so he nonchalantly assumed either role. Today, as we walked cautiously over the frozen waters, he had reverted to being an affectionate favourite, rubbing up against my legs and nudging my hand for a pat. I wasn't sure I wanted the extra weight so close to me on the ice at first, but rationalized this old veteran might know where it was dangerous.

Casey raced all over the river, checking every upturned block of ice for smells and leaving his calling card on most of them. Tyhee tried to both follow him and be with Marsha as well, so the poor black and silver mutt was nearly run off her feet from exhaustion.

Throughout the winter, as the river level fell, the immense sheets of ice split along fault lines and buckled as they settled – often leaving one section tilted and perched hip-high above its neighbour. On the next trips onto the river, when we would bring the toboggans, we would have to pick a gentle route or else shovel snow to form a ramp at these abrupt boundaries. Once in a while, we could look down a crack and see sand or gravel instead of running water. Only then did we know we were over a gravel bar, and not the main river. The total distance across the river plus these bars and islands was about a thousand yards.

"Feels good, doesn't it? That was nerve-racking," I sighed to Marsha as we finally waded into the drifted snow on the other bank. "It's reassuring to know there is something firm under this snow."

We found the remains of a woodcutter's cabin close to the foot of Victoria Rock, the hill that had been blocking our sunlight. Taking a moment to be tourists, we poked through the ruins, delighted to see willow saplings growing from the old

In case the ice breaks under my weight, I've got a pole to straddle the hole.
Of course Casey decides to walk as close to me as possible.

sod roof, which itself lay on the floor. In the corner was the twisted wreckage of a cookstove, half buried by collapsed rafters and snow. There was nothing worth salvaging.

"It's nice to know someone wintered in a cabin smaller than ours," announced Marsha. "I wonder how sane he was by springtime?"

Our itinerary today included finding the mouth of Six Mile Creek and ascending its watershed. Sunlight was the topic most on our minds; all through dark December, we had looked across the wide river and seen the sun shining on parts of this east-facing bank. This seemed like a good location for a cabin. The woodcutter's old building was tucked right up against the north side of a hill.

Maybe it had something to do with the access to the sternwheelers? We pushed on to examine the south half.

At the creek mouth, we found – the dogs found for us – a game trail up the valley. Here we could walk easily, save for ducking branches and straddling the occasional deadfall. The tracks and scats indicated this was a circuit for families of rabbits and squirrels, and also for the odd fox and coyote. When we came across wolf prints and fur-filled excreta, our dogs picked up the scent immediately and crowded close to us. Their ears rotated like radar dishes, and their eyes scanned continually for any visual warning. All three tails were tucked low between their legs. Howling at wolves from home was clearly more fun than visiting in the strangers' territory.

To have an overview of the valley, we scaled the sidehill and sat on an exposed rock outcrop. With Grandad's old WWI field glasses, we could survey the small kingdom of Six Mile Creek, noting where the wood was thickest, where the beavers had dammed the creek and the approximate range of the winter sun.

"This is a grand spot for lunch," I announced, and retrieved the biscuits, sardines and thermos flask from my daypack.

"Nice view, but a little draughty, don't you think?" Marsha was pulling up her anorak hood against the wind.

I poured her some steaming miso soup, noting how cold the outside of the steel flask was on my bare hands.

"I'm glad someone invented vacuum bottles to keep our soup hot," I said, making conversation while fumbling with the opener on my Swiss army knife. Sardine cans have to be the trickiest containers to open and are no easier with mitts on. Again I had to use bare hands.

"Next time, I'll keep the sardine can in my pocket so it is warmer on the finger tips," I resolved. "That would make them easier to spread on the biscuits too."

We settled on eating alternate snatches of fish and biscuit, because I was making a mess trying to mold the stiff little herrings on the brittle hardtack. The miso soup was more successful.

"This would have been a much better location for a cabin," Marsha decided, after a long sweep with the glasses.

"More sun over here where Victoria Rock isn't in the way," I agreed. "Good firewood close to the river and on the islands too. And the beaver dams have already raised the water and warmed it for irrigating a garden."

"Are you thinking of homesteading here?" Marsha asked, giving me a long smiling sideways look.

"Well, maybe someday," I admitted. "But we'd have to win a lottery to be able to afford the costs. Setting up a self-sustaining farm in the North would take an initial cash outlay we may never be able to afford."

"But dreaming is free, isn't it?" she smiled.

"Free. And cold!" I said, making ready to head back to our warm cabin.

On the walk home, my thumbs felt very cold. Unwisely, I'd only brought enough mitts for the conditions prevailing at mid-day, when we'd left Horsefall. Now the sun had disappeared behind a ridge, and the wind was blowing with a vengeance, swirling snow around our bodies. I flexed my fingers and drew up my thumbs into the body of the mitt to rub them on my fingers. For a while, holding my hands in my armpits felt better, but I wanted a free hand to hold a pole while we crossed the river's icy expanses.

Presently, the antics of the dogs and the task of climbing over pressure ridges distracted me from these cold-finger worries and I forgot all about it until that night.

At supper, one thumb felt numb at the tip, but we shrugged it off to *maybe I bumped it on something*. When all the toboggan construction was happening, it was rare when I didn't have a bruised thumb or finger from erratic hammering.

The next time the topic of my thumb came up was four days later. I'd been unconsciously rubbing it on my parka, to relieve a tingling itchiness, and Marsha wondered what was wrong.

"Do you have a hole in that mitt or something?" she asked when she could no longer contain her curiosity. "How come you keep playing with your thumb?"

We clinically examined my digit, carefully comparing it to the other thumb. The itchy one was more reddish and slightly swollen. Its tip was less sensitive than the other's as well.

"Let me kiss it better," Marsha suggested.

She did, and we forgot about it for another two days.

This next time, it was me who raised the subject.

"This damn thumb is getting itchier all the time," I told her. "It feels like I've just been bitten by a bee."

Marsha felt the offending digit and gave her diagnosis. "It feels hot. Must be some healing going on inside there." Never one to miss a good opening, she added in mock seriousness, "I hope you'll live. The best treatment is to soak it by washing the dishes after supper."

By late that night, I didn't feel much like laughing. Now there was a painful burning sensation, which I tried vainly to relieve, initially by sucking on it, then with a cold compress, and finally by soaking my thumb in cold water and baking soda. For most of the night, I lay in bed wishing there was some way to stop the throbbing and the aching. At times, I wanted to cut the damn thing off.

Over the next forty hours, most of the throbbing and painful aching subsided, but the tingling itchiness stayed with me for another week. The top half of the fingernail became black and the skin around the tip had turned white and hard, like a callus. By this point, we'd exhausted all our other theories and pinpointed the cause to frostbite on that sardine picnic to Six Mile. What surprised us both was the time delay involved. The real pain didn't start until the discolouring and callus-forming began six days after the freezing occurred.

Under the cap of dead skin and darkened nail, new flesh was growing, bringing on pins-and-needles sensations and making it hard for me not to scratch the healing thumb. We wondered just how much of the flesh would be regenerated, and if I'd be left with a shortened digit. Sixteen days after freezing, a pad of tough, yellow skin peeled off the very top, exposing more dead skin beneath. The next day, this layer also sloughed off, leaving pink, baby-soft skin. So sensitive was the new tip that even a cool breeze through the cabin felt ticklish. The wool mitts I'd worn all winter were now too scratchy; touching a warm teacup caused me to yelp at the heat. It was another day before I could apply any pressure with my thumb.

With so many projects on the go, I had become quite adept at working with my thumb in the air, using the other nine digits for touching and gripping. To sip my tea, I had to hold the teacup strangely, with the healing thumb arched pretentiously.

"If we ever start a homestead over at Six Mile Creek," Marsha decided, "and invite high society people to tea, we'll insist everyone hold their thumbs in the air, instead of their pinkies." She thought this was all quite funny.

"Okay," I agreed. "It'll be the start of a new fashion in frostbitten fingers."

We could joke about the event now, because my thumb tip was going to fully regrow. This outcome was a happy ending to the lesson I'd been so vividly taught: from now on, we'd take extra clothes with us at all times, to be ready for the worst changes the weather could throw at us. The winter was reminding us to be diligent and – as always – demanding our respect.

CHAPTER EIGHTEEN

NEIGHBOURLY VISITS OVER THIN ICE

Our calendar notes (we had to keep records or we'd lose track of the date) finally began to include the words *finished* and *done*. They shone from the checkered paper like badges of accomplishment, scripted medals for our diligence. After working at the harness-stitching business so long, I half expected a gold watch when we finally retired from cobblering with the completion of number ten, the spare collar.

Three days after that, the second oak toboggan was ready for its first trial. We might have called this a *maiden voyage*, but we were terrified of breaking through the river ice, and were rather superstitiously avoiding aquatic expressions. I'd learned so much building the first toboggan, that this foot-longer vehicle took not half the time.

To make the maximum use of the daylight hours, we set our alarm clock an hour ahead, and took turns waking long before sunrise to prepare breakfast by lamplight. Then we would eat together at the short table beside the cookstove, while watching the slow dawning of the south-eastern sky.

Natural light was at a premium. To prevent eye strain, intricate work – such as sewing – was best done near the window at noon. But these few sunny hours were also the favourite time to be outdoors, training the dogs or doing the wood and water chores. We felt torn, wanting to be everywhere at once. At times, it was frustrating: where were the quiet winter days of which we'd been warned? When would we be *bored and have nothing to do*?

Yet gradually changes were happening. Not only on the physical plane – such as darned mittens and new gauntlets – but mental differences were also emerging. Our attitudes shifted. I had always been *goal-oriented*, since as early in my childhood as I can remember. The emphasis was on passing a test, completing a school project, getting the Wolf Cub badge, winning the game, obtaining a degree; there was always a goal. Now, slowly, I was becoming more *process-oriented*.

As the weeks trickled by, the days started to flow into one another. Time began to slow down, and I was living more in the present. Instead of rushing to finish a toboggan, my energy channelled toward mastering single steps.

Before, I'd been making impossible deadlines for myself and then would race vainly against the clock. Now, a job took as long as was required for it to be done well. By concentrating on *process*, the quality of my workmanship rose, saving us the time spent re-doing or repairing mistakes. Instead of being disappointed about not meeting some arbitrary deadline, we could feel content at day's end that we had worked competently. If a harness was not quite finished, it would be tomorrow. I discovered I was really a good worker after all, and had just been a lousy estimator of the time required to do any task.

Once we felt confident every project would get done in its right time, we took time out to give each other massages, go for a ski or walk along the basalt cliffs. After preparing, building, organizing and cooking for the first excursions, Marsha decreed we needed a full *Day Off* to mentally prepare ourselves and to relax properly. This special day was a lovely moment to space out, write a few letters, read old magazine articles, philosophize with the dogs and simply play in the snow. We believed a day off before a trip might temper any gung-ho, con-quer-the-wilderness feelings, so travel could be a time to appreciate each other and the environment around us. Indeed the dogs seemed to like us better after our day off!

We joked about these time-management revelations, and about discovering the reasons for a *weekend*. Happily, we had control over our lives and could declare a *Sunday* whenever it suited us. Little by little, this cabin experience was contribut-ing to our personal growth in unexpected ways.

Frozen waters were the winter highways connecting everyone who lived and worked in the bush. The prospect of venturing away on the river ice was haunt-ing us: we knew we'd have to conquer our fears or be quite limited in where to explore. So, early one cold January morning we mustered our courage and headed upriver toward Fort Selkirk with one toboggan and four dogs. It was slow going as we thoroughly tested every suspicious patch of ice with our long poles.

About halfway, in a cluster of islands, we came to vast open patches – as large as football fields. The swift water was roiling and steaming, churning slush and ice chunks, and looked absolutely terrifying.

"Gees, it's Twenty-Five Below. What's it going to take to freeze this river over completely?" Marsha asked.

"It doesn't seem to follow any particular logic, does it?" I agreed. "We need to ask Danny if there is a pattern year after year."

We found a solid route past this dangerous section and, after three-plus tense hours, let out a big sigh of relief as the dogs stepped onto a corrugated snowmobile trail. They eagerly followed this path, scampering up a steep ramp to the open townsite. From the far end of town we could hear dogs barking, and then the roar of a gas engine increasing in volume as it approached at high speed. Seconds later Danny Roberts was grinning ear-to-ear beside us.

Danny and I had become good friends during a summer I was based at Fort Selkirk working as a Parks Branch river patrolman. We'd netted salmon together and hunted beaver with my .22 rifle. At summer's end, I gave him that gun.

"Danny, this is Marsha, my girlfriend. Did you bring the *sign-in book*?" I teased him. As caretaker of this national historic site, Danny dutifully logged every visitor's arrival.

"Guess you've got lots of time to sign that book," he laughed. "I heard you moved in at the Frenchman's cabin at Horsefall. How many dogs you got down there?"

"Can you hear us?"

"My dogs sure can. Must be when it's feeding time at your place that my dogs look that way and make noise. You want to have some tea? Abbie will want to see you."

Our dogs merrily followed Danny's machine past abandoned log cabins, schoolhouse, church, stores and shops, to his small house near the parade grounds. Behind it, five huge sled dogs were chained to dog houses, pacing aggressively back and forth. They climbed on their roofs, jumped off, hopped back up, down – bursting with energy and confusion.

"Wow. Those are tall dogs, Danny," Marsha said. "Do they go fast?"

"Guess so," Danny grinned. "I don't use them so much now. I keep them in case this *yellow dog* breaks down." He gestured at the snowmobile.

Just then, Danny's wife Abbie stuck her head out the side door and commanded, "Quiet down!" All the dogs fell silent.

Inside, the small house was toasty warm and fairly dark, so it took a moment to get oriented after the outside cold and brightness. Abbie held court sitting on a cot, with their tiny pet dog Timmy on her lap. She relaxed quickly when Marsha sat beside her and grasped her hand. "There were so many open patches. Aren't you scared when you travel on the ice?"

"Guess so," Abbie said. "These days I mostly sit on the toboggan, getting towed behind that snow machine when we go into Pelly. I try not to look."

We couldn't visit for more than a quick cup of tea because Marsha and I didn't want to take our chances finding our trail home in the dark. As we said goodbye, Abbie asked Marsha to visit again, and Danny offered to give us pointers about training our dogs.

"Come back with all your dogs and you can sleep in that tourist cabin," he said, waving goodbye. "Better bring lots of blankets. It could be cold in there 'cuz it isn't chinked for winter."

The ride back was much less nerve-racking than our outbound trip; Casey had no difficulty following our track. Perhaps he and the other pooches were thinking about getting fed at home since they trotted along nicely. We could both ride and only halted the team to get off and warm up. The temperature was dropping fast now that the sun was almost down. To get warm, there is an Inuit trick of trying to jump up and click your heels together three times before landing. Neither of us could manage more than twice, but we vowed to get better over the winter.

Two miles before Horsefall, when we stopped to get our blood circulating with more heel clicking, we could hear lonesome howling from our other five dogs. It was past their regular feeding time and they felt compelled to lament this injustice to the world. Though I couldn't pick it up, the swivelling of Casey's sharp ears indicated he was hearing responses from Danny's dogs.

A few days later, with both toboggans, a huge pile of bedding and enough food for three days, we arrived again at Fort Selkirk, setting up quarters in the tourist cabin. Wanting to avoid any problems, Danny came down to tell us about his traps.

Traps were a most serious hazard for our teams. Fur-bearing animals were being actively *harvested* in this region, so most trails had leg-hold traps along them plus the occasional snare and conibear trap. We would need to make a point of meeting the closest trappers and learning where their sets were. Most encouraged us to use their trails because the dogs' scent was thought to attract other mammals. To help people spot the traps, each set was generally flagged with dangling fluorescent survey ribbon about twenty yards away. Apparently most animals can't distinguish colours like humans can, seeing more in black, whites and gray, so the bright markers don't tip off the prey. Apart from that help in identifying the locations, it was up to us to guide the dogs past safely.

In the case of a trail set, which was a trap buried under the trail or a snare dangling over it, there was no choice: we had to stop the team and make a path around. Trail sets were the favoured method to catch lynx, whose fur was very valuable. Cubby sets, generally a leg-hold trap buried under a dusting of snow and placed in a twig corral just off the trail, were easier to avoid. For these, I could

Danny Roberts received a small stipend from Parks Canada to be caretaker for the abandoned Fort Selkirk townsite. Many of the cabins still had cutlery and curtains, as if the inhabitants thought the move to Pelly Crossing and Minto might be temporary. [photo courtesy Klaus Ollmann and Tom Funk]

stop the dogs, walk ahead, and then stand between the trap and the trail while the dogs ran past. Eventually, we had the leaders trained to gallop past a cubby set and pull the rest of the team by before they smelled the fish or beaver gland bait. The command was *On by!*

Danny ran a trapline behind the town. He led us along an old roadway on his yellow machine, pointing out where the traps were. For this lesson, we had only my squad with us and were very careful to coach the dogs past each one. Marsha's team we'd left chained beside our Selkirk cabin.

After Danny had roared off back to his house and we were on our way back, we were startled to find Marsha's dog Hinglish caught by a back foot in a number four leg-hold trap. He was so frightened and in such shock that he'd not even eaten the nearby fishhead bait. Somehow the shaggy dog had broken loose from where we'd left him, and had come after us. Curiosity had been his downfall.

We were both quite distraught because Hinglish was such a dear dog and in obvious pain whenever I moved the trap. A number four trap has formidable metal jaws that grasp the animal's leg, with a powerful spring on each side. To open the jaws, both springs have to be compressed, a procedure usually performed by cracking the trap over one knee or thigh. With Hinglish's foot in the trap, I couldn't lever it into position without hurting him.

Finally, with Marsha restraining and reassuring Hinglish, I was able to hold one spring closed with my foot while I squeezed the other with both hands. Marsha gingerly pushed the jaws apart to free Hinglish's leg.

The hide and flesh were cut to the bone on either side, but the foot still moved. The jaws had caught him high – at the ankle – and hadn't broken those big bones. If it had been lower across the toes, he'd have been crippled. He – and we – had been very lucky.

Marsha held the big, black dog on her lap for the trip back to camp. He was so exhausted from his ordeal he submitted readily to this new role as passenger and patient. At Selkirk, we dusted the wound with penicillin powder and gave him an extra helping of supper. He licked his foot for a while, then fell asleep near the heater.

Although it was clearly not his fault, Danny Roberts felt badly about Hinglish when we explained in the morning. He told us about a dog getting trapped when Danny was just a boy out alone with his father's team. The wheel dog stepped on a trail set which all the other dogs had missed. This dog was a big, vicious brute, quite terrifying to a youngster. To be able to work on the trap without the dog biting him, Danny had to hook a chain onto the dog's collar and tie it ahead taut to a tree, so the dog couldn't turn its head. Next, Danny stood on both springs and pulled up on the jaws. Then he could carefully pry the jaws apart with a stick, and the wheel dog pulled its leg free.

Both Hinglish and the dog in Danny's story healed and were able to return to work after a short layoff. We heard how one woman used C-clamps to close the springs when she had no one to help her. We liked this idea enough to include two clamps in the toboggan's tool pouch on subsequent trips.

Hinglish would not have been trapped if we had made our chains properly. The problem was with our gang chains, the long chains that could be fastened between two trees and had side chains branching off for each dog. My mistake was to make this gang chain too fancy. I'd wired clips onto each end of the side chains so we could change their positions along the main line. We didn't realize then the clips could undo when rubbed on a taut chain. Not only was Hinglish free on this fateful afternoon, but so were Tyhee and Big Pete. Peter was a mess, his beige and white fur drenched in blood likely from a disagreement with Jeff. The result of their argument looked alarming, but the damage was fortunately only a couple of minor puncture wounds. We solved the clip problem by wiring the side chains permanently to the main chain.

From my previous time in the Yukon, I had a solid grasp of what was needed in the way of equipment for short winter camping trips, but never before had I the opportunity to fill two freight toboggans for excursions of indeterminate length. We wanted to take little unnecessary gear, but our idea was to maintain our lifestyle on these travels, as opposed to rushing desperately to some predetermined destination and back. With nine dogs to pull us, we could bring a massive payload.

Sitting in their toasty cabin, eating cookies Marsha had made, we talked at length with Danny and Abbie about the outfit they used and the routines they followed when travelling together some twenty years before. Their main trapping route had been along a string of cabins on the old Fort Selkirk-to-Donjek River trail. Their suggestions helped us modify our kit, mostly by reducing and simplifying down to basics.

We wanted to bring a tent and stove, but we planned to make brush camps too, to see how comfortable we could make ourselves under the stars. For their travel Danny and Abbie each had a dog team, varying over the years from four to six dogs per team. They had small line cabins to stay in, plus a canvas wall tent at the far end. We would have the weight of a stove and tent with us, but they had their loads of traps, carcasses and furs. Our situations would be similar – *except* they had grown up at this game and understood every step intuitively.

Abbie's heart was weak now and Danny's lungs were giving him trouble so they would be mushing no more, yet were happy others would want to emulate their old culture. Clearly our presence touched them emotionally. Fond memories were stirred up, they said, each time we brought our two teams into their yard.

"You remind us of us," Abbie said.

The tent we were packing was larger than necessary, so a nice luxury. We bought it in Vancouver at a time when we weren't sure if there would be a cabin for us to settle into or not. With the possibility looming that this purchase might become our only winter home, we thought *big*. It was nine by twelve feet with five-foot sidewalls and had a simple peaked roof. There was no floor. Made of ten-ounce canvas, it weighed about thirty pounds.

The other shelter we would have for our nights on the trail was a ten-by-fourteen-foot canvas tarpaulin. For brush camps, ropes could be tied from the grommets around the edges to trees to fashion whatever shape of lean-to the weather dictated. The excess material would be folded underneath as a floor beneath our bedding.

Our first winter camp, testing equipment before this trip, had been only a snowball's throw from our cabin. After the fashion of the Hudson's Bay Company fur traders, we spent a night outside our home *fort* to check if we had everything before we went too far afield. And – although the history books did not mention it – I bet the traders snuck back inside a warm cabin to have breakfast the next morning just as we did.

What the trial confirmed to us was that we really did need all the bedding we'd planned to take. Our philosophy was no matter how miserable the weather, how exhausting the travel, how harshly the world in general was treating us during the day, it would all be bearable as long as we knew our bedding would keep us warm. Being cold all night would sap energy, changing a holiday into a marathon of endurance. We packed one toboggan half-full of bedding. Apart from the tarp, we had seven camping foam pads and a blanket to put under us. Our immediate cocoon consisted of four sleeping bags and two flannelette sheet liners.

No two people have the same rate of body metabolism. A Yukon expression for a bed partner is *your heater*, and some people's dials must be set higher than others. Curiously, Marsha could generate plenty of heat to keep me toasty while she herself was chilly. After experimenting, we found she was all right on a stack of four pads and the blanket, while I needed only three.

I hadn't figured out what we'd use for a woodburning stove in the wall tent and Danny came to the rescue. He volunteered to make us one out of a 10-gallon fuel drum. It would be a miniature of the 45-gallon barrel pig heater, but with the top flattened for a cooking surface. He had some 6-inch stove pipe to lend us too.

"When you come back, I'll have it made," he promised. "There's plenty of old drums here – no one will miss one," he added with a conspiratorial wink.

See Appendix IX for detail about sleeping bags, the stove Danny built for us, our grub boxes and cooking gear, repair kits and more.

Next morning, armed with directions about the safest route, we headed out to visit Carol and Lew Johnson who had a homestead just up the Pelly a few miles.

The trip could not be direct since the waters at the confluence of the two mighty rivers were open and showing no inclination to ice over.

"It is always a bad place there," Danny told us. "You have to go up the Yukon for a ways, then cross where it is safe. After that you go between islands and sometimes you have to go on the shore along that side of the Pelly."

Fortunately Danny had scouted the route on his snowmobile a few days before, when he'd gone to the farm for eggs and his mail. We could follow his track.

"Some places you better check the ice," he cautioned, "because the ice can open up where it was okay before. And some places you can be safe on a skidoo going fast, but maybe you got some trouble going with dogs."

Danny's advice was not helping our nerves at all.

The dogs appeared more confident than their mushers and happily pulled us some two miles upriver before the track skirted the end of a small island and struck out across a quarter-mile expanse of jumbled ice.

The trail took us into a wide channel called Slaughterhouse Slough – a rather ominous name – and through a maze of small islands. At times, we passed over gravel bars and occasionally up and across an island where Danny had chopped willows to create a trail around a dicey spot. At the river's far bank, our Indian friend had driven up a steep ramp and onto a narrow roadway.

"This is part of the old Dawson stage road," I told Marsha as we stopped to drink some tea from the vacuum flask. "Danny calls it the Minto Road, and says it is quite steep in sections where it climbs over the ridge between here and the Minto townsite off to the south."

Twenty minutes later we came into a clearing near the Johnson homestead, on a high bench perhaps a hundred feet above the river level. There was a log and timber main house with generous windows to celebrate a spectacular west-facing view across to the basalt cliffs on the far side. The exposure to the south was unimpeded – an important factor during dark winter months. Lew and Carol had bought this place a few years before from John Lammers who'd operated an eco-tourism business, guiding visitors who preferred to shoot wildlife with cameras rather than with guns. There were a few outbuildings that had been bunkhouses for the guests.

Two happy part-Labrador pooches bounded up to greet us, setting our nine into an uproar of barking. Alerted by the ruckus, Lew and Carol came to collar their pets and welcome us. They invited us to stay overnight in one of the cabins, and promised tea in the main house as soon as we'd chained the dogs and unpacked.

Lew had been a top government lawyer in Alaska during the oil pipeline boom of the 1970s. Over tea and cookies, he explained how the culture in that American state had deteriorated with the influx of 100,000 pipeline workers and fast cash. The almighty dollar instantly transformed sleepy towns and villages, showing no respect for the environment or the indigenous peoples. Alcoholism, sexually-transmitted diseases and violent crimes increased sharply. He and Carol had come to the Yukon to seek that northern spirit they'd appreciated in Alaska in years past.

The Johnsons called their homestead *Stepping Stone*. They had a large garden plot and grew much of their own food. Rows of large glass jars filled the high shelves in the kitchen, displaying dried homegrown marrow peas and beans. Even their pets got into the home-grown spirit, according to Lew: "In the fall they will wander into the garden and dig up carrots for a snack."

Carol chatted with Marsha about the challenges of aspiring to be vegetarian in a northern culture with its severe winter climate. Moose meat and salmon had fuelled the indigenous peoples for thousands of years. Could beans be expected to deliver the high protein and carbohydrate requirements for working outside all day at Forty Below?

Lew confirmed they brought their town supplies in over the Minto Road during the fall, using a four-wheel-drive truck and occasionally its winch. They'd stocked up so a winter trip by truck on that rough road wouldn't be necessary.

They hoped to venture out more on the river ice next year when their grown son was to move in with them and assemble a dog team. Lew was therefore quite intrigued to see how we'd built our toboggans.

"The key factor is the white plastic base," I told him. "It makes the toboggans almost too fast when the dogs are fresh. It can get scary."

Seeing our dogs pumped with morning enthusiasm, we wrapped chain under the toboggan bases for our departure. Casey was doing his leaping and whining routine and other dogs were yanking forward to test the lifeline's strength. When at last we'd said our goodbyes and thanks to Carol and Lew, I untied and held on tight. In seconds the trees were flashing by, as the team charged back along the Minto Road toward the Yukon River crossing.

Two hundred yards along, when the dogs had relaxed into a trot, I could brake them to a halt and wrestle the chain out from around the base.

Minutes passed, then more time. Finally Hinglish's big head came into view around a corner and Marsha's team was soon crowding around my backboard.

"Did you go back for something?" I asked. "What took so long?"

"I'm still seeing stars," Marsha grinned. "There was a tree root sticking up in

Johnsons' yard, and the brake chain caught on it. Next thing I knew I went ass-over-tea-kettle, somersaulting over the backboard into the basket of my toboggan. A bit embarrassing, to say the least."

"You okay?"

"Yep. I decided to take off the chain. We just barely made it around those hairy bends with the dogs chasing after you guys, but we're here."

Passing through Fort Selkirk, we asked Danny and Abby about a possible expedition on their old trail to the Selwyn country.

"That trail's going to be hard to find in places," he said. "Last fellow to use it was the cowboy, Larry Smith. That was many years ago. He stayed here one winter and trapped on my line. Those big dogs out back he gave me when he got new ones – smaller and faster for racing."

Larry Smith now lived at Coffee Creek, some 65 miles downstream toward Dawson City. He'd gained recognition as one of the toughest dog racers in the north, often breaking trail and setting the pace in the gruelling Iditarod race across Alaska from Anchorage to Nome.

"Could you mark your route on our topographical maps?" I asked Danny.

Danny shook his head slowly. "I never used those government maps," he said. "Maybe I could draw it on some paper. I'll try. And I could give it to you when you come to get the stove next time. You're gonna need that stove if you're going on that trail. Might be a long trip with lots of snow when you get up in the hills.

"Hope you like being a lead dog," he added with a laugh. "You maybe gonna be using your snowshoes lots to make trail in front of your dogs."

Danny had just heard reports over the CBC Radio news about a bear wandering around this winter, first sighted near Carmacks and later leaving prints at Yukon Crossing, well within cruising distance of us. So he explained his father's advice about encountering a winter bear. For insulation or some other reason – perhaps while fishing or crossing open water – the bear will immerse itself repeatedly in water and coat its fur with a thick casing of ice. A winter bear is always *mean* and very dangerous to humans. The suit of ice makes it almost bulletproof except for one place, Danny explained: under the arms where the ice wears off. So, although it was puzzling to me how to get a bear to raise its arm for a clear shot, I was glad to be packing my .30-30 with us for protection.

A winter bear had killed trapper Eddie Wilkinson when all bears should be in hibernation. Biologists and trappers disagree as to whether a bear that comes prematurely from its den can survive or not. Mounted Police accounts of the

Though the ice might be over four feet thick where I was standing, an open patch nearby reminded us to keep checking as we headed upriver to Selkirk.

Wilkinson death stated that the bear was very ill, and died only a short distance away without external wounds and with an empty stomach.

Back at Horsefall that evening, as we unpacked, I carefully removed the .30-30 from its holster against my toboggan's backboard. Try as I might, I couldn't shake off some eerie feelings about that gun. Such a powerful weapon projected a presence all its own, as imposing on an aware mind as a nearby sow grizzly, or a proud bull moose. Merely having the loaded weapon in my hand would alter my perceptions, drawing out emotions of the hunt and the dangers and savageness of nature, instead of the more carefree, benevolent feelings that otherwise prevailed. Strangely I was more conscious of danger to me when I was potentially dangerous to other creatures; carrying a rifle created paranoia rather than alleviating it.

A ghastly calm would fall over the dogs whenever they saw a rifle out of its case, and yet few of them had seen what damage it could really cause. Some sat and stared at me with wide eyes; others hid inside their houses. They could perceive the danger instinctively.

As I stowed this last item in the cabin, none of us could have predicted one of our party would soon be dead – killed by a bullet from that rifle.

CHAPTER NINETEEN

COR

The dogs announced something was amiss. Marsha rubbed a peek-hole in the window frost and looked for the problem.

"One of the dogs is loose," she said, with a hint of disappointment in her voice. We had been expecting Don Mark to drop off our mail, but could understand that he might be holed up waiting for this latest Forty Below spell to break.

"Which dog?" I asked. "Are you going, or shall I?"

"Oh, you can go. I'm busy making supper. Hey – I don't think that's one of our dogs! It's blond and Lucky's chained up…. Now I see a red harness. Where could it have come from?"

The blond dog hesitated then ran toward the river. I'd just stepped out into the dog lot when a full team of huskies burst up over our river bank and charged for the cabin door. The musher called a sharp *Whoa!* and the team – surprisingly to us – instantly responded. A familiar-looking fellow stepped off the toboggan's brakepad and grinned. It was Cor Guimond, an old friend who traps and fishes north of Dawson City.

Seeing Cor was a complete surprise but what amazed me more was that he'd come from the north, where there were no trails and no people living for at least fifty miles. After exchanging *What are you doing here?*, we laughed and got all his dogs, including the loose one, strung out on a gang-chain.

Inside the cabin, we hung up Cor's mitts, sweater and damp bedding, then settled into serious tea drinking. Cor was heading to Whitehorse for *Sourdough Rendezvous*, the annual festival where Yukoners from all over the territory gather to party, race and renew old acquaintances. Cor wasn't travelling by car or truck like the other celebrants; he was going to mush the 460 miles from Dawson along the Yukon River, making his own trail. I asked why.

"Just to do it," he said. "I want to see how fast it can be done."

Four years before, Cor had made this arduous journey, travelling in convoy with three other mushers and two men on skis. This winter, he was on his own, and out to improve on their time of twenty-three days. To this point, he was averaging over thirty miles per day. If he could maintain or better this pace, he would be in the capital in a total of two weeks, right on schedule for the opening ceremonies.

Cor was seated next to the airtight, under a lantern where he could see to mend his moccasins. I bombarded him with questions, many about dogs, of course.

Cor's dogs were bigger than any of ours. He'd picked up a few in the Arctic village of Old Crow, and others in Fort Yukon, Alaska. But they weren't Cor's ideal dogs.

"I want faster dogs," he said. "These ones are good for the trapline, but I want more speed."

His dogs had looked fairly played out after today's haul up from the mouth of the Selwyn River. That is, except the one running loose.

"That crummy excuse for a dog! I should shoot him. And I would, except he isn't my dog. I borrowed him in Dawson for this trip."

"Hadn't you tried him before?" I asked.

"No, and I should have known better. A friend offered to lend me *this great dog*.... He's useless. Less than useless."

"What was he doing running loose?"

"He was fouling up the others and holding them back," Cor emphasized his point by stabbing the awl into a scrap of leather, "so I set him loose to run ahead and inspire the others. I'm trying to get some use out of him. When I get to Carmacks, I'll leave him with someone there."

I mentioned the trouble we'd been having with Jeff, and wished we could fix that somehow.

"I don't like shooting dogs," Cor said, "but sometimes you have to do it. The world is better off without some of these dogs. A *lead pill* is sometimes the best way to solve a problem."

The *pill* Cor was referring to was a .22 calibre bullet.

"I hope it doesn't come to that," Marsha interjected, as she turned Cor's hanging clothing so it would dry on the other side. "We borrowed Jeff."

"Well, it's not a pleasant task," Cor admitted, "but no one can afford to feed a useless dog all year. And if you give him away, then someone else will end up having to shoot him."

A musher needs experience to know which dogs to have patience with, Cor told us. The trouble might be more with the musher than with the dog. "I had one dog that I kept over the summer," he said, "even though he hadn't worked well at all. By the next year he was better, and eventually he got to be one of my best dogs."

Cor had made his own toboggan too, so we traded notes on what we'd learned. *[See Appendix VIII for details of Cor's toboggan building.]* He was making what he called *short trips*, such as this jaunt to Whitehorse and a previous one from Old Crow to Dawson, to prepare himself for his great ambition. One of these years, he wanted to travel by dog team from the Yukon across Canada to his native Québec. By staying near the treeline, he could camp in the style of the woodsman, rather than living like the Inuit on their treeless tundra. As Cor matter-of-factly talked of hundred-mile treks, we couldn't help but believe he would someday successfully make this long solo journey across the North. He had the physique of a bear and the determination of a man with a mission: to travel and enjoy the winter.

I offered to accompany Cor to show him our trail to Fort Selkirk. He readily accepted, saying his dogs should be more excited chasing mine. I was delighted at the prospect of being some help.

Cor told us about having to feed cornmeal to his team at one point along a trip when no other dog food was available. The dogs took a few days getting used to the change in diet, he said, but were soon digesting it fine. While explaining this, he pulled out his bonus fuel to add to the bubbling dog food pot on the airtight: eggs from the king salmon he nets commercially during the summer.

"Lots of good protein in this," he pointed out, plopping frozen clumps into the thick, stinky meal. "If this was for us to eat, we'd call it *caviar*."

We also souped up all the dog food that night with blocks of frozen beef blood to give both Cor's team and mine an extra boost of energy for the morning's run.

Though Cor was friendly with his dogs at mealtime, it was a different story in the morning. While Marsha and I were fussing over my dogs, Cor was all business with his.

"Don't pamper your dogs when they are in harness," advised Cor, "or they won't know this is serious. Keep their play and their work separate. It's okay to be affectionate, but do it after they are through, and on their chains. Then you can pat them and talk nicely. But work time is work time: *be serious*."

Cor's dogs were indeed being solemn, sitting calmly in their traces awaiting his command. My dogs were doing their circus acts, leaping, howling, rolling in the snow, growling at Cor's team – quite an embarrassing display. When Casey led a gang foray toward the other team, a fight was narrowly averted. Cor stepped in and dragged my orange troublemaker away from his leader. It was obvious that Cor wasn't impressed by our discipline – or lack thereof.

Rather than risk another attack, I quickly herded my four beasts down the bank onto the Yukon, and pointed them upriver. The temperature had warmed a bit – to about Thirty Below. Casey knew the trail to Selkirk from our visits with Danny and Abbie, and galloped off smartly, full of energy and enthusiasm.

Within seconds, Cor's leader was sniffing my boots. Squatting on my toboggan's tail, I could watch his team almost eyeball to eyeball as they jogged along, tongues flapping and white clouds of breath puffing from their open mouths.

Of course, while I was looking back, my team decided to have a pit stop. My first indication of this was Loki's yip when the toboggan rammed his rear and pushed him on top of Mutt who was moving his bowels. Cor waited patiently while I sorted out the indignant dogs and kicked snow over the steaming brown pile so it wouldn't get stuck to the toboggan bases.

Now Casey wouldn't run. He kept looking over his shoulder as he walked along the trail, checking out Cor's dogs close behind me.

"Make them run!" Cor yelled. He was understandably impatient to cover as much distance this morning as possible.

But Casey wouldn't be hurried. He walked – or trotted after much cajoling – but refused to run. So Cor took his team past us, and ran them off along the trail. My dogs easily caught up, and Casey kept trying to pass Cor, wallowing off the packed trail into the loose snow. There was clearly no shortage of energy or ability on either team.

Then Cor's leader slowed to a walk and kept glancing over his shoulder. So much for the inspiration my team was supposed to give to the other team! Cor and I took turns running ahead to set a pace. The dogs liked this, trotting merrily behind, but neither Cor nor I was feeling particularly jovial when we pulled into Danny's yard at Fork Selkirk to warm up and sip some tea.

Danny had been expecting Cor. He and Abbie had heard on the CBC radio a lone musher was on his way from Dawson up the river. With the cold weather, Danny had estimated Cor would have made good time and be passing through today. There was a fresh bannock just out of the pan, and a new tin of red jam waiting.

Cor passed on news about downriver trappers. Someone had caught twenty-seven lynx, but his neighbour had beat him handily with fifty-one so far! At three hundred dollars a pelt, it sounded as if everyone down there would be buying new snowmobiles and outboards this year.

Danny lamented the scarcity of lynx on his line. "They're all over on your

Cor Guimond (above) visited on his way to Whitehorse. At left Cor's lead dog picks a route through jumbled ice.

side, Bruce. And Peter Isaac gets them all. I haven't seen any lynx tracks on this side of the Yukon this winter."

To give Cor an appreciation of my friend's trapping prowess, I changed the subject to snaring squirrels. Last year Danny had caught seven hundred. This winter he was aiming at eleven hundred! Somewhere, we all laughed, there must be a lot of ladies wearing squirrel coats.

Danny had been busy with his notebook, sketching a map of his old trapping trail overland as far as the headwaters of the Selwyn River. This would be the route of our first long expedition. There were little squares on the map to mark the locations of the line cabins he and Abbie had used two decades ago. *Cottonwood Cabin,* named after the choice of building logs; *Little Summit Cabin* on the plateau beyond the first grand climb; on and on until *Selkirk Creek Cabin* on the Selwyn.

The cabins would be no use to us now, Danny explained, except as dry firewood. Even the old stoves and kitchenware would be gone now, removed by souvenir-hunting helicopter pilots and game wardens. Nothing was too remote or inaccessible for those scavengers.

"Cowboy Smith said it was pretty overgrown. Maybe now you can't even find the way."

"When was that?" I asked. "When did Cowboy go over the trail?"

Danny looked at Abbie, who was sitting on the bed patting her pet Timmy. Abbie shrugged, "Maybe ten years, maybe more."

But all this talk was keeping Cor from his task. We'd only covered six miles of the thirty-some he wanted to make today.

Back outside, Danny loaded the 10-gallon drum stove he'd made for us onto my toboggan.

"You're gonna be warm in your tent with this," he said. I thanked him and we headed upriver.

I accompanied Cor until noon, taking the odd turn at jogging out front, hoping above all the ice was good and solid where I ran. Cor didn't seem to share my anxieties.

"After a few years, you get to know whether it's thick or not," he explained. "You know where it's safe, and where it's weak." He pointed out a darker patch which he would avoid.

"When you're on the toboggan, the dogs should be able to tell you. They feel if the ice is solid with their pads."

I thought back to our terrifying trip, making a first trail to Fort Selkirk from Horsefall, earlier in the month. Casey had led us on a meandering route – which seemed to indicate he was avoiding weak spots, until he walked right over to an open lead and took a drink! I wasn't so sure about Cor's philosophy.

Cor and I shared a thermos of steaming soup, and ate the sandwiches and dried fruit Marsha had packed for us. The sun was dazzlingly bright out here on the snow-covered ice. The dogs lay in their harnesses, panting and squinting into the warming rays. Cor was wearing only a sweater over his long-sleeved T-shirt, and just one pair of mitts. If I hadn't peeked at the thermometer at Danny's I'd never have guessed it was Twenty Below.

As Cor took his leave, pacing his team up the river, my mind was already on our own first long expedition. Danny's map had brought the concept to life and stirred my enthusiasm. Cor's example encouraged us to venture farther than our circle of close neighbours. He was out having a cruise through the wilderness, oblivious to the cold weather. He had assuaged my fear of weak ice, and had given us good advice about handling the dogs. Now I could hardly wait to be off having fun too.

"Okay, Casey," I called. "Let's go home."

They loped the whole way, right past Fort Selkirk and home in time for supper.

CHAPTER TWENTY

FIRST DAY AND LONG COLD NIGHT

Danny Roberts' old trapline followed a centuries-old walking path, winding overland from opposite the mouth of the Pelly River (where Fort Selkirk stands) to the Donjek River country – connecting with side paths leading to Kluane Lake and the White River. Long before the first white men came to this territory, the Indians were travelling long distances to exchange copper, food and furs between tribes. When the Russian sealers and traders arrived on the Alaskan coast in the 1700s, the commerce increased to include a wider variety of furs, with metal knives and woollen blankets in exchange. For us, the trail's rich history would be a bonus to the mountain scenery and relatively undisturbed wildlife we expected to encounter.

We had already scouted out a trail part-way up Six Mile Creek, the day I froze my thumb, that would join onto Danny's old line at a place well past where he now set traps. After the affair of Hinglish getting trapped on a previous visit to Selkirk, we were leery of being near any trapping activity. Since no one had been over the Donjek route for a decade, we had no illusions about the condition of the trail; it would be unpacked and overgrown.

As we hooked up the nine frantic dogs in the chilly pre-dawn glow, Marsha kept shaking her head. "Too much weight," she said. "We've got too much stuff. They'll never pull it."

There was dog food for two weeks and, honestly, enough people food to last us two months. It was obvious where our priorities lay. A reasonable estimate of the weight would have been three hundred and fifty pounds per toboggan, including the mushers. With such bulky items as sleeping bags, wall tent, stove and dog food, the loads looked intimidating.

"Let's give it a try with all this," I suggest. "We'll come back and repack if the dogs can't manage."

Still shaking her head, Marsha untied her lifeline from a tree and silently mouthed *Ready* to me. Her foot was firmly on the brake.

I untied my restraining rope and grasped the handlebars. "Okay, Casey."

Yikes! The toboggan leapt forward, almost pulling my arms from their sockets, as I held on for dear life. Both feet were on the brake, and my back was arched like a ballet dancer's. The brake claw was furrowing deeply into the snow, spraying a tall wash of flakes in a plume-like fan beside and behind me. For a moment, as the dogs plunged over the bank and turned sharply out to the right, I was airborne. Then the toboggan dropped, slamming hard onto the frozen river, abruptly pivoted on a patch of bare ice, and was yanked on by the anxious crew. It was another hundred yards out onto the river before I could get them stopped, and then only because Lucky and Loki wanted to answer a call of nature.

While they were performing their chores, I could safely look back. Marsha's five were now emerging from the forest, galloping down the slope and scrambling out onto the river. As the toboggan cleared the bank and launched into space, I could see daylight beneath it for two seconds. When it hit, my eyes winced shut.

When I looked again, her dogs were crowding to a stop at my feet and pummelled my legs with paws, wagging tails and sniffing muzzles.

"How's the load?" I called to Marsha. "Think you'll be okay?"

"No," she replied, eyes wide with exhilaration. "I need a bigger brake!"

The rich hues of the rising sun dyed the snow as we snaked across the Yukon River, swinging well wide of the fog-marked open patches and the deeper snowdrifts near the islands. At first, the world was a stark, shivery purple, then an intense orange. Twenty minutes later, when we reached the creek mouth, we'd also travelled through island channels of pale pink, while the mountain tops above us were washed in bright yellow. In time all became dazzling, bleaching white.

Six Mile Creek itself was a wide sidewalk of yellow-stained ice, perfectly flat and solid. Our progress was interrupted after two sharp bends by a beaver dam which tiered the ice at waist height. The dogs found no problem here, scampering up the mound of sticks and branches, dragging the freight toboggans easily after. This dammed pond soon led to another barrier, and above that was another. In all, we passed five barricades. The sound of running water was unsettlingly loud at each dam, but the ice above and below – and the dams themselves – were solid and safe.

"Danny will be interested to know how many beaver there are on this creek," I remarked when we stopped to sip miso soup from the thermos.

"How much are beaver furs worth?" asked Marsha.

"Thirty dollars for a medium size and twice as much for a big blanket beaver," I said. "There is a lot of money here for Danny if all these dams have keepers. I'll bet that's a lodge over there."

Against the bank on our left was a shoulder-tall mound of snow. If Danny had been with us, he'd know what to look for to determine if this residence was still in use. There were no fresh footprints or debris from gathering branches, so we had to assume life was either absent, or totally underground and underwater for these beaver families.

When the creek became too narrow and overgrown with willows, we struck off overland for Danny's trail. Immediately we found ourselves foundering in deep snow. Casey would merrily swim through the drifts, following any hint of a rabbit trail, but his choices for passageways were not of the size the toboggans required. Nor was he too choosy about in which general direction the rabbit trails led us.

I stripped off my parka and went ahead to be both lead dog and lumberjack, picking a convenient route through the poplar forest and chopping away the occasional blockage. Behind me, Casey and Lucky wallowed through loose snow which came well over their shoulders. Their footsteps created a semblance of a packed trail for Mutt and Loki who struggled behind them doing all the pulling. Fortunately we had foreseen the prospect of loose snow and had tightened the curls on both toboggans so that the fronts were bowed very high and could easily ride up over the jumbled snow and any logs across my makeshift trail.

Marsha had a full job just keeping her crew from crawling all over my toboggan as they pulled anxiously, impatient to explore the country ahead. She was taking turns using Peter and Hinglish as leader – following the other team was simple work and would build her lead dogs' confidence.

Dawson was continually twisting up his traces and halting the procession. Jeff had been moved back to wheel position, so Marsha could get to him more easily when he misbehaved. The rascally Siberian had developed an appetite for harnesses and needed constant supervision if we were to break him of the habit before he ate us out of webbing. Tyhee had been promoted forward to behind Dawson; it was hoped that her stint at wheel had corrected her tendency to sniff off to the side and avoid her share of the work.

All through the morning and early afternoon, Marsha and I spelled each other off at trail breaking. We had less success at switching the dog teams around though, as only Casey was about to understand following *behind* – and not *on top of* – the person out front swinging the axe. Fortunately Mutt was working well today, so four dogs were splitting the effort on my squad, and they weren't tiring as fast as we humans were.

When we finally came out onto an old telegraph right-of-way and could forget about clearing trail ahead, I'm sure we heard sighs of relief from the dogs as well! Now my dogs could tromp out a path without my lead. I walked gladly in the wide, smooth toboggan wake, able now to appreciate the forest and to watch for signs of where Danny's old trapline would intersect this telegraph route.

The thick gray wire of the telegraph lay in great coils everywhere, sagging from the occasional erect pole, or dragged and tangled off to the side where some moose or bear had wrestled with it. Some of the glass insulators were still intact, even on poles which had toppled and were barely protruding through the snow. This line was part of the Collins Overland, an ambitious 19th-century communications mega-project intended to stretch from San Francisco northward, spanning the length of British Columbia, the Yukon and Alaska, then under the Bering Sea, through Siberia to Russia, and finally on to Europe. That enterprise went bankrupt in 1867, long before completion when competitors succeeded in laying a submarine cable across the Atlantic. The partially-cleared Yukon section was hastily completed some years later when gold was discovered in the Klondike Valley and the boom town of Dawson City had to be linked to the outside world. Eventually telegraph became obsolete, replaced by telephone lines and microwave relay towers built along the same new highway that had forced the sternwheelers into retirement. Though the old communications right-of-way was long abandoned, trees grew so slowly in the North that this was still the most open route through the forest.

There was no question when we reached Danny's old trapline. He had been over this way lately on his snowmobile to pack a short stretch of the trail for us. I felt privileged to be able to ride the toboggan for even this twenty minutes. The dogs ran across the willow swamp, thoroughly chilling my sweat-drenched body and bouncing me over the mounds of frozen muskeg. Out in this open bowl, we could see ahead the range of low mountains we would have to climb over to reach the Selwyn River watershed. One of the first passes would be the Little Summit of Danny's map, and a later one would be Big Summit. It felt good to be really on our way, actually mushing along this historic overland trail.

As the sun slipped behind one of those distant mountains, we were reminded of the scope of the challenge we faced. The temperature was dropping quickly, far more than the loss of sunshine alone would cause. The air was biting on my cheeks and freezing in my nostrils. We pulled on our parkas and travelling mitts, and thought about making a camp.

We had barely left the snowmobile-packed section when we came upon the first of the trapline cabins.

"This must be Cottonwood Cabin," I said, consulting the sketch map.

"It seems to have lasted pretty well, for all the poor things one hears about building with cottonwood," Marsha remarked.

Marsha began poking about inside. Seeing was no problem because a quarter of the roof was missing, letting in plenty of light. Our minds were fixed on finding a suitable camping site though, so as soon as we'd ascertained this partial cabin wouldn't shelter us, we pushed on.

The dogs were indignant about resuming our trek. Each had trampled and dug out a nest in the snow, and was settled in for a night's sleep.

"Just a little further, you guys," I promised them. "First patch of big timber, we'll make a camp."

Of course, now we were feeling rushed and running out of daylight, all we came across was light poplar forest and muskeg swamp. When we saw two white spruce at the edge of a stand of spindly dead black spruce, we decided this would have to do.

"How about I'll chain out the dogs here in the trail, and you start gathering firewood?" Marsha proposed.

"Sure. There's no time to pitch the tent so we'll sleep under this spruce tree."

"Okay," said Marsha, "but get lots of wood. I'm freezing already."

We scurried about like hyperactive field mice: chopping up dry spruce poles for firewood, shovelling away snow with a snowshoe to make a fire pit, dragging out our grub boxes to place beside the fire pit, cutting boughs to sit on, stretching out the canvas tarp, rolling out the bedding, lighting the fire, gathering snow to melt – all in no particular order except that everything had to be done before total darkness. Even on this, our first overnight trip, we didn't have to talk much. Being veteran campers, most of the work was obvious. In time, we'd have these routines honed to a minimum of time and effort, but today we made up with extra hustle.

Having gang chains greatly simplified the chore of staking out the beasts. Marsha attached my team's gang chain to hers and strung the whole affair in one line between two trees along the trail. Feeding them would be easy tonight, as we would have the packed trail to walk along when doling out the mush.

There were some politics involved in deciding who to put next to whom, so antagonists would not be nose-to-nose, growling all night. Of course those who had worked hard were more interested in eating and sleeping than in fighting. Jeff and Dawson were making a great show of displaying their teeth and proclaiming their energy. These two clowns were suspiciously chipper.

"You two wait until tomorrow," Marsha promised them. "I'll have my eye on you both. You'd better work harder or else!"

The *or else* on this trip was rather limited. We could slap them with a mitt but anything more physical could turn a dog into a cowering neurotic who spent the whole time looking over his shoulder at the musher. Too bad the trick we'd played on Mutt the week before would not be possible on this trip—

When Mutt had misbehaved on a run over to the farm for supplies, I'd left him chained to a tree in the forest by himself. When I returned with the loaded toboggan and the rest of the dogs four hours later, the poor dog had howled himself hoarse. He was so frightened he was trembling. I hooked him into harness again and he pulled like he were a different dog. He seemed grateful for the privilege of working after that lonely spell in the forest. If we had been doing a round trip today, we might have tried this stunt on his brother or Dawson.

By the fire's light, we finally got into dry clothes and started on a meal. With the flames licking high in the air to warm us, I chose to cook over coals drawn away from the main blaze in order not to overcook the moose steaks Danny had given us. Regulating the temperature under the frying pan was a matter of spreading the embers to cool them, or scraping out more hot coals to raise the heat. A pot of boiling potatoes bubbled merrily on another nest of coals. On this first night out, the menu wasn't going to be too elaborate: just steaks and spuds, and lots of herbal tea to replace the perspiration we'd spent all day. Tonight's tea blend was picked not three paces from the fire, under a black spruce at the edge of the muskeg. The leaves of the Labrador tea bush yield a quite palatable drink when boiled for about five minutes. Strangely, the second and third brew from the same leaves tasted better than the first.

Marsha had the dogs fed and the bedding spread out by the time I had our meal ready. She was delighted by the carpet of spruce boughs around the fire.

"These boughs are great for keeping my moccasins out of the slush around the fire," she said. "Did you know I've never camped like this in winter?"

"You mean with spruce boughs?"

"Yes – and with a campfire too," she said, holding her fingers close to the flames. "During our wildland recreation courses, we always camped in provincial and national parks where you can't cut trees. This is pretty nice. I could get spoiled."

"How did you stay warm without a fire?"

"Mostly I didn't," she explained. "You have to take along a small gas or propane stove to cook on, and we slept in pup tents or snow caves, which are only a tiny bit warmer than the outside air."

"That doesn't sound very comfortable," I said.

"Yeah, I was often really cold. We only did it," Marsha admitted, "for two or three nights in a row, then we'd need to find a place to get warm and dry out. This is so different." She was snuggled right up to the fire, the soles of her moccasins steaming. The heat was toasting her cheeks a cheery red.

"Shall we sleep under the stars tonight, or do you think we need the tarp?" she asked after we'd sat warmed by the fire for an hour eating our dinner.

The sky was perfectly clear. When the moon rose, we'd be able to see around the valley quite well with the reflection off the snow. Usually there are no clouds when the weather is very cold, and tonight was certainly chilly: our tea froze in seconds if the cup wasn't within an arm's length of the flames. We decided to gamble on there being no overnight snowfall and cuddled together deep in our double bags with the galaxies looking on.

The air was so nippy there was no question about leaving our faces exposed to star-gaze. On nights like this, I wished for a fur-trimmed hood for my sleeping bag, so at least a portion of the night sky would be visible through the breathing tunnel.

About two in the morning, clouds moved in and a gentle snow began to fall. The light patter of flakes hitting the nylon shell of the bags stirred me from my snoozing.

"It is *too cold* to snow," I told myself sleepily, estimating the temperature at close to Thirty Below by the way it chilled my nostrils. "It'll stop in a second." I snuggled deeper into my bag, and fell back asleep.

The storm had no intention of stopping. When I woke an hour later, the flakes were larger, adding every second to the inch-deep blanket of snow already on our bags.

"*Damn.* We'll have to do *something*," I muttered.

"Not *we.* YOU do something," came Marsha's muffled reply. "I hate being cold – and I especially hate being *cold and wet!*" she added, in case I hadn't quite got her drift.

I got up, stumbled around in my duffle liners and T-shirt, stepping on lost pots and knocking snow on myself from overhanging branches. The snow melted and ran down my neck as I was searching through the fluffy drifts, using a fading flashlight to see by. I found some coiled rope and wrestled half the tarp out from under our bedding, then tied the tarp out over us, running lines to trees all around for support. Then I crept underneath, swept snow off the outer bags with my bare arm, and wriggled back into my now-cold bed.

"*Yikes,* do you have to let in so much cold air?" Marsha muttered from her side. A moment later she added, "Thanks, Bruce."

Sleeping under the stars is not all it's cracked up to be sometimes. We were becoming smarter about this winter camping business with each passing day – and night. Now we knew to put up the tarp, or have it handy, no matter how romantic those stars might be.

CHAPTER TWENTY-ONE

EATING: MORNING, NOON AND NIGHT

As the blizzard continued on into the morning, we felt little incentive to get up aside from the persistent call of nature. If we had been equipped with the hoses and bags astronauts wear, we might never have stirred from under the sagging, snow-laden tarpaulin.

"Don't you have to *go?*" Marsha asked.

"Yeah, but I'm not desperate yet," I said, not wanting to leave my toasty bag. "Do you have to go?"

"I'm not getting up until you light a fire or spring arrives," she muttered. "It must be Forty Below."

"Why me?" This was a good opportunity to tease her, because she was clearly more in need of relief than I was. She was already at the grit-your-teeth stage. "What about women's liberation?" I needled. "You know: equal rights to start the fire."

"Don't make jokes. This is serious business," said Marsha. "This is your chance to be a hero."

When she put it that way, I could hardly refuse. The hardest part of the operation was crawling out and getting dressed without tipping snow down my heroic neck, or onto our bedding. After that, I quite enjoyed bustling about, breaking up twigs, rolling a few newspapers, and finding the stack of split firewood under the blanket of fresh snow. A new snowfall is always a delight for me, stirring childhood memories of the year's first snowball, of making snowmen and angels. This snow, however, would never compact well for snowballs, being far too dry and cold. Marsha had not been far wrong on her estimate: the thermometer on the toboggan backboard indicated Minus Thirty-Eight Fahrenheit. I'd never known it to snow at so cold a temperature.

When the fire was crackling vigorously and no longer needed attention, I started the search for buried axes, pots, pans and utensils. After all were located and accounted for, I could breathe a sigh of relief, and resolved to be more prudent on nights to come. If anything was to harm us on these excursions, it would surely be our carelessness. The lessons had been gentle so far, but we mustn't press our luck.

For breakfasts on the trail, Marsha had packed a variety of grains to cook as porridge, plus sausages, ham or bacon for each morning's ration of energy. Just like the dogs, who each received a chunk of fat for breakfast, we needed some fuel that would burn inside us until well into the day. Mornings were also a good time to drink huge quantities of liquid to replenish what was lost on the previous day. If we drank too much at supper, we'd be up too often during the night to relieve ourselves. Letting out warmth from the sleeping bag, then crawling back in with cold air, was hardly a way to win friends and influence people.

The breakfast grains were bagged in one-morning portions, with a pinch of salt already added to make cooking as convenient as possible. This morning's draw was cornmeal, with a sprinkling of flax seeds. To make it richer, we added shredded cheese and raisins after it was nearly cooked, and some milk powder at the last minute.

"Guaranteed to stick to your ribs," Marsha claimed as she dished it out into our bowls. "You'll be able to break trail all day."

After the bacon was done, we fried our toast in the grease left in the pan. Today we were both cold and hungry, so *bacon toast* was a treat. My father introduced me to bacon toast when I was knee-high, but Mom never really approved. No one could burn that much fat unless they were planning to work hard all day outside.

The bread we brought had been baked in tall, 48-ounce juice tins. After slicing each loaf, we wrapped it in a plastic bag and stored it back in its baking tin for travel. Frozen bread is almost impossible to slice without crumbling apart, unless it is an extremely dense loaf.

While packing the kitchen equipment and food in the grub boxes, I noticed there were a few breakfast bags with granola and milk powder in them.

"Those are for some morning when we are too rushed to wait for porridge to cook," said Marsha.

"It's hard to imagine you and me rushing that much," I laughed. Already it was noon and we were still packing up. The *day off* before we left had effectively mellowed out any abnormal anxiousness.

"I'd rather just cruise," Marsha admitted. "We may not make it to the top of Mount Everest, but I want to notice the trees and birds and animals. We don't have any fixed timetable, do we?"

Camping porridge ratios

Serves 2 hungry people...	(grain : water)	ratio
cornmeal	3/4 cup : 4-1/2 cups	1 : 6
millet	3/4 cup : 2-1/4 cups	1 : 3
cracked wheat	1 cup : 3 cups	1 : 3
oatmeal	1 cup : 2-1/2 cups	2 : 5

- add a pinch of salt before boiling
- if too runny, raisins will absorb the extra water as they cook
- flax may be added for flavour and bulk
- a dollop of butter or cheese added in will make this porridge taste richer

---

Other than the limitations of our food supplies, we were without a deadline. The trick would be to remember this, and not invent time urgencies.

For our lunch, which would actually be a mid-afternoon break because we were leaving so late, Marsha grabbed some dried fruit and nuts, two chunks of cheese, and filled the thermos with chamomile tea. I was pleased to see her pack it away on my toboggan, out of easy reach for her snacking urges during our travel.

We both felt that caffeine and white sugar over-stimulate the body, making some organs work too hard to compensate, and causing a net loss. Over this winter, we were trying to put a few of our unorthodox theories into practice. We'd boldly brought no coffee, black tea, nor white sugar into our cabin, so now the choice had already been made.

In this aspect of dietetics, we were going hard against the grain of rural tradition. The most common staples in most bush camps were refined white sugar, salt, coffee, bleached white flour, sugar-cured, nitrate-treated bacon, canned sweet baked beans, processed canned meat, jam and boxes of candies. Just thinking of that list would have upset us if we had been ardent health food fanatics or vegetarians. We were neither, although we were more conscious about our diets than many people. This winter was an ideal time for us to experiment, trying to note the effects of herbal teas and whole foods on our bodies and minds. If, in the future, we chose to become fanatical about our diets, we would have proven to ourselves why.

"I still wish I had a chocolate bar," Marsha said, as we untied our lifelines. "Or how about some coloured marshmallows? Wouldn't that be *so good?*"

"Okay, I give in. We'll stop at the next McDonald's for lunch."

Danny and Abbie had been right about their trail being overgrown. Only where it wound through tall timber could we be sure we had the right route; in there only the occasional fallen tree would confuse us. Elsewhere, when we crossed muskeg swamps or encountered willow thickets, I had to rely on Casey to pick out the faint clues. Time and time again, when I was sure he'd been stumped and led us mistakenly into a tangle of saplings and deadfall, a peek beyond revealed a clear, straight trail. He'd get a chance to lie down and rest while I hacked at the blockage, his tail wagging to encourage me.

Although the distance we travelled that afternoon may not have been far, we climbed in altitude enough to feel that some of this should be called Little Summit. Danny hadn't drawn his sketch-map to scale, and we were matching his cryptic descriptions of *big hill, good for catching squirrels* and *creek comes in on this side* to every possible turn.

"Maybe we're lost," Marsha said nonchalantly, as we chained out the dogs for the night.

"We aren't lost. I know where we are on these big topo maps," I said. "It's just that I don't know where the old trail fits onto the maps. Danny couldn't draw it onto a topographical map because he has never used them. This sketch is the most map he's ever used. He just *remembers* where everywhere is."

Today we allowed ourselves a full ninety minutes before dark to set up properly. Marsha had picked a sheltered spot amongst big white spruce, where there was less snow on the ground and some dry wood handy in the form of deadfall and standing poles. Using snowshoes as scoops, we shovelled most of the snow off to the sides, and trampled down an area about eight by ten feet. The snow in the North is not like that found in southern Canada's warmer, damper regions. The extreme cold and dryness create a granular snow that was much like white sugar or sand in texture. It would not ball or mold at all. However, it would settle when we stepped on it, then become more firm if left for a few minutes to *set*.

The easiest way to gather spruce boughs was to cut down two or three small trees and trim all their branches. The trunks could then be sawn into three-foot lengths that were stacked to form a reflector wall behind the campfire. Two supports were pushed into the snowbank to prop up this wall of green wood. The wall bounced back heat and light, and also drew the smoke away as a chimney of sorts.

"A reflector fire. This is something out of old legends," Marsha said, basking in the heat. "I feel guilty about cutting down live trees, but I guess a wall wouldn't last very long if it was dry wood. Sure bounces a lot of heat."

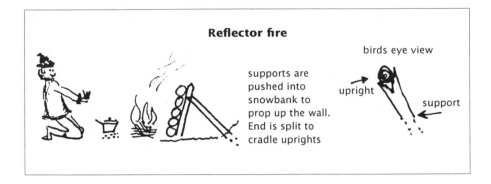

Reflector fire

birds eye view

supports are
pushed into
snowbank to
prop up the wall.
End is split to
cradle uprights

upright

support

"The only part of the tradition we're skipping is spruce bough beds," I said, "and we'd have to murder quite a few spruce trees to do a proper job. The sourdough prospectors wrote of bough beds six or eight inches thick. Our camping pads are more effective and a whole lot less work."

"Speaking of work," she replied, "do you want to get more firewood and I'll be the cook tonight?"

Clearly there was not much time for chatting if we hoped to get everything organized before dark. One of us had to gather the substantial pile of dry wood needed to feed the fire tonight and next morning. It was easiest to cut trees into portable lengths, then carry them back to near the fire for chopping or sawing into fire-size pieces. Most of these pieces would also have to be split, in order to have a hot, less-smoky blaze.

Tonight Marsha assumed the role of cook and tender of the fire. We realized that if the cook had too much to do, the meal might get burnt or tipped into the fire through neglect. Outdoor cooking demanded constant attention, so the cook's only other duty was to gather snow in the big pots to melt for our water and the dogs' meal. Depending on the density of the snow drifts, a potful of snow might melt to anywhere from a tenth to a fifth of a pot of water. We would designate one area as the snow-water source, keeping it clean. The best snow came from the open places, well away from the spruce trees' needles and, of course, well away from the dogs. Digging too deep or in the wrong spot could add unwanted rabbit pellets to the pot. Another reason to set up camp before dark.

When enough wood had been dragged to the site, the woodchopper became shelter maker. The firewood could be cut up and split by the light of the fire, but the bedding and tarp required more daylight fussing. After last night's episode, we'd committed to having the tarp ready for instant erection over us. This meant laying the pads and sleeping bags on one side and folding the balance to the side.

If snow fell, only two corner ropes needed to be fastened to nearby trees to hold up this canvas roof as a lean-to.

Despite the descriptions in old journals about voyageurs and hunters sleeping beside the fire for warmth, I kept our bedding well back, ever wary of the damage sparks and bursting coals could do to our nylon-covered sleeping bags.

Since our own supper was not ready yet, the dogs got their feast at this point. For our expedition up this old overland trail, their food was commercial dog meal, fish meal and beef blood icicles. We felt it important to soak the ingredients with steaming hot water to ensure our dogs didn't get dehydrated.

As soon as I left the campfire with the pot of mush, the dogs sprang from their hollows and threw up a deafening cacophony of pleas, whines, howls, barks and growls, all intended to influence my distribution. But each had to sit quietly in turn before his portion was doled out on the snow. We hadn't brought their dog dishes because it didn't seem at all necessary to pour the mush into their pans, just to have them pour it back out on the snow to cool. Tonight, eight dogs promptly settled back to their snow nests as soon as they finished. Only Jeff was up, jerking on the chain and growling at his neighbours.

"Either he has a lot more stamina than the others," I mused, "or he isn't doing his share."

Marsha was squatting in front of the fire on some spruce boughs, hot mitt in hand, warming the bowls while watching the lentil stew did not burn. It was a thoughtful touch, having heated bowls, because both the food and our hands would stay warmer longer.

"What's your verdict on supper?" I asked her as she passed me my meal.

She had used vegetables from our root cellar we had prepared two days before the trip. They had been washed, sliced, then spread on cookie sheets to freeze

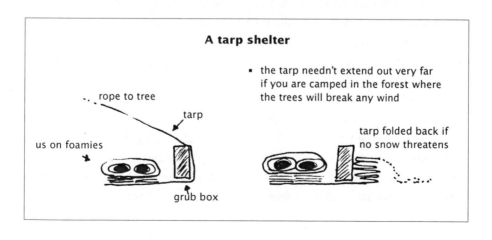

A tarp shelter

- the tarp needn't extend out very far if you are camped in the forest where the trees will break any wind

rope to tree

tarp

us on foamies

grub box

tarp folded back if no snow threatens

outside before packing in plastic bags. Some were in *variety packs* to become part of one meal. Others, like the onions, stayed separate and could be added by the handful to any dish.

"The onions taste super sweet. The freeze and thaw has really changed their flavour," she noted happily, passing me a piece of fried bread to go with the stew.

"The farm potatoes are great," I raved with my mouth full. "How come they didn't go mushy, like when I do them?"

"The trick," Marsha explained, "is to not thaw them before cooking. Just throw them into the boiling water still frozen."

"What else did you learn?"

"The rutabagas are good after being frozen, but these turnips are the pits." She fished out one white cube and flipped it into the fire. "I won't be offended if you don't eat the turnips. *Yech!*"

Supper was late because Marsha's first idea was to make rice, but she had given up trying to keep the heat exactly right for the forty minutes brown rice requires. So, at that point, she changed the menu to a stew, with the rice boiled up in a soup for the second course.

"Rice is too much fuss," Marsha decided. "Lentils taste great and are much simpler. We can scratch rice off the outdoor cooking list and save it for meals when we set up the wall tent and use the stove."

Our meals were more involved than they needed to be, but we enjoyed the time at the campfire and wanted well-balanced meals to keep up our health and strength. Suppertime was a focal point of the day, and we couldn't see ourselves forcing down commercial freeze-dried camping food.

"Thank goodness we've got the dogs, so we don't have to worry about weight. I think freeze-dried food tastes like wallpaper paste," I said smugly. "You'd have to be starving to like it."

"There are other ways to make lightweight food," suggested Marsha. "Maybe not as light as freeze-dried, but much cheaper and far better tasting."

She outlined to me a few ideas she'd used preparing food for backpacking hikes while working as a park ranger. She had grated a variety of cheeses and dried this to make it lighter. If the weather was cool enough to take fresh meat, it was possible to reduce the weight of bacon by par-boiling the strips in advance. Ordinary bread became melba toast in the oven. Beef could be cut into thin strips and slowly dried into jerky in a warm oven. The dried salmon Danny and Abbie had given us was another lightweight, gourmet idea. We could eat it as a trail snack or boil it into a chowder.

Although on a dog-powered cruise we could pack in elaborate ingredients, we did want a few ultra convenient meals for unexpectedly rushed evenings. Our versions of frozen TV dinners were chilli or stew prepared in the cabin and divided into portions large enough to feed two hungry campers. We used a well-buttered frying pan as a mold so the frozen dinner was a convenient size for packing and would thaw evenly in the same pan over campfire coals. A touch more butter wiped all over the disc prevented the plastic storage bag from sticking to it and gave a richer flavour to the finished camp meal.

Macaroni and cheese was another quick meal. It was easier to prepare on the trail than in the cabin because the cheese didn't have to be grated. Frozen chunks of cheddar were so crumbly they readily fell apart in our hands.

Marsha had learned tonight about *burning water*. On her first attempt at melting snow, she immediately put the pot in the flames.

"I guess it wasn't actually the water that burned," she told me, "but the dry pot scorching. As the snow heats up, it turns to steam immediately and is absorbed up into the snow above it. The bottom of the pot must have stayed bone dry for quite a long time, getting really scorched. When there was finally a little water, I had a sip and it had to be the worst-tasting water I've ever tasted. *Yeck!* It was like drinking smoke."

The way to avoid burning the snow, she decided, was to pack down the snow as much as possible, then place the lidded pot near the fire, but not too close to the heat for the first minutes. Even though this was a new batch of water, our tea had a hint of the scorched flavour to it yet.

"Perhaps that's one of the reasons the old-timers liked coffee so much on the trail," I suggested. "Strong camp coffee would mask the flavour of burnt water."

I poured a last cup of tea into the steel thermos flask, just in case one of us was thirsty during the night. Without this precautionary measure, a midnight drink would entail a heck of a lot of work starting a fire and melting snow.

We dumped out the water remaining in the pots to prevent the bottoms from being bulged out when the contents turned to ice and expanded.

Marsha had been chilly last night, so I suggested we trade bags and she could try my home-made super sleeping sack. I didn't realize at the time how hard it would be to get back my toasty home-made bag.

"This sack is pretty nice. A girl could get to like it," were her last words before she dozed off to a well-earned sleep.

Her down bag wasn't nearly as fluffy as mine, but I would have no problem staying warm. We were more accustomed to the cold after two full days outside and could look upon tonight's air as rather comfortable. The temperature had climbed to a balmy Minus Seventeen.

CHAPTER TWENTY-TWO

THROUGH STARS AND BARS

We started early on Day Three, full of oatmeal and good intentions. The sky was cloudless save for the wispy conn-trail from a U.S. Strategic Air Command bomber streaking towards Alaska. Its speed made a mockery of our snail's pace as we continued our tiring struggle to locate, clear and pack the old trail.

My old pet-turned-lead-dog was invaluable with his uncanny sense of where the trail went. Even though Casey was swimming through snow up to his shoulders, climbing over branches and forcing through willows, he kept going for hour after hour. Lucky was also wallowing in loose snow, and his big, floppy feet packed the trail that much more. Mutt and Loki merrily worked their hearts out pulling the toboggan, no easy feat despite it being lightened by the transfer of some cargo onto Marsha's. I tromped behind, axe in hand, frequently high-stepping past my team to attack a deadfall or snowdrift that blocked the path.

Our passing created a hard enough path that Marsha could ride most of the time, and even had to use the brake to keep her dogs back. Casey and Lucky would manage about fifty feet in a burst and have to pause for twenty seconds, then they would charge ahead again. When we lost the way, or a dicey creek crossing forced a detour, I struggled ahead and flailed away at trees with the axe until sweat streamed down my face and soaked my vest. Nonetheless, I believed we were making fair headway along our route.

When it came time to set up for the night, I discovered I had forgotten one critical item at our previous campsite.

"We've got a real problem," I admitted sheepishly to Marsha. "I forgot my team's gang chain this morning."

"Oh, oh! What are we going to do? We'll be up all night with dog fights if they are loose. We've only got one spare single chain, so three dogs will be prowling."

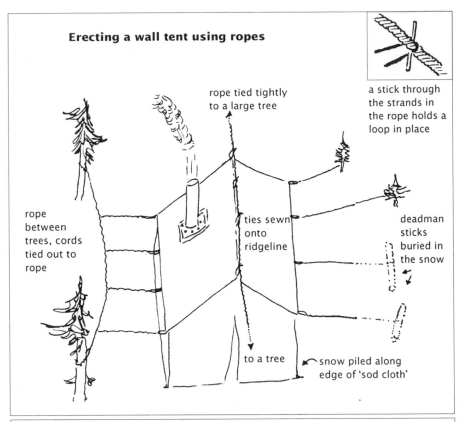

Erecting a wall tent using ropes

a stick through the strands in the rope holds a loop in place

rope tied tightly to a large tree

rope between trees, cords tied out to rope

ties sewn onto ridgeline

deadman sticks buried in the snow

to a tree

snow piled along edge of 'sod cloth'

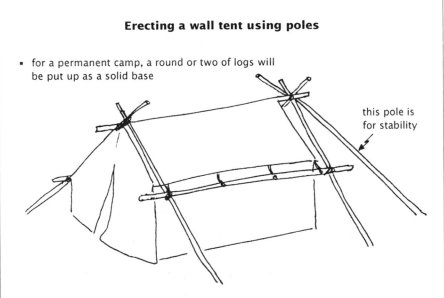

Erecting a wall tent using poles

- for a permanent camp, a round or two of logs will be put up as a solid base

this pole is for stability

"Well, I sure don't feel much like going back," I lamented. "After we've made it this far, it would be nice to make a camp here."

"Oh no, guess what!" Marsha moaned. She was crouched beside her toboggan, one hand inside the curl's cargo compartment. "My chain's missing too. I must have left it back there as well. Now we're in a real fix."

There was no way around it now – one or both of us would have to go back.

"You stay here and start on the camp, and I'll fetch the chains," I offered. "Casey will be able to see the trail even after dark. We'll be back by the time you've got supper made."

I dumped my cargo, taking only parka and flashlight. Though a mite confused about why they were leaving the others, my dogs obediently loped off down the trail. The snow we flattened today had since set into a veritable sidewalk. I had to hang on for dear life as the day's landmarks swept by at an alarming rate. The dogs were having their first chance in two days to run.

Twenty minutes later, we were there. I couldn't believe it. We could not have done more than three miles of trailbreaking all day! Shaking my head in disbelief, I collected the gang chains and headed back up the valley. I was disappointed and amazed our hard work was not as productive as imagined.

"Hey, what are you doing back already?" Marsha greeted me. "Is something wrong?"

"Nothing's wrong. I've got the chains. I've been there and back, that's all."

"But it seemed like—"

"Yep. I thought so, too."

"Let's take a better look at those maps and Danny's sketch tonight," Marsha suggested. "Right now, there's lots to do before dark. I've got the wall tent strung up over here in the trees."

Setting up a wall tent with a complete pole framework is a long process, so we'd adapted our tent slightly for temporary camps.

Marsha had sewn ties onto the tent along the ridge to make it possible for one person to erect the thirty pound tent, using only ropes to support it. If the roof was to be high enough to walk under, the main supporting rope had to be tied high and taut between trees. After this step, the tent could be hung from this line one tie at a time, so the lone person never had to hoist the tent's entire weight up in the air at once. The sides were then staked out to bushes or deadmen sticks buried in the snow. Another way of tying out these side cords was to run a rope between two trees roughly parallel to the side and join the cords to it.

We found this night it was slower in some respects to bother with the tent, but the advantages were legion. Once the tent was up, two candles provided ample lighting for the most intricate jobs, like stitching harnesses or darning mitts, even reading. The rush now was to get the outside work done before dark, such as gathering stove wood and unpacking the toboggans. We could cook a grand meal later at our leisure inside the tent by candlelight.

Sitting by a campfire generally warmed our fronts but not our backs. The heat in the tent was all around. Besides being more comfortable for people, the tent was easier on clothing, too. We ran another rope inside along the peak to hang mitts and socks for drying, a big improvement over the scorching and singeing (and resulting darning) at a campfire. Down-filled sleeping bags and parkas could be dried thoroughly, a near impossibility in front of open flames.

There was no fabric floor in our wall tent. Instead, we used spruce boughs on one half and spread our bedding on the tarp at the other end. Any snow we tromped in filtered down through this matt of boughs, so our moccasins stayed dry. A mitt could fall off the drying rope and not get wet. In fact, after the tent warmed up, we walked around in our socks or bare feet on the insulating layer of greenery.

"This is a far cry from sleeping in a pup tent," Marsha said happily. "Too bad more people couldn't experience camping like this in the south. There would be a lot more people out winter camping."

"Yeah. I could never see how it was supposed to be fun freezing in a tent about the size of a coffin, beside a picnic table on a gravel pad marked Site 35B," I added smugly.

"But at least in a southern park, we wouldn't have to worry about feeding nine hungry dogs!" Marsha laughed as she ducked out the door to check on the dog food fire. We had decided to make a small fire outside to get that chore out of the way sooner and leave the stove top free for melting our water and cooking our supper.

"Oh, Bruce!" she called out. "Come quick."

There was a sense of urgency in her tone, though I could hear no barking or growling coming from the animals.

"What is it?" I hadn't taken time to put on a coat and had only liners on my feet.

"Look at the sky," she said from a spot away from the fire and the glow of the tent walls.

I tried to step from branch to bush, keeping my liners out of the snow. I was forgetting that a touch of wetness would dry quickly in the tent. The last two nights had been so intense I was still acting as if we were camping outside.

Marsha's head was tilted back. I followed the direction of her stare, my eyes now more accustomed to the night. The moon, almost full, was just climbing over the tips of the spruce ridge below us. A million pinpoints of starlight stared back from the dome above us. But the real show was in progress over the western horizon. A wavy band of pastel green light glowed and flickered, extending in an arc fifteen degrees above the mountain tops. Directly above us, a hazy hand of pink wiggled its fingers, each digit pointing, then retracting.

"It's beautiful," said Marsha. "The lights seem to be dancing to music."

"These are as pretty as any Northern Lights I've seen before," I admitted. "This is a real treat to see so much colour."

"There's a hint of yellow over there," Marsha pointed out. "And blue, if you look hard, just below the green. Look for it below the piece that hangs down like a flag."

The green had stretched itself, flickering and rippling like a fabric curtain stirred by the wind. Suddenly, there was no more wind. The hand had dissolved into a cirrus wisp, which dissipated when the blue became more active.

"Do you think there is a message in them?" I asked my partner, only now feeling the night's cold through my light sweater.

"To me, it says, *Relax and Don't Worry*," Marsha whispered. "All this makes me feel so tiny and insignificant compared to the universe. I feel very lucky to be here and able to see these lights."

Indeed, our difficulties in covering much distance did now appear to be ant-size.

"If treats like this are bestowed on even us slow-pokes," I mused, "our trip must be unfolding exactly as fast as it should."

CHAPTER TWENTY-THREE

CHANGING THE PATTERN

On the morning of Day 4 of this trip, we were standing beside our tent, looking across the muskeg at a snow-covered fold in the ridge. This, we were certain, was the ascent into the mountains.

"In a little dip after the top there is supposed to be another cabin," I observed, reading the yellow paper in my hand. "It's called Little Summit Cabin."

"I can't even tell where the top is from here," Marsha exclaimed. "That must be a thousand foot climb! If this is Little Summit, what will Big Summit look like?"

"And how much snow will be on it, is what I'd like to know," I wondered.

"Maybe we should reconsider this idea," said Marsha, ducking back into the tent. "Let's eat a huge brunch and take the day off."

We'd been conscientiously switching tasks, so both could appreciate the joys and difficulties involved with each job. Trading teams, toboggans, even swapping individual dogs on occasion had kept mushing more interesting. A day without the hassle of packing, and setting up camp further on, would be another good change of pattern.

I had been worried our lack of progress was going to weigh heavily on Marsha because she was physically weaker than me and might feel she was holding us back. Though she tended to downplay her own contributions, we complemented each other pretty well. Marsha was teaching me to treat her as an individual, with potential and talents different from mine. In doing so, she was gradually weaning me of my competitiveness. I would have merrily pushed us well beyond our limits of safety and thus was glad to have her moderating influence. If we opted to continue on this old route this morning, it might just develop into a snowshoeing marathon to some drifted alpine passes instead of an enjoyable dog mushing tour. Still, I wanted to give this pass at least one try.

"Okay, let's both take the day off from the dog mushing," I agreed. "How about this afternoon I try that trail on showshoes. I'll go alone, no dogs involved, and just be gone a few hours."

"You'll have a nice break from the dogs," Marsha smiled. "Are they getting to you?"

"A bit," I admitted. "I hate having to yell so much. This trail is so overgrown there is always something wrong or something to tell Casey. How about you?"

"Not so bad. Except Jeff, of course," Marsha frowned. The harness she was mending this morning had been chewed almost through in four places.

We soon forgot about our little hairy friends outside, as we launched into a breakfast fit for a king, and in the quantity sufficient for many kings.

The basis for the meal was pancakes, but we couldn't make simple flapjacks, of course. Marsha had premixed the dry ingredients back at the cabin, as she had done with the bannock mix. (There was little difference between our pancakes and bannocks, except our bannock was fried as a much thicker batter, and there was often cornmeal in with the flour. Some folks mixed up a stiff pizza-crust-like dough and fried that for their bannocks.) There was a generous amount of powdered eggs in the mix, so I was able to add extra liquid to make a tolerable facsimile of French crêpes over the glowing ten-gallon stove. Using scorched butter in the pan – and a splash of Scotch from the medicine kit – helped give a richer flavour. The best part was the topping of frozen strawberries and fried bananas. If we'd had overproof brandy, the dish could have been served flambée as well.

A lovely advantage of winter camping was being able to take frozen foods. Fruit, especially strawberries and rhubarb, would shock the taste buds with a slap of summer. We froze a huge bag of peeled bananas in Whitehorse before coming to Horsefall. Eaten slightly thawed, they tasted like creamy sherbet or banana ice cream. I liked them best after the bananas were browned on the outside in a hot pan with a touch of butter. This way the outside was candied and hot, while the centre was still frozen. A poor man's version of Baked Alaska.

"Not bad for an amateur," Marsha grinned approvingly after finishing a plateful.

"Juice, mademoiselle?"

We had a selection of frozen orange, apple or grapefruit juice.

The next round of crêpes was more plebeian. The jars of peanut butter and honey nestled beneath the stove had thawed sufficiently for spreading. Round three's topping was the dried fruit stewing in a dish at the back of the stove.

Needless to say, I didn't make it out on my snowshoeing excursion that afternoon. Like two overfed piglets, we rolled off into the corner and slept most of the day away. When I finally crept out of the tent in mid-afternoon to grab an armload of firewood, I could see our idea was not unique. Soft snores and low sighs drifted up from the nine curled, sleeping dogs. A grey Whiskey Jack was calmly hopping from spot to spot pecking at the snow for traces of their last night's feed. The dogs hadn't left him much.

"You might as well take the day off, Mr. Bird," I whispered. "Everyone else has."

CHAPTER TWENTY-FOUR

TWO ASSAULTS ON LITTLE SUMMIT

My solo hike up Little Summit was a real sweat-raiser.

I picked up the trail at the base of the slope, where it dodged in and out of the last big trees. Ancient axe blazes assured me this was indeed the old route. Further proofs were the sap-encrusted bruises where descending toboggans had crashed when they overshot the corners. In this partially-sheltered area, the snow was both deep and wildly drifted. Around the trunk of each spruce or pine, the blown snow was tilted sharply down into an eddy almost devoid of snow. In these tree wells, I could see the otherwise hidden forest floor. When obstacles lurking under the snow hooked my showshoes and tumbled me onto my face, I sometimes found myself unintentionally nose-to-leaf with the flora. Mountain cranberry, rock tripe, willow catkins, crowberry, club moss, caribou lichen – the variety of determined, tiny plants surviving in this bitter climate has always amazed me. Ever since I'd learned some names, they'd seemed like old friends whenever I took the time to notice their presence.

The snowshoes I was wearing were almost sixty inches long, and weighed about nine pounds. They were *Faber* brand, made in Quebec. The snow in the North is so fine and dry that smaller shoes are used only in thick brush or for stomping a firm trail in front of the dogs. The Yukon Indians make lighter long snowshoes out of birch and unvarnished rawhide, weighing about five pounds, but they aren't as tough as my neoprene-laced, hickory model. For travel over relatively level, open terrain, the local light snowshoes would have been far superior, but today I might have broken them with all the deadfall I was clambering over.

Where the trail left the forest fringe and curved off into the open, it became a deep rut, barely a snowshoe's width across, ascending the slope at a steep slant. The grade must have been thirty percent in places. Whether the shape of the trail was caused by two hundred years of people and pack animals tromping the muskeg, or by spring run-off erosion, or both, the narrowness created an unpleasant path even with a cushion of snow. The drifts had practically filled the trough so I was struggling over and through waist-high snow. After every step upward and forward, I had to shuffle back and shake the snow from my snowshoes to allow the tip to rise up again. My knees were almost touching my chest with each high step forward. The sweat poured down my face and back, even though I was now stripped down to vest and undershirt.

Yet this workout felt like a treat because I was all alone. My pace was not affected by the dogs' progress. To pass a few hours not speaking a word, not even thinking about dogs, was, in itself, therapeutic.

Finally at the crest, I paused to sit on my anorak, eating lunch while soaking in the outstanding view. Far below was the tiny white square of our wall tent. I was too far away to clearly make out the individual dogs. Off in the distance, the Grey Hunter Peaks of McArthur Game Sanctuary shone distinctly in the bright sunshine. North of them, the next landmarks were the Willow Hills. Volcano Mountain was in the same line of view, but much more spectacular in its lone setting guarding our corner of the Pelly-Yukon intersection. Further to my left was Pyroxene Mountain, a reference point for travellers on the old Dawson Road. From this altitude, it was easy to read the extent of last summer's forest fire along the Pelly. The major burns looked salt-and-pepper; charred stumps and blackened trunks poking through the snow. By contrast, even the deciduous bands of the unaffected forest held a hint of green and brown to show the promise of life.

Turning my back to all this, I headed further over the pass, hoping to discover the cabin that Danny had indicated should be past the crest. However, on the far slope I ran immediately into an area recovering from another forest fire. The blaze had obliterated any signs of the trail. For two hours, I climbed over new growth and decaying, charred deadfall, crisscrossing the clearing for signs of a cabin. The terrain on this side was not steep, more like a creased broad bench tilting slightly to the south. Past this narrow plateau, however, was another intimidating wall of mountain. Up one of the draws, of the four to choose from, the old trail must have ascended. Somewhere over the top was *Big Summit*.

"I'd like Marsha to at least see this view. We can leave the tent where it is for now," I thought. "If I make a good track on my way back, the dogs should be able to pull her."

The snow would have overnight to set into a firm surface. I stomped my feet hard with each step, tromping out wide corners on the steeper sections, with the idea of a wild toboggan descent already amusing me. Little Summit should give us a dandy bobsled ride back to the wall tent.

Marsha and team take a break after hauling through the deep snow.
Though it is around 40° below, Marsha needs to wear
only a light anorak because of all the exertion.

The following evening, Marsha wrote a blow-by-blow description of her assault on Little Summit. She had elected to take her team first, to see how they'd do as the lead team. There was an obvious trail to follow, so either Hinglish or Peter should be able to find the way.

This was her journal entry:

Day 6. I had the lifeline tied around the nearest tree, all the dogs in harness, my mitts back on my freezing hands. With an empty toboggan, I figured this was going to be one nice, easy, fast trip today.

"Okay, Hinglish, let's go!"

I had the whole crew hooked up today: Hinglish leading, then little Pete, then goofy Dawson, then Tyhee, my pet, and last, but not least, was Jeff. Hinglish was not clever at understanding which direction he's being told to go. All he knew was SIT (sometimes), and LET'S GO (even before you said it).

Somehow, when I hollered GEE! he took the correct right fork, and we were flying along the newly-scouted trail. Bruce had yesterday snowshoed up the one-mile stretch to break trail for the dogs and to see whether or not we'd continue on this way. The trail gains about 1,000 feet in elevation.

I lost my balance as the toboggan hit some trail ruts and my feet went flying out behind me. My knees hit the back of the toboggan, and my ankles banged on the brake. I held on for dear life to the handlebars as the crew charged across the muskeg, heading for the spruce forest ahead.

"Oh, no," I thought, "I should have wrapped a rope brake on for the first while."

It never dawned on me to yell WHOA, because my team very rarely listened to a command unless it was the one they wanted to hear. As I was dragged along, I had time to notice the sun shining brightly, and wished we were heading for more open country as the willows and trees closed in around us.

Clunk, clunk, crash!

The dogs piled upon one another and the toboggan stopped just before it flattened the wheel dog. Hinglish had already lost the trail. He'd jumped over the fallen trees straight ahead instead of taking the packed trail to the right.

"Oh, boy! Not a great start," I thought.

After I stomped a path over to the trail, and managed to get the dogs and traces sorted out, I found the toboggan was much too long to clear the corner onto my pathway. It was wedged between two willows. "Oh, boy, again...."

I'm pretty strong when I get frustrated, so it took only a few minutes to free my transportation. As soon as the crew felt slack in the traces, they were off, only I wasn't quite ready. I grabbed my mitts with one hand just as they were about to hit the snow. The toboggan charged ahead into low, overhanging willows.

"This is supposed to be fun?" passed through my mind. I wasn't sure where I was for a few minutes because I had to close my eyes and crouch down behind the backboard. When it seemed safe, I found out we'd managed to go another hundred yards in the right direction, in spite of Jeff who, for some reason, had decided he was not interested in pulling today. He just ran in harness to stay away from the toboggan looming directly behind him, three feet away. I ignored him, hoping he'd decide it was boring when he didn't work.

The trail began to climb a bit as the dogs pulled me along through the black spruce, white spruce, some willow, and finally up into summer creek beds scattered with very small trees. These conifers looked as if they had a hard time through the winters since they were so snarled up and crooked.

We stopped for a rest. The clouds dominated the sky, but so far there wasn't any trouble staying warm because I was so busy. The dogs were beginning to bog down in the deep snow, and Jeff was refusing to pull ahead. He was past the point of walking, and was now tugging back so the other dogs were pulling him up the hill, too. I called his name and told him to get busy and that seemed to work for thirty yards. Then he decided he'd had enough and lay down. We stopped.

I went up to him, untangled his traces, and after cuffing his ears, ran to the back to get us on the move once again. But, oh, no. Not Jeff. He rolled up into a ball and the other dogs dragged him for fifty to seventy-five yards until I got fed up and we stopped again. If you stop the team too often, they lose their momentum and it's hard to get them interested in going again. We were already in trouble as they had stopped very willingly.

This was the perfect opportunity to leave Jeff tied to a tree but I'd forgotten to bring a chain.

When we'd gone about halfway up the hill, Jeff quit yet again, so we stopped. I persuaded him, only to turn around and see Dawson heading up the trail on his own accord. He'd wiggled out of his harness and was off exploring. There was no chance he'd come to my call, as he'd been tied for three months and freedom was freedom!

So we were now three dogs pulling, one dog being dragged, and me. I had been off the toboggan and pushing for much of the last while. We carried on after I removed my anorak and one pair of mitts.

Ten or fifteen minutes later, I saw Dawson bounding down the trail, tail high in the air, and a big, happy smile on his face. This time, when I called him, he decided he'd come, but first he'd go visit with Hinglish and the crew to begin a fight. "Oh, boy...."

They'd only just begun when I came bounding through the knee-deep snow to pull them apart, and Dawson was harnessed up again.

I was ready to pack it in and walk home, but by this time Bruce had arrived with his dogs and urged me to carry on until we could see Volcano Mountain and the surrounding area. I guess the dogs were fed up, too. Even following Bruce's team, my dogs barely crawled up to the view point.

After I calmed down, and Bruce fed me some lunch, I was in a much bet-

ter head space to appreciate the view across the Yukon River valley and far beyond. It was worth it! We could see for miles and miles. Amazing.

Wheel dog Jeff managed to run just ahead of the toboggan on the way down and all went extremely smoothly, except when I lost the toboggan once into a stand of black spruce. Dawson stayed in his harness, and I even got to ride all the way home.

"Yippeeeee!"

CHAPTER TWENTY-FIVE

ONE LAST FLING

W e'd gone about as far up Danny's old trail as the deep snow and our ability to find the trail would permit. Climbing any higher would surely mean spending days and days packing trail with snowshoes through the tall drifts. Another choice, which would take us lower in elevation from this highland setting, was to branch off down Seventeen Mile Creek toward the Yukon River. Our tent was pitched not a mile from this creek's headwater bog.

After checking the scale on the topographic map, I told Marsha, "To reach the river going down the Seventeen Mile Creek valley, it must be about thirty miles as the raven flies."

"How far is that as the dog team wanders?" she asked wryly.

I could tell that, after her *easy jaunt* up Little Summit, she was taking my estimations with a grain of salt.

"I'll go cut some trail in that direction, just to see how difficult it will be," was my suggestion.

"Great. I'll sit here and sew," replied Marsha.

Once again, I strode off on snowshoes, axe in hand and lunch in pocket. By picking a trail just on the margin between the evergreen forest and the willow thickets, there was a minimum of chopping to do. The problem lay where either type of growth petered out and the trail had to be carved through a jungle of willow trees or across a tangle of virgin-growth deadfall. Though I ignored a few huge logs we'd need to lift the toboggans over, my progress down the valley still wasn't fast.

A bonus with this route compared to an alpine trail was the wealth of animal sign. Wolf tracks, dwarfing even Hinglish's big pawprints, threaded their way through the big timber, conspicuously avoiding the trails of the smaller animals. Rabbit tracks, droppings and tufts of fur appeared so frequently I ceased to pay them any attention. There were also fox, squirrel, lynx, marten and what I believed

Though the other dogs on Marsha's team are content to rest,
Hinglish is raring to go!

were old wolverine prints. The latter sobered me somewhat, but I took courage when I encountered no other. Perhaps this wolverine was just passing through the area.

By mid-afternoon, I was exhausted, hungry and ready for a rest. On a low bluff to my right was a perfect vantage point where I could sit in the sun and ascertain exactly how far I'd cut. To add to the intrigue, there was a single set of wolf tracks leading up the snowy bank. I followed his lead.

On the crest of the rise was the object of the wolf's attention. It was a bright orange fuel drum left by a helicopter pilot as a fuel cache. The wolf had peed on it. I brushed snow off a nearby log to sit on and settled into my cold pancakes and dried fruit. This time I'd carried the vacuum flask, so there was hot apple juice to quench my desperate thirst.

The map held rather disappointing news for me. Five hours' exertion equalled only three miles travelled. Ahead where the valley narrowed, the cutting would be considerably harder. It would take at least a week's work to push through to the river. I was just realizing these discouraging thoughts when a curious noise from below caught my attention.

"Now where's he going? Does he think you guys are mountain goats?" It was Marsha's voice. "Let's go, Casey. Give it a try. C'mon, Hinglish, get up there. Attaboy, Loki."

It was interesting to hear Marsha work the dogs. I'm sure she didn't realize how much she was talking, and how loud her voice was raised.

"Let's go, Casey, get up. Go get Bruce. Where's Bruce? C'mon now, you guys, let's go, let's go."

I played dumb and sat on my perch until Casey's head appeared over the crest. He wagged his tail and leaned into his harness to reach my outstretched hand.

"C'mon, Casey! What are you stopping for? Let's go!" Marsha was still out of sight down the bank – four more dogs and the length of the toboggan away. She couldn't see that my pet was on his back, trying to coax me into scratching his tummy.

Marsha looked relieved when I stood on the barrel and waved at her. "Did you call for a taxi?" she shouted.

"Yes, please."

Marsha had come prepared, so we shared an extensive picnic on the barrel, with Casey warming our feet. The dogs she'd brought were a selection of the best from both teams.

"Tell me again why you're so interested in getting to the mouth of this creek," Marsha asked. "I think it is lovely right here."

"Remember that murder I told you about? Where the body was in the root cellar?"

"Uh huh," she replied, obviously more interested in getting a tan on her face.

"Well," I continued anyway, "the murderer's cabin was somewhere near the mouth of this creek, on the bank of the Yukon River. I'd like to find the site and check on how much sunshine he would have received there in the winter. My theory is that lack of direct sunlight tends to make anyone looney."

"What about the victim?" asked Marsha. "Was he looney, too?"

"Maybe. But not from lack of sun," I theorized. "Danny says the victim's cabin was on some island downstream where the valley opens quite wide. I think part of the island washed away so we won't be able to find anything of Smith's place.

But I'd love to find exactly where Davis, the murderer, had his cabin. I want to see how close the hills are."

"What if we go back to the Yukon River the way we came, and follow the ice down to this murderer's cabin?" asked Marsha.

"That's the conclusion I just reached, sitting here looking at the map," I grinned. "But it'll mean lots of travelling on the ice, which could be scary."

Marsha turned the subject back to working the dogs, and I mentioned how much she had chattered to the dogs as they came up the bank.

"We'll *both* have to break the habit," she said. "I guess we both talk like that all the time."

"Do I? I don't mean to."

"How about shouting?" Marsha added. "Do you know how loud you command them?"

Danny had told us if you talk too often, the dogs will stop paying attention.

"I guess if you shout all the time, it loses its effect after a while," I offered.

"Remember Don Mark's saying?" Marsha laughed. *"You don't have to yell at the dogs, they can hear quite well."*

We agreed to remind each other to be quieter on the trail. We had Abbie's suggestion to follow if we had to keep our mouths moving. Back at Fort Selkirk she had told us, "If you gotta talk to your dogs, be like me. I used to sing to my dogs."

The most appropriate song we could think of to sing on the ride back, even though it was long past Christmas, was: *"Jingle Bells, Jingle Bells, Jingle all the way. Oh, what fun it is to ride in a five-dog open sleigh, eh? Oh, Jingle Bells...."*

Next morning as we disassembled the stove and untied all the ropes, I realized how attached we'd become to our tent. This cosy, bright, warm second home had taken most of the struggle out of camping. At night after the stove cooled, the temperature was only marginally warmer than outdoors, but our sleeping bags were dry and we'd climbed into them warm instead of chilled. Our equipment and clothes were all mended, letters had been written, we'd even had a chance to read a few books. We could understand better now how people camped and travelled all winter in years gone by. A big tent, a stove and dogs to pull everything seemed to be the answer for this climate.

If Plan 'A' was following Danny's old trail through to the Selwyn, and Plan 'B' was detouring off down Seventeen Mile Creek, we were now on Plan 'C': heading back to Horsefall and then going down the frozen Yukon River. We hit

Our wall tent camp at the forest's edge. Note that we had poles for the structure this time – sometimes we used ropes between nearby trees.

the trail early. Breaking camp took only an hour, including packing the tent and stove, and harnessing the dogs. They were raring to go, even the lazy ones. We split them into the regular teams, except I traded Mutt for Jeff so that my dogs could try their luck at training the indolent Siberian. We knew Mutt would work his heart out in wheel position of Marsha's team if Tyhee was right ahead of him. Young Mutt had just learned to lift his leg when he peed, but he hadn't figured out yet that Tyhee was an *it*.

"Hang on, Sweetie!" I yelled back to my partner as we freed our lifelines.

"Yippeeeeeeee."

The trail had settled and refrozen so the surface was as firm underfoot as compacted beach sand. The dogs dug their claws in and ran full speed along the narrow track, throwing dry snow into the air as they powered around the corners. The toboggan rocked back and forth like a bobsled speeding down an Olympic course.

Our two brush camps flashed by in quick succession, seeming ridiculously close now that the trail was located, cleared and packed. What took us days to cover on the way in, was slipping by in a tenth the time today. The scariest sections were through the overhanging willows. Here, where the dogs insisted on increasing speed even more because of rabbit scents, branches were whipping at our faces, or rapping our knuckles as we ducked blindly behind the backboards.

As we turned onto our packed Six Mile Creek trail, I noted proudly we hadn't needed to talk to the dogs much at all. When we had, they'd listened.

Out on the Yukon River the dogs trotted happily, their ears up, eyes looking ahead toward Horsefall Creek. We'd been gone all of eight days, and they seemed to have missed their home chains.

With little effort, they scampered across the expanse of ice and hauled the toboggans up the steep bank and into the yard. There was our cabin, exactly as we'd left it, with the windows boarded over and the wheelbarrow propped against the door. There wasn't as much as a footprint from the wolverines against whom we'd barricaded the cabin.

As we began the long job of hauling all the gear into the cabin, the dogs were merrily digging up bits of cow skull stashed under the snow and marking all the trees within reach of their chains. Lucky climbed onto his log shelter, then had a better idea. He started to pace back and forth, staring at the freezer chest, smiling and wagging his tail. The Bacon Burglar was glad to be home.

CHAPTER TWENTY-SIX

HEADING FOR CARMACKS:
CHECKING THE FOOD SUPPLIES

"We could do another camping trip downriver right now," Marsha explained, "but it would leave us with almost no dog food when we got back.

"Or," she continued, "we could go to a store first and be stocked up for the rest of the winter."

I could tell which she preferred. Marsha had a fair amount of squirrel in her nature. She loved to have heaps of food stored away, ready for any eventuality.

She'd calculated the people food so well we could have made it through with what we had. But I'd grossly underestimated how much dog food we'd use over the winter, hoping there would be a few caribou or a moose to help spin out the expensive commercial feeds. We would need an additional four hundred pounds of dog food to make it through to break-up.

"The road out from the farm isn't passable for the truck, but we could make it through to the highway with the dogs," I suggested, "but then the Pelly Crossing Store is closed until summer… We'd need a truck to drive from there to Stewart Crossing or Carmacks."

"How about going to Carmacks along Cor's trail, on the river?" asked Marsha.

The idea would have been unheard of not long ago. It had taken all our courage to make a trail as far as Fort Selkirk to visit Danny and Abbie. Over that six-mile stretch, there were still a half-dozen places where the current was untamed. The sight of the churning, rushing water streaming by, carrying chunks of ice as big as a person, each slammed violently into the ice lip at the lower end of the opening, made me wonder how long one of us would survive in that icy torrent. The unsettling reality was that, like the other floating debris, we would be battered to a pulp, then sucked under the ice surface to drown. Pieces of a body might make it to the Bering Sea, but, as likely, no trace would ever be found.

"It must be at least eighty miles – maybe three days mushing – if all goes well," I warned her.

"We'll be careful," Marsha said with a twinkle in her eye. "And we can rent a motel room in Carmacks and take a hot shower!"

After so many months away from running hot water, that was powerful incentive indeed.

We first had to do a thorough inventory of our supplies and prepare food for the trip. One time-consuming chore would be to grind flour for the bread, muffins and bannock mix that would be our fuel on the trail.

All our grains had been brought to the cabin whole, except the oats which were rolled. We knew whole wheat flour would go rancid over a period of time, so having our flour in the form of wheat berries meant we could still enjoy all the nutrients without the spoilage problem. Before we started to grind our own grains, we had no idea how fast flour became stale and what a difference in flavour freshly ground flour made to recipes.

Our hand-powered grinder was mounted on the back wall of the cabin where it was out of the way and could be left set up. After some experimenting, Marsha determined the optimum height was such that the centre of the handle swing was right at waist level. I lag-bolted the frame to the log wall to make it solid and we covered the hopper with a cloth to keep it clean when not in use.

The exercise involved was great for the pectoral muscles, so much so that a half-hour session raised quite a sweat. We took turns, trying to average thirty minutes per day to keep a little ahead for bread baking days. A good portion of our time spent grinding was passed dreaming about having a bicycle to power the grinding instead. Using our legs would have been much easier.

Read more about grains and other food in Appendix II.

Searching through the root cellar, we discovered a vermin problem. Not only had a weird hole been chewed into a plastic pail of peanut butter, but two mouse traps were missing. Footprints in the sand floor explained that a squirrel had taken the small traps. We promptly set a marten-size leg-hold trap in the crawl space to nab him. Droppings around and on the pail turned out to be from mice who had gnawed all around a ridge of the plastic lid until the centre collapsed. Apparently they couldn't get their teeth into the flat surfaces and had to nibble on the ridge to gain entrance. We set a few more traps for them, baiting them with raisins smeared in peanut butter. At least we now knew what they really liked to eat.

By this late in the winter, the root cellar was definitely lacking in variety and some shelves resembled Mother Hubbard's famed cupboard, yet the cellar had done yeoman's service over the cold months.

Marsha identified a few groceries that would be necessary and added a list of others that would be well-deserved luxuries. Any food brought back from Carmacks would get frozen on the trip, so we would have to gorge ourselves on fresh oranges and the like while in the town. A frozen ham and some chicken would be a change from lynx and grouse (gifts from the trappers), but the trip's real purpose would be hauling dog fuel.

"If we're going to bring back something like five hundred pounds of cargo," Marsha pointed out, "we can't be packing too much of our camping gear along."

"You're right. Just considering bulk alone, there won't be room on the toboggans for everything."

Marsha didn't say anything for a few minutes. It was obvious to both of us the tent and stove would have to be sacrificed.

"Well," she said finally, looking at the bright side, "we'll appreciate that motel room even more after sleeping out under the stars for a few nights. You're *sure* there is a hot shower there, right?"

CHAPTER TWENTY-SEVEN

HIGH OCTANE WITH SIX DOGS

During the darkest times of December, never being in strong, direct sunshine was downright depressing. We had to climb a hill every few days just to catch a noon glimpse of the pale golden globe. All through stark, cold January, the line of sunlight taunted us as it splayed on the cliff face behind us, never dipping down to our flat. The month of February held promising moments, as well as a sprinkle of Forty Below temperatures to keep us on our toes.

Now it was March: Nature exploded with activity and colour. The sun returned gloriously, even triumphantly. Though the nights continued to be nippy, there was no doubt spring's sun was warm on our faces and vitally hot in our hearts. The forest floor became busy with the traffic of little feet as the rabbits and squirrels scampered about, their hyperactivity a celebration of the hotter weather. Birds sang and fluttered in the trees.

At last, it was again pure fun to be outdoors. We sat on the woodpile, feeling healthy and bursting with life. There was less need for knowledge of winter survival techniques to enjoy ourselves under the newly-arrived noonday sun. Like a great weight being cast off, the constant requirement to *keep it together* every moment could now be relaxed a little. For our camping trips, there was less chance of a sudden, dangerous cold snap. And, should it get bitterly cold, we knew it couldn't last too long.

Marsha woke me at dawn on March Third, "We can't go to Carmacks today. You might as well sleep in."

It was a fine idea of hers to wake me to tell me to keep on sleeping. I might have appreciated it more had she included an explanation. "Why can't we go?" I asked sleepily. "We've got everything already packed on the toboggans."

"It's snowing. Big, fluffy flakes. You can't see more than twenty feet through it," Marsha muttered as she crawled back in beside me. "There's about four inches of new fall on top of the two we got yesterday."

The cabin's warmth was bewildering, until I got up and looked at the outside thermometer: it was Thirty-Three Above – just above freezing. Yesterday, before the first wave of storm clouds crowded over us, the reading had been Thirty-Eight Below. With this warmer March weather had come the snows.

Marsha put the unexpected day at home to good use, baking us fruit cake and muffins to eat on the trip. She'd discovered how to substitute for sugar in recipes and still produce a sweet-tasting result. One way was to chop up dates very finely and stew them into a syrup that could be added as part of the liquid to any batter. Skim milk powder was another sweetener. When wheat berries were sprouted, they tasted almost like candy. Besides using them in baking, sometimes Marsha would just roast sprouts on a pan for a sweet snack. She also used blackstrap molasses and honey as other white sugar substitutes. For muffins that were to be eaten frozen with our lunches, an extra amount of fat (butter, margarine or lard) in the batter made them easier to chew when cold and hard.

When the storm blew over around noon, I left with six dogs and a snack bag full of fresh muffins, bound for Wolverine Creek, packing the trail to give us a head-start for the next day. After a three-day rest, every dog was anxious for exercise, but I didn't think I could handle all nine without a load to slow the toboggan. As it was, I had wrapped two loops of dog chain under the empty toboggan before starting and was barely able to hold on for the first mile. Even when one dog had to poop, the others wouldn't stop. Poor Loki had the most indignant look on his face as he hopped down the trail, trying to attend to his business. Only when the two leaders, Casey and Hinglish, heard the call, did the train come to a halt.

"Now that's power," I said to myself, keeping one hand on the handlebars at all times. If they left without me, I might have to walk clear to Danny's before they'd take their next break.

I was still thinking about the difference adding two extra dogs to my usual four was making when we arrived at the Robertses' cabin at the old Fort Selkirk townsite. We'd covered the six miles in twenty-five minutes.

"You getting rich, I guess," Danny chuckled. "Now you got six dogs."

"How many is the most you ever used, Danny?" I asked him as we ducked inside so I could warm up and have something to drink. The dogs sat in their traces, in a long dignified row, except for Dawson, who was doing somersaults and rolling in the snow. It was easier to leave him for now and straighten his traces before we left.

"Eight or nine, sometimes," said Danny, pouring me a cup of jet-black pekoe tea. "But most of the time we used four, five, maybe six dogs. That's all you need."

"Can you imagine how the racers handle a dozen, or up to twenty dogs, like in the Rendezvous races?" I reached for a chunk of Danny's delicious fluffy white bannock. He could fry bread tastier than anyone. I think his secret was mixing in lots of white sugar and *Tang* orange drink powder.

"Must be crazy to do that," Abbie shook her head. "I couldn't hold on to the toboggan." She passed me the red jam.

We got to talking about what they used to eat on the trail if they were going to do a quick, lightly-loaded trip, such as our dash into Carmacks was to be.

"Moose meat," said Abbie. "We cooked it at home or in the tent at the Selwyn. Then when we were hungry, we ate it just like that, or heated it up over a fire."

"What else?" I prodded. "Did you take potatoes or rice or beans?"

"No. Just moose meat, already cooked," she said, "and bannock or biscuits."

To Abbie, fried bread (bannock) was Indian bread and oven-baked bread was the white man's style.

"But what about breakfast?" I wondered. "Did you eat oatmeal?"

"Moose meat and biscuits," said Danny. "Same thing all the time. And tea."

As I untangled Dawson and prepared to continue up to Wolverine Creek, Danny reminded me he had traps set along the bank. With this in mind, I kept Casey up front until we got past the last of Danny's traps. He was quicker at responding to a call of *Let's go. Run. On by!* than Hinglish, so I was more confident he'd pull every dog past the sets even if one was curious. Although Marsha and I had wondered whether Hinglish had learned anything from his experience in a trap last month, I wasn't about to gamble to find out.

Later, I switched Hinglish for Casey, to give the younger one more experience and confidence. The shadow of Cor's old track was barely visible, making a straightforward route for Hinglish to follow. With nary a *gee* nor *haw* to decide for miles and miles, he had a perfect opportunity to lead. Originally, we had him pegged for a wheel dog, since he was one of the biggest dogs and stocky-boned. But Hinglish had such an eager attitude and agreeable disposition, Marsha had moved him progressively forward to inspire the others in her squad. It looked funny to see Hinglish and tiny Peter nose to tail, but they were the two cheerleaders and worked best out front. Today, Peter was at home, and Casey was the one encouraging the big black-and-white mongrel to run his heart out.

The thick layer of new snow was no problem to the dogs, who ran or trotted merrily, pulling me and the empty toboggan easily along the river bank. The sun

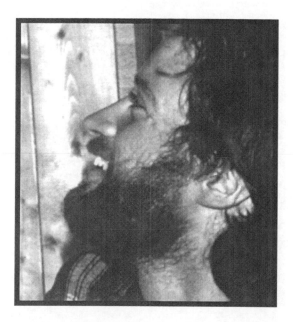

I loved to listen to our neighbours tell tales and explain their lifestyle.

was shining so brightly I wished for sunglasses to cut the glare. In the forest, there were at least some shadows and greenery to moderate the harsh white; out here on the river, I was squinting into an overexposed photograph. When we reached Wolverine Creek, I was relieved to turn for home and put my back to the direct light.

Danny had a snowmobile trail up the Pelly River, past the Johnson homestead to the Bradleys' farm. Though we would be packing yesterday's snow on this stretch also, I thought it would be more fun to return to Horsefall along this route. It would be a chance to check for any new mail that might have been dropped at Hugh's cabin by one of the trappers.

The dogs responded with enthusiasm, running with eyes wide and ears cocked ahead. I switched Mutt up to lead position to see if he had any potential at that spot. After only a half mile, when he baulked at making a gee-haw choice, I moved him back rather than spoil his experience. Though he'd need more time harnessed one back from the leader to gain confidence, I was pleased he would go ahead on the straight stretches. Some of the dogs, like Lucky or Loki, would stand bewildered if put out front. There was less pressure on a wheel or team dog.

Halfway to the farm, I checked in with the Johnsons to see if they had any

*Hugh Bradley rolls a cigarette while we drink coffee and
I get caught up on the farm news.*

outgoing mail. Lew Johnson invited me in to warm up and plunked a mug of
steaming, thick coffee in front of me. It smelled wonderful! Before realizing it,
I was through my second cup and had eaten six of Carol Johnson's cookies and
two pieces of cake.

Carol, who shared Marsha's concerns about nutrition, smiled at my compli-
ments on her baking. "Well, I did use a touch of sugar to make it sweeter," she
admitted, "but not much."

They had been poring over seed catalogues when I arrived. Their vegetable
garden was so productive they had extra rutabagas and potatoes in their root cellar.
We made a deal that I'd swap them vegetables for some cheese we would buy in
Carmacks. We wrapped the produce in newspaper and a cardboard box to keep
it from freezing on my journey home.

"It's okay, boys," I told the dogs as we loaded the cargo onto the toboggan.
"It's veggies; nothing for you to eat."

"Good luck on your trip to Carmacks," Lew said, "and be careful of the ice in
the Ingersoll Islands. If you fall in, you might not get out."

"We'll be careful, Lew. Thanks for the goodies, Carol."

After their rest, the dogs were full of pep again and bounced me to the farm in
no time at all. I had some difficulty persuading them to turn off the river at Hugh's

cabin, because the cattle were further along the ice, drinking from a water hole. From a distance, a cow might look like food to a dog. Up closer, a dog would be more respectful. It took tipping the toboggan to slow them down to a speed where I could run ahead and grab onto their harnesses. After a rap on each snout, they reluctantly obeyed my directions, and walked up to the small cabin on the bank.

"Hello, Bruce," said Hugh, poking his head out the door. "We just had our coffee break, but seeing as you're here, we'll do 'er all over again."

I passed on outgoing mail from the Robertses, Johnsons and us, and Hugh sorted ours from the bundle Peter Isaac had just brought in from the post office at Pelly Crossing. There was a handful of letters from family, and a rejection slip from a publisher. The secretary at the New York firm must have been having a bad day, because she included not only my rejection, but another letter as well that had the spaces for author's name, the title, and a one line comment all blank.

"That one will be handy if you want to fill in your own reason for being turned down," offered Hugh. "It will save you the price of postage next time you apply."

"Well, I wouldn't know what to do with a million dollars if they liked my book manuscript anyway," I announced, and drank heartily from the large mug.

Even mixed half-and-half with fresh cream, Hugh's coffee was powerful. It no sooner hit my stomach, than my whole body began to tingle. I wolfed down a few cookies to settle my stomach, and tried to listen to the conversation.

"Our Don's got three lynx now… Wonder when that mining company is coming through… How's Abbie's health… Did Marsha like the trip on Danny's old trail… How long was Cor's toboggan… The hens are laying again now… Did you water Marjorie's rabbits this morning…"

Hugh's, Dick's, and Peter's voices were weaving in and out of my consciousness. My eyes were having trouble focusing and I felt a trifle light-headed.

"I think I'd better go," I finally mumbled. In my imagination, all the cups of tea at Danny's, the coffees at Johnsons' and here, and all the sweet goodies were lined up in a row and I had to drink and eat them all again. Yet each time one was finished, it reappeared at the end of the line. I was doomed to a dizzying dilemma. The caffeine had been too much after a three-month near-abstinence, and the sugar had topped it off. The dense tobacco smoke in the small cabin was not helping either.

"Gotta go, not much light left." I stood up and felt my head swimming. "Thanks for the coffee, Hugh. See you, guys."

Hugh followed me out to help me swing the team around. I was especially grateful, because it looked to me as if there were twelve fuzzy dogs, strung out as six pairs of identical twins. Grabbing all the handlebars without daring to look at my trembling hands, I gave Casey the *okay* and nodded to my host.

"Drive carefully," Hugh said.

The dogs knew every step of this trail by heart, so I could lean back and close my eyes, opening my mouth wide to draw in that cool, fresh, clean, forest air. Without a word from me, Casey clattered over the ice of Farm Creek, and swung onto the old Dawson Road. By the time the dogs had trotted up the hill and were running across the plateau, my mind was clearing of the dizziness. Instead, the first symptoms of a dandy headache were setting up shop in my skull.

"Neighbours are nice, but I'll have to learn to turn down their coffee and black tea," I said to myself. "I may never make it as a true Yukoner – I can't handle the pace."

CHAPTER TWENTY-EIGHT

TOM, DICK AND CURLY

"*Y*ee*hawww!*" Marsha shouted as her toboggan tilted precariously around the first turn. With half loads, there would be little slowing the dogs today when they really wanted to fly.

Marsha and I were well bundled against the nippy, pre-dawn air. As the dogs' breath froze on their whiskers and fur, it looked as if they too had white wolf trim pulled up as breathing tunnels. It was a treat to be outside during this magical moment of sunrise. The halftones and silhouettes of our high, craggy basalt walls contrasted bleakly with the pastel sunrise washing over the valley floor. Individual snowflakes sparkled in the direct rays, winking millions of eyes at our long caravan. Fissures in the massive ice sheets, and ridges where subsurface pressures had buckled the pans, shone like multifaceted diamonds in the sun, or glowed a haunting, glacier blue from the shadows.

We paused at Fort Selkirk only long enough to drop off mail from Hugh's and collect Danny's shopping list for Roxy's Trading Post in Carmacks.

"We need some more tea," said Danny. "And, make sure it's *BLACK* tea, not that hippie tea or something." He added a big wink after his joke. The neighbours referred to us as *the hippies* because of my long hair and our quirky ideas about nutrition and other topics. We didn't mind the epithet, nor think it disparaging.

"You know, I wish we could come," Abbie said from the doorway, holding Timmy in her arms. "But I'm not healthy any more."

"You and Danny have helped us so much," Marsha replied, giving her a hug, "telling us what to eat, explaining about harnesses and camping, that it will seem like you are with us."

"We'd better be going while it is still cool," I said, nodding towards the southern sky. "It'll be nice to take a break later from staring into the sun." Most of our journey would be south or south-east, a real test of sunglasses.

"How long do you think it will take us?" Marsha asked Danny, as she untangled Dawson's traces and patted Tyhee's nearby nose.

"I don't know," he shrugged, "maybe they got more snow up that way, maybe not so much. I don't know if you're gonna find that guy Cor's trail with all this snow. Maybe you're gonna have to make your own… Three days, maybe four, I guess."

"I'm hoping three," I told him.

"Be careful of the ice through Hell's Gate. Watch where it's darker: could be running water with this new snow over thin ice."

"We'll be careful," Marsha smiled.

"Listen to your lead dog," Abbie threw in. "He's gonna know if it's okay or too weak."

"See you in a week," we called as the dogs tugged eagerly on their traces. "Okay! *Let's go!*"

Each time we came up to one of Danny's traps, I stopped my team well before it, and waited for Marsha's pack to catch up. After all nine were sitting, albeit most reluctantly, Marsha stomped her claw brake hard into the trail, and signalled me with her hand. Then she waited until my dogs had sprinted past the cubby set before starting her team. Having my squad up ahead distracted hers from investigating any fishy smells; when Hinglish got the *okay*, they chased after us at full gallop.

At noon, we reached Wolverine Creek, and stopped for lunch at the end of my packed trail. While the workers sprawled languidly on the snow, we humans chewed on dried bananas and sipped rosehip tea from the thermos. From our perch on a gigantic drift log, we could see a faint track winding across the shimmering snow, and out of sight around the corner. We agreed to keep following Cor's choice of the safest route, unless it led to obviously dangerous sections.

From my summer canoe trips on the Yukon, I recognized the hills ahead. In the valley now blocked from our view were the countless Ingersoll Islands, and along their west limit, a stretch of swift water known to the sternwheeler crews as Hell's Gate. This was the area locals were wary of travelling on in winter. Years before, when Danny maintained a trail from Selkirk to the since-abandoned village of Minto, he had always used an overland route around this part of the river, opting to follow a portion of the Dawson Stage Road. This meant he had to contend with steep grades on the hills, as well as deeper snow at the higher altitudes. We were gambling on the river route because the ice had frozen unusually thick and smooth this year. We would save ourselves the awesome job of packing thirty miles of trail with snowshoes, knocking at least two days off the travelling time.

Also, our flat river trail would be much easier for the dogs with the heavy loads on our return.

"Well, if Cor found a way through, then so can we," I said, calling an end to our break.

The dogs slowly climbed to their feet, stretching and flexing their stiffened leg muscles. Peter yawned, curling his tongue and closing his eyes. No doubt he'd rather sleep all afternoon in the sunshine.

"Did anyone hear if Cor made it to Carmacks?" Marsha yelled from the back of her toboggan.

I thought for a moment, and could only shrug. Even Danny, who listens faithfully to the CBC radio from Whitehorse, hadn't mentioned receiving word about Cor. But he had heard another radio warning of a bear wandering around north of Carmacks. The possible connection hadn't occurred to me before.

"Yikes," I thought, and checked under my toboggan cover to make sure my rifle was handy. "Dangerous ice, blizzards and a winter bear. This is a hell of a way to go shopping."

We paused for a moment so I could scamper up a bank and cut us two long poles. The anxiety was chewing at my stomach. The gee-lines (or *lifelines*, as Marsha called them), which we often had coiled out of the way, were now strung out to their fullest, so the following musher would have the trailing rope to grab should the lead toboggan break through. We were approaching the most dangerous area.

Where the river was narrowest, above Wolverine Creek, one side was wide open and roaring. A cloud of fog hung over the channel ominously. Cor's trail swung over to within a snowball's toss of the sheer edge, and I wondered whether to call off the lead dog.

"Hey! Hey!" Marsha was shouting and whistling to get my attention.

I whoaed my team and waited until her dogs were sitting around my feet. "What's up?"

"That looks scary!" she called, pointing at the churning waters ahead.

We held a conference and decided I'd go ahead with my crew, and check the thickness every hundred feet or so.

Casey couldn't have heard our decision, because he tried to run full steam across the river. Only after jumping on the brake for a ways, and shouting all manner of curses, did I finally get him to stop.

Loki wagged his tail lazily as I inched, hand over hand, along their traces until I reached Casey. If I was to fall through, I wanted a good hold onto at least a harness. I had my long pole with me as well. Casey panted happily and looked curiously at me. He was ready to share my excitement, but a mite confused about how. He offered to shake a paw.

I swung the axe ahead, and let it chop down into the trail. There was a *THOCK* as the steel struck hard ice under the snow. It looked white and solid.

"Is it *okay*?" Marsha called.

"Geez, don't use that word!" I shouted, but the dogs were already moving forward. In a moment, Loki, Mutt and Lucky were crowded next to Casey and me. Lucky was staring at the chipped ice as if there might be food involved.

The ice hadn't cracked under our combined weight, so I felt more confident. Chipping away at the hole until it was ankle deep, I assured myself we had plenty of safety here. The total thickness might have been eight inches to six feet for all I could tell without cutting right the way through.

After that anticlimax, we relied more on Casey's judgment, and I only stopped to check when it looked a bit dicey. Although by following Cor's track we came within a few toboggan lengths of open water, the ice beneath us was never less than the depth of the holes I tarried to chop. Surprisingly, there was usually thick, solid ice right up to the edges of the open leads.

As the river widened out into the maze of islands, we kept to the east for a stretch, winding through gravel bars and willow-crowned islets. When the track suddenly swung west toward the Hell's Gate channel, I looked back at Marsha for suggestions. Her forehead was lined with concern, and her jaw clenched tight. She shrugged and nodded her assent.

"Go slowly," she shouted over the rumble of the toboggans. "Be careful."

At one point, Casey baulked at following the faint track, where it was heading between two pond-like open patches. I didn't question his hesitation, but called him back immediately.

"Good boy, Casey," I told him when he'd swung his mates around and come back to my side.

I took both the pole and axe, and scouted out a wide bypass. I could use the pole to thump the ice ahead to ensure it could support my weight. As I walked forward, I kept that pole tucked under my arm to straddle a hole if I did fall through. A long rope was attached to my waist, leading back to my toboggan. Marsha tended to my dogs until I was beyond the scary section, and then she sent them after me.

"Let's go, let's go," I called as Casey trotted to me. Holding his collar, I steered him onward along the continuation of Cor's upriver track. When the toboggan slid alongside, I stepped aboard and waved to Marsha. She had waited to see if all was safe before committing her five unruly beasts. She caught up within a quarter-mile. How they loved to play catch-up!

Stopping to strip off a layer of clothing. The sun is baking us near Minto.

As the afternoon wore on, this routine was repeated time and time again. In a few places, the trail led right into open water, and out the far side. The river had been eating new leads, and possibly closing others since Cor had been this way.

Once we were past the Hell's Gate, there was another ten-mile stretch to negotiate before the Minto Landing townsite. Minto represented our destination for tonight, and a healthy third of the total distance to Carmacks. Unfortunately, the dogs were much less enthused about getting there than we were. No doubt this endless highway of white was getting rather boring for them. Their pace had slowed to a saunter, marginally faster than human walking speed.

The distinctive hills behind Minto seemed only a hop, skip and a jump away, but were much further on the map. Hours later, we were staring at the same view, hardly any bigger. Small wonder the canines were bored. We played for a while with different leaders, but the enthusiastic ones from the following team mysteriously lost their drive when placed out in the very front and confronted with snow and ice for as far ahead as the eye could see. Hinglish had the most energy, so he led much of this stretch.

When the tumbledown cabins of the deserted village finally came into view, there were eleven sighs of relief and a new spark of life in us all. Awakened by the smells and sounds of the forest, the dogs pranced up the ramp at the boat landing, and trotted anxiously along the old road. Lucky was particularly active, his head bobbing to see past Hinglish.

Since there might be a turn or two to decide before we found our resting spot, I traded back to have Casey head the procession. With the delay, Lucky was growing more and more frantic, tugging at his traces and peering wide-eyed down the trail.

"Lucky must have seen a rabbit," Marsha chuckled. "I hope they all see it and pull us somewhere quickly. It's going to be dark in forty-five minutes."

"If I pass a decent camping spot and you like it, just shout and we'll stop," I called back. "I don't want to be setting up in the dark either."

A hundred yards along the road was a fresh toboggan track, and our dogs scampered along it. Before we knew it, we were parked in front of a big log building, our arrival being announced by five or six chained sled dogs. Our mutts tugged to get at the strangers, but our tipped toboggans thwarted their attempts.

I banged a stick on my backboard to quiet our dogs, and had our portion of the racket under control until the door opened and an old Indian fellow walked out. Immediately, Lucky started warbling and dancing in his traces, which touched off all the others again.

"You sure got noisy dogs," the man said. "Where'd you come from?"

I gave him a babbled explanation of who, what, where, why and when, including a comment that, "If you come from Pelly Crossing, you might know some of the people who lent us dogs."

"Hello, Curly," he said looking past me. "Dawson, what are you doing here?"

It turned out he was Tommy McGinty, whom we'd never met. The dog-lending transaction had all been done through intermediaries, and Dick Bradley had picked up the dogs. We knew this trapper only from stories, and by his generosity.

"Did you call Lucky *Curly*?" I asked him, not sure I'd heard him correctly.

"This dog, here, his name is Curly," Tommy said, not quite sure why I was confused. "And that black dog back there is his brother. Same litter." He pointed to a chunky mutt tied behind a small outbuilding. The two looked no more alike than Peter and Hinglish.

"Curly!" Marsha shrieked. "His name is *Curly*?" She almost fell over from laughter. Lucky was without a doubt the least curly dog in the world. His fur was straight, his body angular, his tail crooked; there wasn't a hint of anything circular in his whole being.

"Hey, Curly," I teased him, but he didn't respond any more to that name than to Lucky. He was being dignified and ignoring me completely.

Tommy must have figured we were both looney, laughing so hard about his dog's name. My explanation about Dick forgetting the real name, and our re-christening him, failed to lift the wary look on Tommy's weather-beaten face.

Surveying his other dogs, I felt embarrassed ours were so much skinnier. Clearly the slur that *Indians half-starve their sled dogs* had little validity; we were far worse culprits.

"I went sixteen miles today with my dogs," he said. "Real hard work, up in the hills. Lots of snow, and the toboggan kept icing up. Hard for the dogs to pull at all. Every mile, I had to stop and scrape the ice off the bottom of my toboggan with a knife."

We'd come over thirty miles today, but had experienced no problems at all with our plastic bases. Tommy pointed to his home-made birch toboggan leaned against the shed: the thick wood base was worn smooth and rounded at the edges.

"Most of the time, I use a snowmobile now," he said, "but it's broke down seven miles up my trapline across the river. That's where I went with the dogs today. I tried to fix it, but something is still wrong with the carburetor, I think."

Tommy reached to touch the hard white base on my toboggan. "Nothing sticks to this?" he asked.

"It seems to slide at any temperature," I replied. "When water freezes to it, you can wipe it off easily."

"How about at Fifty Below?" he asked. Most Yukoners hold a strong suspicion about using anything plastic which might become brittle in the cold. "Does it break when it gets really cold?"

"It was fine all this winter. We've crashed into lots of trees and bounced over logs and rocks," answered Marsha. "This plastic is stronger than the oak."

I offered to send Tommy the address in Vancouver where he could order it, and he said he'd like that. The old trapper blanched, though, when I mentioned the price.

"Birch is a lot cheaper," he smiled. "It grows free."

Tommy had a shack for us to bunk in tonight, saving us the trouble of pitching the tarp. There was a wood stove in the corner for us to cook our supper on. Although he apologized for the mess, we were delighted to have this shelter.

"I'll send my son over to move that moosehide," he said, turning to leave. "My wife uses this shack for tanning hides. That one is almost ready, it just has to dry slowly."

Draped over a pole on the wall furthest from the heater was a massive, creamy-white hide. From close up, we could see the scrape marks of the skinning knives, and the coarse grain of the moose's skin. It had a gentle smell of wood smoke.

"It's still damp," Marsha whispered, "and so soft. Isn't it beautiful? I'd love to be able to tan one like this. Think of how many moccasins this one hide would make. And some gauntlets, as well—"

At that moment a younger McGinty arrived to remove the hide. He told us where they had a water hole chopped through the river ice, should we prefer to use that instead of melting snow for our supper water and the dogs' mush.

Three hours later, dogs fed, people fed, moccasins and mitts hung to dry, kindling split for morning, and a chewed harness reinforced, we settled into our sleeping bags on the rough plank floor, bone-tired after a rather full day. We'd made it over a third of the way to town, and had luckily stumbled across Tommy McGinty's trapping camp. When events fell into place this nicely, I got the feeling we were getting help from someone *up there*. I lay in my bag, savouring the sweet scent of poplar smoke, and feeling very content.

Beside me, Marsha was giggling. Her shaking vibrated the loose floorboards.

"What's so funny?" I whispered.

"Curly!" she blurted. "I can't believe that Lucky's real name is *Curly*. It just can't be." She was still chuckling when I dozed off.

CHAPTER TWENTY-NINE

COUNTING THE SECONDS AND THE DOGS

W hen the alarm clock went off, I caught it before the second ring. On a morning with the promise of new trails, the cold and darkness in the shack couldn't deter me from springing into action. Clad in my parka and boot liners, I shuffled about, lighting candles and tending to a fire in the rusty stove. This heater was simply half of a gas drum with two holes chiselled in the top. One was for the stove pipe and the larger opening was for feeding wood. The bottom, where the drum had been dissected, rested on a bed of sand and gravel. It was crude, but soon was glowing red and throwing off quite a blast of heat.

To save time, we had only granola and toast this morning, and mint tea later on when water boiled and we'd almost finished packing. Though our shack was a fair distance from McGinty's main cabin, we spoke in whispers, noting there was no light on yet over there. Like two burglars creeping about in the night, we silently stowed all the bedding and our kitchen box on the toboggans. Marsha laid out the harnesses in their places and tied our lifelines to bushes. Meanwhile, I tidied inside the cabin, trying to leave everything exactly as we'd found it. We were ready to set off just as the first hint of daylight was stirring through the trees.

Then, all hell broke loose. Casey and Lucky gave the alert, rousing the others from their slumber. Maybe they thought we were leaving without them. When Mutt stretched, he offered a tentative yodel. Peter picked up his cue and howled shrilly. In seconds, all nine were blowing out their lungs, flapping their tails joyfully, and shaking snow from their coats.

We rushed over quickly and tried to hush them, but each had to announce to the world he wanted to be harnessed next. As we led Casey and Hinglish to their places, they leaped and twisted in the air, yanking us across the yard to the toboggans. A light now shone from the main cabin window, and we tried in vain to calm the anxious crew. By the time all were hooked up and ready for business, Tommy had appeared in the doorway to throw out a pail of slop water.

"Thank you so much for letting us use your little cabin," Marsha called, trying to sound cheery.

"You sure got noisy dogs," was all old Tommy replied, before closing the door again.

"Okay, *let's go!*" I called to my team. Marsha's squad followed hard on our heels.

"A fine way to impress the neighbours," I muttered to the dogs as the flush of embarrassment subsided. "Let's hope you have some of this energy left this afternoon. It could be another long day."

Our goal for tonight was Yukon Crossing, another abandoned settlement that, like Minto, had been a stopover for the Royal Mail stages. The old Dawson Road crossed the river at Yukon Crossing, the stages using either a ferry or an ice bridge. There were a half-dozen cabins there, all in various degrees of ruin, but one of them should offer adequate shelter for us tonight. The distance was only twenty-two miles, but with the temperature rising noticeably, it would be tough on the dogs. Above Zero Fahrenheit their fur coats made them too hot, especially out in the sun. Today we would see puddles of water and dripping branches, as the afternoon temperature was promising to rise well above the freezing mark.

By two o'clock, it was obvious the dogs were not going to do much running and possibly little trotting as well. The most I could encourage on some sections was a dog-walk.

I had in front of me, lying open on the toboggan, a copy of the river map book I'd worked on last summer, and our alarm clock. As we crawled past each major landmark on the canoeing charts, I calculated our elapsed time and distance from the previous island or creek mouth. After the speed was worked out mentally, it became clear the dogs were averaging only three miles per hour over this monotonous trail. With breaks for tea and to check dubious spots of the trail, our overall speed was less than 2-1/2 miles per hour, which was only walking pace for a person.

There was a limit to how much prodding a musher could do before the whole experience was miserable for both man and beasts. Without a great deal of experience in the matter, we weren't sure exactly how tired our teams were, or whether they were being lazy. To further complicate the problem, by the time I had calculated our average speed over the past few miles, and was certain laziness was at least part of the problem, the dogs might have picked up their pace slightly. I couldn't berate them for something as abstract as *the last hour's average speed*.

Out on the ice, with the shore up to a quarter mile away on each side, there were very few markers to judge our speed. The pace always seemed quicker when the trail swung over to hug the bank at a bend, though this was likely an optical illusion.

"I wish we had a speedometer, so I could know exactly how fast the dogs are going," I complained to Marsha when we took a break under the first tree we came near in the last hour. "Then I could encourage Hinglish at, say, four miles per hour, and give him heck at three. I'd like to really know for sure, so I'm not chewing him out when he actually is working better."

"It's hard to tell when there are no trees," said Marsha, "but even then I'm never really sure. Sometimes it looks faster and it really isn't."

Five minutes after we started up again, a dark figure stepped out from a spruce-covered island way up the river. I watched it for a while before Casey, who was again leading, noticed the silhouette. His head jerked up and both ears swivelled forward. Then Casey lunged, surging the toboggan forward, even through three other dogs' traces. In seconds, his excitement had been telegraphed to the others and I was being rocketed along the river. If I hadn't been ready, I'd have been flipped off the back when they accelerated.

The toboggan bounced wildly over lumps and whipped around turns. As the distance closed between us, the outline of a wolf became clear. He was casually crossing the river, oblivious to the panic he was creating.

When I dared a glance over my shoulder, I saw Marsha's dogs had caught the vibe and were stampeding after us. Marsha was holding on with both hands, but the smile on her face was hard to miss.

"*Yippeee!* Let's go! Run! Run!" I shouted to my crew, urging them to run even faster. Should we ever catch up to the wolf, there might be a disaster, but I doubted he'd let that happen.

We were only a few seconds from him when he finally turned towards me. With the sun in my eyes, and all the motion of the toboggan, I couldn't be certain, but it looked as if he were smiling at us, in the same way our dogs smile. The mouth was pulled back in a wide grin, and the teeth exposed. Then he moved—

With long, fluid bounds that made a mockery of the dogs' speed, the wolf dashed away from us. He sprinted up the centre of the river, effortlessly increasing his lead, until branching off across to the shore. His paws hardly touched as he danced gracefully over the snow. I've never seen any animal run so beautifully.

The dogs slowed at the point where the wolf had angled off towards shore, and I was able to regain control. They looked full of energy now, tails erect and wagging, not a hint of their earlier posture.

"Wow, was he ever gorgeous!" Marsha said when she joined me. Her dogs were all craning their necks and sniffing the air. A few minutes before we had been making excuses for these presumed walking wounded.

"He sure could run, couldn't he?" I said. "And our guys put on a bit of a show as well."

"Yep, I take back what I said about them being tired. They were just faking it. How are we going to make them work harder?"

"Well, I've got a new idea," I said, pulling a pencil from the day pack. "It'll just take a moment to work out the details."

When we headed on, I had the numbers that were needed. As the lead dog passed a distinctive crack or lump in the ice, or a tree when we were near shore, I started counting off the seconds. There was no wristwatch with a second hand (we only had the alarm clock to tell time) so the old *thousand and one, thousand and two, thousand and three* method had to do. When I was abreast of the same feature, I could determine our speed from the numbers on my paper corresponding with the elapsed time.

The trick was so simple I could have kicked myself for not realizing it sooner. My distance measure was the length of the team and the toboggan, and the elapsed time interval I would count. Distance divided by time equals speed. Each dog's harness and traces were six feet long and I stood about six more feet behind where the wheel dog's traces attached for a total length of 30 feet. So, if I counted off one second for each dog and one for myself, we were going six feet per second or about 4.1 miles per hour. This should be a minimum allowable rate unless we were going up a steep hill. If the time count was four seconds (for four dogs and me) the speed calculated to just over 5.1 miles per hour. A nice trotting speed was six miles per hour which turned out to be about three and a half seconds for the thirty feet.

"Good boys," I called out each time the count was five or less. A few tails wagged tentatively and we plodded on.

When I caught them slowing, though it would have looked the same without counting, I ran forward and without saying a word, lightly slapped every ear with my mitt. Then I ran back to the toboggan and gave the command to continue.

Marsha watched from the second toboggan, amused at all my counting and flapping about. If she'd had the maps, she could have learned we averaged almost five miles per hour for the next two miles, even though my minimum was only four. I think the dogs were bewildered at how quickly I was picking up on their games now.

Our improved speed over these long, flat, relatively dull stretches of river ice

*Jeff was a problem – lazy and stubborn. He had more white markings on his
face than his brother Mutt.*

was not going to win us any races, but it did move us along quick enough so none
of us was bored.

When she became tired of his antics, Marsha traded me Jeff for Loki, so I
could take a turn with our number one delinquent. I put him in wheel position,

right behind Mutt, who was working well, hoping Jeff would follow his brother's good example.

Five miles before Yukon Crossing, the river swung off into a long looping bend to the east. Checking on the topographical maps, I noticed a thin line representing a trail which should cut the distance in half by crossing the peninsula of land and bringing us right to Yukon Crossing. Whether or not the trail was still passable, or ever existed at all, would not be clear until we actually inspected it, because there was no guarantee with maps drawn from aerial photographs.

"Shall we try this short cut on the map?" I called to Marsha. "It looks like it should start just back of the old cabin at Merrice Creek."

"Where's Merrice Creek?"

"Next one on the right."

"Oh, I suppose, so," she agreed. "I hope it's not too deep in snow and full of deadfall."

"It'll be a change from this endless river trail," I pointed out. "Bet the dogs would like something different."

Sure enough, when we came to Merrice Creek, the dogs did perk up. For one thing, there was a snowmobile trail crossing the Yukon River at this point, coming from the highway and winding up Merrice Creek. Casey eagerly swung off Cor's snowblown trail we'd been following, onto this firm track and trotted up to the open doorway of a derelict cabin. When Marsha's team was also up the bank, we tipped the toboggans and told the dogs to sit quietly.

"What was this place, Bruce?" Marsha strode up to the porch and peered into the shadows.

"I don't know for sure. Something to do with a mine up Williams Creek, I believe. The map shows all sorts of little roads leading off into the hills from here."

"Gad, look at this," Marsha called from a room she was exploring in the main log building. "How high is that?"

She was pointing at tear marks in the faded wallpaper. Some animal had shredded the paper and its cardboard backing, reaching higher than I could.

"These must be grizzly claw marks," I offered, lowering my voice a little. "But why would a bear tear the wall apart?"

"Probably after bugs living inside the walls, between the paper and the logs," explained Marsha. "He must have been huge to reach that high."

There were no bear tracks in the snow anywhere around the cabin, and the episode might have happened in the summer, but I checked my .30-30 just in case. The claw marks had reminded us about that winter bear. We were now much closer to Carmacks, not far from where it had been sighted.

Somewhat reluctantly the dogs mushed out of the yard, following the corrugated snowmachine track. Clearly they had been hoping this was tonight's camp.

This conveniently-packed trail was too far from any town to be a recreational avenue. The two most probable reasons for someone to be out in this area were for trapping, and to stake claims at the old mining prospects. With the recent rise in the price of silver, the properties up Williams Creek might have become economically-viable again.

"I'll bet this track leads up to some staking," I called to Marsha. "Someone will be flogging mining stock on a new claim before we get to Carmacks."

The track was following an old bulldozer road, snaking up the side of a cliff. I kept checking the map while we were climbing to see where our little short cut should be. This road seemed to be leading too far inland.

The toboggan slowed. I looked up just as one of the dogs jerked to the side. Only then did I see the strip of orange survey ribbon wrapped around the over-hanging branch. The other dogs stopped.

"*LOOK OUT!*" Marsha screamed. "There's a trap!"

I scrambled around the backboard and made a dive for the errant wheel dog. He was leaned out as far as his traces and the toboggan would let him, pawing at the snow, and straining to get near the smear of bait on a tree.

"*NO!*" I yelled, as my arms closed around his back legs in a flying tackle. He tugged an extra inch and reached with his paw.

I was too late: the snow beneath his outstretched paw exploded. Steel jaws sprang up and snapped hard. A chain that had been hidden under the snow rattled taut as the terrified dog pulled back on top of me.

"Oh, God!" moaned Marsha. "Oh, no—"

Slowly, Jeff opened his mouth and moved his jaws. Not a sound came out. His eyes were bulged and froth began forming on his tongue. When we could finally hear him screaming, the pitch was so high it hurt our ears.

"Help me hold him still, Marsha. I want to see how badly he's caught."

"Be gentle. He's so frightened."

I wasn't sure Jeff wouldn't bite at me because he was so freaked out. Moving off to the side and around the tree, I could see more clearly how his paw was trapped.

"Is this ever gory. One of his toes is barely attached. I can see the bone pieces sticking out." The steel jaws were locked across his paw, holding only the front two toes. Both were badly shattered and bleeding, and one was hanging by only a strip of hide.

"What are we going to do, Bruce? Can we get him to a vet?"

"We're another full day from Carmacks. There's no vet there. He'd have to go into Whitehorse in a car or truck."

"Can we do anything ourselves? How bad is it?"

The toes would either have to be amputated, or sewn back on by a veterinary surgeon. Even if the bones could be pieced together and splinted, there would be no guarantee the muscles would mend well enough for this dog to ever pull properly.

"It would be a major operation, sewing muscles and veins and nerves back together. I'm not sure they do that for sled dogs."

"The poor little guy. I think he's going into shock."

Jeff had stopped screaming and was trembling slightly. His movements were jerky. He was trying to move forward to get his tongue on the trapped paw.

"Would you take both teams around the corner?" I asked her quietly. "I'll unhook Jeff's traces so you can move the others away."

"What are you going to do? Are you going to shoot him?! It's only his foot!"

"Look at it this way, Marsha. He isn't going to be a sled dog again if he's missing toes. And no one wants him for a pet. If we take him back to Pelly Crossing the Hagers will just have to shoot him there."

"How about going to a vet? How much would that cost?"

"We don't know if a vet could help or not. That's really not an option."

"Oh, the poor little guy."

Jeff was lying calmly now, licking at his foreleg, which was as close to the paw as he could get. He looked as if he were moving in slow motion.

A single blast from the .30-30 echoed off the cliffs like rolling thunder. When I slid Jeff's collar off, his skull felt as if it were in thirty pieces. The 180-grain, soft-nosed bullet had done an abrupt and thorough job of ending Jeff's pain.

Jeff wasn't the first dog I'd ever had to shoot, so the actual task was not as disturbing to me as it was for Marsha. When I came around the corner, she was sitting on the curl of my toboggan, crying into her scarf.

The dogs were sitting, or lying calmly in their places. A few wagged their tails tentatively to see me.

"Be glad it wasn't Casey or Tyhee," I said softly, kneeling beside her.

"Oh, I'll be all right in a moment," she sniffed. "But if Tyhee ever gets caught, I'd keep her even with three legs."

"Well, I could never shoot Casey either. But Jeff was not a pet. He was a sled dog; all he was alive for was to work. And he was piss poor at that."

Darkness caught up with us long before we reached Yukon Crossing. It turned out we had gone too far up the old mining road, and had to backtrack almost to the Merrice Creek cabin before we located a trail cut through the forest. This led across the peninsula exactly as the map had shown, but the snow was deep and the way often blocked by fallen trees, as Marsha had predicted. The going was slow, hard work, and our tempers were on a knife's edge. The realization that the river route would have been easier and faster didn't improve matters any. We camped that night off to the side of this so-called short cut, in a terrible spot under poplar trees. I made a crude shelter by leaning poles against a fallen tree and draping the tarpaulin over top, but the snow still swirled in on us as the wind picked up at twilight.

The dogs seemed pleased to get a larger ration tonight, now that Jeff wasn't around to claim his share. If they were mourning, or had even noticed his absence, I couldn't detect it.

We two humans ate our lentil and vegetable stew in silence, poking once in a while at the fire, and thinking about being anywhere else. It seemed there wasn't much to talk about.

CHAPTER THIRTY

TIME FOR CARMACKS

"C'mon, Bruce, wake up. *Wake up.* The alarm didn't go off."

The sun had already risen on Day Three of this shopping trip, and the sky was a clear, deep blue. Last night's winds had blown themselves away, leaving us with what promised to be a scorcher of a day. With my head resting on a rolled sweater for a pillow, and the warming rays now trickling through the poplars onto my face, I felt more like sunbathing than mushing on into Carmacks.

Marsha soon had a fire going and was mixing up some sort of batter.

"This is the last chance for these powdered eggs," she announced, dipping a piece of bread into the bowl. There were other slices thawing on the lid of the tea pot. "They were terrible as scrambled eggs, so I'm trying French Toast."

"They were a little rubbery as scrambled eggs," I agreed. "Sort of like eating a frisbee."

Marsha had made a goo of one part each of powdered eggs and powdered milk and two parts water for today's batter. She fried the dipped bread in a hot pan and managed to come up with an edible breakfast. I think, though, that much of the good taste was the butter and melted honey.

"Shall we try those frozen hard-boiled eggs as well?" I asked. "Let's see if they work out any better."

Somewhere I'd read about thawing out frozen hard-boiled eggs in the tea water while it heated up. I had to wait this morning until Marsha had taken her cupful out of the pot, because she didn't want anything to do with my egg experiment.

"Oh, throw them away. Or feed them to the dogs, Bruce. How can you think about eating those horrible-looking green things? They're all lumpy!"

True enough, these two boiled eggs did look a lot worse for wear. After they thawed and I bit into one, it was obvious the white had separated into layers, each more plastic than the one above it. We both love eggs, and had eaten cases of fresh ones at the cabin this winter, treating them as a convenience food. Yet try as we might to find a good way to take them camping, nothing had panned out (pun not intended). When we took uncooked frozen eggs, it had been too much trouble thawing them before use. If boiled in the frozen state, the outside overcooked before the centre was thawed. With this morning's last attempts, we scratched eggs, powdered or frozen, from our camping food list.

We now had our menu stripped to the basics. From now on, we would pack oatmeal and other porridges, plus some bacon, for mornings. Lunches were muffins or biscuits plus dried fruit and canned fish. Suppers were lentils with home-frozen vegetables and grated cheese thrown in. In these choices, we were actually being fairly sophisticated compared to Danny and Abbie's moosemeat routine or to the policemen's tradition. One long-retired Mountie told me in one word what he ate on his patrols. "Pemmican," he had said.

"Sure. But what else?" I prodded, "Oatmeal for breakfast? Nuts? Dried fruit?"

"Just pemmican," he maintained. "Same for breakfast and supper."

He had made his pemmican from ground dried beef and suet. When it was mealtime, he plunked a chunk in a hot pan and slowly mixed snow with it until it was a thick lumpy gravy. That was it, his whole meal, every meal. Variety would come when he looked in on trappers or miners along his route and enjoyed their hospitality.

With our meal under our belts, Marsha loaded the toboggans and hitched up the eight dogs, while I snowshoed to the river and back to pack the trail. There were still about thirty miles between us and that motel room, so we'd need to hustle.

The pooches were eager to go when I returned. Casey was jumping up and down in his harness, yipping and whining for the big word. The others were standing in place, rocking back and forth, and biting at the snow banks. Loki was snapping his teeth and grinning. Tails were wagging and ears cocked forward.

"Okay," I whispered, and they jerked the toboggan forward. My tracks had only beaten down the loosely-drifted snow and had not packed it firmly, so they still had to wade through, sinking knee-deep in the trail. Yet they pulled well, and Marsha and I rode to the river, saving our strength for the overland section to come after Yukon Crossing.

Our short cut brought us to a ruined cabin nestled behind the last line of trees on the river bank. The building might have figured into the cutting of this trail through from Merrice Creek, but there was little evidence left to indicate what activities had transpired here.

As we took a moment to prowl through the debris surrounding the dilapidated log house and its outbuildings, a familiar sentimental feeling washed over me. Every time I wander into one of these long-abandoned camps, I can't help imagining the efforts someone must have put into homesteading there. We could see where a yard had been cleared for a garden patch, now returned to willows. Each axe and adze mark, each saw cut and spike had taken somebody's time. Their dreams had been wrapped up in this river bank setting for a few years, maybe many. To see their labours' physical results are now worthless, was to be reminded of the futility and mortality of life.

Going out onto the Yukon River ice was now a treat. The snow was not so deep, partly because of the strong winds and hot sunshine over the last few days. If these temperatures kept up, there would be no snow over the ice within a few weeks. The dogs broke into a gallop to celebrate the firmer surface, running along the shoreline for the half-mile to Yukon Crossing. After being in the forest, the dazzling sunshine reflecting off this expanse of white was hard on the eyes. I squinted ahead to make sure we weren't heading too close to traps or open water, but happily didn't have to say a word to the dogs until we were at the old settlement.

There was a line of buildings generously spaced out along the river bank, ranging in size from horse barns and roadhouse to bachelors' eight-by-ten cabins. With all the snow on the ground we had to be careful not to step on boards with nails protruding or stumble into old garbage and outhouse pits.

Soon having had our fill of cabin exploring, we located the old Dawson Stage Road at the back of the settlement and headed off toward Carmacks.

Again we were into deeper snow, but fortunately had Cor Guimond's trail to follow. We could clearly make out his snowshoe prints and the toboggan's smooth track despite a few inches of new snow since he'd been this way on his Dawson-to-Whitehorse trek. Though our dogs could only plod along on this partially-packed trail, Marsha and I were terribly relieved we wouldn't have to do any snowshoeing ourselves. We rode on all but the steepest uphills, finding the dogs able to keep up a fair pace with less need for counting seconds and slapping ears. The loss of Jeff had, if anything, improved our teams. When he had acted up, it affected all the dogs.

I could judge our progress on a larger scale by using the topographic maps and, by the time we stopped for a lunch break, I knew we were halfway to Carmacks. Checking the alarm clock, and figuring the mileage, I estimated us into town by five o'clock if we could maintain our speed.

"Let's not get that specific," Marsha would tell me whenever I gave her a prediction like that. "We'll only be disappointed if the going becomes rougher."

But the route became delightfully better instead of worse. Not long after our lunch stop, we came up to a barrier of snow. When I walked up past the bewildered dogs, I was tickled to see we had come to a junction with a ploughed mining road. Our luck would not have been so good had the grader operator not left a skiff of snow over the gravel.

We now got the dogs to run or trot all the time, though on some of the downhills we would have been as happy with a slow walk. Our brake claws were not too effective on the frozen gravel and we were never sure when we'd encounter a moose or an oncoming vehicle around one of the tight hairpin corners. We strained our ears for warning of trucks but fortunately never met one. As the road threaded around ink-blot shaped lakes, in and out of creek ravines, and up and down steep hills, we began to feel as if this were really a rollercoaster, not a road. To prevent gouging the toboggan bases, we had to steer around random boulders and bare patches. Our arms and thighs became sore from the brute work of tilting the toboggans on edge and leaning to avoid these slalom markers. The dogs were wild about this speedway and galloped for ages, stopping only when their tongues were raining saliva and their bodies trembling from exertion. Marsha and I relished those moments of rest too, because this fast-paced road travel taxed our muscles also.

Twilight was well upon us when the first few buildings of Carmacks came into view. We halted the dogs and then wrapped rope under the toboggans to keep to a pace better suited to traffic. Casey led through the town, and he was clever about turning gee and haw, but neither he nor Hinglish could understand why their teams should only use one lane of the street. We crossed paths with a few pick-up trucks, but no one seemed to mind the delays we were causing. The drivers pulled over to give us plenty of room to go by, and waved and pointed at the dogs.

Carmacks is a small town, barely a village by southern population standards, so there was not far to go. We pulled up to the motel and tipped our toboggans in front of the tavern.

"Whew!" I smiled at Marsha. "That was a wild two hours. A beer will taste great."

"It'll be fantastic to get into a shower. Let's get registered and find a spot for these guys to sleep."

Inside the office I was surprised to find out that it was almost six o'clock, not four-thirty as our alarm clock showed. Perhaps the cold had affected its spring, making it slow down. We would have to either keep it warm in the future, or buy a wristwatch.

We chained out the troops in a vacant lot across the road and settled immediately into the decadent life of civilization. After a flip of the coin, Marsha won the honour of the first hour-long shower. Since everything was damp from the brush camps, I unpacked our outfit and transformed the room into a walk-in dryer. Clothes hung from the curtain rods, sleeping bags draped over chairs, and boot-liners lined up over the hot air registers.

Feeding the dogs was so simple: no fire, no melting snow, merely turn the tap and out came gallons of scalding-hot water. Lights came on at the flick of a switch. We walked over to the hotel café and were amused someone cooked for us, and did the dishes too. Afterwards we settled into a soft bed with a few cold lagers and watched TV.

However, as we lay there in front of the boob tube watching absolutely inane programs, the drawbacks of modern life began to poke through our euphoria bubble. Someone had turned up the tavern's jukebox and the boisterous Friday night drinking crowd began roaring into the motel parking lot, slamming doors and shouting to each other. Ore-hauling trucks roared by on the highway, rattling windows and promising to disturb our sleep throughout the night. Marsha and I did a quick count through our wallets and found them already quite thinner. We hadn't yet been to the grocery store and had already spent a small fortune.

"Life was a lot simpler back at Horsefall," I noted, drawing the curtains and turning off the light.

"Yeah – and cheaper and quieter," said Marsha.

CHAPTER THIRTY-ONE

LIFE IN THE FAST LANE

After months on our own, to be suddenly immersed in society, even in a rural place like Carmacks, was unsettling. We felt uneasy and slightly suspicious of the attention paid to us, and lost or out-of-place when we were ignored. Dealing again in dollars and cents, instead of the barter and favour method of our neighbours, seemed so impersonal and crass. Of course, the system had not changed; it was our viewpoint that was irregular here.

As our day's business of buying groceries and dog supplies progressed, I began to realize what was behind those legends of cranky old-timers living like hermits in the bush, cynical and distrustful of civilization. Life out in the bush, where every day is an adventure, and where brutal winter temperatures can suddenly turn travelling into a life-and-death confrontation, is hard to equate with an office worker's routine. A grizzled trapper might snowshoe through a blizzard in front of his dogs, fall through the ice, and drag himself on into town, where he'd be thought rude for smelling of wood smoke. After coming from the world of Sixty Below struggles for existence, to be suddenly expected to conform to arbitrary social norms is bound to make one cynical. We had only a few dangerous experiences during our season in the bush, but could readily identify with the feeling. We decided not to dawdle in town longer than the time required to arrange our business.

It took all the dog food on hand at both trading posts to fill our order and we arranged to have it freighted with the regular Dawson City transport as far as Minto. Since the freight truck would pass through in the night, only two days from now, we would have to race there immediately with the dogs to meet the drop off. If we missed the delivery, the wolves and ravens would have a considerable feast at our expense.

One supply item that was bulky, and perhaps a luxury, was toilet paper. For the past two weeks, since running out, we'd been using newspaper, but we pampered ourselves now with the real thing. We couldn't imagine what the proverbial old-timers used in winter time, when there were no leaves, the moss was buried under the snow, and paper birch trees few and far between. At low temperatures, snow wouldn't form into a ball to use, and would be as raspy as sand. Perhaps they carried a cloth especially for this use. None of the alternatives seemed very attractive, so we took this one civilized advantage with us, ignoring the space it would take on the toboggans and the departure from tradition.

At the tavern, we learned Cor Guimond had passed through town in fine form although his dogs were ailing. They were having problems with cracked pads. Having dogs with tough feet is critically important, especially when working them at extremely low temperatures. The problem had delayed the hardy trapper for two days, the pretty waitress said with a mysterious smile, but he had nursed the team into Whitehorse in time for the Sourdough Rendezvous festival, right on schedule.

Other inquiries revealed the winter bear was either much further afield, dead, or gone back into hibernation, because no further sighting of bear or tracks had been turned in to the game warden's office.

Our last purchase was a wristwatch to help me with our dilemma of the unreliable alarm clock. It was an acquisition that flew in the face of our conscious attempts to downplay timetables and deadlines in our lives. Although having another timepiece would undoubtedly influence us to be *watching the clock* more, we'd had a good respite from the world of punch clocks and schedules, so felt able to reintegrate this timer into our lives.

"If you insist on telling me the time every ten minutes, though, I'll take it away and hide it," was Marsha's warning.

My defence was I'd never be able to remember to wind the darn thing.

If the temperature had been in the bitter range of midwinter, wearing a metal watch on my wrist would have been tempting frostbite. At those extreme conditions, it would have to be stowed in an inside parka pocket to keep the springs, gears and oil warm enough to run smoothly.

The following morning, we set out at dawn, retracing our steps toward Minto. Again, Lady Luck had smiled on us, or at least had shook dandruff from her godly hair, because there had been a fresh dusting of snow overnight to smooth the ploughed gravel road. The dogs were chipper after two extra-large meals and a day's inactivity, and picked up our race-to-Minto spirit. We ran up the hills beside the toboggans to save their energy for later, and the strategy paid off; the unploughed section of the old Dawson Road had our well-packed, in-bound track on it, so we could hustle along at a lively pace despite the warm afternoon temperature.

When we pulled into Yukon Crossing, there was still plenty of daylight left, so we continued on over our short-cut route and made camp at Merrice Creek. The dogs had done so well, and been so well behaved, Marsha gave each one a back rub as a special treat. It was amusing to watch the reactions of both the recipient and the onlookers while this was happening. When Casey was being rubbed, his eyes would close to thin slits and his ears fall back. He'd ripple his muscles and flex his shoulders, while sighing audibly. There would be a rash of tail-wagging approval from the others at his performance. When it was Mutt's turn for a massage, he nearly twisted himself inside out each time Marsha touched him. This little Pelly Crossing dog had been the hardest to teach to sit, and was entirely frantic about being touched. Although much better now than in November, he was still half-wild.

Hinglish found the contact overwhelming as well, but responded by flopping down and offering his tummy to scratch instead. Peter decided this was worth a comment and started barking from his chain spot. Lucky/Curly turned out to be an eye-closed leg-leaner, and Loki couldn't help snapping his teeth a few times to show his emotions were stirred up.

I tried to rub Dawson's back, but had a hard time keeping up with him as he rolled and twisted, and tried to stand on his head for approval. The little brown youngster should have been in a circus instead of a dog team. When Marsha let Tyhee off to run freely for her treat, she came right over to Dawson and started a ferocious, but harmless, play-fight. I retired from the massage business since neither would pay me the slightest interest.

Having extra time to set up camp, after travelling thirty-odd miles, with hardly a harsh word spoken all day to the dogs, made this a special day. Finally, we had ourselves and the dogs tuned to travel, and it was becoming great fun. The doubts we'd shared in midwinter of whether or not we'd ever see this point were now far in the past. I confess I felt more than a little proud.

The next day, mushing over those long, straight stretches of Yukon River, we ran into one peculiar problem. Our track from the trip upriver was higher than the rest of the snowy surface, because the packed snow hadn't melted as quickly as the loose snow beside it. The dogs' feet were punching through six inches of wet snow on our track but would only sink an inch or so, to the ice beneath, if they walked off the trail. Yet, despite the easier traction there, Casey refused to go beside the trail. It must have disturbed him considerably that I wanted him to walk *off* the trail now, after disciplining him all winter not to wander.

Hinglish was no better, so we tried Peter, then Mutt. No luck. Finally I took a long pole in hand and jogged ahead, leading like Cor had done. If I stayed away from our track, the dogs happily followed me, easily pulling now, their tails all high and waving. With the warm temperature, I was wearing pacs instead of moccasins that would have been wet in no time. Running in these huge, lined boots was not easy, but I was happy for the exercise. It was invigorating to be moving my muscles and feeling my body flow, after the tense anaerobic work of driving the toboggan. Being in front made me feel more a member of the team, and I shared their relief there was no bossy musher behind nagging us to go faster.

The distance fairly flew by, and I only hopped on for a ride again when our old trail was right beside a bank and in the shade. There, our track was still firm enough to support the dogs' feet. Our progress was slowed slightly by a strong head wind, somewhat of a novelty for us because it had been, as a rule, calm during the cold months.

The warmth brought on yet another problem for a few of the dogs: *snow balls*. Hinglish and Peter were especially prone to snow compressing and packing into icy balls around the hair between their toe pads. When these balls became big enough, it was painful for the dog to walk. Hinglish would flop down without warning and start chewing and licking at his feet. Little Peter had to wait for the team to be stopped before cleaning his, or he would be dragged along on his side. The best solution seemed to be for Marsha and I to check their paws quickly every twenty minutes, and pull off any balls that were forming. If we allowed the affected dogs to lick their feet, their saliva seemed to hasten the formation of new balls, so we tried to be quick and get the team rolling immediately. Snowballs affected our silky-haired dogs more than the coarse-haired ones. Trimming the hairs between their pads at lunch time didn't alleviate the problem during the afternoon, so we were stuck with our twenty-minute checkup routine.

We found dogs could get rested in a much shorter time than humans could. After a sprint, or climbing a slope, they would need only about twenty seconds for their purple tongues to become fresh pink, signalling they were ready to gallop on. A longer wait tended to bore them and distract them from the business of pulling.

By four-thirty we had reached Minto and found Tommy McGinty's camp closed up and deserted. The freight truck would come to the Forestry's summer airstrip with our load, so we set up a brush camp in the trees near there. The race part of the trip home was now behind us. There remained ahead the uncertain business of freighting all the cargo we had, plus the dog food delivery, to Horsefall Creek. We went to sleep praying for colder weather.

CHAPTER THIRTY-TWO

THE HOME STRETCH

Half-dreaming and half-dressed, I helped the trucker unload the mountain of dog food and few cartons of groceries. The eighteen-wheeled Kenworth rumbled and hissed and shone its lights brightly in my eyes, appearing much more intimidating now than it would by day. The throbbing, smoking energy was startling and bizarre for someone whose mind was still asleep and whose spirit was firmly in the world of sled dogs and snowshoes. Nonetheless, come morning, we would be grateful this noisy, nocturnal visitor had saved us and the dogs so much work by bringing our cargo this far.

"What time is it?" I asked the driver as he flipped through his papers to find the correct form for me to sign.

"About two-thirty. Sign here and here," he said. "And you keep the pink copy." He peered off into the darkness where we had the tarpaulin tied and eight dogs chained. "Do you live here?"

"Thirty miles downstream. Just past Fort Selkirk, we have a cabin on the river."

"You got a skidoo to haul in this stuff, or what?"

"No, just eight dogs. And two toboggans."

It was quite a heap of twenty-kilo sacks. I wanted to go back to sleep rather than think about it.

"Someday I'm going to get me some of them sled dogs," he said without much conviction. "I'd like to try some mushing. Do they go very fast when they have a big load like that?"

"We'll know after tomorrow," I replied. "This will be their biggest cargo so far."

"I'd better be going. Got a few hours driving yet before I can grab some shut-eye." He swung up into the brightly lit cab. "Good luck," he called as the door closed.

Then the giant truck-trailer unit crawled away, taking its daylight and noise along down the road. My ears were ringing as I climbed back into my sleeping bag. *Freighting has come a long way since the Gold Rush days* was my last thought before falling asleep.

In the morning, after juggling sacks from pile to pile and unpacking and repacking everything, we decided on a plan for loading the two toboggans. All four hundred-plus pounds of dog food and our box of frozen meat went on one toboggan, which we planned to have the four bigger dogs pull. Our clothes, camping equipment and bedding, plus the groceries, were piled onto the other, making a slightly lighter load. I could barely move the bigger load when I heaved on the traces, so we weren't too sure how this was going to turn out. The sun was up already in a cloudless sky, threatening to turn our trail into soup and bake the dogs through their thick fur coats.

However, the dogs threw themselves into their work with their usual morning gusto and dragged the toboggans at a respectable speed along the road and down the bank onto the river. Marsha and I smiled and kept our fingers crossed inside our mitts. The old track had a good crust on it from yesterday's thaw and last night's hard freeze, so we didn't have the problem of paws punching through this morning.

I continued to remind the leaders whenever our pace slipped below my minimum of six feet per second and they soon adopted this as their normal rate. For the first two hours, Marsha and I rode all the time, getting off only for our snowball checks and to jog behind when chilled by the wind. With these twenty second breaks every twenty minutes, the dogs didn't seem to be tiring at all. We were impressed. Landmarks slipped by: Big Creek, Devil's Crossing, an ancient homestead, and then we could see the head of Hell's Gate.

Here we ran into problems. The unseasonable weather was causing the ice in places to be flooded with an overflow of slush. Detouring around these dark patches disrupted our travelling pace and did nothing to bolster our confidence in the general strength of the ice. Twice we came to spots where our southbound trail was blocked by open water. In both cases, the new leads were extensive, forcing us to backtrack and pioneer new routes through the islands.

When the wind picked up and the dogs began to tire, we switched them around. We tried five dogs hauling the heavier toboggan, followed by the other three pulling the lighter one. The second team would work desperately hard to keep up, perhaps not wanting to be left by themselves. Casey pulled especially well when substituted into the second squad, so much so that his tongue would

Checking out an ice bridge near the shore. Though there were open patches only a dozen feet away, the crossing was solid.

go blue and his eyes begin to bulge. It amused us to see him exerting himself so hard, because he wouldn't always do his fair share when leading the first crew on these long stretches. He was one of those leaders Danny had referred to when he told us, "Some lead dogs just lead, they don't pull. You can see their traces hanging sometimes. You got to try to get a dog that will pull *and* lead. Then you got a real good lead dog."

Hinglish was turning out to be a *real good lead dog,* working harder than any of the rest if we could judge by the amount of panting he was doing.

By mid-afternoon, we'd made eighteen miles after only four hours. Marsha examined our options at this point, while the dogs sprawled in the sunshine. Though the temperature was still rising, we could make it all the way home today if we pushed ourselves and the dogs, and were willing to travel in the twilight. We were through the Ingersolls, the wind had stopped and we felt comfortable in our own territory now.

"Then again," said Marsha, sweeping off her sunglasses dramatically and posturing at the sun, "it is also important for a blonde to get a tan. We could stop here

With our UHMW toboggan bases, heavy loads could be pulled much easier
than if we'd been using the traditional birch or oak bases.
Much of our big loads was dog food.

for an early camp and leave a half-day's travel for tomorrow morning. Wouldn't that be nicer?"

"The dogs are going so well, perhaps we shouldn't wear them out. Sure, let's stop now."

"Good. That island over there looks perfect because it's the closest. I vote for that one."

What had been a problem when we were moving was now an asset for camping. An open channel provided us with fresh water, saving us from melting snow. Today, when we had extra time for such chores, our water supply was delivered right to our doorstep. We set our camp at the edge of a spruce grove, facing west so the sunset would be our evening's entertainment. All through the poplars, where we staked out the dogs, were tangles of rose bushes, still sporting a few rose hips. We gathered some for tea and ate others raw, sucking on the pulp and spitting out the seeds.

By the time the sun was down, the three-quarter moon was shining brightly over the spruces. There was a pile of firewood cut, enough to last for days, and our tarp was hung perfectly. Even our sleeping bags were dry and fresh, having been aired in the sunshine for half the afternoon. If anyone had happened along at this moment they'd have thought we were super campers. It helps to have a generous quantity of both time and sunshine. Spring camping wouldn't be hard to take.

Come morning we were able to roll out early, being well rested. Again there was a firm crust, thanks to the cold night air, and the toboggans slid much better. At Fort Selkirk, Danny and Abbie were waiting an early lunch for us. My appetite perked up when I saw some moose steaks sizzling on the heater.

"I thought you would like to eat some moose," said Danny, passing Marsha some fresh bread. "I put them on when we heard you were coming."

"Who told you we were coming? Didn't see anyone out on the ice."

"My dogs always let us know when somebody is coming. They could hear you about an hour ago, maybe just when you started. Sound carries far in the winter."

I thought back to Tommy McGinty and knew exactly what Danny's dogs had heard: *You guys sure got noisy dogs.*

On the last leg to Horsefall, the dogs actually ran for two stretches. With the heavy loads, our job of steering – and keeping the toboggans upright on the corners – took every bit of muscle and mechanical advantage we could muster. When I lost the balance just out from our cabin and the toboggan toppled on its side, the dogs went frantic with impatience waiting for Marsha and me to pry the toboggan and its cargo back upright. Had it been any heavier, we'd have needed to unpack the load in order to right the toboggan. It was a relief to have it all finally at our little cabin, and my new watch told us that it was only 1:30, leaving us half the day to get settled in before dark.

Marsha, who was quite worried before making the long trek into Carmacks, now had a new perspective on mushing to share with her mother in this letter:

Have been wandering around the house, busying myself with unpacking clothes and food supplies, hanging up sleeping bags and gathering snow from around the house to fill up the dog pot for their evening meal. Was really glad I had split lots of cookstove wood before we left 'cause I sure don't feel like doing it now.

Bruce has already hooked up two dogs and has gone to fetch four pails of river water from one of the open spots in the ice only a quarter-mile away. I noticed those two dogs left their cosy circles with much less enthusiasm than they showed us seven days ago. And the other six dogs seemed quite accepting of the fact they had not been chosen for this chore. They have all begun to settle into their rediscovered bones and the idea of being home.

There are so many things to do my mind races from one, to the other, and then back again. My body says, 'Take a break', and so my mind has chosen to settle into these thoughts and write them down.

You'd think a person could relax after seven days on the trail, and a lot of it being less than desirable. As my mind races over the events of our trip, I seem to be able to come up only with such good feelings about having done it, and the accomplishment makes my head swell! Wow... I know others have done many more gruelling trips and suffered through many more hardships than I did, but I'm still proud! Already I'm planning the food we'll take next trip. Coming to the North is the best thing I could ever have done for myself!

CHAPTER THIRTY-THREE

RELAXING

The warm weather continued for a week, peaking with a high one day of 50°F. Our snow was disappearing at an alarming rate; we hoped for a respite in order to do more camping. It hardly seemed fair that we now had the dogs in fine working order, and winter was deserting us.

Our furry buddies had to be exercised, so we hauled driftwood logs from various logjams for a spring firewood supply. After the greater thrills of this winter, the dogs were definitely not enthused about this mundane work. When given a chance to have a sprint for a few miles on the river, they responded with an eager gallop, then appeared disappointed when I turned them back for home.

In the cabin, we got our spring cleaning done, Marsha baked cookies, crackers and bread, and I finally had a chance to do a little woodcarving. Once all the laundry was performed, and the two of us thoroughly bathed, fed and rested, we actually began to run out of *things to do*. After being so focused to put ourselves into this position of readiness, we felt a tad uneasy with the unaccustomed luxury. We wondered what a couple would do on their second winter in the bush, unless they ran a trapline. Our scramble to build our equipment, ready our cabin and train our teams – starting last summer and only now complete – had supplied us with a reason for existence, or, at least, had left us no time to wonder about such a reason. If our quest here was to explore, we would need colder weather to continue. We crossed our fingers, and hoped at least one of the two-and-a-half remaining weeks of March would be cold.

One day, we saddled up six of our charges and mushed up to Fort Selkirk to visit with the neighbours. Abbie had promised to teach Marsha the basics of beadwork, and Danny wanted a hand with supplies he was having trucked in to the Bradleys' farm. A mining company was running heavy equipment on the usually impassable side-road, so a pick-up truck with chains on its tires could manage the trip in from the highway. Danny and I would take his snowmobile to

*We overnighted in this cabin at Fort Selkirk a few times while visiting
Danny and Abbie. The cabin was built by members of the Pelly Band
to shelter summer canoeists and needed better chinking for winter use!*

do the freighting, giving me an opportunity to assess the value of this *whiteman
dog team* as he called his machine.

I sat behind Danny on the snowmobile, with my heavy parka fastened tight, but
was still chilled by the wind. The noise was an annoying whine, loud enough to
make conversation impossible, save for the odd shouted word or two. The speed,
however, was impressive. In a fraction of the time it would have taken with the
dogs, we zipped from trap to trap, island to island, on our way to the Pelly River
mouth.

Where Marsha and I had kept rigidly to our tested trails through this section,
Danny drove seemingly where he pleased over the ice surface. I was somewhat
unnerved at Danny's apparent lack of concern about weak spots.

"Is it safe here?" I yelled into his ear as we passed between two channels of
running water.

"Lots of ice here," Danny said, slowing the machine so I could hear better.
"But over there where it is darker and sort of sunk, I wouldn't go there."

He took me on a grand tour of the islands at the confluence of these two rivers,
pointing out where he had a cabin once and was caught during a spring flood.

"We had to put everything up on the roof, and let the dogs loose. The water, it

Fort Selkirk schoolhouse in the foreground – the church behind it. 'I sat right here at the back,' Danny said, gesturing to a desk beside the furnace. 'It was warm near that heater. A bit hard to stay awake sometimes.'

came up pretty fast, and I thought for a while we were going to get washed away. But then it went down before it got right up to the roof." He laughed heartily, "Abbie and I don't want to spend another break-up on an island. Better to be on land, where you've got some place to get away if you are flooded. Here, we had no place except up on the roof."

For each landmark, Danny had a story to bring it to life. Some were about white settlers and trappers who had lived at the various islands and creeks, others were about Indian legends or hunting incidents. He had seen a moose on one cliff and heard it bark, "just like a dog. When that happens, the old people say something bad is going to happen."

"What happened that time?"

"My Daddy died down near Dawson," he said quietly. "If that ever happens, you should try to shoot the moose. Maybe that can stop the badness happening."

We were amazed at the hive of activity at the farm that had replaced the isolated, calm atmosphere we had become accustomed to. One of the back fields had been transformed into a temporary camp for the mining company, Territorial Gold. Flashy trailers were lined up along one fence. A squadron of dozers, loaders, tractor-trailers, pick-ups and a grader were parked with motors idling, ready to push on along the old Dawson Road towards a gold claim on the Stewart River. People we'd never seen before were walking everywhere, talking about a truck stuck at some creek, and another broken down near the highway.

We quickly loaded Danny's cargo and headed back down the Pelly to his home, and our simple life.

With a toboggan full of supplies being towed behind, the yellow dog wasn't nearly as peppy. I teased Danny about this and he quickly agreed.

"Sometimes when Abbie is in the toboggan and there is a full load, we can't make it up that steep ramp at Selkirk." He smiled and added with a twinkle, "When that happens, Abbie has to get out and walk up the hill, and with her bad leg, she sure doesn't like to do that!"

"Could the dogs make it up there?"

"Every time. They never let you down. That's why I'm thinking about going back to dogs... except they are lots slower."

To distribute the weight to best advantage, Danny had me stand at the back of the toboggan instead of sitting behind him on the snowmobile. Even though the speed had been reduced because of the load, it was plenty fast enough for me. I crouched to keep the centre of gravity low, and that perspective made the ride more unnerving still. We bounced over the ice, sliding on the corners, with the toboggan yanking the snowmachine's tail around. Danny seemed unconcerned by the swaying of the toboggan, though when we reached his cabin he confessed, "I go a little slower with Abbie on the back."

There was still time for Marsha and I to mush home before dark, but Danny had another suggestion: "You two stay and eat supper with us. We're going to have moose steaks. Afterwards, there's going to be a big headlight coming up so you can see the way home fine."

The headlight, to which he was alluding, was the full moon. As the sun set, it was rising large and stark in the south-east. Marsha and I looked at one another and then at the meat sitting on the counter thawing. Danny got down four tea cups and uncapped a bottle of rye whiskey.

"Want a shot?" he asked.

"You bet," I replied and we settled in to have a small party.

"Good medicine, eh?" Danny muttered. There were a few more bottles tucked in with the supplies we'd brought over from the farm. I kidded him about taking his medicine before the sickness in this instance and he chuckled.

"Are you going to be here for spring beaver hunt?" he asked. "We could go together and Marsha could stay with Abbie."

I didn't like to be reminded the winter was almost over and our stay on the

Yukon River would be drawing to a close. We had come to feel comfortable with our environment, our neighbours and ourselves. This would probably be the last time we'd see Danny and Abbie until after the ice left, and we would then be moving away to find work. Danny had offered to ferry our belongings out from the cabin to the road in his long riverboat. The interval between now and break-up might be as long as two months, a thought that made this evening an extra special moment.

After our feast of meat and potatoes, Danny pulled out a battered guitar and played a few cowboy songs while Marsha and I tried to sing along. Abbie sat on the bed, rocking gently and smoking cigarettes. Her little pet dog, Timmy, hid under the bed.

When Marsha's eyelids began to droop and the bottle was nearly empty, we took our leave and stumbled out into the cool evening air. The temperature on Danny's outside thermometer indicated we were in for a good hard freeze tonight. Already the snow was crunchy underfoot.

Although the air was sobering, the atmosphere remained romantic and nostalgic. The six dogs we'd brought today were lying patiently in their harnesses, exactly as we'd left them before we decided to stay for supper.

"They must be hungry by now," Marsha whispered. "It's a few hours past their regular feeding time."

"Let's hope they'll run home all the faster for it."

"Are you going to drive?" she asked as I unhooked the single chain on the lead dog's collar.

"Do you think I'm impaired?" I giggled.

"Yes," she said, climbing into the toboggan basket and settling onto a cushion of blankets, "but there probably won't be any police roadblocks between here and Horsefall."

"I'll blame any erratic driving on Casey."

"I'll be your lead dog," called Danny, now feeling no pain. He jumped on his snowmachine and roared off along the trail.

"Well, here goes," I whispered to the furry parka hood in front of me. "Are you set?"

"Yep. Hang on yourself."

"Okay, Casey! *Let's go!*" I shouted and the dogs bolted after Danny's tail-light. I waved to Abbie in the cabin doorway, and almost fell off on the first bend.

After a moment, I located the brake with my clumsy feet and slowed us to a less terrifying pace. At the top of the long, steep ramp down onto the river, I stopped them completely so Marsha could get out to help me ease us slowly down this treacherous spot. There was quite a ski-jump of piled ice at the foot of the incline and I realized there was a fair chance of me coming undone if the dogs hit this at full speed. Should I lose them at this point, they wouldn't have stopped until they were home. On my wobbly legs, the six miles would be a fair hike tonight.

Danny was zipping back and forth on his yellow dog, a broad smile visible in the moonlight. When we were out on the river and pointed for home, he threw the machine into a series of donut skids and then gunned the motor for his cabin. We exchanged waves.

In a minute, his noise had petered out in the distance and we were alone with only the soft creaking of toboggan boards and the rasp of the snow underneath. As we passed patches of steaming open water, we could hear the water hissing, *"Husssshhh."*

The dogs settled into an easy lope, running with their heads up and ears cocked forward. With only the two of us as load, the toboggan wasn't a hard pull, and they would have us home quickly without tiring. In fact, they were friskier now than they had been for days. The full moon must have excited them too.

As Danny had promised, the moon was illuminating the river valley with blue, flat light similar to a car headlight. Its position high above us made the scene glow with a romantic, gentle softness; the patches of snow and angled ice reflected the moon's brilliance in an iridescent array of colour. Though all was screened in blue, the hues of the evergreens and the metallic sheen on the basalt cliffs stood out vividly on this magical tableau.

"It's so beautiful," Marsha whispered, her voice low in reverence to the setting.

"Like travelling through a dream, isn't it?"

Whether the dogs were running for their suppers or had picked up on our thorough contentment, they needed no words from us to keep their pace for home. After months of having to nag and encourage them continually, this midnight cruise was a rewarding jewel. We spoke ever so quietly, to not distract them, or ourselves, from the mesmerizing panorama.

"Moonlight full on the Yukon River," whispered Marsha, holding my mittened hand in hers. "I'll never forget this."

CHAPTER THIRTY-FOUR

THE BODY BELOW

There was a thick, ominous-looking letter from the Royal Canadian Mounted Police in the bundle of mail I had picked up at the farm when Danny and I had gone for his supplies. I didn't open it until the following morning, when we sat down to eat breakfast.

"Do you have a secret past?" Marsha asked with a mouthful of toast. "What are the Mounties after you for?"

"It's okay, partner. You can relax about this one," I tried to sound like Bogart in *Casablanca*. "The boys in scarlet and funny hats got their man fifty-five years ago this month. And—" I flipped to the last page of the photocopied report, "he was arrested and taken to court in Dawson City."

"Who was, and what for?"

"Do you remember me mentioning a murder that happened down near Seventeen Mile Creek? Where the body was stuffed down the root cellar?"

"Sure. I think of it each time I have to go down into our root cellar," Marsha admitted. "It gives me the creeps."

"This is the investigating policeman's report, sent to me by the RCMP Historical Section in Regina. I wrote two months ago for any information they might have about the case."

"Well, might as well tell me about it now. Your toast is already cold."

"Okay… The Mountie's name was Constable Arthur B. Thornthwaite and he was stationed in Carmacks. On the evening of February 26, 1926, he got a message from Mr. Marshall, the owner of a wood camp at Seventeen Mile, saying a woodcutter was missing from his cabin further on downriver at 27 miles below Selkirk. The missing chap was Charles Smith, an old-timer.

"Thornthwaite and a tracker he hired at Selkirk, Joe Menzies, went down to investigate. It says here he and Menzies arrived at the cabin of Harry Davis, 21 miles below Selkirk on the left limit of the Yukon River, at about 7 p.m. on March

3rd. They questioned Davis about Smith because the two had been known to visit back and forth, and to walk into Selkirk together on occasion. Smith was apparently well liked, and Davis quite the opposite.

"Davis is quoted in the report here as saying, *'The last time I saw Smith was on the 12th of February. He came up to my cabin to have a plaster put on his back. I gave him some caribou meat, he put this in his haversack and packed it back to his cabin. I haven't been down to Smith's since January.'*"

"So did Davis do it?" asked Marsha, impatiently. "Did he kill Smith?"

"Wait until the end. I'll tell you the whole story as I read this," I scolded, knowing she was the type who reads the last page of a book first so she wouldn't be scared at the climax.

"The Mountie and Menzies went on downriver to Charlie Smith's cabin. There was no Smith, but his snowshoes, two rifles and watch were still in the cabin. Smith's revolver was missing, and the water barrel and perishables were frozen.

"So Constable Thornthwaite and the trapper spent the next three days combing the area for signs of the missing man. Smith's cabin was on an island, but he had a small trapline on the shore. The two men followed all his lines and found no fresh prints in the 50-square-mile area they searched."

"How did they know he didn't fall through the ice?" Marsha asked.

"Well, the report mentions that. There was only one hole in the ice, but it had been made when an Indian broke through after Smith was reported missing. And, the river wasn't deep there because the Indian had gotten out all right."

"So these investigators didn't know much, except that he was missing and not on his trapline."

"There was one clue they picked up on in Smith's cabin," I noted, feeling this had the makings of a detective thriller. "Smith's calendar had been crossed off up to and including February Twelfth, so they knew the date he had left his cabin last."

"He crossed off the Twelfth, so he must have left on the Thirteenth, right?" Marsha interjected. "That's the day after Davis saw him."

"Nope. That's what I'd have figured, but the Mountie knew better. Thornthwaite had stayed overnight once with Charlie Smith when out on his long dog team patrols and had watched the old man carefully. Every morning, the first thing Smith did was cross off today's date. So our clever constable knew Smith disappeared sometime between the morning of the Twelfth and that night.

"Now where was Smith on the Twelfth?"

Constable Arthur Thornthwaite of the Mounties was determined to get his man. [photo courtesy A.B. Thornthwaite Collection, Yukon Archives]

"At Davis's place, getting a plaster on his back and then walking home with some caribou meat," said Marsha.

"Right, at least according to Davis's story. So the two investigators mushed back upriver to pay another visit to Mr. Davis."

At noon on March 7th, 1926, two dog teams pulled up to Davis's log shack. Menzies walked back into the forest, as if to relieve himself. But while Constable Arthur Thornthwaite was inside seemingly interested in filing Davis's claim for welfare rations, Menzies was really searching the area and exterior of the cabin for clues. If Davis had done Smith in, he would need to dispose of the body. There wasn't much that could be hidden from a veteran trapper: wherever Davis had walked, Joe Menzies followed the trail like a bloodhound.

Inside, the young policeman had allowed the topic to drift back to his main investigation. Davis repeated his story, changing a few details, adding others but sticking to the date. Davis gave this detailed description of Smith's attire on the date in question: *a dark flannel shirt, a leather belt about 1-1/2 inches wide, with a Colt Automatic attached; he wore a little dark blue toque, and Indian moccasins, and a khaki haversack, U.S. Army style.*

While Davis was talking, Thornthwaite was glancing about the cabin, trying to visualize the two men: one applying the mustard plaster, perhaps a fight. But how would Davis kill Smith? And why would he want to?

Then the constable noticed a calendar hung in the corner. He crossed the room and casually flipped the page back to February. The Twelfth was the only date *not* crossed off! What could have upset Davis's routine so he would have left that date?

Davis was now claiming he hadn't had *any* meat all winter, because he had no money to buy ammunition for his .30-30 rifle. Marshall had only recently given him some shells. This contradicted Davis's earlier statement about giving Smith some caribou meat, but Thornthwaite let it pass. He was allowing Davis time and room to hang himself. And the shifty suspect did indeed give himself away: not by what he did or said, but by what he *didn't* do – he didn't ever move.

When Thornthwaite asked permission to *make a routine check to ensure there was no hidden supply of food, and that Davis was truly destitute,* Davis agreed, but stayed himself in the very centre of the cabin throughout the search. Even when Menzies entered and the three men were crowded uncomfortably close together, Davis didn't step back. The Mountie now knew where to look for clues.

He asked Davis to step back and sit on the bed. Then he got down on his knees and began wiping away dirt and silt from where Davis had stood. In a few seconds, he found a two-inch-diameter stain on the peeled spruce pole floor. It could have been blood. Menzies soon uncovered another area that might have recently been washed and scrubbed: hardly in keeping with Davis's housekeeping standards.

"You say you've had no meat this winter?" Menzies asked.

"No, and I need food," Davis maintained.

Thornthwaite looked to his helper and asked what he'd found outside.

"Nothing amiss," Menzies reported. "No sign of a food cache – or of anything else at all."

Thornthwaite glanced down again, noticing a faint pattern in the sand, silt and ashes partially covering the pole flooring. With a finger, he traced the lines, then used a piece of kindling to scrape dirt from the crack. It was a trapdoor.

"I haven't been down in the cellar since last September!" Davis cried out.

But the Mountie was already prying up the cover. He was not looking for a food cache: he had a bigger mystery to solve.

Constable Thornthwaite was halfway down the crude ladder when Davis made his move. He grabbed for his .30-30 leaning against the wall. But Menzies had beaten Davis to the draw.

"You might be able to shoot the Mountie," he told Davis calmly, "but I'll make sure you die, too." Menzies held a revolver pointed at the suspect's chest.

Davis placed the rifle on the floor and raised his hands. "I give up. I killed Charlie Smith," he admitted.

Thornthwaite, caught in the middle of this exchange, glanced down into the cellar and saw a man's legs. He climbed up and formally arrested Harry Davis for the murder of Charles H. Smith. No one had any doubt about the date.

Menzies and Thornthwaite took turns guarding the prisoner so the other one could identify the body. Charlie Smith's head had been bashed in and there was a bullet wound in his chest. A plaster was still on his back. The revolver was missing, but there was over $400 on the body.

"If Davis had killed Smith for the money, why hadn't he taken it?" Marsha wondered.

"Harry Davis made a statement which is quoted here," I said, "claiming he had put a mustard plaster on Smith's back, but that it was too hot and had burned Smith's back. Davis describes the fight they had next:

Smith said it was too hot and reached out and grabbed my rifle, which was against the wall near my bed, and hit me twice with it, across the left hip and left temple. We then had a fight, and I hit him over the head with a piece of wood, and got the rifle away from him and hit him over the head with it, and then when he was on the floor, I shot him. I was about six feet distant from Smith when I shot him. I got Smith over to the cellar and lowered him into it and washed the blood from the floor where I had shot Smith."

"So it was self-defence," Marsha stated. "Except he didn't have to shoot him, did he? Davis had already knocked him over the head and had Smith lying on the floor."

"That would be up to a jury in Dawson City to decide. First these two sleuths had to get Davis into Fort Selkirk without him doing them in as well. Constable Thornthwaite describes the root cellar as actually being an abandoned mine shaft, so there was plenty of room for Davis to store more bodies down there. And remember, they didn't know where Smith's missing Colt handgun was. They had to watch him every moment, even when Davis wanted to relieve himself.

Harry Davis was photographed after his arrest by the Mounted Police constable. [photo courtesy A.B. Thornthwaite Collection, Yukon Archives]

"Davis now described how for days he had felt the dead Smith's eyes watching him from the cellar. This little gem of information must have convinced his captors Davis was quite looney. The report merely states Davis was taken to Fort Selkirk, but I'll bet they made him walk out front where he couldn't pull any tricks on them."

"They would have come right past our cabin, bringing the body, too," Marsha said, glancing out the window towards the river. "What an unpleasant thought!"

"Actually they took in the prisoner on this day, and Menzies and another fellow returned for the body on the next day. Davis was kept in a room in back of William Schofield's general store under constant guard so he couldn't escape or commit suicide.

"A week later, Constable Thornthwaite, accompanied by Constable J.R. Purdue from Whitehorse, escorted Davis to jail in Dawson City. This time they travelled on the Royal Mail stage coach over the old Dawson Road, and they brought the body along for an autopsy."

"Great," moaned Marsha. "So this murderer and the dead body were taken in a horse-drawn sleigh along the road behind us. We're surrounded by old ghost trails here."

"Want to know what happened at the trial?"

"Sure."

"Me, too. But the report ends with the prisoner being remanded for trial. We'll have to write to the archives in Whitehorse, or visit the Dawson Museum for microfilm copies of the newspaper accounts of the trial. It may take a few weeks for a written reply."

We cleared away the breakfast dishes and began our day's chores. The temperature was back down below freezing, so we were thinking about camping destinations again.

"I know already where you want to go," said Marsha.

"Well, wouldn't a nice trip downriver be fun?" I grinned.

Marsha didn't say anything for a moment, turning the idea over and over in her mind. Eventually, she sighed and reached for a sheet of paper to start a food list.

"Just promise me one thing, Bruce," she said.

"Name it."

"Promise me there won't be another dead body."

CHAPTER THIRTY-FIVE

ALMOST ANOTHER

Although the murder cabin was only fourteen or so miles downriver from us, we packed our full winter outfit, including the wall tent and stove. Marsha organized a full week's supply of people food, and I measured out a similar amount for the dogs. The trail, or more to the point the lack of one, would slow us, and we wished to explore without feeling rushed.

Since the warm spell, we were more leery about bears, so we spent part of the last day at home building stronger shutters for the windows. These boards might slow down a groggy bruin fresh out of hibernation, although a determined intruder would eventually dig through the plywood roof with his claws.

Come morning, the sunny spell was only a memory. The temperature had dropped significantly, vindicating our earlier decision to pack our warmest clothing. Fat, grey clouds grasped the clifftops, dusting us, as we harnessed the dogs, with the occasional sprinkle of flakes and hinting of worse to come. However, the dogs were bouncy and happy to be leaving once again, so Marsha and I were soon caught up in their enthusiasm. They raced out of the yard and onto the river, rattling the toboggans over the icy trail and shaking any cobwebs out of our sleepy heads in the process.

We headed across the Yukon to Six Mile Creek on our old trail. Beyond, there might be a trace of Cor's track from a month ago, but the combination of snowfalls and sun melt since didn't lend much hope.

Casey led us to a narrow ice bridge across a strip of open water that looked dangerous, but when I checked it with the axe, there turned out to be a good margin of solid ice. Two minutes later we came to another bridge that collapsed in front of me when I poked at the band of snow and ice with my long pole. The detour up onto an island past the open flow held us up for a half-hour before we could regain our old trail and trot again. A consolation for our axe work clearing this bypass through the willow brush was we'd have a safe route for our return journey.

Casey was only able to follow Cor's old track for ten more minutes before it petered out in the centre of the river. For a while I let him follow the shoreline, but this forced us through deeper snow than in mid-river and also took us on a longer winding route. My leader would happily follow the shore *or* cross to another land point, but he was reluctant to strike a path straight down the wide river. Other mushers had told me their leaders also got confused when presented with the task of heading across a huge lake or river, and would not lead in as straight a line as their mushers might wish. Telling the dog, *Gee, just a bit,* or *Ten degrees to the Haw side* was not going to work, at least with my old pet. We tried Hinglish, but he was even more intimidated by the expanses of white than Casey. Before we lost all our momentum, and their enthusiasm, I strapped on cross-country skis and assumed the role of lead dog myself. The surface area of these long, birch touring skis was enough to distribute my weight to a point where I wasn't too worried about plunging through the ice myself. To check for the crowd following hot on my heels, I would stop and chip at the ice with a ski pole.

At Black Creek, about six miles below Horsefall, we paused for a sip from the thermos, giving the dogs a chance to relax, lick their paws and nap in the snow. Marsha unpacked her camera and took a few photographs of the sprawled bodies. Despite the cover of cloud, the air had warmed to Zero Fahrenheit.

"I'd like to reach the mouth of Seventeen Mile Creek to make camp," I told her, as we prepared to press on. "We can explore from there."

"Why are you so interested in these old cabins? It's almost an obsession for you."

"I don't exactly know," I confessed. "It's eerie, isn't it? As if there were ghosts or spirits involved. I wonder if someone who is now dead is luring us down there? I can feel the suspense building with each mile as we draw closer."

"Do you seriously believe Davis's or Smith's ghost is promoting all this?" Marsha was sceptical.

"Well, if it is Davis's ghost," I offered, "let's hope he hasn't got anything dangerous in mind."

Our destination was south-west from here, because the river had begun a long swing to our left. As we descended, passing through the Three-Way-Channel Islands, the light breeze picked up force and began pummelling us with hard pellets of snow. The valley had widened considerably, granting the storm ample room to have a hardy run at us. As the gale increased, we put on more layers of clothing, but decided against stopping. While we kept moving, we were warm

The Yukon was more than a half-mile wide and frozen over four feet thick in most places, yet the ice was dangerously thin in spots.

and our equipment was protected under the toboggan covers. If we stopped to set up camp, the driving snow would soon be into everything. The wind would fan a campfire through cords of firewood in no time at all, and steal all the heat as well. The best course of action, for the moment at least, seemed to be pushing on, hoping the storm would blow over by the time we reached our destination.

Marsha had to manage both teams when I was skiing ahead. Whenever the first bunch got caught on a block of ice, she ran ahead and set them right, then brought her troop past the same obstacle. Each ice ridge we crossed was a bout of hard work for her, especially if the toboggans tipped and needed to be wrestled back upright. From my vantage point out ahead, she appeared to have the worse job. When I suggested we switch periodically, she quickly declined the offer.

"You go first," she said. "I'm scared stiff about falling through the ice. *Please be careful!*"

As I squinted into the gale and chose what I hoped would be both a safe and a relatively level route across the pressure ridges and scrambled jams, the images of dog teams from long ago flashed through my mind. When Constable Thornthwaite and tracker Joe Menzies were driving their teams down here to search for Charlie Smith, there would have been a well-used trail to follow. In most years, the river froze much more jumbled and uneven than this winter, often creating a surface chocked with blocks and slabs of ice taller than a man, and pushed together like wrecked cars in a scrap yard. The two men would have probably been fighting through and over mounds and struggling to keep their toboggans from tipping into the crevices. We were encountering obstacles of this scale only at pressure ridges and the odd bend where the ice pans had buckled.

Reports and photographs of the early Mounted Police patrols which travelled from Dawson City over the mountains to Fort McPherson in the North West Territories indicated these groups were usually composed of three or four dog teams, tended by four or five men. The extra man would be able to go ahead on snowshoes to pack trail, and there would still be a man to manoeuvre each toboggan over the rough ice. Today, we could have used an extra person to help Marsha.

Arthur Walden, who wrote a book called *Dog Puncher on the Yukon* about his experiences freighting and running the mail at the turn of the century, ran as many as twenty-seven dogs and three sleds, with only one helper (called a swamper) on the last sled. The three sleds were attached in tandem and the swamper had a brake to help slow them down. At hills, they would sometimes haul up one sled at a time if the climb was very steep, and wrap chains under the runners or base for the descent.

For me, the most thrilling image was of the great annual treks of the Indian families, who routinely came from the Mackenzie district to the Yukon, and back. Apparently it was the women who managed the dogs. All the men went ahead to pack trail; they would take turns charging into the deep snow to beat down the high, loose drifts. This was extremely hard work, and as each one exhausted, another would race past to do his turn. The Indians travelled with the whole family including grandparents and infant children.

The storm became more intense with each mile we covered, until we could barely see across the river. From my canoeing charts, I knew the next major landmark would be Whalen Island, behind which we should find the creek mouth and, nearby, the cabin of Harry Davis. For today, I would be quite content to locate any dense stand of forest for overnight shelter from the wind, and leave the ghosts to themselves for one more day. I waited for Marsha to catch up and told her of my intention. She too wanted to stop as soon as we came across a suitable location.

Whalen Island was mostly wooded in poplars, promising neither the shelter nor dry wood we needed, so I swung off toward shore. Our way, however, was effectively blocked by a raging canal-like channel close up to the bank. The open water stretched back upriver for some distance, so I led us further downstream, hoping to find the end or a safe bridge soon.

For another half-hour, we followed the black water, staying well away from

Picking our way through jumbled shore ice to locate a safe route – I'm ahead testing the thickness before calling the dogs to bring up the toboggan.

the sheer edges. Looking across the swirling flow, we could see that the ice shelf on the far side was easily two feet thick, but we avoided approaching closely to check the near edge.

Finally, we came to where the hungry current had bent over to the island, but had left a hundred yard wide bridge of ice near the bend. Our choices were to trample across the island and continue downriver; to turn back upstream and go – possibly over a mile – to the head of this stretch of open water; or to attempt the bridge. Tempting us across the bridge of ice was a dense stand of evergreens on the shore for shelter and fuel.

We stood for a moment weighing the possibilities, and looking at the ice. The current had obviously undermined this ice crossing, because its surface was sunken some three or four feet lower than where we stood. Still, the colour was no darker, and the width made us think the centre portion must surely be safe.

I went out on my skis to cautiously check from close at hand.

Marsha wrote this version of the subsequent events in a letter to her Mom, who no doubt was happier not knowing at the time what risks her daughter was taking:

I was the one to stay behind and wait 'til the ice bridge was tested safe... My guards were down... I was vulnerable...

It was either cross here, or retrace our steps back miles, or go out around the island to get to the tall timber so we could make camp. We'd travelled twelve miles today into a cold wind blowing upriver. The sun had taken the day off and the snowfall added a greyness to our travel. We had a decision to make. The crossing was definitely a closer route to setting up camp. The wind and snow was blowing around me, wicking away little by little my body heat. I'd already put on my winter parka.

Bruce had gone ahead on cross-country skis, poking at the ice as he went, stomping sometimes and poking, two or three times at all places, ahead, beside him, and on the other side and ahead again. All went well as he reached the other side and stomped a path a bit beyond the crossing place so the toboggan would be pulled across and not stopped short of safety. Whew, I felt better!

I dumped my toboggan over on its side to anchor my team where it was, and climbed on the back of the lead toboggan to drive it across. Bruce had come halfway back so the dogs would go to him and then follow his trail exactly across to the other side. Seemed like a good idea.

'Okay, let's go,' I said, with a lump of fear in my throat. The dogs were anxious to go as they'd been stopped for ten to fifteen minutes so there was no problem getting them on their way. Before I knew it, we'd crossed over the dip to the higher side and all was okay.

Bruce said he'd ski over and get the other team, but I felt we needed one person to drive the team and another person for them to follow, because of the exact tested trail they needed to stay on. So we both proceeded back toward the other side.

By this time, I'd had time to catch my breath and make a few jokes about falling in because the fear had lifted from my throat and gut, and all seemed routine from here. I even had my arms stretched out from my sides, saying, 'I guess this is supposed to be what to do,' when down I went—

A hole had formed about three feet in diameter where I once stood. I was suspended on my outstretched arms. Water was swirling at my feet, legs and waist. I felt the current pulling at my boots and heavy wool pants. I looked ahead at the very thin ice my arms were on. I was too scared to move—

I called and called for Bruce. I couldn't see or hear him, and the more I envisioned my situation, the more panic I felt. I had to get out!

I don't know how I managed to pull myself out of that hole... because my feet could not touch the bottom. Yet the next thing I knew, I was squirming up on that thin ice. First on my elbows, then my chest, my stomach, and soon my legs felt free of the rushing water and I was rolling away from the hole. I didn't dare stand up, in case I fell through again, so I rolled and rolled and rolled away from the hole. Then I felt safer and ran up the slope to my tipped toboggan.

The wind was still howling and the snow coming down. My body felt like I was encased in an ice cube. It was a burning cold sensation I'd known from before when I'd gone swimming in a glacial lake one summer.

There was no cover from the wind and my pack with the dry clothes had already gone across to the other side with the first team. Bruce was now with me and insisted I move around so my clothes wouldn't freeze solid and prevent any movement while we figured something out. The only trees nearby were the poplars on the island, which would be useless for starting a fast, hot fire or for any shelter.

Just when we were a bit stumped, Casey, Hinglish, Curly and Loki pulled up beside us with my pack and Bruce's toboggan! Yikes, we didn't have time to be afraid for them as they'd decided there was too much excitement on this side which they weren't going to miss for anything. So they walked back across on their own time and own trail, arriving safe and sound to get into the action.

'Thanks, guys!' I said through chattering teeth.

At that point, Marsha stripped off her icy clothes while I unpacked wool sox, dry liners and moccasins for her feet, fresh long johns and wool pants, and two sweaters, mitts and my big parka. In a minute we had her bundled up in enough clothes for Sixty Below. After she ran around in a circle for a while and jumped, her circulation was back to all extremities, and she actually had to open the parka to let out heat. With the danger now past, we fell into each other's arms and hugged ourselves silly. After being that scared, we felt light-headed to be safe once more. We laughed and kissed, hugged and rolled in the snow, and danced with the dogs.

Then we pulled ourselves together and directed the teams upriver. There was only an hour of daylight left and we had camp to prepare.

We backtracked, following the open channel back to where it began, and then went another good distance before crossing to the shore. There we found a dense stand of mature spruce on a high bank, which would become our home for the next few days. We oriented the wall tent so the doorway looked onto the river, and stretched out the gang chains parallel to the bank so every dog would be tethered with a view. There was enough firewood to last us weeks within fifty paces of the tent and a mountain of blue ice to melt right below us on the river. The camping spot was ideal, and we felt our luck had returned after a near-fatal lapse.

When we had the dogs looked after and our lentils simmering on the stove, I asked Marsha to remember specific details of her adventure.

"Did my feet touch the bottom? I remember my feet being dragged downstream by the current. I felt panic at the suspended feeling of my body being *nowhere*. My feet felt very heavy in my boots."

"Did you feel wet, or just cold?" I wondered.

"The sensation of being wet never really occurred to me until I raised myself back out of the hole and the wind hit me. Before that, I knew I was wet, but an actual wet feeling, I don't remember."

"Did you look down ever?" I prompted.

"No, I don't think so. I don't remember ever looking down, just at the thin ice level and higher," Marsha explained while stirring the supper. "I don't think I ever looked behind me or even twisted my head. I was too scared to move because the ice under my arms was so thin."

"That's why you didn't see me," I explained to her. "I was behind you and was reaching out with a ski pole for you to grab. You couldn't have heard me either."

"You know, the falling through happened so fast, I don't remember falling. I was just there. In the water. Hanging on.

"I was on the verge of tears, total helplessness," she continued. "I had thoughts of closing my eyes and having this whole escapade vanish. I thought, *It isn't true! What do I do? Wait for help? Get out myself? Move? Be still? What if the ice broke more?* I was almost in a dream world, not totally conscious of anything. I reacted on pure instinct to get out."

She dished out our supper, and poured the hot apple juice with an amazingly steady hand. I would have been shaking still, had it been me in that hole.

"As soon as I got free of the river," Marsha continued, "I wanted to run, run, run… run away from the uncertain ice below my feet… run away from my cold, wet clothes and freezing legs… run away from the foolishness of the whole adventure. I didn't feel like crying, except maybe when I was in the hole."

Marsha hadn't cried, but I felt like bursting into sobs at that point, listening to her calmly talking about such a horrifying experience. She was so brave and I felt so very privileged to be with her.

CHAPTER THIRTY-SIX

ENTERTAINMENT AT SEVENTEEN MILE CREEK

An aftershock from Marsha's dramatic adventure rippled through us in the morning. From the moment we awoke, we were confronted with reminders, such as the wet woollens hanging to dry near the stove. Marsha's parka had been soaked up to the armpits, a soggy line testifying to the desperation of her situation in those icy waters. We ate our morning mush with our eyes and conversations averted, intent on avoiding any reference to death, danger, drowning or bodies. When I suggested, finally, that we postpone by twenty-four hours our search for Davis's cabin, Marsha readily agreed.

"I feel more like spending today quietly," Marsha said, lying back onto the pile of bedding. "Let's stay close to the tent all day, and not plan anything specific so there is time for napping, a chance to appreciate each other.

"Life seems so temporary and fragile," she added, "we should make the most of each other while everything is in our favour."

The kettle was boiling, so I dropped in some chamomile flowers and put it aside to steep. Chamomile would be a calming influence for the quiet morning.

"What exactly did you have in mind?" I asked her with a hint of lust in my voice.

"Well, to start with," she laughed, "you can massage my shoulders for at least an hour. I feel a bit stiff."

Outside, the grey clouds trailing after yesterday's storm cast a foreboding gloom over the countryside. The dogs lay curled in the hollows they'd dug for themselves in the snowdrifts, rising only to stretch, sniff and relieve themselves. Occasionally, the ice would crack with a sound like a cannon shot reverberating across the valley, ricocheting off the far hills and echoing from the cliffs behind us.

We stayed inside our white room, emerging only for more firewood and to feed the dogs. At dusk, when I stood on the top of the bank, holding the empty dog pot in my hand and watching the moon rising from upriver, I realized the skies had cleared. A few stars were beginning to twinkle through the last wisps of cloud on the eastern horizon. This had been one of the few days all winter we hadn't been intimately familiar with every nuance of the day's weather. So much time indoors seemed a shame, I thought, then quickly refuted the idea.

"We are part of Nature, too," I mused. "Being in love is simply another way of appreciating our world." Pleased with that rationalization, I ducked back inside.

By next morning, our spirits were restless again, and we resumed the hunt. The return of the sun had certainly contributed to our rekindled energies; it washed over the tent, making the inside blindingly bright. We chose to do our day's wanderings on cross-country skis, staying on land where possible. Following the river bank, we came across evidence of violent flooding in some previous year's spring break-up. Willows along the shore had been flattened, some uprooted, and others clinging to life but tilted drunkenly, their upriver sides deeply scarred from the bulldozing ice blocks. A huge spruce with most of its roots intact had been floated back sixty paces from the bank and was now lodged in amongst a grove of poplar trees.

I stomped ahead on my skis, forcing a trail through the saplings and driftwood piles. Marsha's manner along this path was a reflection of her dissimilar character: she ambled slowly, examining driftwood logs from all sides and angles, picking up spruce buds and curls of poplar bark, for no other reason than *they were pretty*. In this aspect, we complemented each other's personalities, helping one another see more of the environment. When the Indians lived in the bush, they rarely wintered without women in their camps and on their travels. It was only the white men coming later who believed they could survive independently of other company and help. Harry Davis and Charlie Smith were two all-too-typical examples of loners for whom the strain had proven too much. The fight that ensued ended Smith's life and sent Davis to trial for his.

We paused at the creek mouth, and thoroughly tested the ice before venturing up its flat road-wide surface. In a few minutes, we came to a telegraph line drooping to shoulder height where it crossed the creek. There had been no, or few, poles in this section that we could see. Instead, glass insulators on short wooden arms had been spiked to the trees to support the line.

The right-of-way was overgrown in willow, making it harder to travel there than through the evergreen forest flanking it. We skied parallel to the line, looking for signs of human habitation, but finding only evidence of a healthy squirrel population. These little critters had piled huge mounds of pine cones and chips

Taking a day off to smile and cherish life – camped near the Harry Davis cabin site, downriver from Horsefall.

beneath a few ancient trees which had escaped the hunger of the sternwheelers' boilers. Their snow homes were riddled with tunnels and trampled pathways, but the residents we saw chose to scream and chatter at us from safer spots high in the branches. Their tone was unmistakably rude: our presence was *not* appreciated.

We followed several blazed trails fruitlessly, finding each petered out into a game trail at the far limit of the spruces. From the number of scars on the trees, we figured someone had gone wild with a hatchet, marking everywhere, until we realized the river had once flooded this high. Faint traces of silt in the bark revealed these scars were made by the ice, not by humans.

We tracked for hours, discovering a swampy, muskeg pond where moose had been yarding, but no sign of a cabin. The depressions in the snow indicating a cow moose's and her calf's bedding spot were recent: their hoof-prints had not been melted much by the sun. Out here in the open, last summer's tall grass shone golden in the sunshine, poking through the patchy, ultra-white snow. The field was dimpled and pimpled with the mounds of muskeg, the snow throwing a thin skin over the whole.

By two o'clock, we'd still not found any sign of Davis's cabin and decided to turn and search again over the ground we'd covered.

"Let's split up, so we can examine more area," I suggested.

"Fine by me," said Marsha. "Just be careful. Don't fall down some old root cellar hole!"

She chose to sweep along the shoreline, and I kept further back almost to the wall of rock that loomed over the flat. I stumbled upon a section of old road, but it led only to the creek, and apparently had been a wood-hauling route.

On the upriver side of the creek, the white spruce forest thinned out, changing to spindly black spruce that marched up the Seventeen Mile Creek valley, no doubt continuing all the way to our old camp at the base of Little Summit. This creek was the one we'd attempted to descend weeks ago from its alpine source.

A common neighbour of the black spruce is the Labrador tea bush, and this creek valley held good to the rule. I picked handsful of the pubescent leaves, stuffing my pockets until they bulged uncomfortably. The thought of such quantities of tea lying here in fields, free for the picking, prompted me to call for Marsha.

"Hey-ay! *Hey-ay!*" I shouted towards the river and whistled shrilly.

"Hey-ay, yourself!" came the spoken reply from the other side of a clump of spruce. Marsha had followed my trail from where I'd crossed the creek, and was picking tea only a stone's throw away.

"What a gold mine, eh?" she remarked, showing me her harvest of leaves. "Did you notice these leaves are redder than the ones near Horsefall?"

"Now that you mention it, I do. Must be something to do with the different soil on this flat. Most of the tea we picked this winter was from higher levels, up on the plateau off the trail to the farm. It'll be interesting to see what difference this will make to the flavour."

Marsha had found another road in her wanderings, this one parallel to the telegraph line, but closer to the river. We headed along it towards our tent. The route was fairly easy to travel since much of it cut across swamp that hadn't grown back in willows. We skied in the deep ruts, wondering if the last users had dragged their wood sleighs with the help of dogs or horses. Likely this was one of William Marshall's trails. Marshall had been Charlie Smith's employer and the one who had turned in the alarm about the missing man.

When the old road veered away from the river, we struck off through the forest aiming for the shore close to where we estimated our tent to be.

"Look at this, Bruce," Marsha suddenly called out. She was pointing with her ski pole at a log I'd just passed. "This looks like a notch for the corner of a cabin, doesn't it?"

Sure enough, there was a neat axe gouge out of this log and, as we discovered by sweeping snow away, a matching notch was carved out of another log beneath it. We were so close to the river that I'd dismissed these as driftwood from the floods. We prowled around now until the trail of logs strewn across the forest floor led us to a suspicious mound. Part of a door frame and section of a wall protruded from the snow and the sun glinted off metal.

From close up, the features of an old cabin were obvious. We could make out the outline of roof beams and poles which had collapsed over the rest, burying most of the interior in dirt and sod. There was a smashed cookstove: a tiny model that was combination airtight heater and stove. Beside it was an enamelled wash-basin, which looked intact until I poked it with a ski pole and found there was no bottom.

Marsha found a milk tin and pieces of milled planking lying under the snow nearby. Further excavations rewarded us with discovery of battered kerosene tins and a well-rusted saw blade. We noted everything was covered in fine grey-brown silt, but there was no way of discerning whether the flood had been before, after, or the cause of the cabin's destruction. So little remained intact of the cabin itself we couldn't even be sure of its exact original location or orientation. If there was a deep root cellar beneath the pile of wall and roof, it was inaccessible to us. The only other possibility in the immediate area was a shallow depression about the size of a bath tub. This wasn't much like a mine shaft, though it might have once been deeper.

"Do you think this was Davis's place?" Marsha's tone was sceptical. "Isn't it too far upstream?"

"It is about the correct size," I said, pacing off the length of a wall log lying near the depression. "And it isn't far from the river bank. But who knows? It might have been one of Marshall's shacks instead."

Laying the map out on the snow and aligning it with my compass, I could triangulate our position fairly precisely with a bearing on two hills. The elevation scale on the map verified what would be obvious on a midwinter day: this was a poor location for sun exposure. A cabin here would have received even less direct light than our shady cabin at Horsefall Creek. The hills to the south of this site were as high as and much closer than our Victoria Rock. This would be a most depressing place for over four months.

"But what if Davis lived further down?"

"Check out the map, Marsha. All along the bank for the next half-dozen miles, the exposure would be as bad. The sunniest spots would be on islands, like where Smith lived, or over on the far shore."

At suppertime, we had a chance to sample Seventeen Mile Creek's Labrador

As long as its roof was intact, a cabin could last many decades without the walls rotting. The pole roof on this old cabin had partially collapsed and the whole structure was deteriorating.

tea, and tried to imagine Harry Davis doing the same in his squalid shack by the bank.

"It may be my imagination," I told Marsha as we crawled off to bed, "but I think this tea is quite different from the stuff we've been drinking all winter."

"I noticed it tasted a bit stronger, but it was still pleasant," said Marsha, sleepily.

"What I mean is, that it might be a bit *stronger in its effect*," I whispered. "You know how Labrador tea has a reputation of being a mild *narcotic*. Do you think maybe Harry Davis drank this stuff all the time and—"

"Bruce, you have more weird theories than I have patience," Marsha said firmly. *"Please go to sleep!"*

CHAPTER THIRTY-SEVEN

SETTING OUR SIGHTS HIGHER

Marsha's misadventure three days ago quashed any thoughts I'd been entertaining about further river travel. We'd been idly curious about our next-door-neighbours some sixty miles north but now realized we might never meet them. The river ice had become too dangerous.

Those neighbours were trapping at Ballarat Creek, and their access was from Dawson City, further along down the Yukon River. This put them at the southern end of a long string of trappers and homesteaders who live along the river. The combined traffic from all the dog teams and snowmobiles travelling in and out of Dawson creates a major trail on the ice in that region. Had we reached Ballarat earlier in the season, we could have mushed confidently from there to the famous Gold Rush town.

There was, however, another idea up our sleeves for this last week of March. We held a planning conference while eating our oatmeal porridge.

"Let's get off this river and do a dry land jaunt," insisted Marsha. "How about up Volcano Mountain? There should be trapline trails most of the way."

"Sure. If Don is through trapping for the season, we won't have to worry about his traps."

"And I won't have to worry about falling through the ice anywhere," sighed Marsha.

"Except for crossing Volcano Lake," I corrected her, but quickly added, "which shouldn't be any problem. There is no current, so the lake ice should be a few feet thick everywhere."

"Okay, when shall we leave?"

"If we go back to Horsefall today, we could go tomorrow," I suggested. "Is that pushing us too much?"

"No, I'm game and the dogs are well rested," Marsha declared. "And, the sooner we get back to Horsefall and are off the river, the better I'll feel."

We hauled down the tent and were underway two hours later. Our trail from three days past was a shiny ribbon across the matte river plain, easy for the lead dog to pick up, so I could ride instead of skiing ahead. The dogs ran as far as Black Creek, where we halted for lunch. The sun was beating down from a cloudless sky, slowly turning the snow surface into mush, but not enough to worry us. There were only another five miles to Horsefall, and the dogs still felt fresh.

"With all this sun, I hope there is some snow left in the bush," I worried to Marsha, while she piled cheese onto some biscuits.

"The air temperature should be cooler at the higher altitudes," she assured me, "and there was more snowfall up off the river. I'll bet there will be lots left on Volcano Mountain, maybe too much."

I could tell Marsha was looking forward to being on solid ground again. Why, she was even smiling at the idea of stomping through deep snow up a steep mountain.

There was one minor detour to make near the mouth of Six Mile Creek, where one of our ice bridges from the trip downriver was washed out. When this bypass operation was over, we thought we were home-free, as our creek was now in sight across the Yukon. However, at closer inspection, we found our usual ramp up off the river was blocked by a narrow but effective barrier of open water.

"No more chopping holes to get drinking water," Marsha called out cheerfully, as I directed Casey downstream to try another approach. "Think of all the time that will save."

We cut across a sandbar, over a well-frozen slough, and onto the creek flat from the west. Though this ramp off the river was considerably steeper, the dogs eagerly charged up the bank as though the toboggans were empty.

We were unpacked and repacked in an hour, leaving us much of the warm sunny afternoon to enjoy in holiday style. Marsha set up a picnic for us on the wood pile, spreading a bath towel over a square of plywood to make our table. We sat on logs, basking in the sunshine, eating popcorn and drinking the last two beers from the root cellar. When we'd left the cabin for any long periods, I'd dug a hole in the sandy cellar floor, and buried the beer and few remaining perishables under an insurance layer of earth. With a few dog food bags piled on top, the treasure had been sufficiently insulated.

We departed for Volcano Mountain early next morning, now carrying snowshoes instead of skis, and only the tarp for shelter. The food box contained just enough for an overnight trip. There was one meal's ration of dog food plus eight chunks of fat in a sack on Marsha's toboggan. This was the lightest we'd ever travelled,

Our two toboggans parked outside Horsefall cabin in this late-winter photo. The sunshine on the snow would be dazzling – sunglasses were very important to prevent snow blindness.

and it made a big difference. Even though we both rode, the dogs could still trot up all but the steepest grades.

Our route coincided with the path of the miners travelling in from Pelly Crossing over to the Stewart River. The bulldozers and grader I'd seen parked over at the Bradley farm had passed by on the old Dawson Road, grading the snow smooth, and widening the way by knocking down willows and small bushes at the sides. What had been a quaint, somewhat overgrown, horse-drawn sleigh's pathway was now a wide cat road. It was ironic this route had been created eighty years ago to service a gold-mining town, and was now being stripped of its heritage flavour by machines on a present-day search for the same precious metal.

The toboggans slid well over the few gravel patches, but the rocks took their toll with gouges and scratches on the bases. Where the earth was exposed and slightly wet from the sun, however, the white plastic grabbed and was harder for the dogs to pull. To help them out, we would tip the toboggan onto one edge and hold it balanced on this *skate* until back onto packed snow. After a few miles, all of us – dogs and people – were happier when we branched off onto Don Mark's trapline trail heading toward the mountain.

"Hang on to your hat," Marsha shouted. "Don said this trail is pretty crude."

"It's beautiful compared to the trail those dozers leave in their wake," I yelled back, leaning the toboggan hard to knife around a tight corner. Don's light sled was two-thirds the length of our toboggans, and he'd cut his corners accordingly.

The trail wound up a hill, meandering to take advantage of partially cleared game trails and any natural breaks in the forest. We could see where Don had set his traps, though the actual leg-holds and conibears were no longer out. He must have collected them all early, when the weather became too hot for the fur to be prime. Although he could have legally continued until April First, Don would get a better price if he waited until next season to trap the animals when their fur would be denser and longer again. The uncaught animals would also form the breeding stock for future years' catch.

As we travelled farther over Don's trail, we could see evidence of his hard work. This trail could not have been easy to create. In places, we snaked through thickets of willow so dense I couldn't see more than thirty paces on either side. We traversed hillside choked with spindly black spruce, growing as close as quills on a porcupine. Every stump had to be cut well below the snow-line so the harnesses and sled wouldn't get snagged. Some areas would have been impassable swamp until the ground froze hard, so all cutting would need to be done well into the winter, when the days are short and the air bitterly cold.

At the summit of this hill, through breaks in the trees, we could see a white disc of lake with Volcano Mountain looming large and magnificent high above it. By the day's end, if we made the summit, we'd have gained over three thousand feet in elevation over the valley floor.

"Too bad we couldn't go straight across in space, instead of going down to the lake level and then climbing again," Marsha lamented. "I don't think the dogs like all this uphill or the heat."

The thermometer at Horsefall had read Fourteen Above when we left in the morning, but the air had warmed considerably under the clear skies and brilliant sun.

"They'll like this part going down to the lake," I predicted. "Are you going to chain up?"

"Naw. Let's go for it without the extra brakes."

"Okay, but give me a good head start."

Don must have been tired of chopping at this point or he was developing a Wild Slide as an amusement, because the trail didn't traverse the slope at all to reduce the grade. We faced, I discovered too late, a straight shoot with only a slight jog near the bottom. Trees crowded both sides of the narrow trail, leaving no room to manoeuvre. I pumped the brake and dragged a foot behind, but was still going far too fast to turn that corner. I knew I should do something – so I closed my eyes.

If the trees had been thicker, or the toboggan curl not set so high, something on the toboggan would have snapped. Instead, we sheared off two wrist-diameter spruces and came to rest perched part-way up a third.

From the comments drifting down the slope, I gathered Marsha's toboggan hadn't made it far before climbing a tree of its own. The tone of her voice told me I could be most helpful by minding my own business, so I collected my own shattered nerves and continued on down.

When Marsha and her crew joined us on the edge of Volcano Lake, I noticed she'd fastened a chain underneath after all.

"Even with this chain, I didn't make that last bend," she grinned. "My scar is a bit lower than yours on that tree."

I checked the lake ice near the edge with my axe, but ceased to worry when it was still solid at a depth of nine inches. Likely it was many feet thick. Don had told us to head straight across the windblown lake surface and then look to our right for the trail to resume, but we had little success explaining *straight across* to Casey the Poofer, who once again proved not useful on wide open spaces.

"Casey would never do in the high Arctic, where everything is flat," Marsha teased me.

"He'd need an Inuit to teach him directions with a long whip, I'm afraid. If you aren't in a hurry, he'll lead us around the edge instead."

"Fine," said Marsha. "I like the scenery near shore better myself. And it won't be as far to swim if we go through the ice," she added dryly.

When we came at last to the far side, Casey immediately picked up dog scents, locating Don's trail where it mounted a steep bank. Once we were into the bush, where the snow hadn't drifted as much, the packed trail became plainly visible again.

Not far up the trail, at a point where the slope increased dramatically, we came across a pole cache where Don Mark and another trapper, Ron Woolven, had stored some gear. We could see a bundle of canvas that might be a wall tent, a box of spikes and a roll of plastic. They were progressively moving supplies and equipment farther in on this trail, so they would eventually have another base camp for overnight stops on the line. Some trappers have the luck to have a highway or at least an old road for access to their fur. These two fellows were having to pioneer a route starting virtually from scratch.

Read more about trapping in Appendix X.

We passed more trap locations as we slowly climbed the steep trail. In these sub-alpine areas, where the game was not dense, the trapper would have to cover great distance to catch a few animals. The inaccessibility of much of the ground would ensure no one could over-trap even if they wanted to.

By now we were well up on the shoulder of Volcano Mountain, dodging in and out of the treeline, across open meadows and through stands of birch and lodgepole pine. Where the trail began to descend to the next valley, we found a few spruces to camp beside and chained up the dogs. From here we would ascend on snowshoes. After listening to their pleas, we gave in and let Casey and Tyhee come with us.

We removed our snowshoes early in our climb, finding the angle of ascent too steep. Instead, we waded through the knee-high drifts, picking our route to take advantage of any rocky outcroppings blown bare of snow. We had hoped the two dogs would break a trail for us, but our frolicking pets leapt through the snow, making paths in grand circles, leading every direction but straight ahead up. Marsha selected a ridge to aim for, which, when we reached it, proved to be better walking. The surface was alternately free of snow or wind-packed hard enough to support our weight. The climb took over an hour.

At the rim, we could look hundreds of feet down into the heart of this ancient volcano. We didn't dare approach the edge too closely, since it wasn't obvious how much of the crusted snow lip was supported by rock and what was corniced out precariously over the void.

The volcano's wall facing the Yukon River was intact, but the back portion must have been consumed by the explosion and molten flows. The western face of this mountain was draped in black lava rock extending clear down to a corner of the lake, looking like food that had boiled over and baked onto the outside of a casserole dish. We found it hard to fully comprehend that all the land we could see, stretching to the Yukon and Pelly and far beyond, had once been a sea of molten rock, yet the evidence was irrefutable. The basalt cliffs along the rivers were igneous rock, and this was the closest source of such volcanic material.

Our view over the Pelly River valley was stupendous. The forest extended down the slopes below us like fingers of a giant hand, probing into the stubbled

We're at one of Peter Isaac's line camps and Casey is telling the team it's time to go! PULLING FORWARD might have been helpful, but his jumping nonetheless did inspire forward movement by the others.

burn we'd seen from up on Little Summit. Last summer's massive forest fire had marched in from its source near Pelly Crossing and had been halted just short of the Bradley farm. At one time, the heat was so intense flames had jumped across the Pelly River to torch huge tracts of timber on the far shore. The Johnson homestead had been spared only because of a last-minute shift in the wind. Eventually, it was the weather that extinguished this monster fire when a week of steady rain poured inches of water over the entire valley, doing a job hundreds of aircraft passes and an army of firefighters couldn't. Don had been fortunate his trapping territory hadn't been affected as others' had been. In the heart of the burned area, the fur-bearing animals would not rejuvenate to their former populations for ten to fifteen years.

We ate our muffins and cheese, sipping from the thermos, delighted to be high as the gods on Olympus. Our mortal servants, sitting attentively at our feet, sniffed out every crumb that fell from our lips. The entertainment, we soon realized, would be a snow squall rushing at us from the south. Grey, billowing clouds were being swept towards us by a fierce wind, the gusts pushing the curtain of precipitation beneath to an oblique angle.

"*Yikes*, what do we do now?" Marsha asked. "There isn't any shelter here to speak of."

"It can't last too long. I can see the sun shining behind the clump of clouds and the whole system seems to be moving really fast. It'll be upon us before we could make it down to the first trees, so we might as well stay right here until it's over – and try to enjoy it," I grinned.

"I suppose we deserve to get blown off the mountain for not paying attention to the weather behind us," said Marsha, pulling up her parka hood and fishing out mittens. "I haven't watched a good storm from this perspective since last summer on the fire lookout tower. Let's hope it doesn't get too windy and blow us into the crater!"

As the first breezes of the storm's front were chilling our cheeks, a huge raven swooped down, and nearly brushed my toque off with his wing tips. Casey woofed fiercely, and a tiny object fell from the bird's claws. It landed beyond us, just over the crest of the lip, and rolled for a distance over the wind-packed snow crust. Casey moved to give it chase, but I tackled him before he could dive over the lip. We weren't sure that a dog's weight mightn't avalanche the snow, taking him down over the sheer drop into the depths of the volcano.

"I think it's an old rabbit bone," reported Marsha, checking with the binoculars. "I can see a fluff of fur and something white, like bone."

"Do you think the raven dropped it there on purpose, as bait?"

"It sure looks like a dangerous spot for a dog or coyote or wolf. If they fell over that precipice, the raven could feast on their remains at the bottom."

From our vantage point, we couldn't tell if the snow where the bait had dropped was a cantilevered cornice. There was no rock visible to prove it otherwise. We held firmly onto our pets' collars so they couldn't explore the question further.

As the full fury of the storm hit, we could do little besides wedge ourselves into a fold in the rock and hide our faces from the wind. The dogs curled into balls, tucked their noses under their tails, and closed their eyes. Tyhee appeared to be nonchalant about this whole experience to the point of dozing off to sleep. Casey peeked at us, his brow furrowed, telegraphing his disapproval of our choice of resting spots. We would agree with him this was far too drafty for comfort. The driving snow pelted our parkas, making a raspy sound as the flakes chafed over the fabric. The wind flattened us, pressing on our bodies like a hundred hands.

When I raised my head for a curious, but imprudent survey of the scene, a gust caught my parka hood as if it was a spinnaker and fairly lifted me to my feet. I quickly twisted away from the wind and tumbled to the ground to cling frantically to the rocks.

"Geez, Bruce, be careful," Marsha shouted at me, barely audible over the howling. "*You'll be blown over the edge.* Lie still!"

I didn't need her warning now. For the next five minutes, I gripped the rocks with renewed conviction, patient to wait out the blow.

Then, as suddenly as it had struck, the storm passed, riding on a carpet of high-altitude winds, dusting the far side of the crater with the final flurries of its wake. The sun shone in our faces and the air was again calm. We saw the sparkling miniature forests below us once more, and wondered how the other six dogs had appreciated the brief storm. Thoughts of them reminded us about the work of setting up camp awaiting us when we got back down.

Descending was certainly easier and faster than ascending had been. If we'd brought pieces of plastic or cardboard, and had courage, this would have been a dandy slide right to the treeline. Even so, we were skidding down the slope at a respectable speed on the soles of our moccasins. Marsha, with her background in downhill skiing, made a decent showing of moccasin skiing over the snow. My movement down the ridge was less dignified, but still fun with the snow to cushion my falls. Marsha brushed the snow off me at the bottom and told me I'd get better with more practice.

The sky was beautifully clear for our evening's sit around the campfire. As the sun set, we watched the deep indigo of twilight ease across the Pelly Valley, creeping like a gentle flow of sleep over the tiny trees and strip of ice. The heavens were rich mauve, almost red, save for a diminishing band of fierce gold on the western horizon.

When the galaxies finally appeared, their light was enough to outline the vast panorama. We lay under the stars in our sleeping bags, warm from the dry birch fire, watching the tongues of flame flicker and dance. This was certainly as fine a camping spot as anyone could hope for, as long as the weather stayed clear. We could feel the volcano's powerful aura around us, yet were comfortable in its grasp.

CHAPTER THIRTY-EIGHT

GIMME A BRAKE?

Dawn came early to our camp on Volcano Mountain. We were finished our porridge, and huddling over our tea, before the shadows had fled the river valleys. The air had a bite that made the campfire that much more hospitable. One by one the dogs raised their heads, yawned and settled back to sleep. Peter had the innate talent for making every move, even yawning, a show of grace. He opened his tiny jaws wide, coiling and stretching his slender tongue, and displaying pearly rows of sharp teeth. His long-lashed eyes blinked sleepily, then he rolled over to lick himself cat-like, grooming the silky hair on his legs.

"He's such a cutie," Marsha whispered.

"Do you think he'll like going back to Pelly Crossing and being Peggy again?" I asked idly.

"He'll always be *Big Pete* to me," she chuckled. "And he'll have Mutt as company at the Hagers' place. They'll probably feed him more than we did, and work him less. He'll love it."

When we had the crews in their harnesses and pointed downhill, it was Peter who was the best behaved, sitting daintily, eager to go but waiting obediently. The others – frantic to get moving – were squirming and pawing at the snow. With the awesome descent facing us, we wished they were a little less enthusiastic.

"Have you got your chain brake on?" I asked Marsha.

"Two wraps near the back. Hope that's enough."

"We'll see," I smiled and gave Casey the *okay.*

Two minutes later, I was lying in a snowbank, quite sure that two wraps hadn't been enough for my toboggan. On a sharp bend, I had overshot and driven on the wrong side of a tree. The dogs, with their four-legged traction, had kept to the trail, and been jerked to a rude halt. Now the toboggan was rolled on its side, held from tumbling into a ravine only by the wheel dog's straps.

"Oh, what fun it is to be a musher," I muttered, crawling back up to the trail.

244 • BRUCE T. BATCHELOR

Snow was melting off my face and running down my neck. I looked around for
Marsha, to whom I'd addressed my last comment, and realized she hadn't come
down this stretch of trail yet. I cleared my team off to the side.

Eventually, Peter's head appeared over the crest of the hill, and then Hinglish's,
then Dawson's and Tyhee's. They were all pulling hard, but the toboggan wasn't
moving fast. On the back, Marsha was covered in snow, and grinning gamely.
She was hopping up and down on the brake and calling out *Slowly, Slowly* to the
dogs. They crowded to a stop beside us, tails all a-wag and tongues dripping.

"Did you pile snow on your head to cool off, or did you wipe out, too?" I
teased.

"Oh, we had a dandy crash back there," she said, flipping back her hood.
"Wiped out three or four little trees, and almost knocked myself silly falling over
the backboard into the basket again. I didn't realize the trail was this steep when
we went up it yesterday."

"How'd you wipe out when you were going so slow down this part?"

"The clips broke on the chain brake. All I had left was the claw brake and my
dogs were just a-bootin' 'er trying to catch up to you. I knew we were going to
crash, it was just a matter of *when*, and into how many trees."

"You okay now?"

"Oh, I'm fine. Just bruised my dignity big time, landing on my head inside
the toboggan. After that, I wrapped another chain and some rope under the base.
I wasn't going to take any more chances."

I looked at her toboggan and saw all the brake loops. Her dogs looked pooped
from pulling it down the hill.

"I'll wrap mine up the same," I said. "I've had enough thrills for today."

That's when I noticed my own brake chain was dangling to one side.

"You broke a clip on yours, too," Marsha pointed out. "No wonder you missed
that corner."

"I thought we were going pretty fast," I admitted. "If I'd known the chain was
busted, I'd have been *really* scared."

On this one part of Don's trail, three steel clips had been demolished in the
space of thirty seconds. We had used the same steel G-clips for the harnesses and
all the tethering chains, but hadn't had one break on us all winter. Obviously the
strain on a chain brake was far more than anywhere else.

"With trails like this one, I know now why Don has spent half the winter
repairing his sled," Marsha laughed.

At the lake shore, I instructed Casey to lead us around the other half of the
perimeter, so we could examine the main lava flow from close up. The path of

the molten rock had been quite obvious from the summit: a strip totally bald of trees, down the mountain side extending along one edge of the lake and out onto the plateau.

"This looks like the moon's surface," I pointed out, standing on a tall mound of porous black rock. There was a layer of snow over all horizontal surfaces, but the vertical faces were exposed and holey as Swiss cheese.

"To me, it looks like burnt egg white," Marsha suggested. "All black and crusty and full of bubble holes. When do you think this happened?"

"One book said thousands of years, and another mentioned volcanoes on the coast might have been active in the seventeen-hundreds. Maybe this one was stewing at the same time."

We crawled over the strange formations while the dogs waited impatiently on the ice. The sun had climbed high, and would soon make the snow sticky, so we cut short the inspection. There were about six miles to cover on the way home.

At the Dawson Road, we noticed tracks from various pick-up trucks in the snow, and realized the entire stretch in from Pelly Crossing must be clear, and passable for light traffic.

The bulldozers and grader crews must have repaired or replaced any creek bridges on the side-road into the farm to keep their supplies rolling in. Their labour meant we could get our truck, Furd, out to the highway now if we wanted to return dogs to Pelly Crossing. The ravages of spring run-off on the road had been a nagging concern to us over the past weeks when we'd made our plans. However, as had so many other details of this winter, events were opportunely falling into place. Early April would be the right time to scout for summer jobs, sell some of our outfit, find homes for Loki and Hinglish, and perhaps check through the Dawson Museum records to find out what happened to Harry Davis at his trial. A week or so later, we could return to watch the ice break-up, and then, with Danny's riverboat, freight out our remaining equipment and supplies. We mulled over this plan while the dogs trotted for home.

There was water running down Horsefall Creek ravine. It was merely a trickle, snaking under patches of snow and through the gravel, but clearly a harbinger of the run-off torrents to come. South-facing, exposed slopes were practically bare already, though the snowpack in the dense woods and north-facing pockets was deep and would last weeks yet.

"We'd better leave in a few days," I joked to Marsha, "or we'll need wheels on our toboggans."

"Wheels, or maybe pontoons," she replied. "I think the ground will get a lot wetter before this snow is all gone."

We tied the dogs at their shelters, noting the dog lot looked disgustingly cluttered. The debris of five months was poking through patches of packed snow and ice. Bones from the farm's cattle lay everywhere: fragments of leg, tips of hooves, chunks of skull and jaws still sporting a few green molars. Recent stools that had been buried by sudden snowfalls had now thawed and were lending a decidedly unpleasant aroma to the yard. Small cream-coloured discs lay everywhere, at first puzzling us about their identity.

"Oh, those are *parsnips!*" Marsha exclaimed. "I *knew* they wouldn't like them."

Two months ago, when we found some of our vegetables were at the end of their storage life in the root cellar, Marsha and I had washed, sliced and bagged all the parsnips, turnips and carrots for freezing. The ends and questionable pieces had gone into that night's dog food. I had been sure the dogs wouldn't notice the bonuses in the dark, but Marsha had been as certain they wouldn't like parsnips.

"They eat in such a disgusting frenzy when it's Forty Below," I protested, "how did they pick out the parsnips?"

"Let's clean them up," Marsha decided, "before they rot and stink. The whole yard looks like a compost pile."

Together we shovelled up the maligned vegetables, the excreta and most of the bones, taking four wheelbarrow loads to our heap in the meadow. Most of the stools piled there over the winter had turned chalky-white, and had little smell.

After supper, waiting for bath water to heat, we walked to the bank and watched the sun set down the river. The channels of running water were inky-black streaks below the shiny gray columnar cliff walls. Overhead, the low hooting of a Great Horned Owl alerted us to his presence somewhere in that fiery sky. Borders of the wispy clouds reflected colours from the vanishing sun: indigo and rose, orange and royal blue. The jumble of hues seemed both unlikely and natural. Our experience over the winter had taught us the North is a mixture of the unusual and the unbelievable. We watched the exposition of light with a touch of sadness in our hearts.

"Nothing left but packing now," I sighed, putting my arm around Marsha's shoulders.

"If life's that dull," she whispered, "I'll be very surprised."

CHAPTER THIRTY-NINE

THE CONGENIALITY AWARD GOES TO—

At midnight, the temperature was a nippy Fourteen Fahrenheit, but the following noon saw a rise to Forty-Six Degrees. We had been prolonging our freezer's usefulness by stacking ice blocks inside and around the tin-lined chest. Marsha threw an old blanket over it all to give this spot beside the door a bit of shade from the harsh afternoon sun.

Despite our efforts, the freezer's days were numbered. The ice we could haul from the shoreline was now candled into long icicles which shattered into thousands of pieces, and did little to cool the chest's contents. The air entering through cracks in the sheet metal was well above the freezing mark from mid-morning until after sundown. Even if we'd been planning to stay at the cabin over the next few weeks, the food inside the freezer would have to be dealt with.

Some of the problem was easily rectified: the choice pieces of meat, and all the frozen fruit, we ate over the next three days. We cooked hamburgers over a campfire outside, and stewed rhubarb for dessert. The next night's repast was lynx steaks, followed by strawberries and yoghurt made from powdered milk. Unfortunately, there was a limit to what, and how much, we could devour immediately. Some twenty pounds of various frozen vegetables would go to waste if left in the freezer, as would odds and ends of lynx meat, bacon and home-made liverwurst. Our dogs definitely wouldn't help with the frozen parsnips but were eager for any donation of meat. One of them in particular kept reminding us of this option.

Old Lucky-Curly no longer looked as emaciated as before, but his routine hadn't varied. Two or three times per day, until one of us would go out and hush him, Lucky would do his one-two-three shuffle dance accompanied by that raspy bark. He longed for a rerun of his break-in to the freezer chest.

We decided to play up to his fantasies. Marsha formally presented the lanky blond mongrel with an award for being *Mister Congeniality*. Lucky was the one dog who rarely fought when all the others had a brawl; he certainly deserved some recognition. The reward was a package of Gainers Bacon we'd bought in Carmacks.

"I hope he doesn't mind all the nitrates and other chemicals," I said. "And too bad it isn't Oscar Mayer brand, so this could be a real *Oscars* ceremony."

"We'll see if he complains during his acceptance speech."

Thoughtfully, she had sliced the plastic wrapper so it wouldn't get consumed with the prize. Lucky shook hands like a real gentleman and ate one pound in two bites.

"Congenial, but terrible manners," Marsha scolded him. "You shouldn't *wolf* down your food like that."

Lucky sniffed all around her until convinced there was no other bacon. Then he grabbed the package and would have swallowed it whole had Marsha not wrestled it from his jaws, and taken it beyond his chain's reach.

The other miscellaneous pieces of meat were split up democratically amongst the eight dogs. Our homemade liverwurst had a touch of ground parsnip in the recipe, but either the dogs didn't notice, or they couldn't eat around the minced vegetable. Whatever the case, we heard no complaints, except about the quantity: everyone wanted more.

Loki's guard-dog experience came in handy when we processed the frozen vegetables. We thawed these carrots, beets, parsnips and onions, and spread them on sheets of plywood and metal to dry in the sunshine. Loki wasn't the least bit interested in eating the vegetables, but fiercely defended them against any raids by Whiskey Jacks or juncos. He lay importantly in the centre of the array of drying trays, turning his head slowly side-to-side to watch over what would become dried soup mixture. When the old dog's eyes began to droop and his head nodded sleepily, we moved the operation over so he could be in the shade while on duty. He accepted the work as a great honour and, although he dozed off occasionally on the job, he did that too with much dignity.

The drying took three days. We stirred the vegetables every hour or so during the day and brought everything inside at night. When they were crispy dry, we broke them into tiny pieces and mixed in barley, salt, sage, powdered garlic, basil and cayenne. The resulting conglomeration could be added to stews or soups, or cooked in with rice or lentils during the time we'd be off in the Dawson area.

While the veggies were drying, we kept busy. Marsha baked goodies to take along: bread, cookies and granola bars. I made a sturdier metal collar for the wall tent's stove pipe opening. Marsha hand-sewed a skirt to wear, in case the spring weather in Dawson was too hot for her jeans. We raked the yard clean, and burned garbage galore in the trash barrel. It was a joy to work outside, wearing only a shirt and never even thinking about mittens.

Loki and Dawson invented a dog version of *Snap* to liven the last days at the cabin. We had them tethered side-by-side in the dog lot, though of course not close enough to touch one another. They took turns nonchalantly parading, then suddenly rushing to chain's end, snapping terribly and snarling as if their favourite bone had been stolen by the neighbour. Loki was doing so much snapping I was worried his well-worn teeth might fall out during all the fun.

If Marsha and I were playing a game these long spring days, it was *I Spy* from the basalt cliffs. With Grandad's binoculars, we watched the dark snakes of open water edging further across the Yukon River with each passing day. The ice was melting quickly around the gravel bars and logjams but the vast central expanses showed no signs of weakness. The few bad areas along the base of the basalt wall, which had remained unfrozen all winter, were now spreading longer and wider under the insistence of the relentless sun. We picked out our sled trails, winding across between the islands, shining icily against the pocked, patchy snow. Our cabin's green roof made it easy to spot, but we had to stretch our eyes, and imaginations, to see smoke wisping from the cookstove's stack. Not content to merely spy on the dogs, we talked to them, waiting for their reactions when the sounds reached them two seconds later. Loki wagged at us and snapped at Dawson; Tyhee stood and double-pawed the air at Marsha's call; Hinglish looked large and bewildered even at this distance. Mutt rose, stretched, and then collapsed on his doghouse roof. The others were hidden by the trees, but we knew Casey was awake by his shrill yips in response to my whistling.

We scanned over the hills towards Minto, the white peaks near Carmacks, the parade square near Danny and Abbie's at Fort Selkirk, and up Six Mile Creek where we had eaten lunch the day I froze my thumb. Further up that creek valley was Little Summit and behind it was the Big Summit we never reached. Downriver, our trail wove through the jumbled and sunken ice in a slough, then around the corner of the valley. Past that point, we could not see the Yukon itself, only the hills that were above us on our trip to Seventeen Mile Creek investigating the old murder story.

Marsha whispered softly, feeling the grandeur before us, "I feel like this is all ours, like we own it all." And for that moment at least, we did.

Our isolation had been a chance to put ourselves in perspective with the world. Life had been much easier here: not as confusing, not at all money-oriented and people-busy like town life. The times alone had been an opportunity to meet ourselves: the adventures together a chance to explore one another while seeing the country. We'd known the winter would make or break our relationship. We had made it.

"There is a beautiful cabin on Lake Lebarge," I told Marsha, suddenly reminded of another person's winter, "built by a young American a few years back. He had just been discharged after action in the Vietnam War, and chose virtual isolation, camping on the uninhabited side of Lebarge. There he patiently, purposefully, almost reverently, crafted a lovely log cabin on a cliff overlooking a small bay.

"The task took him a few seasons to finish, but when the cabin was complete, so was the builder. The quiet months had been a transition for him from the horrors of wartime. He was now ready to live with people again: he had rediscovered himself."

Two days before we left for the spring, I ran the dogs to and from the farm to check on mail and receive an up-to-date report on the condition of the side-road. The trip, using six dogs with Hinglish leading most of the way, was remarkable only because of its brevity. The total travelling time, there and back, was under three hours.

"I left the farm exactly seventy minutes ago," I announced triumphantly to Marsha. "And part of that time was coming downhill with the chain brake."

"Hinglish must have seen lots of rabbits on the trail ahead," she teased.

"There were lots of little critters out sunning themselves, for sure," I laughed, one secret of our success revealed. "Do you remember the time for my first trip into Horsefall with Casey, Loki, and Mutt and Jeff in November?"

"Four hours? Five hours? This is quite an improvement. One more year and you'd be ready for the races."

"Would you do another year of this life?" I asked her, half-seriously.

"Only if we could plan it so there wasn't so much packing to do! I feel I've been packing and unpacking for eight months solid. And we're off again now for maybe two weeks, then back here to pack it all again—"

"I've got a feeling this is leading to something," I smiled.

"You bet," Marsha grinned. "I packed all day today while you were having a run with the dogs. Tomorrow, how about you finish while Tyhee and I sit on the bank and work on our tans?"

"What can I say? Except that your pet appears to have a head start."

CHAPTER FORTY

FOUR DOWN, TWO TO GO

W e left the cabin before daybreak, aiming to have completed the drive over the side-road out to Pelly Crossing before the sun made the road too soft. Athough each night we'd been having a solid frost, the daytime temperatures were turning bare ground into gumbo.

The dogs were delighted at another pre-dawn departure. There was something conspiratorial about the hour that made us speak in whispers, and stirred the dogs' enthusiasm. We made them sit for an extra few minutes while Marsha ran over the lists one last time, making sure we had everything for a two-week absence.

"Ssshhh! Sit still and be quiet," I said to the dogs in a stage whisper. Tyhee grunted a few times, and Casey yawned noisily, yet the two rows stayed amazingly still.

The cabin was boarded up and the door nailed closed, so Marsha's tour was only a check of our two loads. When she was satisfied, she untied her lifeline and winked at me.

Then she yelled OKAY! at Hinglish and was off bouncing and sliding across the clearing. Her team hit the trail first, setting a blistering pace across the flat and hardly slowing at the ravine. I'd have loved my team to keep hard on their heels, but Loki, then Lucky, then Casey had to stop for a morning dump.

Marsha waited at the top of the hill.

"I think your dogs will go faster if they can see mine ahead of them," she smirked. "We don't mind waiting for you slow pokes."

Hinglish and Peter bounded off along the trail in the lead, their heads high, looking for rabbits. These hardly seemed like the same dogs we'd brought in five months before, when they had been as green as we were. Marsha drove her dogs as if she'd been doing it all her life, and the eight workers moved us along with the style of veterans.

"Too bad," I thought wistfully, "we couldn't stretch the calendar and have another month of mushing. When all goes well, there isn't a finer way to travel."

As we left the plateau and started our descent to the Pelly, the bare patches outnumbered the areas of snow. The farm creek had a healthy skim of ice from last night's frost over an ankle-deep run of overflow and slush. We galloped the dogs across, the ice breaking under the weight of my toboggan, but we were on the far side before the water had a chance to rush into our wake.

Our old servant, Furd, was parked where we'd left him beside the hen house, still clad in his tire chains. We brushed wet snow off the hood, and shovelled off the dog boxes. Hugh had warmed the battery in the barn in anticipation of our arrival, so we had no problem starting the old pick-up.

"I don't think you'll need those chains," the farmer advised, "because those mining fellows have got the road graded smooth right through to the highway. Hardly any snow on it at all, I'm told. The only spot you might have trouble is Caribou Creek."

We collected the outgoing mail and loaded the dogs into their kennels. The lucky ones found old bones from November's trips, likely tasting better now to a dog's palate. I lashed one of our toboggans on top of the load, with the hope we could sell it in Dawson.

"You may find enough snow further north to use that toboggan again," Hugh said, tucking in a dangling rope. "But I'll promise you there won't be enough around here in two weeks. You'll be walking or boating when you return to Horsefall for your outfit."

The side-road was as easy travelling as Hugh had predicted. At Caribou Creek, we had to drive through water almost up to the floor boards, but the truck never hesitated, bouncing and splashing powerfully across the boulder-filled creek. At the Klondike Highway, we breathed a sign of relief and let the dogs out one-by-one to relieve themselves.

Next stop was Pelly Crossing village, where four mutts would be returning to their owners. The streets were already deep in dust, and busy with the traffic of bicycles and toy wagons. Litter from all winter lay limply in the brown snowbanks lining the route to and from the post office hut. The concept of *garbage* was a relatively new cultural phenomenon to this native people whose complete life's possessions were biodegradable a generation ago. The tatters of plastic, glass bottles and tin cans emerging through the melting snow like spring flowers, had been sniffed, chewed and again abandoned by both wandering dogs and the huge black ravens.

We weren't stopped at the Hagers' house for thirty seconds before the rug-rat telegraph had alerted Jimmy and his buddies of our arrival. They ran up from the river bank, gasping for breath and crowding around the two dogs we held beside the truck.

"There's Peggy! There's Peggy!" one of them shouted, grabbing for a tail. Peter looked scared and ducked behind my legs.

"And Mutt! Or is that Jeff?" Jimmy hollered, grinning from ear to ear.

"This is Mutt," Marsha said, handing over the jittery dog's chain and harness. "His brother is dead. He got caught in a trap and we had to shoot him. His foot was too badly smashed and—"

But no one was listening to her as more Indian boys arrived, bunching around the dogs, patting, poking and dragging them around by their chains, shouting, laughing and jumping up and down. Someone produced a child's toboggan and the dogs were immediately pressed into service. On his first attempt, Jimmy put Mutt's harness on upside-down, but realized his mistake before I had a chance to offer advice. Peter and Mutt looked confused and nervous with all the tiny hands holding them, but let their former owner manhandle them into the collars without squirming too much.

Then – with one boy pulling Peter, another out ahead, one on either side of a concerned Mutt, two on the toboggan and the others running in circles, flapping their arms, shouting *Go! Mush! Come on!* – this strange, happy gang moved off up the river ice, never smoothly, never fast, but everyone having a grand time.

"Goodbye, Pete. Goodbye, Mutt," Marsha called and waved. "I hope they'll be all right," she whispered.

We tied Lucky-Curly and Dawson behind the McGintys' house with their other dogs. This caused a great deal of barking, peeing on trees, scratching the ground and sniffing. We noted Tommy's dogs still looked fatter than ours, despite our efforts to bulk them up over the past month. No one was in the house, so we cruised the village until an old man pointed two figures out to us, way out on the river ice.

Here at Pelly Crossing the river cover was completely intact, showing no signs of weakness even at the edges. Tommy and his wife were sitting on a bench in the sunshine, watching and giving light-hearted advice to the children around them who were fishing through a half-dozen holes. We talked for a spell about dogs, toboggans and trapping, but the hot sun kept drawing our conversation away to more spring-like topics: the ice break-up, Grayling in the creeks, and moose having their calves. Everywhere around us that afternoon were handsome, happy children, so full of life and energy we thought them lucky to be living in this village. The sense of community was strong and the adults found time to share with the youngsters.

Driving the truck on the highway was strange; the speed was quite startling after a winter of travel at one tenth the pace, or less. The mileposts flashed by with delightful punctuality; the wheels turned for every corner without a word of command. When we stopped at Stewart Crossing Lodge for gas and a snack, our truck waited patiently without fighting the other vehicles. The snag was Furd's appetite: gasoline cost over two dollars per gallon and this beast gobbled a gallon every ten miles. Ever the mathematician, I calculated it was cheaper to feed eight dogs to pull the same distance.

Near Dawson City three hours later, we dropped in on our friends, Greg Skuce and Sally Robinson, who owned a cabin on Bear Creek. We planned to discreetly inquire as to our welcome with *four well-behaved, quiet dogs who could be chained further down the road and wouldn't be any trouble.* However, Sally owned an English sheepdog, a long-legged, mop-faced female named Maggie. Maggie didn't wait until our truck was stopped before provoking a tumultuous outcry from the kennelled four. She stood on her hind legs and thrust her hairy head into each dog box, eliciting growls and snarls. Furd was rocked on its springs by the imprisoned mutts' frantic struggles to get out and tangle. Maggie barked and ran in circles, delighted by the uproar.

Greg walked up to my cab window and said, "This must be a *love me, love my dog* visit. How many did you bring?"

"Only four," I answered weakly. "We can all camp down the road if they are too much hassle here."

"Oh, don't worry about them," Greg laughed. "If we can put up with that nutty sheepdog, we can handle yours. You can chain them out back across the slough, and they won't be in anyone's way. How long can you stay?"

"A few days anyway, Greg," Marsha said. "We want to look for jobs and find homes for two of these dogs."

"There's a dance on Saturday. You'd better stay that long," he smiled. "I hope you can stay longer and have a real good visit. But, there's one thing—"

"What's that?"

He glanced back at the dog boxes, where the racket had settled to a dull roar. "Promise you'll take all the dogs with you when you go. With Maggie around, any more pets would drive me nuts."

While we unloaded the truck of its frenzied cargo, and walked each one through

Loki was a dear old veteran –
missing a few teeth and always hopeful for an ear rub.

the deep snow to his temporary quarters out back of the cabin, Greg explained the job situation for the season ahead.

"The price of gold is way down over last year, so many of the claims won't be worked this summer. Three of the biggest employers have already announced they aren't opening up at all. Jobs will be scarce, even for equipment operators and experienced gold miners. You can put your name in around town, but don't count on anything coming up for quite a while."

"We'll go back in to our cabin until break-up, then bring out the rest of our outfit," I told him, struggling to hold Casey steady so Greg could attach a chain to his collar. "So our plan is to try to line up jobs for next month, or June. If nothing's happening just yet, we can spend more time finding good homes for Hinglish and Loki. Loki is a good watchdog, and a fine wheel dog. Hinglish has too much talent as a sled dog to not go where he'll be part of a working team."

"Maybe Hinglish wants to be a pet dog instead," Greg chuckled. We looked where the shaggy mongrel was digging. He had a pile of snow balanced on top of his head, and his fat tongue hung pink and dripping to one side.

"I know his calling is to be a sled dog," I insisted. "He was one of our best."

Sally had a suggestion for Hinglish's future, and explained it at suppertime.

"Grant and Karen Dowdell have a dog team. They use them all winter on Grant's trapline, and to get in and out of town," she told us. "If Hinglish is that good, maybe Grant will want him."

"But they live upriver quite a way, Sally, right? How would we get there to find out?" I was hesitant about any more river travel.

"They are only about a dozen miles upriver and the Yukon River ice is still safe here," Greg pointed out. "Dawson is about a hundred miles further north of where you wintered, so the ice is thicker here. The ice bridge across the river is open for vehicles and will be for weeks yet. We can check around town to see who's been on the trail lately, but there shouldn't be any problem."

I looked over at Marsha, who was staring out the window. Memories of her dunking must have been passing through her mind. I wanted to visit Grant and Karen's homestead, but not if it meant taking chances.

"They've got a radio telephone," Greg suggested, "so you can phone them to ask about the trail, and to see if they want another dog."

That evening we raised the Dowdells over a very poor radio connection. Through crackling static, we thought we heard Grant assuring us the trail was still safe, and that we were most welcome to visit. About a new dog, he gave an answer that was drowned out by noise on the line. The connection deteriorated further and we could barely hear him signing off.

"Well, Marsha, shall we go upriver and see them?" I asked. "He said the trail is safe. People are using it every day."

"I suppose we could go to find a good home for Hinglish," she answered solemnly, then added cheerfully, "We can leave tomorrow morning and take freshly-baked cookies for their sons."

CHAPTER FORTY-ONE

SUPERDOG ON TRIAL

W e stood at Dawson City's waterfront, looking out over the confluence of the Klondike and Yukon rivers, assessing the condition of the ice surface. Far off to our right downstream, we could see vehicles driving along a built-up strip of ice, roaring across the river as if this were an ordinary length of highway. Even tractor-trailer units hauling giant bulldozers and back-hoes to mining sites were making the crossing.

The trail we'd take upriver wound along the shoreline at the front of town, with branch-paths giving access from various streets and buildings. Past the Klondike River, where all upriver traffic funnelled together, the trail looked as wide as a country road.

"But how safe is it?" Marsha asked, looking at mist rising where the Klondike River was babbling over a gravel bar. A raven was playing with some bit of soggy matter he'd plucked from the dark water.

As if to answer her question, a snowmobile appeared in the distance, coming this way. Within seconds, the driver had driven past our position and whined on to the centre of town.

"We'll be no heavier than he was," Marsha admitted. "Let's get on with it then."

We had only our sleeping bags and a sack of dog food as a load, plus Marsha, who volunteered to be the rider. She bundled herself in a blanket and sat on the bedrolls, content in the role of non-paying, first-class passenger. The dogs were deliriously happy about having some exercise. They twisted and jerked on their harnesses, whimpering to be loosed for a good run. I made quite certain all was ready before I untied the lifeline from Furd's bumper.

They charged up the wide packed trail, heads held high, running on tiptoes to see ahead. I gripped tightly, hoping our whole trip could go at this pace. This trail had been beaten rock-hard by the winter's traffic, so the toboggan bounced and skittered wildly. My bent knees were absorbing the jolts for me, but Marsha found her ride less than comfortable.

"I want my money back," she griped, "the suspension on this coach is terrible."

"This hardly seems like we're on a river," I said. "Spending a winter along this section of the Yukon River would be quite different, more like living beside a road."

Yet, even as I was speaking, the trails converged. By the time we'd lost sight of Dawson City behind us, there were only two parallel tracks winding up the river, passing around islands in long gentle curves. We were now away from the roar of traffic and the hum of the town's diesel power generators, having slipped back into the world of spruce trees, ice pressure ridges, sparkling snow and peaceful quiet. Our ears heard only the familiar sounds of dogs' feet on snow and the creak of toboggan boards.

"It is so nice to be away from civilization again," Marsha said, surveying the valley from her bedroll perch. "I didn't realize how noisy Dawson was until we left it behind."

Rounded rocky hills, their sides deeply creased by small creeks and pup-creeks, crowded close to the shores. Bottom land in the valley was limited to the wide, flat islands and a few narrow benches at the creek mouths.

Nowhere did we see the basalt rock formations so common to the Fort Selkirk region. The Yukon River here was also two or three times wider, the flow having been enlarged by waters from the Selwyn, White, Stewart, Sixty-Mile and Indian rivers.

"This seems like a different river, doesn't it?" I spoke in a whisper to not distract the dogs, who were trotting along at a pleasing clip.

"I was thinking that myself. How much further?"

"Next chain of islands. We'll see some sort of trail up the bank."

Five minutes later, the dogs pulled us up a steep pathway and onto Grant and Karen's island. We were right into their yard, halted beside the house, before Grant's dogs noticed our presence. They belatedly announced our arrival from a dog lot in the trees beyond.

"That's a sleepy bunch of watchdogs," Marsha said. "But why not, in this sunshine?"

Grant, Karen, and their two youngsters came out of the log home to greet us. As Northerners are wont to do, they inspected our team, noting the home-made harnesses and toboggan. The boys, Jonathan and Daniel, wanted to know if the dogs could be petted.

"It's okay, as long as you move slowly and don't scare them," Marsha instructed. "These dogs haven't been around people your size too much."

"Your timing is perfect. We were just sitting down to tea," Karen announced. "Come on in, Marsha, and let the men chain up the dogs." They trooped off into the house, leaving us to talk dogs and catch up on an old friendship.

"Your place sure looks different, Grant. You two have been busy: last time I was here, you were just starting the house and had stumps all over the fields. That must have been three years ago."

"Four and a half," he corrected gently. "Karen and I figured it out last night after you called. Your parents were with you on a canoe trip."

"That's right. And I think you had only one dog at that point."

"Well, I've got six now," he said, glancing at the trees where his dogs were staring our way. "Karen and I calculated we can't afford to feed more than that. But which dog was it you wanted to give away?"

"Hinglish, the shaggy black one. He may not look like he'd be good, but he was our best puller and has lots of enthusiasm."

"I see you've got him leading."

We talked about Hinglish's history and about our other dogs for a few minutes while clipping them to a gang chain. Grant took me on a tour of his team, and then showed me his array of toboggans and sleds. One sled was on loan, another was old; this toboggan had just been built, the other was a spare now; he had a vehicle for every purpose and condition. For trips to town, on the hard-packed river trail, he could take a sleigh, which cut the surface friction substantially over using a toboggan. In particular, I was intrigued with the way his main towline attached to the sled. There was a chain bolted to both sides of the bow, and the towline was fasted on to it by a quick-link coupler. The beauty of the system was that if the trail was tilted, as on a sidehill, or if the load wasn't centred, the towline could be moved over one or two links of the chain to compensate for any tendency to steer off to one side. The single hook-up meant, of course, that either the dogs would all be pulling in siwash harnesses on one towline, or that a tandem-harnessed wheel dog would need a singletree behind him. I asked Grant which type of harnessing he used.

"I used to have collar harnesses, like yours," he explained, pulling a bundle of siwash harnesses from the basket of his toboggan, "but switched to this type of webbing harness a few years ago. I'd never switch back now."

"How come?"

"The dogs might be able to pull more weight with the collar type, but this other type never gets tangled. When my dogs were hooked in tandem, they were forever getting fouled. Now, it hardly ever happens. For that reason alone, I prefer the webbing type."

Our enthusiasm was kindled to the point we had to immediately take both teams out for a run. It would also be a trial for Hinglish, we decided, just in case Grant wanted to keep him after all. We stopped in the house long enough to have some tea and explain our mission.

"You two have fun playing outside," Karen called to us as Grant and I ran off, teasing in a tone she used with her pre-school-age sons. "And Marsha and I will sit here all afternoon and drink tea. The boys have discovered Marsha's cookies so they are busy too."

Grant harnessed five dogs, leaving one rather dejected Malamute sitting on his house. This was Bing, his old pet, who had feet trouble.

"I've hardly been able to use him this winter," Grant admitted. "But I couldn't bring myself to get rid of him: he is a loyal old friend. Yet even when he can run on those feet, he isn't as fast as the others."

I could tell what Hinglish was up against. He had to be so good Grant would keep him, and get rid of his old pet to stay with six dogs – or break his rule and feed a seventh worker.

"We can put Hinglish in with my team to give him a real test." Grant suggested, "and I'll give you one of mine."

He selected a bitch who would cause the least problems with Casey, Tyhee and Loki, and then led Hinglish over to his squad. I expected a fight, but Grant's dogs only wagged their tails cautiously and growled to themselves, allowing Hinglish to pass without incident.

"You can use him as leader if you want," I offered. "Hinglish isn't too clever about *gee* and *haw* yet, but he'll move along at a nice pace."

"Mostly I want to see if he can keep up with the others," Grant called over. "I've already got two leaders." He had installed Hinglish in a siwash harness at wheel position.

"Ready?"

"When you are."

I had an embarrassing moment with Casey who decided to come back and check out this new female, but eventually got my team headed along the path towards the river. Grant was holding his dogs back, giving me a healthy head start.

After we were down the bank, I pointed Casey upstream and urged them to run. I felt I was also on trial, and wanted all four dogs to perform well. When they had picked up an easy lope, I turned to watch Grant's team come onto the ice.

His leaders came scrambling around the corner like they were chasing a moose, snow flying and the light sled bounding behind. Grant was tucked down to keep the sled more stable, riding like a driver in the Rendezvous sprint races. His dogs hadn't run for a few days and were eager to catch up to us. I urged Casey to go faster. The chase was on and we had a twenty-second lead.

When we had hooked up, Grant explained to me the origin of the curiously parallel snowmobile tracks on the river trail. Usually the winter trail was a single path, with pull-offs wherever one team or machine had curved off into the deep snow to let another pass by. This fall, though, a large crawling tractor with two tracks had driven up the frozen river to a mining claim on the Sixty-Mile River. Since then, there was a packed trail for each direction of traffic. My team was running in the right-hand lane and Grant's was gaining on us in the left.

"Let's go, Casey, come on, *run,*" I yelled, milking him for every ounce of effort. *"Let's go!"*

I turned to watch Grant's team and nearly fell off the toboggan in delight at what I saw. Hinglish had heard my calls and was turning on the power. But he hadn't been content to run in the left track behind the others, and had leapt across to our side. With a siwash harness, he wasn't connected directly to the other dogs, only to the main towline.

I stared, mesmerized by his determination as Hinglish dragged Grant and the sled across the loose snow into our track as well. When the sled was again on packed snow, he lengthened his strides and came after us with renewed vigour. For a while, he was pulling the sled single-handed and threatening to pass Grant's other four galloping dogs. From the smile on Grant's face, I could tell he was impressed.

"You may have won yourself a new home, Hinglish," I said under my breath, and called on my dogs to stop.

"I was worried about how your dog would run," Grant said when we had all nine dogs sitting quietly, "but he seems to be keeping up fine."

"He must have caught the *following spirit*," I chuckled. "I think he wanted to catch up to his buddies. How about you going ahead for a spell so these guys get a chance to chase?"

We took turns leading and luring the other's team into running faster, gradually working our way a few miles upriver to Bell Creek before turning for home. By the time we were approaching Grant's island, my dogs were tiring noticeably. The extra distance they had covered, coming this morning from Dawson, was taking its toll. Casey would no longer run, but brought us in still trotting. I was proud of how they'd lasted against Grant's fresh team.

If Hinglish was to find a home, he'd have to earn a spot on Grant's dog team. How would he compare?

"Did you decide about Hinglish?" I asked Grant when he handed the panting dog back.

"I'll have to talk it over with Karen and tell you in the morning. Will that be all right?"

Grant was able to give me an immediate answer about another matter, though.

He purchased one of our two gang-chains, to use when out trapping, or visiting along the river.

"I've always wanted a stake-out chain, but never got around to making one," he told me.

We were selling all our equipment at the cost of materials, so Grant got a wholesale price on the chain and clips. He outlined another way to make a tethering line for temporary stops.

"One fellow upriver makes his out of 5/16-inch aircraft cable. He attaches clips directly to the cable by their swivels. If the dogs are only hooked there temporarily, side chains aren't necessary; the dogs can be fastened right to the cable," Grant explained. "First he heats a 5/16-inch nut red-hot, and slides it onto the cable, then crimps it down in position while still hot. Then he slides on a washer, the clip, another washer, and a second red-hot nut."

The result would weigh only a fraction of what our heavy link chain did, an important consideration for racers, especially those who have to stake out a dozen or sixteen dogs. A cable would not be as comfortable for overnight use, but the dogs would eventually get used to it.

Grant showed me another musher's aid commonly used in his area. He had made a rattle out of a fan-belt and beer caps. This belt-rattle was used both to discipline lazy dogs and to inspire them. When a dog heard the caps clattering, he'd run faster to keep the sound at a distance.

Over supper, the four of us exchanged stories and tips on dog care and cabin living. Marsha had won the two boys' hearts, and they hung on her every word. Afterwards, they wanted her to play and see their books and toys.

Meanwhile, Grant showed me his toys: plants growing in flats and trays in the southern portion of the farmhouse. The Dowdells support themselves by market gardening for the townsfolk of Dawson City. I asked Grant if this was a good line of work for new couples moving to the area.

"Terrible," he said. "If we had more competition, we'd all go broke. The market is very limited here, and the area couldn't handle another producer. Selling vegetables in town can't be everyone's answer."

"How about your trapline? Does that bring in much money?"

"Last year I made enough as an assistant trapper to pay for the dogs' upkeep for the year, and no more. But if I can do that each year, I'll be happy. It means we get free transportation in the winter."

Marsha and I slept in the living room beside the tiny bedding plants, and woke early to the sound of children's excited voices.

"Do you think they're awake yet?" said one shrill whisper.

"I saw her move."

"You two leave them alone," came their mother's voice. "Let them sleep if they want to."

It was a delightful way to be wakened. We hadn't been around children all winter, and were happy about their presence. Marsha lay on her back and smiled.

"It must be killing the boys to have to wait," she said. "Let's get up."

"Or, we can stay in bed and invite them to come visit," I suggested.

The boys pounced on us, anxious to tell us the news. They blurted out their parents' decision.

"We're getting a new dog!" Jonathan said.

Note: *Grant Dowdell re-named Hinglish, calling him* Hing *as a tribute to Grant's first sled dog, Bing. Four years later, Grant's team won the 1985 Percy DeWolfe Memorial Mail Race – a gruelling Dawson City-to-Eagle, Alaska contest – and established a new course record, with Hing as a leader.*

CHAPTER FORTY-TWO

LOKI GOES TO WORK
AND DAVIS HEADS FOR JAIL

There was a message awaiting us when we returned to Greg and Sally's place. A letter I'd sent had brought us the hoped-for answer: Loki was wanted by some friends who were house-building just south of Whitehorse. Dave Nugent and Paulette Dufour had known Loki from when they'd helped build Mel and Laurie's ferro-cement boat on Vancouver Island. Now they had embarked on a construction project of their own, and needed a watchdog.

"Loki's dog team talents might get used," said Greg, who had taken the call. "Nuge just bought a puppy from Jon Rudolph that should turn out to be a big dog. Maybe Loki can show him the ropes."

Loki could ride to the territorial capital with Jon and Carol, who were coming for the Saturday night dance. Suddenly, we owned only two dogs again.

Marsha looked a trifle melancholy.

"What's up, Marsha? Why the long face?"

"I guess it's because all the dogs are leaving or have gone," she said quietly. "I feel like I've lost my children."

"You've still got two," I replied. "Casey and Tyhee will still be with us."

"Yup. And I love them," she sniffed, "but it is still sad."

At the Dawson City Museum we located a microfilm copy of the *Dawson News* for Tuesday, June 22, 1926. The headline declared *DAVIS SENTENCED TO LIFE IMPRISONMENT.*

"I'll read you the first lines," I told Marsha. *"After an hour and five minutes of deliberation, the jury in the Smith murder case returned a verdict of Manslaughter against Harry Davis who clubbed and shot Charles H. Smith, woodchopper—"*

I turned the viewer dial to focus on a later column.

"Davis will be handed over to serve his sentence in the penitentiary of the

RCMP outside," I read. *"One of the outstanding features of the trial was the manner in which Constable Thornthwaite handled his share of the responsibilities in connection with this important case—"*

"What do you think happened to Davis?" Marsha wondered. "Do you think he was ever paroled? He'd be old but could still be alive."

Forty minutes later, my eyes bloodshot from looking at the whirling microfiche, we had the answer to that question, too.

"HARRY DAVIS, LIFE PRISONER, DIED MARCH 5," I read out the headline. "He was in prison less than a year."

"That's good to know," said Marsha, taking a deep sigh. "Now I'll be able to go into our root cellar without wondering."

CHAPTER FORTY-THREE

DOG PACKING THROUGH GRIZZLY COUNTRY

After a week and a half in the Dawson City area, Marsha and I were anxious to return to Horsefall Creek. We realized the side-road would be a mess by this point, with the low sections flooded by snow run-off from the hills, and possibly some of the creek crossings washed out by erosion. The mining company would have stopped using the road, their permit to move over frozen ground now expired. We could count on driving as far as Crosby Creek, about halfway home, but might have to walk the remaining sixteen miles overland, carrying clothes and supplies on our backs. To lighten our loads, we planned to have the dogs carry packs too.

We started in from Pelly Crossing after midnight. We had waited for the temperature to drop enough to re-freeze the road's surface. Our way would be lit by an almost-full moon.

Trapper Don Mark, our friend and sometimes mailman, was living at Crosby Creek in a wall tent while building a log home. Our plan of operations called for an overnight stay at Don's, then a day spent stitching a saddlebag-style canvas pack for Tyhee to use. Casey already had a pack from years before.

"Don is a real night owl," Marsha pointed out. "He'll probably still be awake listening to his shortwave radio when we get there."

The moon painted the forest in a wash of blue and grey. As the truck crunched over the frosty road, we caught glimpses of the Pelly River, its surface glowing silvery white, a snowmobile trail appearing as a metallic thread. Gaps in the frozen covering, where open water would be lapping and gnawing at the ice edges, were harmless blots of black ink from this vantage point. Three rabbits, who were mesmerized by our high beams, waited until the last split-second before leaping acrobatically out of our path. Swooping low in pursuit came a Great Grey Owl, his five-foot wingspan blocking our view of the road as he narrowly missed colliding with our windshield. The night held both a fairy tale air and a full-moon ominousness that kept us on the edge of our seats and totally alert every moment of the drive. When we reached Crosby Creek, we realized how tense we were.

"—I won't have any trouble sleeping," Marsha sighed. "I feel like I've been driving through a dream already."

Don was awake, reading through magazine reports of the space shuttle *Columbia*. He treated us to an amazing bombardment of information, switching from dog sleds and pioneer homesteading, to nuclear age technology, and back again at the drop of a hat. His team had placed second in the Freight Race in the Mayo Carnival and he was as proud as punch about that.

"Next year, I'm going to take my dogs to the Whitehorse Rendezvous races," he declared. "They were really burning up the track in Mayo."

I smiled at his appreciation of dog speed while looking at the rocket statistics he had just passed to me. "Everything has a purpose," I thought sleepily. "And it is a wonderful world if one has the option to choose his own place."

Next morning we were able to leave without sewing Tyhee's pack. Don had one to lend us that his old leader, Raisins, had worn in her younger days.

"You can try out this one and see which style is best before you make Tyhee's," he offered. "Raisin's pack was made from a Tahltan Indian design."

"Casey's was sewn like those used by the Teslin Indians," I pointed out. "Let's hope any new pattern we come up with for Tyhee will combine the designs better than the two tribes got along."

"What do you mean?" asked Marsha.

"The Teslins and the Tahltans were neighbours whose idea of population control was to have a good war every generation or so and wipe out half the young men."

"Yuck," she said and stooped to lay the canvas and moosehide bundle over her pet's back. "Will she mind this?"

"Casey has never protested," I was happy to report. "I think it makes him feel important."

As if he had heard a stage cue, my orange-and-white mutt rose to his feet and strode solemnly in front of us. He held his head rigid, kept his tail proudly high, and would look to neither left nor right.

"He's at work now," I explained to the two bemused humans while I loaded his pouches, "so this is *very* serious."

Soon we were walking along the shore of the Pelly River, Casey by my side and Tyhee at Marsha's. Each dog was carrying over twenty pounds of cargo, which was all we dared load on the first trip of the season. They would be able to carry this much easily, though the packs would slow them down to about a person's walking speed on the flat. Climbing hills, the weight would have considerably more effect, especially as they weren't conditioned to it yet. We had the packs well secured, so the load couldn't flop or poke at them, and was balanced side-to-side. The weight, I'd been taught, should bear over the front legs, not further back.

"Keep Tyhee right by you," I advised Marsha. "If you can impress upon her from the outset this is serious work, there won't be a problem later with her wanting to wander off exploring or swimming with our precious cargo on her back."

Tyhee was learning to control her puppy enthusiasm and kept beside Marsha while being attentive to all the sights and smells we passed. Casey, on the other hand, was the picture of pompousness. He took short steps and held his head high, like a sergeant-major leading a parade.

We found we could walk safely on the shelf ice beached along the river bank, stuck on the gravel shore. The sun reflected off the snow, ice and the golden sand cut-banks, sending up shimmers of heat, and making us feel thick-headed from the warmth. The walk along the river was a substantial short cut compared to the cooler, forest-shaded side-road.

We were at the day's halfway mark, the Bradley farm, by lunch time. Dick's wife Marjorie served us tea and cake while we rested our stiff muscles. Although we'd been getting plenty of exercise early in the winter, we'd become somewhat spoiled after the dog teams jelled and could pull us everywhere. This morning's effort of both hiking and packing had left us already tired and foot-sore. We sipped our tea at the dining-room table and gathered our energy for the remaining nine miles.

"With the river ice so thick this year," Marjorie said, "we may have a spectacular break-up. The ice can jam anywhere and the river will flood very quickly. You'd better be careful where you'll be when the ice starts to go."

"Do you ever get flooded here?" Marsha asked her.

Marjorie told a story of how the farm flat had been flooded one spring before she had met Dick and moved to the farm. Dick and Hugh had been forced to evacuate the farm, herding the livestock ahead of them. It must have been an interesting sight to watch all the different animals stampeded to escape the rising waters: cattle, horses, chickens and pigs all in one pack. Later that night, the waters receded and Dick, Hugh and their animal menagerie could return safely.

Concerns about break-up flooding gave us food for thought as we hiked up the steep trail from the farm flat and onto the plateau. A brief sun-shower cooled

Walking along the shore ice down the Pelly, with rifle in hand. The dogs have just enough load so they would keep up but not bound off.

our sweaty brows for a few moments, but the solitary cloud soon drifted on. Our winter trail was now a motley strip of mud, last autumn's fallen leaves and patches of mushy snow. Although the air was quite warm, the trees were not yet in bud. We scanned the naked poplar branches as we walked, hoping to identify new species of birds migrating into our region, but found this rite of spring was not yet in fruition.

Four miles from Horsefall, we stopped for a brief hiatus. Tyhee was merry, licking our faces and rubbing against us, while we sat wearily on a log, sharing a grapefruit and mustering strength for the final push. Casey was parading ahead down the path towards Horsefall, impatient to continue his work, when he suddenly stopped, turned toward the bushes and let out an alarming *WOOF!*

Instantly Tyhee was beside him, snorfling and sniffing at the ground, her long nose racing back and forth, trying to gauge the direction of the scent.

Marsha and I pulled on our packs and joined the investigation. I located one clear track in the mud, and our hearts jumped as we made the identification. A more textbook-perfect grizzly bear print would be hard to find: the claw marks were long and deep.

"Look at how big this fellow is," I gasped, placing my boot inside the depression and noting room to fit two fingers on either side.

"What gets me is where he's headed," said Marsha. "His track comes out of the bush here, turns onto the cart-road and is headed in the same direction as we are. He's right ahead of us!"

The dogs were anxious, almost frantic, as we continued on. They tugged and jumped at the short leashes we tied to their collars. I stopped to check the action on my Winchester, assuring myself I could lever a live round into the chamber at a moment's notice.

The tracks were less than an hour old, having been made since the last rain shower passed over. We surmised this bear had not been long out of hibernation because his trail wandered and veered on and off the road for a stretch as if he were confused. Then he struck out purposefully, following one cart rut, moving with large strides, not even stopping to sniff at old lynx sets.

"He must have just remembered a good cabin to raid," moaned Marsha.

The dogs urged us on, smelling the ground and lower branches, eyes wide and their ears sweeping the air for the slightest sounds. Fear had diverted our minds from fatigue. Not wanting to surprise the bear, we talked in loud, happy voices. When we ran out of things to say, we began singing instead, alternating between *The Bear Went Over the Mountain* and *The Teddy Bears' Picnic*. An Indian friend had told me his people believed bears were cousins to people because a skinned bear looks quite human. Apparently bears can telepathically hear whatever you say, so we were careful not to speak anything disrespectful.

The last hundred paces to the cabin were the worst. There was a chance this grizzly might still be inside, rooting about and smashing into the cellar for the last bag of dog food. Marsha held both dogs while I took off my pack and cocked the rifle. My voice was almost hoarse from thirst and all the singing, but I kept up a loud banter to announce my presence. Step-by-step, listening for sounds in the bushes, ready to shoot at whatever moved, I advanced on the cabin. The grizzly's trail went across the dog lot, right towards the door. There were no shutters broken on this side but my view was restricted to the one wall. With my heart in my mouth, I peered around the corner to check the front of the cabin. Then a flow of relief flooded my body: the tracks swung away from the door and out into the yard. For some reason, the grizzly had not bothered with our cabin.

"Hold on to the dogs, Marsha," I called over my shoulder, "while I see where he's gone. He's not in the cabin."

I followed the prints into the forest until they branched onto one of our wood trails, and headed off to the far end of the Horsefall flat.

"Maybe he heard us coming," Marsha suggested when we were finally settled down inside our cosy home. "Good thing we emptied the outside freezer box."

"Something put him off," I agreed. "Let's hope he stays put off. I'm afraid we may be sharing this creekmouth with that grizzly for a few weeks, and I'll feel better if he keeps to his own end."

"Well, I hope he kept going and crossed the river," Marsha replied. "But just in case he comes near, we'd better keep the dogs close to home."

"Yes, I don't think they would get along. But speaking of dogs, why don't we make a pattern for Tyhee's new pack while we have the ideas fresh in our minds?"

"Okay, Raisin's pack worked well but let's alter a few details."

See dog pack instructions in Appendix XI.

CHAPTER FORTY-FOUR

A BAD WEEK FOR HEELS: MARSHA'S AND CASEY'S

Marsha had a large, ugly blister on her left heel, a souvenir of the hike in. Usually she takes some *moleskin* tape to protect friction spots on long walks, but had forgotten on this occasion. She showed me a trick she'd learned when working as the park ranger for the Bugaboos Park in southern British Columbia.

"I picked this up from the climbers," she explained. "They wear stiff leather boots and are always plagued with blisters. If you leave all the fluid under the skin, eventually it ruptures and tears, exposing very tender skin and an area that easily gets infected. So, the idea is to pierce the blister, drain off the fluid, and leave the drain open for any new fluid to run out."

She had a piece of dental floss and a sewing needle. After sterilizing the needle in a candle's flame, she threaded on the floss and poked right through the balloon-like sore. A clear liquid spurted out as the needle entered, then trickled out along the floss she left hanging from the deflated blister.

"You leave the floss dangling so the fluid will run out along it. Cotton thread or floss works well because liquids will wick away from the wound," she continued. "The old flap of skin should be able to adhere back onto the heel, so you miss the tender pink stage this way. It looks kind of gross to have a string hanging from your heel, but it works."

While we were inside attending to Marsha's heel, the dogs had started their spring project. It appeared to be an all-out war on rodents, but we saw no casualties except a few innocent bystander bushes uprooted in collateral damage. Casey was the chief excavator, scooping out earth with his forepaws and flipping it between his back legs in an awesome spray that splattered bushes and trees for twenty paces in any direction. He burrowed so far he could crawl right down until only the white tip of his tail was visible. His quest after ground squirrels and mice was turning the yard into a maze of trenches, craters and mounds. On rainy days, he looked like a coal miner, his face and legs darkened with silty mud. Tyhee was the supervisor, barking into the holes, and scurrying around the yard to sniff in every hole to see where the enemy might be massing. Whenever she got bored with the lack of action, she would attack her buddy instead, chewing at his legs or neck, bothering him relentlessly until he devoted a moment to playing with her.

With only two dogs, we dared to let them be loose in the daytime, keeping them near the cabin. Most of the time, they play-fought for a few minutes, then Tyhee would sleep in the sunshine while Casey enlarged his burrows. If we were outside, they would stay beside us, trying to help, but mostly getting in the way while we did chores. After a winter of work, I imagined they missed being useful.

To minimize the danger of the pets tangling with a porcupine, we chained them at night. Casey, in particular, was so habituated to being tied at night, he would wander around restlessly in the evenings, whimpering periodically until I fastened his chain. Then he promptly fell asleep.

After a few days of close attention and occasional disciplining, we felt they had understood our message: *stay in the yard.*

"They seem to be sticking around the cabin really well now," I noted to Marsha. "Do you think they've made the full transition from working beasts to house pets already?"

"I hope so," she said, "because I hate to see them chained up."

Our soft hearts nearly cost the dogs their lives. One morning, perhaps a week after we'd returned to Horsefall, the dogs were both mining for mice, throwing sand and soil over the woodpile, while we sat on the sawhorse drinking tea and rubbing the sleep out of our eyes. Today, we agreed, would be another sun-tanning day, hot enough perhaps for a few dramatic movements in the rotting river ice. Then Marsha noticed the dogs were gone.

We called, but they did not respond.

"Must have seen a rabbit," I offered.

"They'll be back by lunchtime," Marsha predicted.

But they weren't. We called and whistled some more, to no avail. Doubts crept into our minds.

"How come they haven't returned? Surely they can hear us anywhere on the flat."

"Maybe they've gone to the farm?"

"I guess there are hundreds of things it could be," I muttered, angry at myself for letting them loose. "They might be chasing a caribou or a moose."

We sat down to lunch, but without much appetite. Supper came and went – still no dogs. We called and called, our voices echoing off the basalt cliffs, but to no avail.

In the morning, after a restless night, I put the thermos and two leashes in a day pack, and picked up the rifle. There was one main trail leading off the flat up the ravine to the plateau, so we headed that way, calling, then listening… calling, and listening.

Every bird rustling in the bushes gave a false hope. Any clatter of branches, or bleating call of some small animal, we took as sounds from our lost pets.

"Are there wolves around at this time of year?" Marsha wondered aloud. "Would they attack two dogs?"

"Oh, they've probably gone to the farm to kill chickens," I tried to sound reassuring, but didn't believe it myself. I had been with Casey for five years and my eyes watered at the thought of him dying in a circle of wolves. We walked on, calling frequently.

Near the fork to the Black Creek trail, Tyhee stepped weakly out of the bushes. There was dried blood all over her face and she was trembling. Marsha ran to her and hugged the injured pet tightly, tears running down her cheeks and pooling with the blood on Tyhee's face.

"Where's Casey?" I kept saying. *"Where's Casey?"*

I called and called, terrified my brave companion was dead. I felt guilty for treating him like the rest of the workers this winter. He had been so important when he was our only leader. He was special: he was my long-time friend.

"Casey! Casey! CASEY!" I called and called. *"CAAA-SEEEY!"*

"There he is!" Marsha cried out. *"Oh, my god!"*

I spun around. He was barely mobile, staggering and dragging his back legs. Then he collapsed on the trail. His ears were right back; his head rested on his paws. I dropped the rifle and ran to hug him. A spray of dried blood showed vividly on his white collar fur, and his back legs were drenched in bright red. He had come back and he was not dead. I was so relieved.

We sat with the dogs for a half-hour, patting them, gently rubbing and probing their fur to find the wounds. Tyhee's nose was split at the nostril, and her cheek had an inch-long gash right below the eye. Her nose trickled blood, but the flow would flush the wound, so we left it alone. There were two tears in the hide over her hip. She reacted to our touching as if there were muscles injured inside, so we didn't upset her with too much probing there. She licked the holes, cleaning them in dog fashion.

Casey had two holes about a hand's width apart through his neck hide. They resembled bullet wounds, where one could be the entrance and the other the bul-

*Our pet dogs Tyhee, on the left, and Casey – they enjoyed their challenges
being put to work with the other dogs and seeing miles of winter travel.*

let's larger exit. It was his legs though that were more alarming: both Achilles
tendon areas were injured. There was a puncture the diameter of my finger right
through one leg between the bone and tendon. A large flap of hide hung off the
other heel, exposing the tendon and much of the joint. I couldn't tell immediately
if any of the inner working parts had been damaged.

After the initial assessment, we walked home very slowly, the dogs under
their own steam but moving with measured steps. There was never a thought of
needing the leashes; these two troopers had been lucky to survive the battle with
whatever it was, and had very little energy left.

With our truck parked at Don Mark's tent camp, any evacuation of the dogs
to a veterinarian would entail a walk of 16 miles. That exertion would do neither
dog any good, and they were far too heavy for us to carry over that distance. We
would have to be our own vet.

The dogs' natural healing mechanisms were far more powerful than any major
doctoring we could do, so we tried only to support them. We didn't stitch any of
the wounds, but did dust them with eye-and-wound powder, hoping the penicillin
and sulfa drugs would help fight off infection. We also confined the dogs to their
chains so they would rest in the sun's warmth. Marsha souped up their rations,
adding powdered milk and vegetable oil, and we made sure they always had full
pans of water.

"They need love and attention most of all when they are healing," said Marsha,
"to keep their spirits up."

Not until we were dusting Tyhee's hip on the second day did we find three
more holes under her dense fur. These ones were fairly small, each about a pencil's

diameter across. Now, we could see the pattern: five claw marks in a curved line. The span was far greater than my outstretched hand.

"It was that grizzly," I said, instinctively looking to see the bear wasn't now approaching. "They are lucky to be alive."

"The grizzly must have had Casey by both legs, and Tyhee distracted him," Marsha imagined the battle. "She got her nose and cheek clawed with one swipe, and her hip ripped with another blow."

"That scenario explains the wounds," I said, and glanced over at the sleeping Casey. "Thank you for rescuing him, Tyhee."

CHAPTER FORTY-FIVE

BREAK–UP!

While we nursed the wounded and packed our winter possessions, a grand drama was beginning. Upstream from us, a thousand miles of the Yukon River and its tributaries, and a million acres of lakes held a mind-boggling quantity of ice. At Horsefall Creek, for example, the river was over a half-mile wide and covered, judging from our water holes, by about four feet of ice. In the sloughs and lakes, the frozen covering could be twice as thick. All that mass of ice would soon be ready to move.

Every day the sun and rain melted the ice plus snow on the hills, causing the river level to rise. Ice sheets that had settled against low banks and on sandbars when the water level dropped after freeze-up, were now being re-floated. If one section broke loose and collided with another, the momentum could gather, like a snowball rolling down a slope might trigger an avalanche. But the loose pieces might instead jam into others and lock together, damming the flow and awaiting a larger shove. Whether the result would be colossal or miniature was determined by the interrelationships of weather, snowpack, ice thickness and luck. The scale of damage the moving ice would cause depended largely on how much ice had melted before the whole system let go.

Near the end of April, the ice along our shoreline melted and was undercut by the strong current until there was a seventy-foot-wide, open channel stretching for about a mile. The exposed edges of the ice sheet gradually crumbled from the wash of the current and the pummelling by floating ice chunks. Within a few days, the width had doubled.

The small patches of ice clinging to our bank were all candle ice. A cake that was over three feet thick and seemingly solid, would break apart at the poke of a stick, tinkling into a pile of slender icicles, each as tall as the original block.

By now, the river water had turned quite murky, as snow melted on the sidehills, bringing soil matter with it into the creeks. Our Horsefall Creek, which had been dusty dry in the autumn, was now gushing forth a respectable torrent of rusty-red water.

"I made a water level gauge," I informed Marsha one afternoon, and led her to the shore to inspect a notched stick lodged in the mud. "This way we can know exactly how much the river has risen. I carved lines on this side and numbers at every tenth mark."

Though she submitted to a brief lecture on how to note the level and where to mark it on a chart, with the date, time and temperature, Marsha really had little interest in my pseudo-scientific study, and offered her own measuring method: "When the water level comes above the bank, then I'll know it is flooding," she said.

We made a betting pool, guessing the date of break-up though we had only a vague idea of what the event itself would be like. My choice was May Third and Marsha picked lucky day seven. The prize would be a back rub from the loser.

On the twenty-eighth of April, I noted the river had risen three feet between dawn and mid-afternoon, straining the ice sheets' grip on land and flooding over them in places. Through the binoculars, I could see out near the centre where a new lead was being cut. The surging current and tumbling loose ice were wearing away at the sheet, attacking the edge of the hole with a furious roar. As chunks broke off, they were either sucked under the sheet or pushed up on top. With the sudden influx of afternoon run-off, brown water spilled over the main ice, forming an incongruously calm puddle over a hundred yards in length. I called Marsha, so she could join me in the front row of the peanut gallery.

"Look at that big guy," Marsha shrieked, as one ominously large floe bobbed up to the heaped ice marking the main sheet's edge and spun around in the current. Suddenly it was gone, pulled under the sheet, and swept downriver like a submarine.

Smaller blocks danced up to the divide and were spurted up onto the sheet, where they floated around in the brown puddle like lost rubber ducks.

"That one coming now shaped like a coffin must be as big as a pick-up truck," I remarked. At the critical spot it stood on end, tottered, then slid smoothly under the sheet. Others coming behind, fragments from some large piece upstream that had broken free, charged along the lead and smashed one by one into the submerged barrier and piled on top. The combined weight was too much and a section of the sheet gave way, tipping drunkenly. Then it hopped up onto the next section. The movement's fluidity belied the size of the ice pieces: each section was as big as a suburban house lot. More and more ice crowded in, grinding and whomping about, some of it diving, but much being spewed onto the heap of blocks marking the extent of the widening brown lake.

We watched for hours, until the sun began to set. As the day's heat abated, so did the run-off. When the river level dropped, the puddle was cut off from its source. Over the course of an hour, the dark slick shrank upon itself, its water melting down into the sheet ice, and the silt filtering out to dye the surface and clearly mark the extent of the flooding. The huge rubber-duck blocks were abandoned here and there around the stain site. The stage was again calm.

Each evening over these weeks, a new flock of geese or ducks or swans would check out our channel for a possible camping spot, although only ducks took up our hospitality. Groups of mallards swam about, paddling up onto the island below us and waddling around in last year's tall grass.

The geese came over in huge flocks, easily numbering a thousand in three or four waves. There was a constant jostling for position amongst the individual birds, so their vees were never stable for more than a few seconds. On a relatively calm day, the central ones could flap enough so the outside birds would coast in the slipstream. With a following wind, the whole flock would glide, flapping occasionally to correct course, in the manner of cruising eagles.

The Tundra Swans seemed a cautious lot, maintaining such altitude we could only tell they were not geese by their distinctive song. Their call was a musical whistle, more shrill than the honking of Canada Geese.

The eroding and puddle-flooding of the river cover went on for a week, entertaining us with the odd surges yet seemingly having little effect on the total expanse of frozen water. Occasionally the ice sheet would crack, making the now-familiar sound of artillery fire, but we were beginning to think all might calmly melt away, depriving us of the spectacle we'd hoped for.

Against our shore, the open channel crept wider day-by-day. One afternoon, there was a two-hour parade of small cubes and slushy ice, encouraging us to speculate on the goings-on upstream.

Another week of waiting passed by. My lists of gauge readings proved the obvious pattern of afternoon rises, and little else. The air temperature was fluctuating extremely, freezing at night, yet in the high Seventies during the day. We were snaring rabbits to spin out our food supplies, not at all certain how long we'd be waiting. We baked the skinned rabbit in a casserole dish of dried beans, with lots of onion and garlic – delicious! My predicted date came and went, and so did Marsha's guess. We each got a back rub as consolation prizes.

Marsha is surveying our domain from the basalt cliffs above Horsefall Creek. Fort Selkirk is on the low plateau in the distance across the Yukon River valley.

Marsha was sun-tanning on the roof and I was trying to write (but thinking more about having lunch), when a deep rumbling sound demanded our attention. Looking through the line of trees, it appeared our creek flat was moving, but this was an illusion: actually the entire background was in motion! We ran to the shore, just in time to see our channel squeezed shut. The whole river's cover of ice, a sheet half a mile wide, had slid sideways and was jammed tightly to our shore. Incredibly, the surface was perfectly intact: we could see our dog trails and water holes exactly as they had been, only a hundred yards closer to us.

"The river level is higher than it has been all week," I whispered to my partner, awed by the sudden silence. My gauge stick was nowhere to be seen – crushed under a hundred-ton pan of ice.

"So much for the statistics," Marsha teased. "We'll go with my measuring method."

Past the closest downstream island, the ice had not budged. There was still a channel along the near bank, and in it we could see blocks bobbing along, no doubt broken off by our big shift. For the moment, as the river paused to contemplate its new configuration, this was the only motion visible. Though there was no sound, the air hummed with potential energy. I thrust a new stick into the bank and watched the level gradually lap up higher and higher, minute by minute.

It was a few hours later before the river rumbled again. This time the ice had fractured along a few faults. The pieces of this massive puzzle ground and strained against one another, prodded and pushed by bigger upstream sheets no longer anchored and now anxious to get to the Bering Sea. But, after travelling only a few hundred yards, everything pinched to a halt. A new icescape, fitting tightly to both banks, was resting uneasily before us. Only at the boundaries was the ice grinding and breaking up. The large surfaces would sometimes flex and ripple wave-like, but they remained essentially intact.

"If you can judge by the edges near us," I figured, "only about a third of the thickness is candle ice. The rest looks quite solid."

"That means there is an incredible amount of ice out there," Marsha agreed, "and a whole lot more upriver."

"If you imagine ice backed up clear to Lake Lebarge, all this thick and all ready to go, it's terrifying, isn't it? If the momentum gathers too fast, we can kiss our cabin goodbye."

"This is so huge," said Marsha, uneasy over my last remark, "I feel quite helpless. Let's hope the river goes down a little and the ice melts slowly just where it is."

When we examined my latest gauge stick under the fiery glow of the setting sun, it indicated the river was indeed dropping. In response to the lack of support below, the ice began creaking and settling, making resounding *whooomps* that shook the evening air, echoing between the cliffs, and startling the dogs to growl in alarm.

Well after dusk we stood watching a glowing riverscape lit by a silver first-quarter moon. Around that satellite was a distinct double halo, foretelling of both subfreezing temperatures tonight and extreme heat tomorrow. We went to bed, but slept with our ears open.

Some of the river ice we'd mushed over was no longer solid – as the sun and warm air melted the exposed surface, that water had dissolved through, creating candles *up to 3 feet long.*

"The temperature has already risen thirty-one degreees since the overnight low," I announced at ten o'clock next morning. "It is Fifty-Five degrees now, and not a cloud in the sky. Heat waves are shimmering off the ice, and the water level is rising steadily."

"Any other scary news?"

"Come see."

During the night, the determined current had again gobbled open a channel against our bank. Our usual observation perch was only five feet above the surging brown flow, close enough for us to identify each twig, stick and broken ice candle as it swirled by. We were startled and delighted at one point when three Merganser ducks swam by, oblivious to the blocks around them and to our presence. The water was steadily undermining the forested bank, the ice chips and chunks polishing a spruce's bared roots, sanding off any colour until they looked like spaghetti noodles instead of the foundation for a century-old tree.

When the ice sheets again broke, it was not so much the sound, but the quaking that alerted us. The air held a whiff of ozone like before a lightning storm. The dogs barked frantically. Trees along the bank were swaying. We dashed from our brunch to watch, but were cut off by a moat of icy water across the path. Our flat, laced with old river channels, was being invaded.

"Try by the other boat ramp," I shouted and we raced for it, hopping over a probing finger of water. When we could finally look out on the river, we instinctively grabbed for trees to brace ourselves.

The slow-motion moves of yesterday were playing at full speed today. Everywhere we looked sheets were grinding and buckling, suddenly sliding up and riding over the neighbour. Huge pans the size of whales reared up, the baleen-like under-layer of candle ice streaming water as the monsters muscled about. With awesome power, these masses were passing by us, jarring slabs off the sheets and destroying themselves in the process.

Soon the river was a choking mass of blocks, many as big as railway flatcars. The blocks jostled as people do in a stampeding crowd.

"Look what's coming!" Marsha pointed upstream.

The broken ice had been merely a vanguard for more sheets, these ones larger than football fields, cramming each other and battling as they contorted to fit the curves of the river. For a moment they locked and hesitated, three of them spanning the river, too wide to pass on, the weight of water and ice building behind them. Then the force heaved them free. Along the bends, gravel bars were scooped out like so much salt. Willows toppled from the banks into the river and were ground to matchsticks. Tremors under our feet were building in tempo. We were so close, we could have stepped onto a sheet. The trees on both sides of us quivered as their roots were torn by ice gnawing the bank. Frantically, we surveyed an escape route, in case our lookout ledge collapsed, but we couldn't leave yet: we were mesmerized and transfixed.

The floes surged past at about four knots – faster than walking pace. Through all the motion, the surfaces of some sheets had remained marvellously unaffected.

"Isn't that where the trail crossed over to the island with a big drift log?" Marsha pointed to one familiar-looking pattern on a passing sheet. "I think I recognize the way the trail wiggles."

"If that's where that sheet wintered, then we've only seen one mile of river go by," I replied. "About nine hundred and ninety-nine more to come."

"When some chunks come by with cow pies on them, we'll know the Pelly River's ice has broken, too," she laughed.

The river was so completely crowded with slush and floes it gave the illusion one could walk across on the moving ice, hopping the occasional fault line. The idea, however, was not the least bit tempting.

A thunderous crack or deep woomping sound would come from the shifting ice sheets, and we'd hurry from the cabin to see what was happening. If the jams held, we'd need to flee soon to higher ground.

I looked over the scene with the field glasses, but had trouble believing the enormity of what was coming next.

"You are not going to believe this," I whistled, handing Marsha the binoculars.

"I can already see it without those. That's *big!*"

Pushing behind these sheets was the granddaddy of them all. One vast piece, easily a half-mile square, moved down and plugged the river with a touch of finality. When ice behind it began to pile up, nothing budged. There was deathly calm. Through the glasses, we could see the upstream floes heaping up, forming a ragged line to mark the boundary of this flat iceberg. We were abreast of the centre of the gigantic blockage, assured of a prime seat when the plug was pulled.

"The river is clear downstream, right to the corner," I reported, after a long scan north. "There are dawdling sheets hung up on bars and islands, but the main channels are open."

"Look at the ice popping up beyond this block in the open water," Marsha pointed out. "They must be getting pulled underwater and bumping along under the sheet. Imagine what they are doing to eat away at the underside."

The chunks making the subsurface trip were as wide as our cabin, but were dwarfed by the size of the blocking sheet itself.

We were standing on the bank, maybe four feet higher than the ice, watching the water trickling around the base of the sheet. My second gauge stick had long ago vanished under the scouring press of ice. For a few moments, the height of the thin slip of water near us actually dropped, but then a surge brought it back to the previous level. Water seeped in, steadily pushing, pulsing and breathing like an immense trapped animal. We waited, expecting the pressure to float the iceberg, but it was wedged tight.

Minutes passed, then two hours, the tension mounting.

"What about the animals in the valley?" Marsha mused. "Do you think they are all watching this happening, drawn like we are? This is so magical. I've never seen this much natural power from this close."

"Maybe that grizzly is sitting on the bank at the far end of the flat as dazed as we are," I replied, the image of rabbits, squirrels and a bear all sitting at the shore to watch providing comic relief to the emotionally-draining display before us.

"Let's see how our dogs react."

When we released them, Tyhee tried to climb out onto the iceberg, her nose quivering and her eyes wild with enthusiasm. We quickly grabbed her, and called for Casey who had disappeared. He came eventually, wagging his tail, his face and paws covered in dirt from his favourite rat-hole. That made fifty-fifty results on our theory testing: Casey was clearly not very impressed by the power of break-up. To play it safe, we chained the dogs again, but fastened Casey closer to his diggings to make him happy.

Once again, the first change was the cutting of a channel against our shoreline. A steady progress was made, right past our viewpoint, until the lead reached the head of our slough. There the hammering current ate a path through the tumbled shore ice and inundated the back channel, transforming it into a raging rapids. We raced through our yard for a closer view of what had been dry ground, one of our sources of driftwood for fuel.

"Now I can see how those piles of drift logs got there," I stated. "They were perched so high above the winter ice level it was hard to imagine the water ever being so high."

The rising water threatened to breach the banks, the river level easily fifteen feet higher than when we'd driven our toboggans on it a month before. Into the slough poured a deluge of silty run-off, its surface thick with rotten ice and erosion debris. A few fallen trees, white spruces sixty feet tall, were manhandled along rudely, their roots amputated and the trunks stripped of branches. Large patches of bark were skinned off by the lathe-like action of the tumbling ice. The entire river seemed to be funnelling into our narrow slough, indifferent to route, heeding only the draw of gravity. Although our cabin site was now less than eight feet above the raging current, the release of water through the slough seemed to be taking some of the pressure off. The level held steady for hours before we quit watching for lack of daylight. Inside the cabin, we checked the root cellar and discovered it had a foot of water in it. Our ladder could now be the flood level gauge.

"If there was a dead guy in the cellar, he'd be drowning now," I observed.

"Everything will be fine, I just know it," Marsha decided as we nibbled a late supper. The interior of our home was a mass of cardboard boxes: our possessions wrapped and labelled for the eventual move south. Even the propane lanterns were packed, so we were navigating by candlelight. Marsha carried one over to the bedside and slipped under the sheets.

"There's nothing we can do about the river anyway," she murmured sleepily and blew out the candle.

Marsha, who was usually the worrier of this partnership, promptly fell sound asleep. I was so overwhelmed by the day's events I dozed fitfully. Three times I got up with a flashlight to check at the river's edge for reassurance. The level hadn't risen, but it had also not dropped as it had during previous nights.

When we peered out the window at daybreak, the river was in full march. The iceberg had disappeared, and in its place was a teeming flow. The ice was not a single layer of blocks now; there were blocks on slabs on more blocks. We stood on the shore speechless and wide-eyed. There was no water visible at all, even though we could see five feet down into the cracks. If this much ice was floating above the water, so much more must be moving beneath, supporting it.

As a witness, I felt insignificant. We were eye to eye with the top of parading ice piles.

When we checked the boat landing, we found blocks of ice as big as the riverboat had floated through the trees during the early morning and were scattered about like volunteer additions to our landlord's fishing fleet. The landing was mostly dry again now, protected from the river by a towering dike of packed ice, ten feet high and twenty thick. This was a solid wall, yet all the original pieces were obvious, their dimensions easily distinguished by the direction of the grain and the silty stains.

The current is eroding a channel along the near bank.

Checking on our slough, we found it similarly dammed across its head and dry, exhibiting a motionless, grounded collection of ice and debris. We poked at the closest blocks with poles, delighting when one would collapse into a heap of icicles. The sound was a tinkling, though not like crystal: more like a plastic beaded curtain's rattle.

For hours the grand march continued. Millions of tons of ice passed us and the flow appeared endless. We had begun to relax and were having a bite of lunch when suddenly we both sat upright, listening. It had not been a noise that caught our attention, but the sudden quiet. Until that point, we had not appreciated how noisy the river had been. We could see through the cabin doorway what had happened: the ice had jammed.

I raced to the bank and checked the ground beside the wall of ice. The puddles under the ice were filling fast. The river was locked, this time full of piled ice higher than the bank. As far as we could see upriver and down, ice was packed tightly. We waited for an hour as the water rose steadily and the jam held fast.

When the water began lapping over the banks and climbing the sloping bench towards the cabin, we started our evacuation procedure. There was only three feet of elevation left.

"You carry the sleeping bags," Marsha was organizing, "and I'll take the food in my pack. We'll need matches and an axe, and you'd better take your rifle—"

A low rumbling interrupted her, signalling the icejam was moving on. The water's frightening advance towards our door abated, relieving us from frantic escape preparations. We splashed through shallow water to the shoreline.

"What is all this doing to the islands downstream?" wondered Marsha. "The front of this jam would have the power of a hundred bulldozers."

"I guess there will be a few less islands and some new gravel bars in their place," I offered. "That ice could wipe out a forest of trees as if it weren't there."

"I don't think I'd like to live on an island, like Grant and Karen and their boys. I hope they are all right, and Hinglish too."

"This jam will have smashed itself to bits by the time it reaches them," I replied, "though there will be similar jams happening all along the river these days. Let's hope they get off lightly."

For an hour the thick flow continued, then it tapered off to intermittent patches of mushy ice and the occasional lonely sheet the size of a tennis court. Even a mass this large looked paltry after the spectacles of the previous days. The dike walls were still heaped up on the shore, the most obvious evidence of the jam now. The river level on the far side of these barricades was down to a height that let us breathe many sighs of relief.

The danger of break-up was over. It was time for our summer to begin.

WHAT TO DO ABOUT A DREAM

A week later, when the river was safe for his boat, Danny Roberts ferried us and our mountain of possessions to Crosby Creek on the Pelly River, where our truck was waiting. We stopped in to say goodbye and thanks to Abbie, then the Johnsons, the Bradleys and Don Mark. Everyone was caught up in the new season's spirit, so the main topic of conversation was planting gardens and fields.

In Whitehorse, we held a yard sale at Debbie and Don McArthur's house, and were able to sell all our northern equipment, including Furd, our truck. Marsha had received an offer to work a forest fire lookout tower near Burns Lake, B.C., which meant we couldn't dawdle in the Yukon any longer. On May 26th, Casey, Tyhee, Marsha and I climbed into a black 1965 Ford Comet (named *Fred*) and drove back down the dusty Alaska Highway.

The dogs' wounds healed completely over the following weeks and they settled easily into being pets again. Marsha had a new mountain to live with and I had this book to write. Our lives had come full circle, from a dream I'd had beside a northern lake, to a reality, to a memory. Already, parts of it seemed surreal.

We were standing outside her fire lookout building, peacefully watching rainbows form over Babine Lake, when Marsha brought forth her latest idea.

"Next summer," she said, putting her arms around me, "how about we go riding in the hills and take along pack horses? You know, it could be a *nine-horse summer*."

Marsha spent the summer on a fire lookout tower before we moved to the BC coast to work on a fish farm.

APPENDIX I

MAKING FREIGHTING COLLARS AND HARNESSING

See related diagrams and comments in Chapter 2.

Our harness designs were a combination of ideas, based on books about Arctic exploration and horse saddlery, plus an old dog harness relic provided by Danny Roberts. Our collars were formed from tanned leather stitched to a thin steel rod and stuffed with oat straw.

Some old-time dog collars, I read, had cane instead of steel. One saddlery text opined that rye straw was the ultimate stuffing, but we settled on oat straw because that's what a nearby farmer was growing. Moose or caribou hair had been used as stuffing in the past, and was thought by Hudson Bay Company traders to be superior to straw because it didn't break down as fast. One could use discarded nylon pantyhose as padding as well.

One reference to making horse cab collars said the leather should be soaked, then stretched over a wooden frame to mold it into a smooth contour. But other sources simply said wet it, sew and stuff, so we did this and didn't worry about a few minor wrinkles in the leather.

To simplify the manufacture, we had less variation in bulk between the fat draught area on the sides and the thinner throat area, as compared to a scaled-down model of a horse collar. We were encouraged in this by seeing examples of Native-made dog collars that were completely uniform in bulk all around, like a donut. We made a few contoured collars before creating our first donut-shaped one – the latter was so much easier, the next ones were all donut collars.

The contoured collars had an exposed seam, but that seam was off-centred so as not to rub against the dog's shoulders. We found that a lighter-weight leather was required for the contoured collars to minimize wrinkles. In this version, the rod was bent before the second seam was sewn. As the stitching progressed up the sides, stuffing was jammed in to stretch the wet leather to the desired shape. My favourite stuffing implement was a T-shaped chainsaw wrench/screwdriver tool, while Marsha had success using chopsticks.

For each collar, a rectangle of leather about 23 by 7 inches was needed.

Almost twenty feet of traces was required per harness. Historically, traces were made of thick belt leather and attached with conway buckles, rivets and linen stitching. We decided to substitute nylon webbing for the leather strapping at a fraction of the cost. It was easier to work, as strong and would be less tasty to the dogs. By selecting stiffer webbing, your harness will be stronger and less prone to getting tangled than with limp webbing. The trade-off, however, is that stiffer webbing is more difficult to stitch.

We eliminated the conway buckles normally used for adjusting the hame-tugs

---

Making a contoured collar

- This pattern for a dog with head 17" to 19" circumference, measured at base of ears. For larger (or smaller) dog, change the length but not the width.
- Draw a rectangle for pattern on 24" by 7" leather

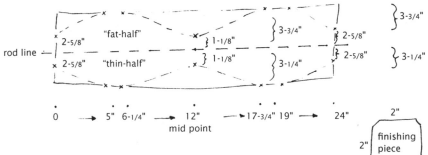

rod line

"fat-half" 2-5/8" 1-1/8" 3-3/4" 2-5/8" 3-3/4"

2-5/8" "thin-half" 1-1/8" 3-1/4" 2-5/8" 3-1/4"

0   5" 6-1/4"   12"   17-3/4" 19"   24"   2"
         mid point

2" finishing piece

- Mark rod line and reference points (x) on leather, connect with smooth curves and cut out. The "fat half" will be on the inside of collar.
- Lay rod on line, fold over leather (rough side inside) and stitch entire length, tight to rod. Bend rod to oval shape, then bend ends back and tie them. Make sure exposed seam will be on outside.

Cross section views

second seam first seam
stuffing (rod)

hame-tug

- Stitch across centre, then up both sides. Stuff after a few inches, packing tightly and pounding leather with mallet to force desired shape. Second (exposed) seam must be away from dog. Match pattern reference points (x) as you sew. Keep leather wet with sponge while working it.
- Add finishing piece as per instructions for donut-shape collar.

Note: if stuffing with nylon stockings, it will take eight pairs per harness.

Making a donut-shaped collar

1.

7" x 23" leather (rough side inside)

adjustable belt tongue
(about 4" out from rod)

belt buckle

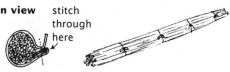

rod is 2-1/2 feet long

1" seam

- stitch close to rod in five spots to hold
- attach belt pieces

2. Cross section view   stitch
through
here

- Straw is twisted and tied in roll, about 22" long, 5" circumference but thinner at centre
- centre the roll on leather, fold over, then thoroughly wet leather with sponge
- starting at centre, pull leather tight with pliers and stitch through the three layers, minimum 4 stitches per inch. Work toward ends, re-wet leather as needed
- at ends: trim straw, sew closed

3.
- Bend collar a bit at a time over bannister or broom handle [don't try to use dog's neck!]. Desired shape is slight oval, taller than wide

- use pipe to help bend rod back tightly

- tie rod ends with thong or wire, cut off excess with hack saw or file

4.
- Try on dog, loosen thong/wire if necessary

underside view
of top join

- add finishing rectangle of leather to cushion under join. Stitch at ✷✷ marks, leaving one corner loose for minor adjusting
- make hame-tug slits halfway up each side, 1-1/2" slit for 1" webbing

Cut between
seam and rod

Note: Instead of using rolled straw, the collar can be sewn from the centre up both sides simultaneously, stuffing after every few inches. Use moose hair or nylon stockings. Or use straw this way: cut half-dozen straws 9" long, give 1/2 twist, fold double and jam in with stick or wide screwdriver. Pack tightly each time so collar is solid.

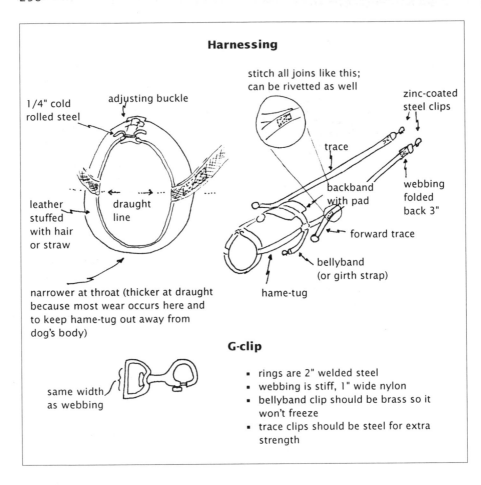

Harnessing

stitch all joins like this;
can be rivetted as well

zinc-coated
steel clips

1/4" cold
rolled steel

adjusting buckle

trace

backband
with pad

webbing
folded
back 3"

leather
stuffed
with hair
or straw

draught
line

forward trace

bellyband
(or girth strap)

narrower at throat (thicker at draught
because most wear occurs here and
to keep hame-tug out away from
dog's body)

hame-tug

G-clip

same width
as webbing

- rings are 2" welded steel
- webbing is stiff, 1" wide nylon
- bellyband clip should be brass so it
  won't freeze
- trace clips should be steel for extra
  strength

and backbands, both to save a few dollars in cost and because, once fitted to a
particular dog, a harness wouldn't need adjusting. This meant we left the stitching
of the tugs and backbands until we had the dogs in front of us.

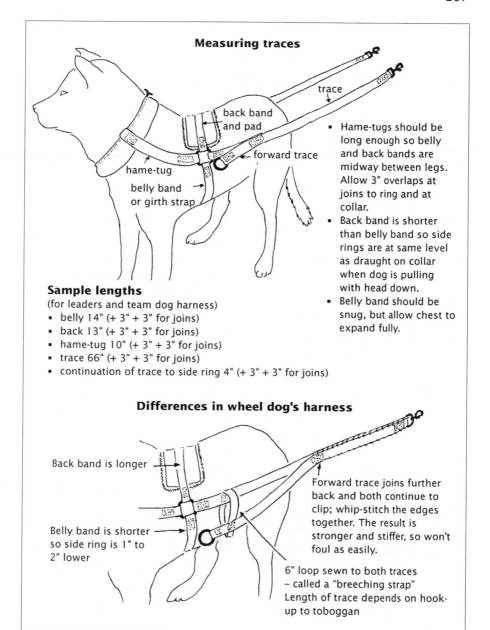

Measuring traces

trace

back band and pad

forward trace

hame-tug

belly band or girth strap

- Hame-tugs should be long enough so belly and back bands are midway between legs. Allow 3" overlaps at joins to ring and at collar.
- Back band is shorter than belly band so side rings are at same level as draught on collar when dog is pulling with head down.
- Belly band should be snug, but allow chest to expand fully.

Sample lengths
(for leaders and team dog harness)
- belly 14" (+ 3" + 3" for joins)
- back 13" (+ 3" + 3" for joins)
- hame-tug 10" (+ 3" + 3" for joins)
- trace 66" (+ 3" + 3" for joins)
- continuation of trace to side ring 4" (+ 3" + 3" for joins)

Differences in wheel dog's harness

Back band is longer

Belly band is shorter so side ring is 1" to 2" lower

Forward trace joins further back and both continue to clip; whip-stitch the edges together. The result is stronger and stiffer, so won't foul as easily.

6" loop sewn to both traces – called a "breeching strap" Length of trace depends on hook-up to toboggan

APPENDIX II

HOME MAKING AT A YUKON CABIN

See also Chapters 9, 21 and 26.

S tuffing or *caulking* the cracks in the cabin walls was an on-going, almost obsessive activity over the first weeks. The logs had been roughly flattened along their length to nestle together fairly tightly, but the gaps around the corner notching were fist-sized. As soon as the outside temperature dropped, the sources of cold drafts became obvious. Even if we had not felt the biting jets of cold air, the buildup of frost and ice around air leaks signalled their presence as effectively as a white flag. We stuffed the offending spaces with pink fibreglass which we called *pink moss* as a joke. Fortunately, there were bundles of this insulation left over from the cabin's roof construction. The traditional materials for caulking the seams between logs were moss and oakum rope. Moss had the great advantages of being free, handy and not particularly attractive to animals. Our pink moss was forever being pilfered by mice and squirrels for their own homes – we even found one practical squirrel who had made his nest inside a bundle of pink fibreglass, hollowing out a small cave and stocking it with dried mushrooms and pine-cones.

The cabin floor was made of chainsaw-milled boards, with no insulation below except an air space between the joists. Marsha banked sand around the outside of the cabin, and filled in the excavations made by mice and squirrels under the base logs. Later, when there was enough snow, we banked this against the walls too.

Noticing after the first snowstorm how fast the snow melted off the roof, we decided to double the layer of fibreglass insulation between the rafters. Also, to make this insulation more effective, we added a poly vapour barrier to the ceiling.

Our door was very drafty, but I didn't feel up to building a full porch onto the cabin. This would have given us a place to hang snowy clothing where it wouldn't become wet from heat, but there was a limit to how much time we wanted to spend on renovating the cabin. Besides, after caulking and re-insulating, the cabin would stay comfortably warm and was even – at times – too hot and stuffy. A neighbour told us: "We spent the first two winters plugging every crack, and have been making ventilation holes ever since. It was just too hot."

There was always a certain amount of smoke emitted when loading or adjust-

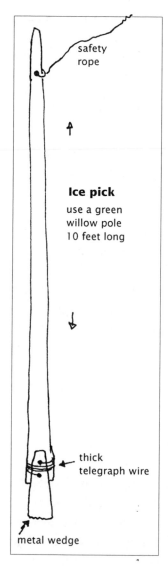

Ice pick

safety rope

use a green willow pole 10 feet long

thick telegraph wire

metal wedge

ing the heater and stove. With no way out, this blue haze would hang at eye level as if the cabin were a smoky tavern. The solution, we determined from looking at the old homestead ruins, was to make a small opening high up in a gable end, with a trapdoor remotely operated by a long cord.

Some fresh air had to find its way into the cabin if we weren't to get carbon monoxide poisoning from the wood combustion in progress. To control the source and, in so doing, eliminate other drafts, we installed a copper pipe to bring outside air directly to the airtight. When this pipe was wrapped around the heater, and angled upward, the incoming air would expand while it heated, and blow into the cabin like the blast from an electric hair blower.

A fire in our airtight heater could last all night if dampered right down, but that didn't produce enough heat to keep the cabin warm. So we had to operate it slightly hotter, and someone had to get up and add more fuel during the night. Grant Dowdell, whom we visited later in the winter, had a solution to eliminate the nightly reloading ritual: he installed a second barrel stove beside the regular one in his farmhouse basement and could leave two fires idling all night. The two together threw off as much heat when dampered as one barrel burning at a faster pace.

In digging our water holes through river ice up to four feet thick, an axe was useful for chopping through only for the first half. When the hole was deep, we switched to a heavy, chisel-like pick, and used a long-handled pot to scoop out the ice chips. The pick had to be long enough to reach the full depth of the ice without the worker bending over. We found a green willow pole handle was heavy enough to shatter ice with its own weight, yet not a strain to lift. At the farm, the Bradleys used heavy metal pipe handles, and much narrower cutting edges on their picks.

When the pick finally broke through, the water underneath would rush up to fill the hole. Since it was difficult to enlarge the bottom of the hole with the water cushioning the pick's impact, we cut out the full diameter at each level, leaving only a thin disc to be punched out when the first water gurgled in. If we had created a hole shaped like a cone, the narrow end would have frozen solid overnight and we'd have had to start all over again.

We chipped away down the sides each day to forestall the eventual freezing of the hole, but resigned ourselves to cutting a completely new hole every week and after any trips away. To insulate the hole from the cold air above, we covered it with a sheet of plywood and a sack of straw, then shovelled snow over top.

Our upstream neighbours at Fort Selkirk, Danny and Abbie Roberts, used ice for their water supply all winter. Danny hauled blocks of river ice with his snowmachine and put huge cubes into a galvanized 45-gallon drum behind his wood stove to melt.

I was surprised to see one homestead had an uninsulated hand pump out on the river bank which worked all winter. As long as the source could be below the frost line (which could be a long way in the Yukon), and the water drained back down properly after each pumping, this had to be the best answer to the whole water chore. If we had been planning on staying a second winter at Horsefall, a hand pump – ideally for inside the cabin – would have been my first purchase.

Our work on the cabin passed quickly when we listened to music. We had a cassette tape deck which sounded superb because of the fine acoustics of the log walls. There was also a short-wave radio, though we could only pick up a few stations. Ironically, we could not receive Radio Canada International, but Radio Australia, Radio Moscow and Voice of America came in loud and clear. The blatant propaganda and politically-biased *world news* reports on these stations were especially absurd to us in our lives of simplicity and isolation – ours was such a different world. Eventually we used the radio only to find out the time to set our clock.

To power our cassette deck and radio, we had an old 6-volt car battery. It lasted for five months before needing a recharge at the farm's generator.

Temperature will grossly effect the performance of any battery: warm batteries produce more power. If fully charged, a wet-cell battery won't freeze, but it will not have much power until thoroughly warm again. However, if not charged, the fluid inside can freeze and crack the casings. We put our battery in the root cellar when we left on trips if there was a possibility of the cabin interior freezing.

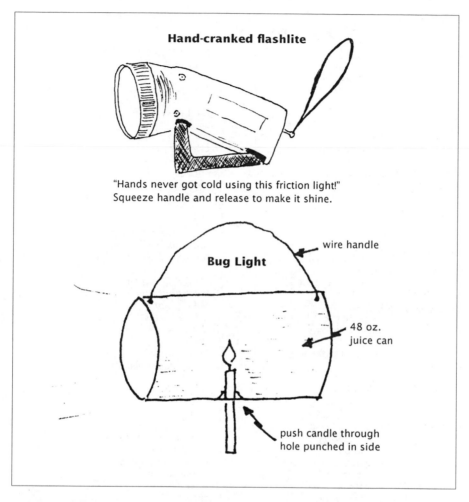

Hand-cranked flashlite

"Hands never got cold using this friction light!"
Squeeze handle and release to make it shine.

Bug Light

wire handle

48 oz.
juice can

push candle through
hole punched in side

Because flashlight batteries lasted only a few minutes at very low temperatures, eventually, we weren't using regular flashlights at all. Instead, we had one hand-crank flashlight and made candle lanterns. The handcranker was a cheap, plastic-encased device that worked like a child's friction toy. Until the plastic parts broke at –50°F, we found this an ideal alternative to battery power; we wished there were sturdier, metal models for sale. Our candle lanterns or *bug lights* were made from large juice cans: we removed the top, punched a hole halfway down the side for the candle to poke through, and added a wire handle.

We hand-ground our flour. By adjusting the pressure on the stones, it was possible to regulate the coarseness of the final product, right from whole wheat pastry flour to cracked wheat. For special, delicate recipes, calling for white cake flour,

OUR WINTER SHOPPING LIST

DRIED FOODS
- assorted beans
- brown lentils
- green peas
- dates
- bananas
- apples, pears, apricots
- prunes, peaches, etc.
- powdered milk
- coconut
- sunflower and sesame seeds
- walnuts, peanuts, almonds
- pecans, cashews, etc.
- raisins, currants
- popcorn
- alfalfa seeds
- mung beans
- variety of noodles
- herb teas
- "Inka" (chicory drink)

GRAINS
- wheat berries
- rolled slow oats
- millet
- long-grain brown rice
- cornmeal
- bulgar
- soymeal
- triticale
- quinoa

CANNED FOODS
- pineapple
- grapefruit
- home canned fruit
- tomatoes
- tomato paste
- mushrooms
- evaporated milk
- UHT milk
- corn
- seafood (salmon, tuna, mackerel, sardines, oysters, shrimp, clams)
- lemon juice in bottles
- pickles
- frozen juices (apple, orange and grapefruit)
- miso
- mayonnaise

FRESH OR FROZEN FOODS
- potatoes
- carrots
- onions
- celery
- rutabagas
- apples
- parsnips
- oranges
- squash
- eggs
- cheese
- meat (bacon, sausage, ham)

SPICES
- salt, pepper, curry, garlic, dill, oregano, basil, sage, cinnamon, nutmeg, dry mustard, parsley

BAKING & CONDIMENTS
- baking powder
- baking soda
- brewers yeast
- baking yeast
- vanilla
- lard
- blackstrap molasses
- honey
- peanut butter
- butter
- jams
- Tabasco
- tamari soya sauce
- carob chips
- buttermilk powder
- apple cider vinegar
- olive oil
- tapioca
- arrowroot
- freeze-dried yoghurt starter
- powdered eggs

MISCELLANEOUS
- toilet paper
- matches (wooden)
- dish soap
- laundry soap
- hand soap
- candles
- wicks, mantels, globes
- tinfoil
- wax paper
- small plastic bags
- sewing kit
- toothpaste

Marsha would use a sieve to separate out most of the flaky wheat germ which could be used in other baking. She determined that using coarse flour meant a bread recipe would require extra flour and turned out heavier as a result. Coarse flour was not great for thickening sauces or gravy.

The wheat we used was Red Spring Wheat. We also ground flours from soya meal, millet, triticale, rice, lentils, cornmeal and oats. Also, we ground spices, such as anise, cloves and caraway seeds. Compared to health food stores, feed dealers were a far cheaper source of whole grains, but the quality was not guaranteed. Feed destined for animal consumption may be brought through packing facilities not as well cleaned and inspected as those used for processing human food. Also, a higher proportion of weed seeds, mildewy kernels, dust and rodent hair are allowed for animal standards. We were assured in a letter from Buckerfields nutritionist A.M. Hicks that, *"if a fungicide or other treatment is used on it, the chemical must contain a marking colour so it is visually apparent that the wheat has been treated."* Our wheat was #3 grade, half the price of human grade #1, and it baked into the best bread I'd ever tasted. We ate a full 88-pound sack over the winter.

Spartan apples had kept for four months in our root cellar and were still fine and crispy. Oranges and grapefruit had gone woody after six weeks, but they were mostly eaten by then. Celery was fine for about a month, and cucumbers as long. Eggs that we bought by the case from the Bradleys' farm would have kept for six months, but were usually eaten in as many weeks. Root crops, such as potatoes, turnips, rutabagas, carrots and parsnips, were stored in the sand to help preserve them right until spring. When we went off on our trips, we piled sacks of dog food over the produce to insulate it. Despite the low temperatures, that tactic worked fine.

We had varied results when storing ginger, garlic and sourdough in both the root cellar and freezer chest. The ginger went woody if frozen and lost most of its taste. Garlic bulbs could be frozen without affecting texture, but the flavour decreased with each freeze-thaw cycle. We elected to keep our supply of both these plants in the cellar, where they preserved well. With sourdough starter, the opposite choice was better. When we left this bread-leavening agent in the cellar, it continued to work, eventually fermenting beyond a palatable point. After being frozen, however, the starter bounced back when thawed to produce weaker results, but of excellent flavour. With subsequent uses, it recovered all its potency.

APPENDIX III

MAKING GAUNTLETS AND DUFFLE LINERS

See also Chapter 10.

The leather Marsha used to make my gauntlets was the deer hide we'd tanned back in Qualicum Beach. Being home-tanned, it would breathe well, like the Yukon Indians' smoke-tanned moosehide. Later that week, we pieced together gauntlets for Marsha, using the backs from old moosehide gauntlets I'd worn out years before and cutting new palms and thumbs from the deer hide.

The gauntlets were made for wearing over mitts, duffle liners or gloves. They saved wear and tear on the warm, more fragile, woollen underlayers and helped keep them cleaner and therefore warmer.

Our duffle liners were made from the same pattern as the gauntlets, just cut smaller to fit inside. Duffle cloth is woven and matted wool that comes in different weights and colours and is like dense blanket fabric. Some mitts we saw in the Yukon were actually cut from Hudson Bay blankets. The weave in duffle cloth gives the material more strength than felted wool would have, but a special stitch was still required to make the seams last. First, Marsha stitched the seams with a polyester-cotton thread to secure the edges tightly. Stitches were alternately long and short to distribute the strain over the weave of the duffle. Next, she re-did all the seams, using wool, taking larger and longer stitches to further spread the strain. This wool stitch was the one that showed decoratively, so a colour that contrasted with the duffle was used.

To further prolong the life of these liners, Marsha sewed thin leather onto the duffle, extending from the palm up to the thumb flap. This is much easier, she learned, if done before the liner was assembled!

Even with reinforcements and the best of care, wool mitts wore out quickly. Fortunately, Marsha had foreseen this and brought a bundle of *dead sweaters* scrounged from second-hand stores and saved after laundry disasters. These she purposely shrank and matted by repeated hot washings and quick, hot drying. The resulting material she used like duffle cloth to make gauntlet-pattern liners and mitts.

Gauntlet instructions

1. Cut four pieces of the main pattern and two of the thumb. Make sure correct sides are cut if leather is smooth on one side.

2. Cut a 3/8" lace for making welted seam. This can be cut in a spiral from scraps. All seams will be sewn with a welt, using a whip stitch.

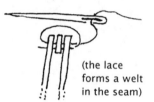

(the lace forms a welt in the seam)

Use sinew or waxed thread (or dental floss) and either a glover's needle or an awl and rounded needle. To end a thread, stitch back over previous stitches and snip off.

3. Cut on 'cut here' of palm. The opposite piece will be the back (do not cut it for a thumb!). Fold up the thumb flap just cut, and match it with thumb insert, 'right' sides (outsides) together. Sew, stretching palm leather as necessary to make the two fit. Use whip stitch and lace for welt.

4. Place right sides of back and palm together and stitch, using whip stitch and welt again.

5. Turn inside-out and trim off excess welt.

Cont'd overleaf

Pattern pieces for leather gauntlets and duffle liners

Palm pattern
cut 4 pieces:
(2 palms, marking thumb cuts)
(2 backs)

cut here on palm pieces only

cut here

cut here

make wider across here to fit over coat sleeves if very bulky

extend to length desired

Thumb insert pattern
(cut two)

wrong side

right side

stretch

wrong side

Making quick "Dead Sweater Mitts"

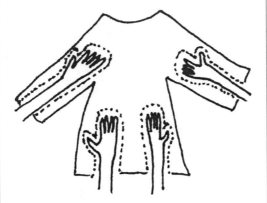

- mark, sew, *then* cut out
  (so the material will not unravel before
  you get it sewn)

Tips about reinforcing the duffle liners

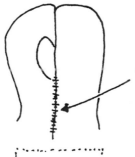

- alternate the
  stitch lengths
  (so the stress
  is over a
  larger area)

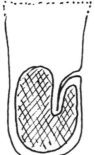

- sew on thin
  leather palm
  to protect
  the liner.

Gauntlet instructions (cont'd)

6. Add any fringe, braid, rick-rack or fur desired to cuff.

 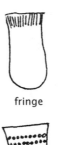

fringe   braid

zig-zag   fur
trim   (often beaver)

Add beading or embroidery
wherever you like!

7. Attach **'idiot strings'**
   before you lose the
   gauntlets. Braided wool
   makes attractive strings.

- gauntlets can be removed,
  and folded behind back to
  keep them out of the way
  yet still handy

- junction of the harness is
  close to armpit

- idiot
  string
  length is
  length
  of
  arm

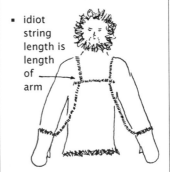

For quick, crude mittens that we used for chores around the cabin, such as dishing out dog food or carrying water pails from the ice hole, Marsha had a simpler pattern. She would trace around her hand on a double thickness of dead sweater material, leaving enough for a seam allowance. Then she would pin the layers together, sew on the chalk line with her handcrank machine, and *then* cut out the pattern. The finished mitts weren't beautiful, but they were quick. In fact, most of these were downright ugly, because Marsha couldn't bring herself to take decent-looking sweaters from the thrift stores. She liked the grotesque ones which no one would ever wear. The only criterion was there be a substantial percentage of wool in the fabric so it would shrink and matt well to make thick, warm mitts.

The year after our Horsefall Creek winter, Marsha and I met Arthur Thornthwaite, the Mountie who solved the Charlie Smith murder mystery. Long retired, he was living in Victoria. He told us the police, when on their extended dog-team patrols, always packed dress-up clothes (braided and fringed gauntlets and uniform hat at minimum) and some bells and coloured tassels for the dogs' harnesses. As they approached a trapper's remote cabin or an Indian encampment, Thornthwaite would halt the team and strip off his work parka and mitts, switching to the fancy clothes. After he classed up the dogs as well, they would parade into camp. This ceremony was done, he said, to respect their hosts.

APPENDIX IV

BUILDING FREIGHT TOBOGGANS

See also Chapter 11 for more information on making toboggans.

We procrastinated a bit when it came to making our freight toboggans. The customized children's model was still holding together and I wanted to gather my thoughts and my confidence. My first attempt at this project during the summer had been a dismal failure of splintered wood, and we had only enough materials for one more try at bending boards.

Learning about the process of bending wood had taken me into the field of shipbuilding because, although no one was making dog toboggans on Vancouver Island, every shipyard had tradesmen with experience in steam-bending ribs and planks. I jumped the gun, buying oak planks before I thoroughly understood the critical factors involved. The lumber purchased was unsuitable for bending because it was kiln-dried, wasn't clear of knots, and was sawn on the wrong angle. The

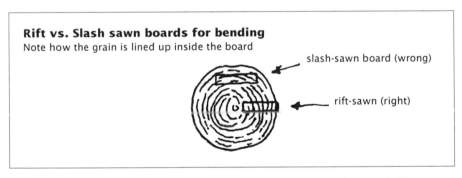

Rift vs. Slash sawn boards for bending
Note how the grain is lined up inside the board

slash-sawn board (wrong)

rift-sawn (right)

choice wood would be air-dried (or still green), straight-grained and rift-sawn.

Not only did I have poor material, but the frame I'd made to wrap the steaming planks around turned out to be too flimsy, breaking apart on the first attempt. After the frame was beefed up, the oak boards began snapping when I forced them to curl. Obviously, this approach wasn't going to work. To salvage the expensive hardwood, I ordered the remaining planks resawn into thinner and narrower strips (cut from 7/8" x 8" to be about 11/32" x 4") which I hoped would bend more easily. When we left the Island for the dusty drive northward, I was still reading and asking questions, planning my next attack on what I'd initially figured was a straightforward carpentry project.

The first dog teams into the central Yukon were possibly those of the Hudson Bay Company, pulling birchwood toboggans laden with fur trade cargos. Apparently the famous *couriers-de-bois* who worked for the English company made these vehicles from local wood when no imported hardwood was available, bending the sawn or adzed planks after they had been boiled to make them supple. Joints were fastened with rawhide babiche and wooden pegs. In those early days,

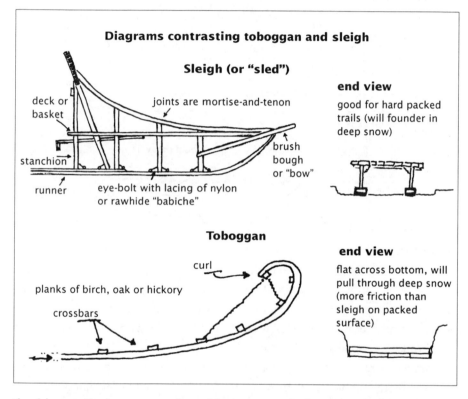

Diagrams contrasting toboggan and sleigh

Sleigh (or "sled")

deck or basket

joints are mortise-and-tenon

stanchion

runner

eye-bolt with lacing of nylon or rawhide "babiche"

brush bough or "bow"

end view

good for hard packed trails (will founder in deep snow)

Toboggan

curl

planks of birch, oak or hickory

crossbars

end view

flat across bottom, will pull through deep snow (more friction than sleigh on packed surface)

the driver walked or ran, steering with a rope attached to the curl of the toboggan (called the *head rope*). The only passengers were the sick or feeble.

On hard-packed trails, a heavier load could be transported using a sleigh instead of a toboggan because the sleigh's runners would have less friction on the snow than a toboggan's broad base. Off a travelled trail, however, a sleigh would be difficult to steer and would founder in deep snow.

For much of the 20th century, trading posts in the Yukon carried pre-bent oak and hickory boards imported from Eastern Canada. Trappers would make a toboggan by buying boards of the required length and width, bolting on hardwood crossbars and threading through side ropes and head rope.

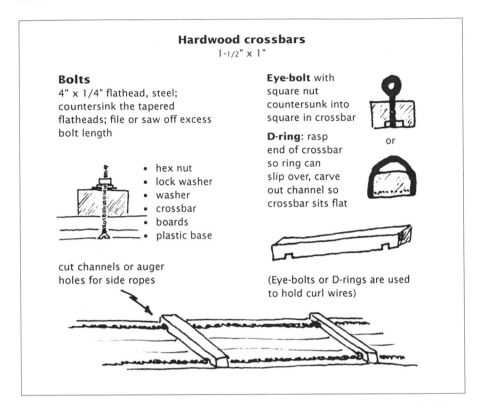

Hardwood crossbars
1-1/2" x 1"

Bolts
4" x 1/4" flathead, steel;
countersink the tapered
flatheads; file or saw off excess
bolt length

- hex nut
- lock washer
- washer
- crossbar
- boards
- plastic base

cut channels or auger
holes for side ropes

Eye-bolt with
square nut
countersunk into
square in crossbar

D-ring: rasp
end of crossbar
so ring can
slip over, carve
out channel so
crossbar sits flat

or

(Eye-bolts or D-rings are used
to hold curl wires)

The old-time Yukoners' other option was to start from scratch with a birch log, cutting out planks with a rip saw. If only a slight upsweep was desired, the green wood could be bent without steaming or boiling, and left to dry over a form. For a higher, tighter curl, the wood fibres had to be loosened by being kept in boiling water or a steam box before bending.

Birch was reputed to be the fastest surface in extremely cold weather, but oak was more durable. Birch grows in the Yukon; oak had to be imported from Outside. In the spring, when crusty snow could quickly rasp away the base, iron runners were bolted onto the bottom for protection. These metal runners also pulled easier than wet wood at temperatures near the freezing mark.

Early photographs of the toboggans used by the Royal North-West Mounted Police showed neither brakes nor handlebars. The drivers could pull, steer and brake with the head rope (also called a *gee-line*) or with a pole fastened to the curl, but mostly they just plodded along ahead of the dogs on snowshoes to pack a trail. Travelling in a convoy of three or four teams on long patrols, one man might stay back to guide the toboggans around a tight spot or down a steep bank. If the going was particularly smooth, the men could sit on top of the load for a

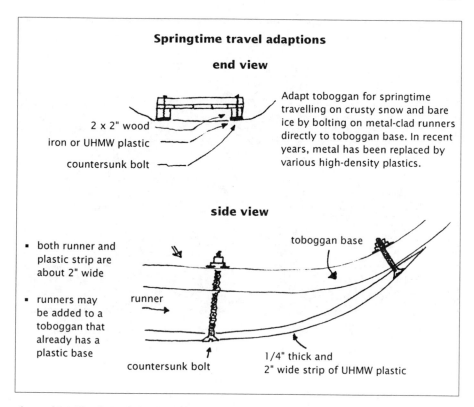

Springtime travel adaptions

end view

2 x 2" wood

iron or UHMW plastic

countersunk bolt

Adapt toboggan for springtime travelling on crusty snow and bare ice by bolting on metal-clad runners directly to toboggan base. In recent years, metal has been replaced by various high-density plastics.

side view

toboggan base

- both runner and plastic strip are about 2" wide

- runners may be added to a toboggan that already has a plastic base

runner

countersunk bolt

1/4" thick and 2" wide strip of UHMW plastic

short ride. To slow the toboggan on dangerous descents, chains or ropes would be wrapped underneath to drag in the snow. Only in the late 1920s did brakes and handlebars come into widespread popularity.

During the mid-1970s, the Teslin Indian Band in the Yukon village of Teslin opened a woodworking factory that produced hardwood toboggans as well as sturdy cedar-strip freighter canoes. Their toboggans were made of Arkansas oak, using one inch by eight inch planks steamed under pressure and bent into a high, three-quarter curl. They were very sturdy, and heavy enough to be used as cabooses behind snowmobiles, called *skibooses*. The factory sold them without uprights or attachments; it was left to the buyer to design whatever brake and handlebars he wanted. Unfortunately, the factory had been closed for a few seasons before our trip north in 1980, and Teslin toboggans had become a scarce and much-coveted item. If we could have bought two of these vehicles when we passed through Teslin, my construction project could have ended right there.

The booming hobby-sport of dog racing brought a few new options to the world of working dogs: various rigid plastics began being used in the early 1970s as bases

Constable Arthur Thornthwaite mushes his dogs up a ramp from the river. One dog's tail is held high – an indication that husky is not pulling his hardest. [photo courtesy A.B. Thornthwaite Collection, Yukon Archives]

Two police patrol teams on the Yukon ice below Dawson. Note the dogs in tandem freight harnessing and the lack of backboard and handlebars on the toboggans. [photo courtesy Glenbow Museum]

on sleigh runners. P-Tex, a product developed for downhill skis, and UHMW [Ultra High Molecular Weight] polyethylene were two of the most popular, because they are so strong and slide easily on snow. Soon, entire sleds were being made from these plastics, aluminium tubing, electrical conduit and nylon cord, with only part of the runners being wood. The reports I had received on the UHMW were so favourable that we purchased a four foot by ten foot sheet of this rigid plastic on our way through Vancouver to use as a base under the boards of our toboggans. We had instant appreciation of the slipperiness of this material when we wrestled to secure the quarter-inch thick sheet securely to the trailer.

When we passed through Whitehorse, Norm Rudolph (Jon's father) had a solution to my worry about a suitable process for bending our thin oak planks when we got to Horsefall. He urged me to *boil* the wood, explaining boiling had been a preferred method of bending ships' timbers in the Maritimes for centuries. Because our oak had been kiln-dried, it was too brittle to ever bend properly with steam; boiling was the only way. Norm gave me a chest-high length of six-inch diameter iron sewer pipe. We were to plug and bury one end in the ground, pour in water, then build a fire around the pipe. This we did at the cabin and the technique proved completely successful.

Our thin planks required thirty minutes of boiling to loosen up. At that point though, the change was amazing – the wood suddenly became limp and pliable. After I rushed the steaming board to our bending frame, Marsha would pin the end in place and then drop dowels into the holes as clamps while I walked the plank around the frame. [See diagram on following page.]

Bending the thin planks was not hard, though we needed to work quickly to have a board completely pinned before the winter air cooled it. The tighter the wood was clamped at each spot, the less chance there was of splitting or feathering. Although our results were satisfactory, the forming would have been gentler on the wood if the outside surface had been compressed with a metal or canvas strap during the bending, and if the inside of the frame had been a continuous form to distribute the strain more evenly.

Had we not planned on adding a plastic base under our toboggan boards, it would have been essential we have boards with straight grain and bend them so each one had the grain aligned so it would slide, rather than grab on the snow. Wood with scrambled grain and occasional knots, such as ours had, would never have made a good final base.

We were elated when we had our first success pegged to the bending frame

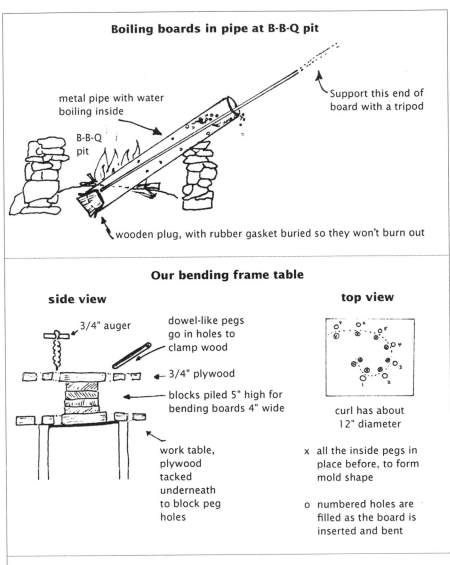

Boiling boards in pipe at B-B-Q pit

metal pipe with water boiling inside

B-B-Q pit

Support this end of board with a tripod

wooden plug, with rubber gasket buried so they won't burn out

Our bending frame table

side view

3/4" auger

dowel-like pegs go in holes to clamp wood

3/4" plywood

blocks piled 5" high for bending boards 4" wide

work table, plywood tacked underneath to block peg holes

top view

curl has about 12" diameter

x all the inside pegs in place before, to form mold shape

o numbered holes are filled as the board is inserted and bent

Grain direction concept

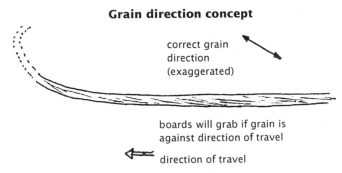

correct grain direction (exaggerated)

boards will grab if grain is against direction of travel

direction of travel

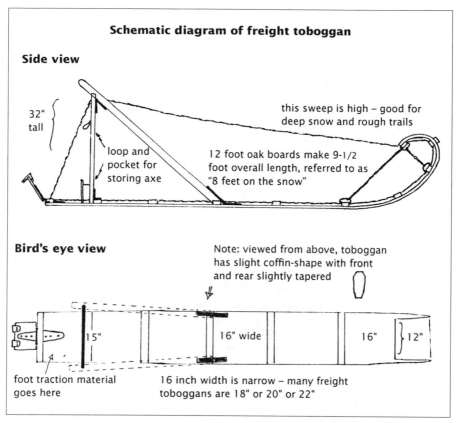

Schematic diagram of freight toboggan

Side view

32"
tall

loop and
pocket for
storing axe

this sweep is high – good for
deep snow and rough trails

12 foot oak boards make 9-1/2
foot overall length, referred to as
"8 feet on the snow"

Bird's eye view

Note: viewed from above, toboggan
has slight coffin-shape with front
and rear slightly tapered

15"

16" wide

16"

12"

foot traction material
goes here

16 inch width is narrow – many freight
toboggans are 18" or 20" or 22"

and anxiously waited for it to dry. After thirty-six hours, we removed the pins and the curled plank popped off. Then we bound it with rope to preserve the shape while the next boards were boiled and bent in turn.

Toboggans were generally between sixteen to twenty-two inches wide. Four of our boards gave us the narrower limit, well-suited for travel through the bush behind tandem (single file) dogs. Most toboggans we saw were made of three six-inch or two eight-inch boards. Twelve-foot-long boards would yield a vehicle over 9-1/2 feet in length, which was a practical size. Of this overall length, about 8-1/2 feet would be *on the snow* because the rest would be the upsweep of the curl that allows the front to ride up and over loose snow.

Before we boiled our boards, we selected which would be the outside ones and tapered them so that the resultant vehicle would be slightly coffin-shaped. The narrower curl ensured that the ends of the boards would be tucked well inside, away from snagging branches. The tail's taper made the toboggan easier to steer.

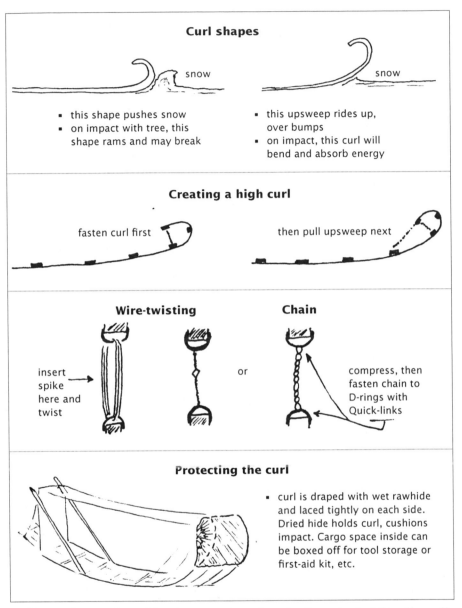

Curl shapes

snow

snow

- this shape pushes snow
- on impact with tree, this shape rams and may break

- this upsweep rides up, over bumps
- on impact, this curl will bend and absorb energy

Creating a high curl

fasten curl first

then pull upsweep next

Wire-twisting   **Chain**

insert spike here and twist

or

compress, then fasten chain to D-rings with Quick-links

Protecting the curl

- curl is draped with wet rawhide and laced tightly on each side. Dried hide holds curl, cushions impact. Cargo space inside can be boxed off for tool storage or first-aid kit, etc.

The curls were bound in place at two angles, the first wire holding the curl's half-circle, and the second fixing the amount of upsweep. A fancier-looking method than using twisted wire was to use chain and link fasteners. Traditionally, the curl was draped and laced tightly with wet rawhide, but we had missed our moose this winter and had to omit this step.

When assembling the boards, crossbars and plastic base, we found it important

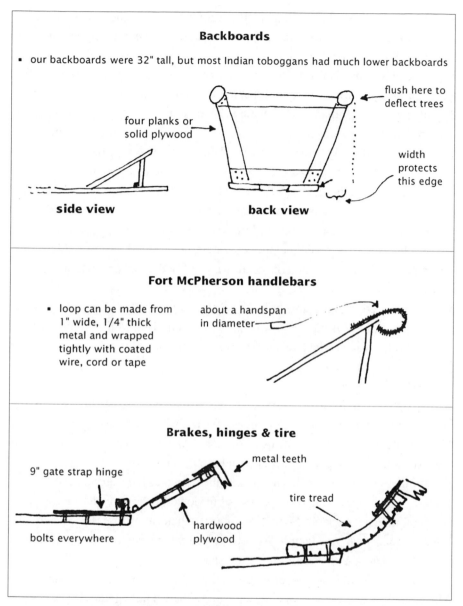

Backboards

- our backboards were 32" tall, but most Indian toboggans had much lower backboards

four planks or solid plywood

flush here to deflect trees

width protects this edge

side view   **back view**

Fort McPherson handlebars

- loop can be made from 1" wide, 1/4" thick metal and wrapped tightly with coated wire, cord or tape

about a handspan in diameter

Brakes, hinges & tire

9" gate strap hinge

metal teeth

tire tread

bolts everywhere

hardwood plywood

to have the plastic warm to ensure a tight fit. After the completed craft was taken outside into the cold, the plastic contracted more than the wood and was drawn up snugly.

The designs of handlebars and backboard varied widely on the toboggans we saw. Those at Pelly Crossing had a low, wide backboard with handlebars so low one had to stoop to hold on. Keeping the weight low made the load more stable, which was especially important if the toboggan was to be used on occasion as a skiboose. Some of their backboards were solid plywood, like ours were, but others were made of four planks, bolted together and to a crossbar at the bottom. The resulting opening was covered with canvas, or left open for access to the load. Handlebars on the Indian models were fastened to the backboard with telegraph wire or strips of galvanized metal. At the lower ends, the handlebars were wired to a crossbar or directly to the baseboards themselves, with wire passing under the toboggan in a recessed groove. Another method – which we adopted – was to use hinges to fasten all these points. Because of the strain, the hinges had to be super sturdy ones with locked hinge pins, and with bolts used in lieu of screws.

Our handlebars were simple willow poles, but we saw a unique design from Fort McPherson that solved the problem of getting speared during sudden stops. Their handles ended in a loop of metal, wrapped with tape for a better grip.

Our brakes were metal claws bolted to a square of hardwood plywood, which was in turn hinged (using a 9" strap hinge) to the tail. Don Mark used a tire tread version which was as effective until the weather became very cold and the rubber became too stiff to bend.

Losing one's footing could mean a long walk home if the dogs didn't care to stop, so we improved the traction on the area of the tail where the musher would stand. We saw old toboggans with strips of tire tread or rough matt fastened here, but we liked a macramé rope net for grip under our moccasins.

Another safety measure against losing the dogs was the trailing head rope (or lifeline, or gee-line). This was also useful for lowering a toboggan down a steep bank, or pulling it back out of the trees or a snowbank after a missed corner. Fifty feet was a practical rope length. We usually tied this rope to a tree while harnessing the dogs, to guard against premature starts.

Following the Indians' pattern, we wired our curls to the top of the backboard. Then the sides were woven in with rope, tying the whole together like a suspension bridge. The toboggan could flex and snake along a trail, but each spot was supported to keep it from bending too far. A canvas or moosehide tarp laid out and fastened to both wires formed a basket into which the cargo was placed. Moosehide is much more durable than cotton canvas, but there was synthetic canvas called *polyduck* which was almost as tough as hide.

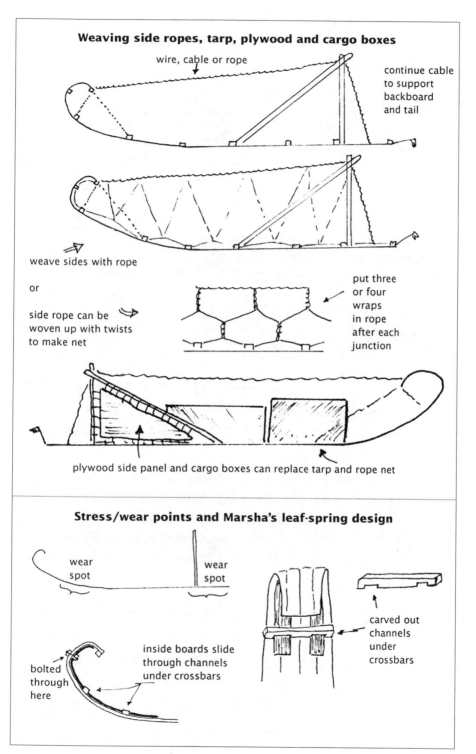

Weaving side ropes, tarp, plywood and cargo boxes

wire, cable or rope

continue cable to support backboard and tail

weave sides with rope

or

side rope can be woven up with twists to make net

put three or four wraps in rope after each junction

plywood side panel and cargo boxes can replace tarp and rope net

Stress/wear points and Marsha's leaf-spring design

wear spot

wear spot

carved out channels under crossbars

inside boards slide through channels under crossbars

bolted through here

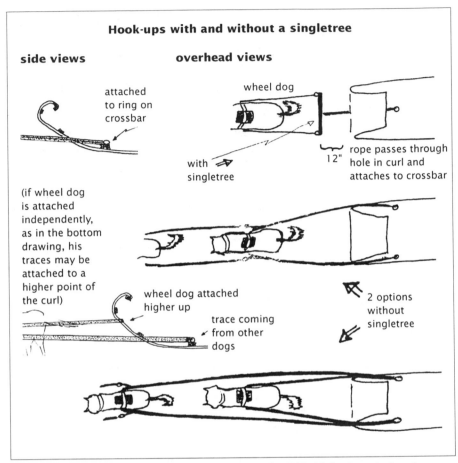

Hook-ups with and without a singletree

side views   **overhead views**

attached
to ring on
crossbar

wheel dog

with
singletree

12" rope passes through
hole in curl and
attaches to crossbar

(if wheel dog
is attached
independently,
as in the bottom
drawing, his
traces may be
attached to a
higher point of
the curl)

wheel dog attached
higher up

trace coming
from other
dogs

2 options
without
singletree

Toboggans built in pre-plastic days were usually 7/8" thick, though they became thinner with use. A few trappers told us the Teslin toboggans were best after a few seasons, when the wood had *loosened* and there was more flex in the base. Checking out retired toboggans, wear was most obvious in two places: from the backboard to the tail (beneath the musher's weight), and where the upsweep starts. We reinforced our toboggans at these points to compensate for the thinness of our oak planks. By doubling the boards at these stress points we had the stiffness comparable to a well worn-in heavy toboggan. Where we strengthened the upsweep, it was important to leave in the flexibility, so we used a leaf-spring system Marsha devised after the first few crashes. The reinforcing boards were left to slide through channels in the crossbars. On impact, these inside boards absorbed and dissipated much of the shock.

The finishing touch to the complicated construction was attaching the dogs' harnessing to the curl. Mushers seemed to be divided into many schools of thought on this matter. If the dogs were to be run in siwash harnesses off a single towline, the line was usually passed through a hole near the base of the curl, and fastened to a ring on a crossbar. The dog closest to the curl (the wheel dog) may or may not have been hooked directly to the top of the curl, depending on the musher's preference.

If the dogs were in the tandem freight harnesses we were using, there were at least three options. There could be a singletree spreader bar behind the wheel dog, from which a single rope or chain passes through a hole in the curl; or the wheel dog's traces could be extended to pass on either side of the curl, hooking onto a crossbar about where the upsweep starts; or the traces from the rest of the team could bypass the wheel dog whose traces attached independently to the curl. We tried a few different ways and didn't notice very much difference. It would have been interesting to know how the wheel dogs themselves rated the options.

Whatever hook-up was used, all mushers we spoke to agreed the wheel dog must be close to the curl to help steer. *His back leg, if extended, can almost touch the curl* was how one trapper measured the distance.

APPENDIX V

CARING FOR THE DOGS

See also Chapter 13 for other information about dog feeding and care.

Feeding our dog team regular dog food would be expensive, so we examined the alternatives before we moved to Horsefall. Commercial dog meal was very heavy, and bulky to haul to the cabin. A dog of Loki's size (50 lbs.), if fed straight dog meal, would need roughly his own weight in food per month, an amount that would cost us about $20 back in 1980. In cold weather, and especially when the dog was working hard, that would have to be supplemented by fat, such as a pound of raw beef fat per week.

Traditionally, dog teams along the Yukon River were fed dried salmon and whatever game was available, plus skinned carcasses from fur-trapping activity. There are two salmon runs each year on the Yukon: the kings (chinooks) come in July and August, and are netted for human consumption; the *dog salmon* (chums) start being caught in September, and were saved primarily for dog feed. In recent years, as the price of smoked salmon has risen, the second run has been netted increasingly for people food. When fishing for their teams, river residents would dry the chums while the weather permitted. After it got colder, the catch was simply stacked like cordwood on the bank to freeze. The dogs love them in this form, gnawing on a fish as if it were a huge popsicle.

We got to our cabin too late to fish because – although the dog salmon were still running – there was too much ice flowing in the river to risk putting out nets. Fortunately Peter Isaac was doing well on his trapping and could bring us skiboose loads of lynx meat for our team. "Only the leg bones are dangerous," he told us, "because they splinter badly."

Besides fish and trapping carcasses, another alternative to commercial meal was buying various feeds from a livestock dealer and mixing our own formula of dog food. This was cheaper and gave us an opportunity to experiment with the effects of difference ingredients. We bought rice, rolled quick oats, soya meal, fish meal and corn meal from Buckerfields farm supply store, plus dog meal. The grains, we were warned, have to be soaked until soft before serving or they will pass right through the dog. Most mushers cook their dogs' evening meal – or at least soak the ingredients in hot water – which ensures all the ingredients are digestible. Enough heat will also kill worms and parasites in game meal that otherwise might be passed on to the dogs.

When we wrote to Buckerfields' head office, asking for advice on concocting our own recipes, their nutritionist sent this reply:

> I can see some dangers in uncontrolled extending of our dog food with fish meal and/or soybean meal and/or oats. My main concern would be with the calcium:phosphorus balance as soybean meal and oats are high in phosphorus and very low in calcium. Fish meal has a good balance and, therefore, does not present the same problem. However, if soybean meal is used to replace the fish meal, and oats are also used, there could be a problem. Therefore, I would suggest you do not use these products to make up more that 10–15% of the dogs' ration and I would use a mix of about 25% fish, 25% soybean meal and 50% oats.
>
> —A.M. Hicks

We took extra fish meal with us on camping trips to mix in with our recipe because this powder was compact and very high in protein (65%). Fish meal was as close as we could come to the tried-and-true trail rations of dried or frozen river salmon. Mounted Police directives from the 1920s advised packing: 'Fish, about 6 lbs. per diem per dog, green. Fish to be well thawed at camp fire before feeding.' Or, patrols could take '3 pounds of dog pemmican per diem each.'

The Mounted Police's recipe for dog pemmican was as follows:

> Coarse odds and ends of beef, to be first dried, then ground or shredded. Fat of beef to be rendered and whilst hot poured over the beef, which is to be well stirred. The mass should then be put in bags of convenient size for packing on dog sleds.
>
> —from a letter sent to us by S.W. Horrall,
> Historical Section, RCMP, Ottawa.

For a working dog to gain weight and put on muscle, meat was the best food. Trappers regarded beaver carcasses very highly, because of the high fat content in beaver meat. Ground chicken (bones, feathers and all) was being used as a base for feeding many Alaskan racing teams. In our case, we were fortunate to have access to the leftovers from the fall slaughter of beef at the neighbours' farm. The heads, stomachs, reproductive tracts and frozen blood, along with Peter Isaac's lynx meat, helped our teams get into shape before our camping sessions got into full swing in the New Year.

Sled dogs can subsist on a surprisingly low ration but they will tire after only a

*Mounted Police members Allie (lead dog) and Constable Arthur
Thornthwaite at Rampart House in the northern Yukon. Sixty years after this
photo was taken, Thornthwaite was retired in Victoria, BC. This photo was
on his wall.* [photo courtesy of A.B. Thornthwaite Collection, Yukon Archives]

little work. They needed much more food, up to twice subsistence levels, to work all day in the cold. What we thought early in the season were lazy or stubborn dogs, turned out to be excellent workers when we upped their rations. We learned to check their condition by feeling their bodies. One place to notice was over the pelvic bones, which should have a little fat over them. By pinching the skin, we could also tell if a dog was dehydrated. If the skin didn't spring right back, the dog needed more fluids. Though the dogs ate snow and we served their meals soaked, occasionally (especially on long, tough trips) they required more water. A few spoonfuls of melted lard or bacon grease added to warm water would coax any of our dogs to lap up a drink.

The cheapest dog bowls we could find were bread pans from the second-hand stores. In the dead of winter, when the rations were larger than the capacity of a bread pan, we poured the extra on the snow, and never heard a complaint.

The Mounties gave their dogs a feed of hot oat mash once a week, to keep them from binding up on the steady meat and fish diet, as well as to flush out worms. This was the same procedure the police used to de-worm their horses. [Incidently, all the police team dogs were given regimental identification numbers, just like the horses and the men themselves.]

The first sign we had of worms was flat, white segments in the dogs' stools. Most dogs got worms once in a while, from a piece of rabbit left on the trail by a generous fox, from game carcasses that weren't thoroughly cooked, or from another dog's stools. We promptly treated all the dogs with pills, but new cases cropped up all winter. The pills were *Canoids*, a prescription worm-poison. As with most worm treatments, the procedure had to be carried out once to kill the adult worms and two weeks later to kill the newly-hatched next generation.

The dogs' hide was certainly tougher than my skin – as I learned whenever I attempted to intervene into a dog fight without wearing heavy leather gauntlets. Their healing system was also superior and quite different to mine. Deep tears in their hide, which would have meant dozens of stitches if the wound was on my arm, healed amazingly quickly if the dog was left alone. A human wound will scab over, so the knitting of flesh and skin by scar tissue happens unseen. Then, one day, the scab sloughs off to reveal repaired skin. By contrast, a dog's cut won't scab over. Instead the wound continually weeps a little blood and clear fluid to flush itself. The patient will instinctively lick the wound to help this flushing action. Meanwhile, new skin – complete with hair – grows in slowly around the edges. The wound stays open and weeping until the new skin finally closes the gap. For a novice who has no experience in the matter, the dogs' wounds look alarming: they were always *open and still bleeding* – which was actually fine.

If we believed a wound might infect, we dusted it with *Eye and Wound Powder* (from Ayerst Laboratories), a veterinary-use-only penicillin powder. Because this brand also had sulfa in it, we followed Hugh Bradley's advice and limited the dustings to three consecutive days to guard against burning the new skin.

The rate of healing was hard to believe. Tyhee was admiring Mutt's bone one day on her way to be harnessed. Mutt took offence and tore a gash in her belly I could easily have put a fist into. We considered going out to a veterinarian for this wound, but the trip would have taken days and been none too gentle on the nosey and seriously injured pet. Instead, we dusted the wound and confined her. Amazingly, within a week the opening had reduced to the size of a penny, although

Chain designs: gang and individual

wired on permanently

to tree

rope to tree

Gang chain
- 7' between side chains and at each end
- side chains 18" long; clip must have swivel
- ends may be tied with rope or chained to trees
- other names are *stake out chain* and *tether line*
- be sure last dog can't reach rope to chew it

Individual chain for at home
- clips attached to chain with twists of wire
- 10' long is generous
- 2/0 lion-link is strong enough if there are swivels so chain isn't twisted

clip or wired   swivel in centre   clip with swivel

Making semi-slip collars with 2" rings and 1" webbing

top view   **side view**

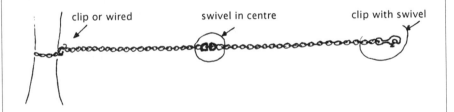

[X]   first ring

second ring

1. Measure circumference at base of dog's ears ('big circumference')
2. Measure circumference of throat ('small circumference')
3. Amount needed is twice big plus 6" minus small
4. Stitch on one ring with a 2" overlap
5. Measure along big amount and mark webbing [X]
6. Pass free end through ring well past mark [X]
7. Slide on second ring to the mark [X] and fold back webbing and stitch 1-1/2" square to secure second ring
8. Measure back from this square the amount 'big minus small' and stitch down, creating gap along which first ring slides.

it was still open and looked like a brand new puncture. After a few more days' rest, Tyhee was back in the line-up.

Danny Roberts, our neighbour at Fort Selkirk, recommended sewing a wound if there was a big flap hanging down. He once had a dog nearly scalped in a fight, so he stitched the flap back on in a few places. By pinning it back in place, yet leaving gaps for drainage, he helped the skin heal back on.

Sewing a dog's hide was not easy, as I'd found out when helping a friend piece a pet back together after it fell out of a truck on the highway. Poor Mittie had been dragged by her chain before my friend heard her cries and spotted her flopping in the rearview mirror. The repair was like stitching thick leather. We had to use a glover's needle, dental floss for thread, and pliers to push and pull the needle through. Mittie didn't appear to feel much pain while we did this, partially due to being in shock. We noted that a dog would go into a stupor after being wounded, another part of their natural healing process. While they were mentally drowsy, the body was mending itself faster. This stupor would last for a few days if the injury was severe.

We learned at Fort Selkirk [see Chapter 18] when Hinglish and others got loose from their gang chain, to wire the side chains onto the main chain permanently with a swivel. Grant Dowdell explained another way of building gang chains – using aircraft cable – in Chapter 41.

The same stiff, nylon webbing that made the best harness traces made dandy limited-slip choke collars. The idea was to make a collar that could slip closed enough to choke the dog a bit, yet wouldn't open so wide as to come off without the musher's assistance. We needed two rings like those used on the harnesses and from 26 to 29 inches of webbing for each collar, the length depending upon the circumferences at the dog's ears and throat.

APPENDIX VI

FIREWOOD

See also Chapter 14.

Four years before our winter at Horsefall, I was chopping wood to heat my little geodesic dome cabin near Whitehorse, figuring I was an expert woodsman, when Barry Barlow tactfully took me aside and clued me in.

"You're splitting your wood wrong," my longtime buddy insisted, "and your axe is too sharp."

He drew a diagram in the snow to illustrate the different ways to sharpen axes, each for its own purpose. My splitting axe was razor sharp and finely tapered, so it was forever getting stuck into the rounds instead of wedging them apart. A finely-tapered blade, he explained, also has the danger of being chipped or dented.

Barry then demonstrated the proper technique. If I'd had one of those monstrous ten-pound splitting mauls to pop apart my wood, I might never have received this other half of Barry's impromptu lesson. All I had was a general purpose two-and-a-half-pound axe, and I was becoming very frustrated trying to split some knotty spruce rounds.

"What you need to do," he said, lining up at a huge block of wood, "is be more efficient with your energy. Give your wrists a little turn as the axe hits, so some of the impact is directed sideways. You want to pop the wood apart, not cut through it."

By twisting it this way, my axe didn't get stuck in the wood at all. After a few tries, I was popping the wood apart like a professional. It was now great fun!

Next Barry showed me where to aim the blows. The heartwood at the centre is softer wood and often pithy. This part isn't holding the round together, so aiming the blows at the outside rings is more effective.

Marsha and I had a small chainsaw as well as swede saws. Neither of us particularly liked using a chain saw but we sacrificed some of our peace and tranquillity in order to have the wood chores done sooner.

The only size of chainsaw with which Marsha felt confident was advertised as a mini-saw or one step larger. We bought a Husky 32, only partly because Jon

Sharpening axes for different purposes

carpentry edges...

bench axe   notching   general purpose   splitting maul

(only on
one side)

Bending the knees during swing

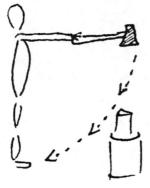

- a miss will strike your feet
  (not good)

- now a miss will hit chopping block
- bending knees also increases the
  velocity of the axe head!
- remember to give axe a slight twist
  when impacting to *pop* the wood apart

Cutting logs without a saw-horse

- cut almost through

- then roll over

- and break apart with axe

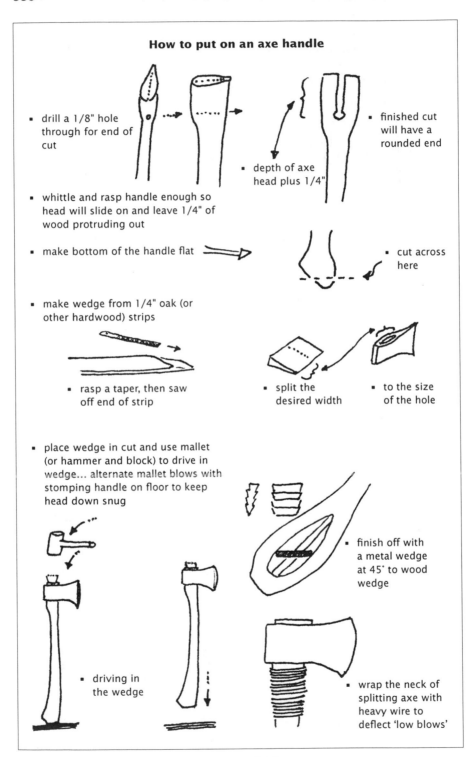

How to put on an axe handle

- drill a 1/8" hole through for end of cut

- whittle and rasp handle enough so head will slide on and leave 1/4" of wood protruding out

- make bottom of the handle flat

- depth of axe head plus 1/4"

- finished cut will have a rounded end

- cut across here

- make wedge from 1/4" oak (or other hardwood) strips

- rasp a taper, then saw off end of strip

- split the desired width

- to the size of the hole

- place wedge in cut and use mallet (or hammer and block) to drive in wedge... alternate mallet blows with stomping handle on floor to keep head down snug

- finish off with a metal wedge at 45° to wood wedge

- driving in the wedge

- wrap the neck of splitting axe with heavy wire to deflect 'low blows'

Rudolph had the local franchise for Husqvarna. It was small and lightweight, equipped with a fourteen-inch bar which was ample for the trees in our region.

The secret to keeping small saws running, Jon warned us, is to keep the chain always razor sharp, so the engine doesn't have to labour too much. He advised storing the saw indoors between uses during cold weather, and keeping the gas topped up to minimize water condensation inside the tank. A teaspoon of methyl hydrate added to each tankful of gas mixture should keep the gas system clear of ice. Filtering all gas is a wise additional safeguard.

After we wore out a bar and chain rather quickly, a friend advised us to thin our chain oil with kerosene during the very cold weather. This would make the oil capable of lubricating all the way around the bar. The abrasive silt that was in the driftwood we cut must also have contributed to the wear on bar and chain.

APPENDIX VII

ASSEMBLING OUR WINTER COSTUMES

See also Chapter 15 and Appendix III.

O n our feet we wore either boot pacs or moccasins. When the weather was warmer than Zero Fahrenheit, the snow would be too wet for moccasins. One temporary solution was to put a plastic bag inside each moccasin so at least the liner would stay drier. We also saw people in Pelly Crossing wearing toe-rubbers over their moccasins for the warmer days, but the liners would eventually become wet from condensation when the leather could no longer breathe.

When we bought our pacs, we noted some styles came with steel toes and shank plates to meet construction safety requirements. The heat-conductive steel would have been an invitation to frostbitten toes in our climate.

In making our moccasins, Mrs. Lizzie Hager of Pelly Crossing used a pattern that called for two pieces of leather, though a moccasin maker further north would have followed a four-piece design. The northern pattern yields more moccasins per hide because it uses smaller pieces which can be cut from trimmings. As another advantage, this latter style has a simple sole which can be replaced without remaking the entire moccasin. We didn't get a chance to compare the two patterns through a winter's wearing because we only used the locally-preferred two-piece design. Ours gave us no problem at all; in fact, they were wonderful!

Before the white man appeared on the Yukon scene, the Indians apparently stuffed their moccasins with dried grass to insulate them. No doubt they used furs for liners as well. After trading with the Russians began via the coastal tribes, woollen blankets were introduced and used for all sorts of clothing, including moccasin liners. Woven wool proved durable and extremely warm. With this fibre, moisture could wick away to some extent from the feet, and pass on out through the leather. Coarse duffle (thick woven and matted wool) made the best liners, and were standard issue for the Royal North-West Mounted Police.

The best were doubled duffle liners: two separate liners – one slightly smaller – sewn together at the top and tucked one inside the other. To dry this style, the inside half is pulled out. The Canadian Army used these double duffle liners, so we got ours through a government surplus store.

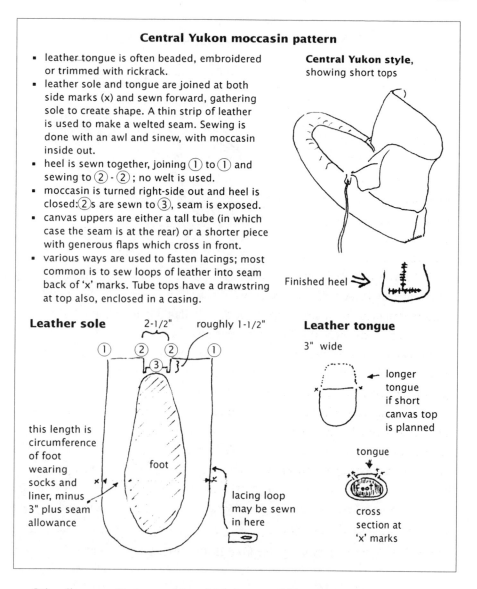

Central Yukon moccasin pattern

- leather tongue is often beaded, embroidered or trimmed with rickrack.
- leather sole and tongue are joined at both side marks (x) and sewn forward, gathering sole to create shape. A thin strip of leather is used to make a welted seam. Sewing is done with an awl and sinew, with moccasin inside out.
- heel is sewn together, joining ① to ① and sewing to ② - ②; no welt is used.
- moccasin is turned right-side out and heel is closed: ②s are sewn to ③, seam is exposed.
- canvas uppers are either a tall tube (in which case the seam is at the rear) or a shorter piece with generous flaps which cross in front.
- various ways are used to fasten lacings; most common is to sew loops of leather into seam back of 'x' marks. Tube tops have a drawstring at top also, enclosed in a casing.

Central Yukon style, showing short tops

Finished heel ⇒

Leather sole

2-1/2"   roughly 1-1/2"

① ② ② ①

③

this length is circumference of foot wearing socks and liner, minus 3" plus seam allowance

foot

× ×

lacing loop may be sewn in here

Leather tongue

3" wide

← longer tongue if short canvas top is planned

tongue ↓

cross section at 'x' marks

Other liners we had were felt, which is matted fibre. Felt liners that had a high ratio of wool to other fibres were almost as warm as wool duffles, although the felt was not as durable as duffle cloth because it wasn't woven.

Each night at our cabin, we'd take out the liners from our moccasins and hang them to dry. It was handy to have many pairs so we could wash them occasionally. Without the accumulated dirt, and after they had been fluffed again, the liners and moccasins were noticeably warmer. The woollen liners required a cool wash-water temperature to prevent shrinkage and the felt had to be handled carefully

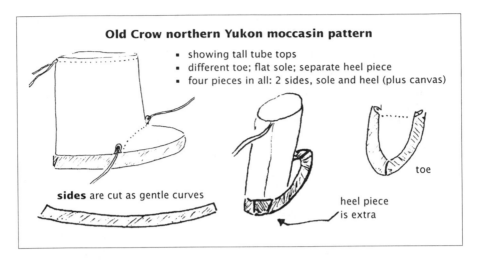

Old Crow northern Yukon moccasin pattern

- showing tall tube tops
- different toe; flat sole; separate heel piece
- four pieces in all: 2 sides, sole and heel (plus canvas)

toe

sides are cut as gentle curves

heel piece
is extra

because this material is not strong when wet. Since liners took many days to dry out after being thoroughly saturated, we'd wash our liners a full week before a trip. Out camping, we'd stow that day's slightly damp liners inside our sleeping bags to have them dry and warm come morning.

With all the liners hanging near the airtight, it was easy to get Marsha's confused with mine until Marsha brought out some bright embroidery thread and stitched *M* on all hers and *B* on mine.

We bought our socks literally by the dozens; they were economical, mostly-woollen work socks. By each day's end, we could count on having our socks damp from condensed sweat, so we needed a big supply, especially for camping trips. Drying socks over a campfire takes careful attention and much patience if the socks aren't to be scorched. This task could be avoided altogether by bringing along a change of socks for each day. Marsha reinforced our work socks when

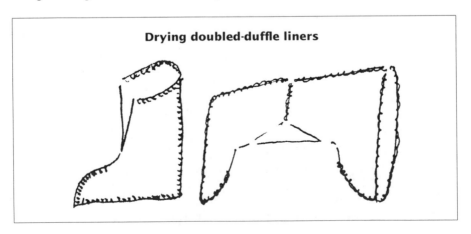

Drying doubled-duffle liners

they were new. She darned synthetic yarn across the heels and toes to protect the original fibres and to add a touch more warmth.

Winter underwear comes in many styles. The one-piece *union suit* – with a trap door in the back – is less draughty than two pieces but the whole outfit must be removed if only the ankles get soaked. And with two-piece suits, one has more options, such as wearing woollen bottoms and cotton thermal top, for example.

We didn't buy any quilted down underwear, having been warned against it. When the down is compressed or damp, it has very little insulating value. Quilted polyester was also available, but we found it adequate and simpler to have only cottons and woollens, the traditional choices.

When the weather was severe, the underwear went on in layers, with cottons first. Cotton thermal knit underwear was very comfortable, and did not feel itchy, as wool did. Thermal knit has many small holes which trap air next to the skin. Some of our underwear had up to 15% synthetic fibre blended in, which was just enough to reinforce without much loss of insulating value, and yet not so much synthetic that we felt clammy.

Workmen's baggy coveralls were handy to have to throw over other clothes if the outside work became grimy, or if the temperature dropped.

The aristocrat of winter shirts is made from *Vyella* cloth, an expensive 50% wool, 50% cotton material that feels like soft cotton. Marsha sewed one for me, and Grandad donated to her one of his that had shrunk, so we each could wear one and feel like nobility once in a while. Otherwise we made do with cotton shirts, avoiding ones with any synthetic fibres. I found that even a small amount of synthetic in the tight weave of a shirt stopped it from breathing properly, and left me a soggy, stinking mess.

I practically lived in my down-filled vest; it was warm, comfortable, easily removed if conditions or temperature changed, lightweight and could breathe away body moisture. Marsha was satisfied with her vest made from *Thinsulate*, a synthetic insulating material that passes body moisture fairly well.

We made use of a whole wardrobe of wool sweaters. For example, packing two thin ones for an outing gave more flexibility for temperature changes than one thick one would have. For afternoons spent training the dogs, I usually wore a Cowichan-style west coast sweater with a canvas anorak over it to break the wind. If I was still cold, I'd hop off the toboggan and jog behind to warm up.

Marsha's *Thinsulate* parka was substantially cheaper than goose down, yet still cost $160 in 1980. Marsha was quite pleased with the warmth of the synthetic filling, and noted it dried quicker than down and didn't clump up after being washed. The outer shell was a cotton/polyester blend, and Marsha added a wolf fur ruff to the hood to make a breathing tunnel. Wolf and wolverine were the only furs good enough for the Indians' parka ruffs.

Abbie Roberts, our Indian neighbour at Fort Selkirk, was kind not to comment on the raccoon (!) fur ruff which adorned my old parka. This was a last minute replacement for a lovely wolf ruff that had become moldy in storage. But even this poorer grade fur helped keep my face warm and the breathing tunnel from frosting too badly.

Much later, I learned the moldy wolf ruff I had discarded could have been salvaged. Sally Robinson of the Dawson City Museum showed me a technical bulletin from the National Museum which dealt with the problem of leather artifacts becoming moldy. A thorough drying, followed by vacuuming to remove the mold, will restore fur or leather. Then a spraying with ethyl alcohol disinfectant, such as *Lysol*, prevents the mold from recurring.

I had a huge *Pioneer* brand parka for the coldest days and a lighter *Sprung* model for the balmier weather. When I put an anorak over the lighter parka, it was almost as warm as the big canvas-covered, down-insulated Pioneer. Locals referred to the Pioneer coats as *DPW parkas* because, although they are too heavy, bulky and hot to wear when doing physical work, they are ideal for standing around, like the proverbial Department of Public Works employee *working*. On camping trips, we always took our big parkas along, just in case the temperature dropped. For the long miles of travel on lakes or flat trails, standing almost motionless on the toboggan, the warmest of coats was needed. Whenever we stopped and had much physical work to do, our parkas would be removed and placed on the toboggan until we were underway again.

Similarly, we had big mittens and gauntlets which were only for travelling in. Marsha's gauntlets were moosehide and mine were deerskin. Not everybody wore gauntlets; some locals dismissed the long cuffs as *snow scoops* and a nuisance. We appreciated how the extra material added considerable warmth to the wrist area, a great help during inactive mushing spells.

When doing chores, we wore half-wool, half-nylon mitts with short leather mitts overtop. For the thumbs and fingertip areas on work mitts, knitted wool alone was not durable enough, and a purely synthetic mitt would have been too cold, so the 50/50 blend was a reasonable compromise.

One trapper wore green gardening gloves to set his traps, but wool and leather for travelling between sets. Surveyors wear silk gloves to protect their fingers from cold metal while they quickly adjust their instruments. Many of the whites in town who didn't have access to the Indians' craftsmanship, wore mitts made for skiers, which had polyester-lined palms and down-filled backs. Again, the great disadvantage with these mitts was the inability of the chrome-tanned leather to breathe away hand moisture.

To save on the number of repairs, we sewed a thin leather palm and thumb onto some work mitts. Others we darned in advance, as we'd done with the socks. With a few mitts hanging to dry, others in the laundry bag, a couple awaiting darning, and some lost under the snow until spring, we needed every pair we'd bought and could have used another half-dozen pairs. If Marsha hadn't been knitting new ones and making others out of shrunken sweaters and bits of blanket [see Appendix III], we'd have run out long before spring.

To protect our necks and heads, we had woollen scarves and toques, plus the parkas' hoods. Marsha modified my toque by crocheting on ear flaps I could pull down for colder days.

When we slept outdoors in our sleeping bags, we wore our toques to preserve body heat. Marsha tied a chin strap of braided wool onto hers to keep it in place as she moved in her sleep. This strap also saved her toque from being snatched away by low branches as she rode through the forest.

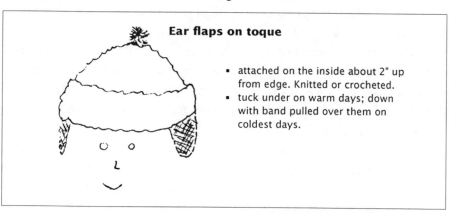

Ear flaps on toque

- attached on the inside about 2" up from edge. Knitted or crocheted.
- tuck under on warm days; down with band pulled over them on coldest days.

Another option for headgear is the balaclava-style toque, such as our trapper friend Don Mark wore. It could be rolled up like a regular toque or pulled down to cover his neck and most of his face.

APPENDIX VIII

COR'S TOBOGGAN

See more about Cor's outfit in Chapter 19.

Cor Guimond, who visited us on his Dawson-to-Whitehorse trek, had made his own toboggan. He'd cut and milled birch for his boards, leaving them to air-dry from midsummer until December. Though they were one inch thick, he only needed thirty minutes of boiling time before bending each board. Our kiln-dried oak, a third as thick, required just as much boiling. His air-dried wood was more flexible than any kilned lumber, and might have been stronger if he'd steamed the planks instead of boiling them. Both steaming and boiling loosen the wood fibres, allowing them to stretch and slide past each other, but boiling tends to rearrange the natural alignment more, making the result more brittle. Using only steam, it *may* be impossible to bend some kilned wood which has already been weakened by intense drying temperatures. In stubborn cases, where boiling in water isn't enough, one oldtimer said that boiling in raw linseed oil might work.

On the coast, shipbuilding wood was always soaked overnight before steaming. The simplest steamer we saw was a plastic dry-cleaning bag draped over a long frame with an electric kettle underneath. According to shipbuilding manuals, Cor's green planks might have needed ninety minutes of steam to become pliable.

Cor's bending frame was a flattened log, curved up at the end, with a section of log crosswise on the top. He mortised in two-by-fours to have spots to clamp the six-inch wide planks. He bent all three planks on the same day, then left them to dry for three days before attaching crossbars and a base of UHMW [ultra high molecular weight] plastic.

Because Cor had different conditions and intentions in mind, his toboggan was both wider and longer than ours. For marathon trips along the river he needed a low, stable load; because he was often alone, he needed the length to pack more cargo. The overall length of his boards before bending was 14 feet; this was over 11 feet *on the snow*. A toboggan that long would never have made it on narrow trails but was ideal out on the river ice. Cor was using tough polyduck synthetic canvas for a covering over his load.

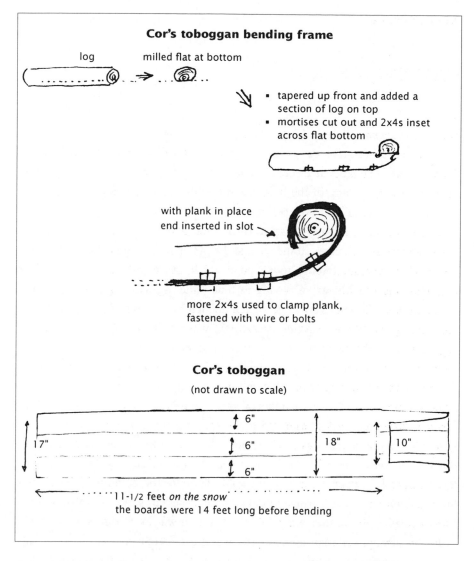

Cor's toboggan bending frame

log　　　milled flat at bottom

- tapered up front and added a section of log on top
- mortises cut out and 2x4s inset across flat bottom

with plank in place
end inserted in slot

more 2x4s used to clamp plank,
fastened with wire or bolts

Cor's toboggan

(not drawn to scale)

17"　　6"　　6"　　6"　　18"　　10"

·······11-1/2 feet *on the snow* · · · · · · · · · · · · · · · ·
the boards were 14 feet long before bending

Cor told us the white UHMW plastic was very popular in the Dawson area, so much so that some mushers were building toboggans without *any* baseboards, relying on the strength of the plastic to hold everything together. Laminated wood runners were bolted directly onto the *bottom* of the plastic to give it the necessary shape, and these runners were also clad in UHMW. Don Mark was building one along these lines to try on his narrow trails. These plastic-base sleds were called *scooters*.

APPENDIX IX

CAMPING GEAR

See related commentary in Chapter 18.

O ur canvas wall tent was 9 feet by 12 feet, with 5-foot-tall sidewalls. An eight by ten size would have been adequate for camping trips, but I wouldn't have wanted to sacrifice any of the height. Even with five-foot sidewalls, there was barely room to stand up in the centre.

Danny made us a camping stove from a ten-gallon fuel drum, using a cold chisel and an axe to make all the cuts, and a punch to pierce holes for the bolts. We could fit three sections of stove pipe inside the stove without collapsing them flat. This was a real blessing, saving us much fiddling with cold metal at nippy temperatures. The relatively large 6-inch diameter of the pipe for this size stove ensured a good draft for starting fires. There was a cast-iron damper in one pipe section to slow the outflow of smoke when needed.

To control the inflow of air through the bung-hole in the door, we hung a small tin can over the lip of the hole and suction helped keep it in place. By using different tins, with various numbers of puncture holes, or using no tin at all, we could basically regulate the rate of burn and the cooking surface temperature. This scaled-down pig heater was tremendous at burning all sorts of dubious quality wood, even rotten stumps and split green logs. It produced enough heat to give the tent a tropical atmosphere, even at the coldest outside temperatures. It could not, however, maintain that thermal output all night. The tent's canvas walls provided little insulation; soon after the stove burned out, it was as cold indoors as out.

Each evening, before turning in, there was the ritual to be performed of arranging the morning's fuel close by the stove, matches handy, so the morrow's first chore could be as brief as possible. With all this prearranged, I needed merely to partially emerge from my bag to get the day rolling. I could then snuggle back down for a ten-minute snooze while the tent warmed.

To prevent the hot pipe from burning the canvas roof at its exit point, I fashioned a sheet metal collar which held the canvas back. Asbestos cloth collars were still available for this purpose but – wary about asbestosis – we passed up on this particular tradition.

If we were staying in one spot for a while, banging on the stove pipes with a

Danny's ten-gallon stove

star-shaped edges bent up to hold pipe →

top flattened for cooking surface

place on two green logs with a few nails to suspend hot stove →

← bung for intake draft vent

- three 18" sections of pipe can be stowed inside the stove when travelling

- a bent nail secures damper assembly

- other damper method: slide a tongue of sheet metal into a slice in pipe

Sheet-metal stove pipe collars

or

- use enough pipe so sparks won't fall on tent roof. Four 18" sections may be needed
- pocket is sewn onto roof; canvas cut back for 4" minimum clearance – but still keep the pipe from getting red hot!
- small holes around main pipe hole are to help dissipate heat

- pipe hole is cut out as an oval because pipe passes through roof at an angle

stick would dislodge most creosote accumulation. When we were moving about, the creosote all got knocked out during the packing process. To separate the chimney into sections for storage inside the stove, we simply dropped it on the ground and the sections would pop apart.

Marsha owned an expensive *Camp 7 North Col*, down-filled sleeping bag and had a lighter synthetic bag which she could use as an overbag. An overbag was important for dealing with condensation. Body moisture condenses wherever the cold outside air meets the warmer air inside the bag or bags. If we'd only used one bag, the goose down filling would soon have become damp, lose its loft and insulating value. However, adding a second layer of insulation – in the form of an outer sleeping bag – meant the condensation point occurred somewhere in the outer bag. Some man-made insulators, such as *Hollofill* and *Fiberfill*, are not much affected by a moisture buildup, so they are good filling for an overbag. Encased like this, the inside goose down sleeping bag could remain dry and lofted for many nights.

Marsha sewed tube-shaped cotton flannelette sheet liners to keep our bags cleaner and cosier. Sheets were far easier to wash and dry than the bags themselves. Some stores sold liners that had ties everywhere which would fasten to ties sewn into the sleeping bag, locking the liner in place. With our tie-less ones, we had to climb into the liner first and then wriggle into the bag wearing the liner. A joy of having flannelette was that we avoided the terrible initial coldness of the nylon sleeping bag shell as we settled in for the night.

For my own bag, I wanted the best I could find. My choice was a kit of pre-cut nylon pieces, measured pouches of goose down, a dozen spools of thread and a hefty instruction booklet. A Colorado-based firm, *Frostline Kits*, sold the package for $152, a bargain price for an expedition-calibre bag in 1980. I chose this model primarily because of the design of the internal baffles. The down was held in interlocking vee-shaped tubes so it couldn't shift or settle as much as in the standard box or slanted-box designs. As on all good bags, there were no seams sewn right through anywhere.

The vee-design was too intricate for commercial seamstresses to sew without pushing the retail price out of sight. Thus, a do-it-yourself kit was the only option for owning this type of bag. If I had been very rich I would have paid someone to sew this project for me – making the bag took well over a hundred hours. I was no whiz on the sewing machine, but could make steady progress. We used Mom's old *Singer* electric for a week before we left Qualicum Beach. Marsha spelled me off whenever my eyes began to cross and the seams wandered. Yet when it was time to leave, the bag was not completely finished. Back everything went into the carton and we hauled it to the cabin that way.

After Christmas, we stuffed the down from their plastic pouches into the baffled compartments, stitched the remaining seams on Marsha's handcrank sewing machine, and pulled out all the pins. It was magnificent. It would have been hard

Cross-section of sleeping bag baffles

"vee-shaped"

- overlapped baffled
  compartments

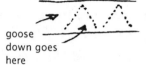

goose
down goes
here

"box baffle"

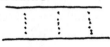

"slanted box"

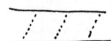

These are standard baffle designs

Examining cross-sectional measures of joined sleeping bags

Bruce in bag   Marsha in hers

 +

too much
room! too
cold!

 =

one bag   another

[Assume: sleeping bag cross-sections are approximately round]
Area = π times radius squared
Circumference = π times diameter   Diameter is twice radius
Now: call the area inside the bag A, its circumference C, and its radius R
We know that A = π (R)² and C = π (2R)
To find the area inside the doubled bag **A** (with circumference **C**, radius **R**), we
must determine **R**.
Since **C** is twice C [see above diagram], then **R must be twice** R.
Therefore: A   = π (R)²
                     = π (2R)²
                     = π 4(R)²
                     = 4 π (R)²   = 4 A .... four times the area of a single bag!
So we have four times the old volume (length is a constant, so volume varies
directly with the area), yet only two people! Our solution? See diagram below.

Examining cross-section of one-half-bag-overlapped

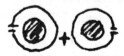 + =   or =

The new circumference **C'**   = 3/2 times the single bag circumference C
So, the new radius **R'**   = 3/2 R
So, new area **A'**   = π (R')²
              = π (3/2 R)²
              = 9/4 π (R)²
              = 9/4 A ... just over twice the single bag area
                       ... creating just over twice the volume

to appreciate all the details involved or the miles of seams required in the construction of an expedition-calibre sleeping bag if we hadn't done it ourselves.

After sewing this bag, we replaced the zippers in Marsha's two bags and my overbag, so they all matched. This way we could zip the two down bags together and the outers as well if we so desired. It hadn't occurred to me, however, that joining two bags would make a large bag with four times the volume of a single bag (rather than twice), and we were only two people (not four) to put in it.

Somehow, mathematics had put a damper on our hot idea. The alternative, without actually cutting up the single bags, was to leave one zipper open and overlap about a half bag under us. This solution gave us slightly over twice the volume of a single bag (continuing to consider the cross-section as round). The overlapped material was no problem, just extra insulation beneath our bodies. [For the mathematics behind this, see diagram on previous page.]

On the coldest nights, we could retreat into separate bags, but keep the outer overbags joined to share some communal body heat. In our own inner bags, we could pull up the mummy hoods tightly around our heads for maximum warmth.

Using a mummy-shaped sleeping bag felt restricting to me until I learned to stop fighting the bag when I rolled over or curled up. The trick was to bring the bag with me when moving, instead of trying to move inside a stationary shape.

On early Arctic and Antarctic expeditions, explorers soon determined that goose down sleeping bags were impossible to keep dry. An igloo was a poor place to dry out damp clothing or bedding. So they looked at what the Inuit [Eskimos] were doing and soon switched to bags made from caribou hides with the hair left on. Each morning, bags were taken outside, and the moisture allowed to freeze, then shaken or brushed out. We would have loved to have caribou sleeping bags, even if they were bulky – and no doubt quite odiferous – but we had no access to hides. Caribou hide is so warm because the hair is hollow. My experience with caribou to that point consisted of sitting on a hide for a toboggan ride once and having to get up after ten minutes because my bum was too hot. This gave me a lasting appreciation of the Inuit's favourite clothing resource.

Closer to our home, the native Indians had slept in fur robes, some made from muskrat fur, and others of braided-then-woven rabbit fur. My grandfather described the robe his father brought back from the Gold Rush as *entirely made from the soft belly fur of muskrats, and large enough to accommodate many children.* There was a distinct odour, he remembered from playing in it with his brothers: *It smelled like family.*

We needed stuff sacks for packing our sleeping bags, so we created some on the trusty handcrank sewing machine. Even in the warmth of the cabin, we could vividly imagine how miserable it would be to stuff cold nylon-covered bags into sacks with our bare hands at Forty Below, so we made these sacks large enough to pack while wearing mittens.

For insulation under us at night, we brought seven 3/8-inch-thick, closed-cell foam pads. Four were blue polyethylene foam and three were the similar but more expensive *Regalite*. Both types were reliable well below Minus Forty. We very consciously didn't have any of the white *Ensolite* pads. One bad experience stuck too vividly in my mind—

The winter before, I'd been persuaded to take eleven teenagers on an overnight camping trip. They were participants in the Katimavik program for Canadian youth. They were all anxious to experience Paradise Below Zero, but weren't prepared when the temperature suddenly dropped to Thirty-Five Below. With a group that size we needed three fires so everyone could get close and warm. After eating a smoky but hearty meal, they began to lay out the sleeping gear.

One boy was clowning around and dropped his Ensolite foamie. It broke in two. I couldn't believe my eyes; usually these pads are soft and limp.

Beside me, a young Québeçois was holding a plate-size piece of foam in each hand and saying, "I'm sorry I broke this. How are you supposed to unroll it?"

I took his roll and tried to slowly open it: it broke like a crisp potato chip. This was the first time I'd used the white foamies at such low temperatures and it was obvious they'd be of little use.

Everyone nestled tightly together that night but only a few in the centre got a decent sleep. Without adequate warmth below, many had to get up and huddle around the fires until dawn. Fortunately, none of the Katimavikers suffered frostbite. When I later reported this incident to Mountain Equipment Co-op, their staff was horrified and promptly instituted a temperature rating system for their sleeping pads.

To solve the problem of how to safely pack all the cooking equipment and food on the toboggan, I built two sturdy plywood grub boxes. Cardboard boxes would get soggy and disintegrate. Also no good were canvas or burlap sacks that would settle, gradually sprawling off the toboggan to be worn away by the passing snow.

With wooden boxes, we could be assured that fragile items would be intact and also that mice and squirrels couldn't raid us at night.

In sharp contrast to what a back-packer would take camping, we took a cast-iron frypan and huge pots. Only a thick, cast-iron frying pan could give us a fighting chance at not burning food when cooking over an open fire. Because we would be melting large quantities of snow or ice chunks for water, big containers were necessary. Sturdy, one-gallon steel pots could be settled right in a campfire

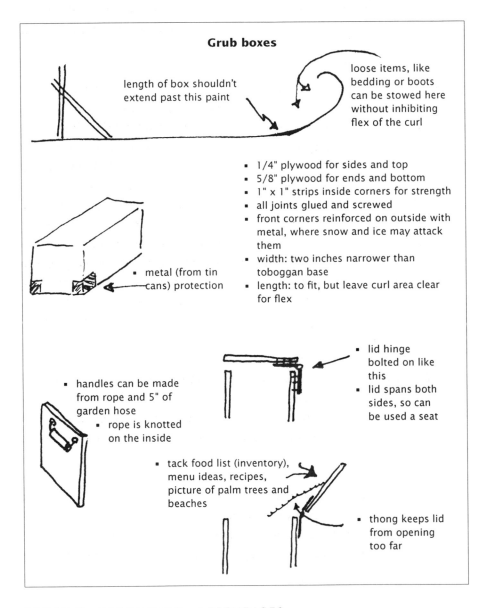

Grub boxes

length of box shouldn't extend past this paint

loose items, like bedding or boots can be stowed here without inhibiting flex of the curl

- 1/4" plywood for sides and top
- 5/8" plywood for ends and bottom
- 1" x 1" strips inside corners for strength
- all joints glued and screwed
- front corners reinforced on outside with metal, where snow and ice may attack them
- width: two inches narrower than toboggan base
- length: to fit, but leave curl area clear for flex

- metal (from tin cans) protection

- lid hinge bolted on like this
- lid spans both sides, so can be used a seat

- handles can be made from rope and 5" of garden hose
  - rope is knotted on the inside

- tack food list (inventory), menu ideas, recipes, picture of palm trees and beaches

- thong keeps lid from opening too far

without worry of them tipping or burning out. Each evening we would need about 3 gallons of water for our tea, supper, dish washing, personal washing and for adding into the dog pot. When packed away, the pots and pans were stowed in kraft paper bags to keep soot from getting everywhere.

The rest of the kitchen gear was: lids for the pots and pans, wide-mouthed tea kettle, metal mixing bowl, wooden stirring spoon, flipper, wash basin, French knife in its sheath, hot mitt, dish soap, scratchy pad, tea towel, two plates, two bowls and – in a small denim bag – three forks and three spoons.

Tucked in a corner of one grub box was a pouch containing candles, matches, a can of *Sterno* for starting an emergency drying-out fire and extra flashlight batteries.

Another pouch was home to toilet paper, a face cloth and a bar of soap. Face washing sounds like the last thing one would want to do outdoors, especially with all the warnings about exposed flesh freezing in so many seconds at such-and-such wind chill factor. Yet it was important to keep clean, washing all the sweat salts, smoke and soot out of our pores. Perhaps more advantageous was the uplifting mental effect of baring skin and wiping off with a steaming cloth – for a moment forgetting the winter and feeling only the wet flush of heat. It never failed to perk up our spirits.

Washing dishes was actually a privilege on a camping outing. We recalled how my sisters vied for the job on a summer canoe trip a few years before. Jill, who prides herself on her grooming, was horrified to see how grimy her hands were becoming from campfire soot and the aluminium paddle.

"How come your hands are so clean looking?" she demanded of Nora, the younger sister.

"Probably because I do the dishes all the time," was the matter-of-fact reply.

After that there was a contest after each meal to see who could be first to immerse their hands in the steaming dishwater.

For us, after a long day of mushing, it was heavenly to soak our hands for a few moments while wiping the plates, letting our fingers soak up the welcome heat.

Without a doubt, the few moments before a fire was lit and underway must rank as the coldest of all. Bare fingers numbly piling little twigs and shavings, kneeling in the snow to puff gently on glowing splinters of wood... it brings to mind Jack London's famous tale about a man who froze to death when an overhead branch tipped snow on his kindling and last matches. We had read the story and agreed to cheat instead – into the grub boxes went a BiC lighter, candles and newspaper.

Three bundles of the *Whitehorse Star* had been in the load of supplies we trucked into the cabin in October. Having newspaper saved us the chore of splitting ultra-fine kindling with cold hands. The easiest method was to roll a single sheet and then tie it with a simple overhand knot. Three of these rolls plus one crumpled sheet for a starter would create a blaze sufficient to ignite small branches, avoiding the twigs-and-shavings stage altogether.

The only minor drawback to using newspaper was the printed stories. I was so news-starved Marsha would catch me reading the paper instead of rolling it. This even though every paper we had *was the same issue* – October Tenth!

Other equipment we packed included a three-gallon dog food pot, into which fitted a measuring scoop, the long gang chains, a single spare chain and a few coils of rope. Each toboggan had a holster built up against the backboard: for an axe and swede saw on one, and an axe plus the rifle on the other. Strapped onto each backboard was a small canvas packsack which served as a daypack, holding sunglasses, maps, pencil and notepaper, camera, lunch fixings, sweaters, extra mitts and a vacuum flask.

Our first aid kit was small, fitting into a toboggan curl. In it were two 3"-wide tensor elastic bandages, a handful of band-aids, a roll of adhesive tape, gauze pads, some alcohol swabs, moleskin to prevent blisters, two gauze rolls 2" by 5 yards, a package of tampons, dental floss and a container of *Eye and Wound* powder. The latter contained penicillin and sulfa, and we used it for both dog wounds and our own. We felt we could improvise around this basic kit, using the sewing implements from the harness repair kit to stitch up any wounds bandages couldn't handle. Marsha had Backcountry Ranger training in First Aid and certainly enough courage: she once sewed three stitches in her own leg to close a wound after a climbing accident in the Bugaboos! Just in case anyone needed tranquillizing, sterilizing or inspiring, we included a mickey of Scotch whiskey in the kit.

For mending clothes, we included woollen yarn and darning needles, scraps of canvas and denim with linen thread and needles, and folding scissors. The inevitable harness repairs required an awl, blunt harness needles and coarse waxed thread, plus extra webbing, rings and clips. So we would have a little leeway about *when* to do those repairs, we took a spare harness and choke collar. For mending a toboggan or anything else, we carried extra 4" bolts and nuts, pliers, clamps, hay wire, snare wire, rope, cord, leather thongs, a file, a few nails and a roll of electricians' tape.

The drawstring bag for this repair paraphernalia was the leg of a blue jean, amputated at the knee. We tucked it away in the curl of my toboggan, hoping not to have to use it, but scarcely a night would go by when we did not pull it out to darn a mitten, sharpen an axe or repair a harness. Our friend Cor Guimond told us the best repair kit was to *Build it sturdy the first time!* Though our gear did need frequent attention, we certainly knew how to fix it because we had made most of it ourselves. It was a wonder the dogs could pull it all.

Travelling long distances in the Yukon winter means you'll be mushing in low-light and extreme cold. Cor Guimond warned us to make our gear strong because our lives would depend on it.

APPENDIX X

TALKING ABOUT TRAPPING

Marsha and I had become more aware of the realities of a trapper's life through Don Mark's visits with us over the winter. Since this was his first year at the business, he was still mulling over the moral and philosophical questions intrinsically linked to this profession. Even as isolated as we were in the Pelly and Yukon valleys, the increasing pressures from animal lovers in the south of Canada and the United States were threatening to change or even wipe out his job through consumer boycotts and new government regulations.

Although various government agencies and Ban-the-Leg-Hold-Trap groups had been searching for years for the ideal humane trap, the best alternative so far was the conibear trap. A conibear would kill the animal instantly – snapping its back or neck – as long as the animal entered the set from the correct angle. A disadvantage for the trapper was that this type of trap was much harder to arrange perfectly every time. Also, when an animal was killed, its fur could freeze to the metal. The trapper had to take the trap back to his cabin or line tent with the animal still attached to thaw both out if he wanted to save the fur from having a long bald strip. Because of this, the trapper had to have twice as many traps. With a leg-hold trap, the animal was usually still alive when the trapper came. If it had died in the meantime, the jaws gripped at the ankle, where a bald patch wasn't important. By leaving the leg-hold trap still attached to the tree, and handling it as little as possible, the trapper's own scent didn't get onto the trap as much as it would from bringing it back into his cabin.

The instant kill of the conibear also meant the dead animal was fair game for mice and birds. These scavengers would strip off the fur for their nests or peck holes to eat the flesh, making the animal's death in vain. A live animal in a leg-hold trap could defend itself until the trapper arrived to dispatch it.

"The other pressures," Don had explained to us one evening at our cabin, "are proposed rules that you have to check each trap every day. Already trappers in British Columbia have to check every seventy-two hours and the humane societies are pushing for every twenty-four hours."

"Do you think whatever happens in B.C. will become law in the Yukon soon after?" I asked.

"That's usually how it works. If I had to check each trap every day, I could hardly cover any line at all. Some days the weather is too bad. Some days you're broke down. I have to cut wood, make new trails, skin what I've caught and look after the hides. Trapping isn't as easy as most people imagine. It's godawful hard work, for damn poor money."

"But what about these great prices we hear? Like six hundred dollars for one lynx?"

"Sure, some guys get a few lucky years and make money while the lynx cycle is at its peak, but there are poor years, too. And it is pretty expensive keeping up cabins and tents, snowmobiles or dogs. It would be a lot easier to sit in town, and collect welfare, or unemployment insurance, or be a civil servant, but I like this life better. But if there are too many new rules, it'll be hard to make a go of it."

"How do you justify what you have to do, killing animals just so a fashion-conscious woman can own a fur coat?" I prodded.

Don laughed. "I refer to it as *murdering cute, furry little animals for some rich bitch in New York City*. Well, I don't enjoy clubbing animals any more than you would. When they look up at me with those big round eyes, I feel like a criminal, murdering them like that. I have to think about *managing the resource*, just like the cattle at the Pelly Farm are a resource. The cattle are killed, skinned and eaten. The difference for these wild animals is they have a free life unless they put their foot in a trap."

On our trip to Volcano Mountain, we followed Don's trapline trail. He said the last trapper harvesting the sub-alpine forest on that mountain moved away thirty years ago. That trapper had been Jared Wilkinson, who left for remoter territory far up the Pelly, then moved near the headwaters of the Stewart River. Jared and his brother Eddie obviously loved living and working in wilderness so removed and different in time, space and thoughts from city life. In this new age of helicopters, electronic communications, and anti-trapping activists, we wondered if younger trappers like Don would get the chance to live out their lives in the same seclusion as the Wilkinsons had. Ironically, trappers themselves were becoming an endangered species.

APPENDIX XI

DOG PACKS

See related commentary in Chapter 43.

We use a hybrid dog pack design – part Teslin, part Tahltan. Essentially, the pack was two box-like pouches, joined by a back piece. We added a chest band, a flap to cover the load, and two rows of loops for lashing down the cover flap. Marsha suggested we allow one-inch seams as canvas tends to unravel easily.

I helped lay out and cut the canvas, while Marsha operated the handcrank sewing machine. She used the largest stitch size, and the seams held well to our tug testing.

"If I ever make another pack," Marsha commented, "I'd want to use coloured canvas and trim it with braid. And if the machine has a zig-zag stitch, that would be stronger than a straight one."

"The polyduck canvas Cor used for his toboggan cover would be good for packs," I suggested, "because it is so tough and waterproof. That would save us the trouble of sealing the bottom of the packs with a hot linseed oil and paraffin mixture to protect them from all the water and mud the dogs' legs splatter up."

"Maybe we could attach mud flaps onto the dogs," kidded Marsha. "Little rubber ones that say *Keep on Packing.*"

The simplest way of securing the pack is with a single band that is attached to one pouch, passed under the dog's belly and cinched to two rings, then wrapped around the cargo and cinched at a second set of rings. This is roughly the Tahltan method. A lashing rope crosses back and forth on the top holding the flap down over the load.

Their perennial rivals from Teslin Lake area didn't use a chest band, relying on one long rope to secure the back piece to the dog's body then wrap around the outside, snugging it tightly against the dog's sides.

When I wanted to show Marsha this roping technique, the dogs were asleep outside and we didn't have the heart to waken them to be models. So I had to get on my hands and knees instead, wearing Tyhee's almost completed pack and pretending to be a pack dog.

"Keep still," Marsha laughed as she passed a rope under my armpit and gave a little tickle. "You're the silliest animal I've dealt with all winter."

Making a dog pack

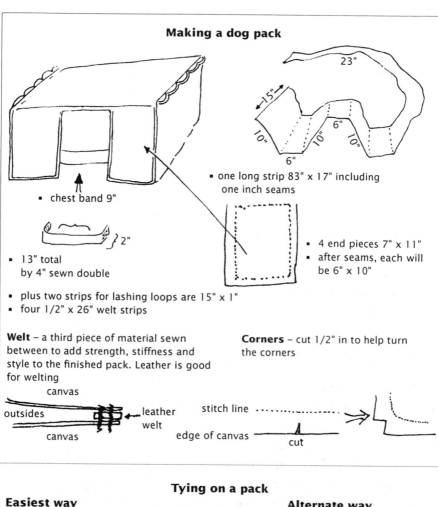

- chest band 9"

}2"

- 13" total
  by 4" sewn double

- one long strip 83" x 17" including
  one inch seams

- 4 end pieces 7" x 11"
- after seams, each will
  be 6" x 10"

- plus two strips for lashing loops are 15" x 1"
- four 1/2" x 26" welt strips

Welt – a third piece of material sewn
between to add strength, stiffness and
style to the finished pack. Leather is good
for welting

Corners – cut 1/2" in to help turn
the corners

canvas

outsides ← leather
welt

canvas

stitch line ·····················→

edge of canvas ————

cut

Tying on a pack

Easiest way
- one band, cinched at two
  points with buckles or
  double rings

End view

cinch here to
hold pack tightly
to body

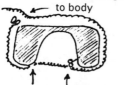

sewn here   cinch here to
             tighten across belly

Alternate way
- hold dog's head between
  your legs
- make loop, hold it at 1,
  pass free end back and
  down, crossing under dog's
  chest to come up behind
  the dog's left 'armpit'
- bring rope over top of pack
  along that side to 2 then
  down, cross back under
  chest to right armpit, and
  up to join loop at 1
- from there, pass rope around outside of
  pack, returning and tying at 1

front

ABOUT THE AUTHOR

BRUCE T. BATCHELOR

B ruce Batchelor came to the Yukon in 1973, planning to stay just long enough to earn money for a trip to Europe. Instead, he fell in love with the wilderness and its people, and stayed for most of the next eight years. He has written three books about his stay in the North.

Marsha McGillis, heroine of *Nine Dog Winter*, agreed to marry him in 1983. Their son Dan was born in 1992. They live in Victoria, B.C., with a white lab-husky cross named Tyhee Too in honour of the Tyhee in this story.

Bruce and Marsha own Agio Publishing House, where he edits and directs marketing, while Marsha designs the books and Dan takes photos.

Photo above: Bruce Batchelor with dog team on the old Dawson Stage Road, beside a carved wooden milepost.

LaVergne, TN USA
29 October 2010
202819LV00002B/12/P